CW01239310

EXPERT DETERMINATION

THIRD EDITION

By JOHN KENDALL
Solicitor,
formerly partner, Allen & Overy

Assisted by CLIVE FREEDMAN
Barrister
3 Verulam Buildings, Gray's Inn

"Experto credite"

Virgil

LONDON
SWEET & MAXWELL
2001

Published in 2001
by Sweet and Maxwell Limited of
100 Avenue Road, Swiss Cottage London NW3 3PF.
http://www.sweetandmaxwell.co.uk
Typeset by
J&L Composition Ltd, Filey, North Yorkshire.
Printed in England by
MPG Books

First published 1992 as Dispute Resolution: Expert Determination

John Kendall has asserted his right under the Copyright, Designs and Patents Act 1988 to be identified as the author of this work.

A CIP catalogue record for this book is available from the British Library.

ISBN 0421 703008

All rights reserved. Crown Copyright legislation is reproduced under the terms of Crown Copyright Policy Guidance issued by HMSO. No part of this publication may be reproduced or transmitted, in any form or by any means, or stored in any retrieval system of any nature, without prior written permission, except for permitted fair dealing under the Copyright, Designs and Patents Act 1988, or in accordance with the terms of a licence issued by the Copyright Licensing Agency in respect of photocopying and/or reprographic reproduction. Application for permission for other use of copyright material including permission to reproduce extracts in other published works shall be made to the publishers. Full acknowledgement of author, publisher and source must be given.

Material in Appendices B, D and I is reproduced by kind permission of the Law Society, the Royal Institution of Chartered Surveyors and the Centre for Dispute Resolution respectively.

Non natural forests were destroyed to make this product, only farmed timber was used and re-planted.

@ Sweet & Maxwell
2001

EXPERT DETERMINATION

AUSTRALIA
LBC Information Services
Sydney

CANADA and USA
Carswell
Toronto – Ontario

NEW ZEALAND
Brookers
Auckland

SINGAPORE and MALAYSIA
Sweet and Maxwell Asia
Singapore and Kuala Lumpur

FOREWORD TO THE SECOND EDITION

This book is in the rare category of original legal texts. All subjects have their beginning and this still slender volume remains the first systematic treatment of a subject with enormous potential.

Expert determination has existed in the shadows for well over two centuries, rubbing shoulders uneasily with the law of arbitration and certification. Like some forms of commodity arbitration it seems to owe its survival to the simple fact that it works and is found commercially useful—A and B agree to abide by the decision of C. The system is infinitely flexible: there need not be a dispute, no writing is necessary and any form of procedure can be adopted. Yet what happens if C is thought to have made a mistake, or admits that he had done so? The law inevitably steps in and begins to create a jurisprudence, curiously taking many decades to resolve even these simple questions. But the subject had clearly arrived and seems to achieve belated respectability with the Court of Appeal's decision in *Jones v. Sherwood Computer Services*.[1] Curiously the case is still not included in the Law Reports, despite the case which it overruled being so reported.[2]

The thrust which has pushed expert determination into prominence is the recognition that all, or at least many, of the disadvantages and technical pitfalls of arbitration can be circumvented by substituting an agreed expert determination. At a stroke the peril of appeals, intervention by the court, or allegations of misconduct (or serious irregularity in the new parlance) can be put to one side and replaced by an expert procedure almost devoid of technicalities and contractually binding. Perhaps this is how arbitration was always intended to work. Such a course is now firmly underpinned by the approach of the courts, as exemplified in the *Channel Tunnel* case: "those who make arrangements for the resolution of disputes must show good reasons for departing from them".[3]

John Kendall's admirable book, and particularly this new edition, has arrived at a propitious time. Parties to unavoidable commercial

---

[1] [1992] 1 W.L.R. 277, [1992] 2 All E.R. 170.
[2] *Burgess v. Purchase & Sons (Farms)* [1983] Ch. 216.
[3] *Channel Tunnel Group v. Balfour Beatty* [1993] A.C. 334 *per* Lord Mustill.

disputes are searching with ever more discrimination for bespoke dispute resolution systems, free from technical pitfalls. With arbitration and ADR enthusiastically setting out their stalls, but each with a track record far from spotless, expert determination will form an ideal counter-balance, offering real opportunities to those in need of the particular qualities and facts which are ably described in these pages. This book is to be welcomed as a unique contribution to the literature of dispute resolution and a valuable source of new ideas.

John Uff Q.C.
Nash Professor of Engineering Law
King's College, London

PREFACE TO THE FIRST EDITION

I had a traditional legal education in the early 1970s. The courses contained little or nothing about dispute resolution, and I had never heard of arbitration. As an articled clerk (as trainee solicitors were then called) one of my tasks was to proof-read agreements. I then encountered, for the first time, the phrase "as an expert and not as an arbitrator".

Lawyers from a number of different disciplines encounter expert determination. Property specialists can refer to Bernstein and Reynolds' *Handbook of Rent Review*; statistically rent review is by far and away the most significant application; but other uses of expert determination are not covered in any book. Some of the arbitration textbooks touch on the principles of expert determination, but only as a side-issue to the central topic. Law libraries do not have a separate category for this subject, and it is usually treated as a subdivision of arbitration, from which it is rather different.

Further confusion is created by the use of the word "expert", which makes most people think of an "expert witness" which is hardly surprising given the great importance of expert witnesses in modern dispute resolution. The function of the expert to whom issues are referred is not, like the expert witness, to give evidence about those issues to a tribunal, but to determine those issues himself. The word "expert" does have to be used for our topic because "valuer", the only real alternative, no longer covers all the applications of the procedure, particularly those which have been developed more recently.

So, finding frequent enquiries being made to my firm about determination by experts in applications other than rent review, I decided to write this book. I hope it will be useful to practitioners from all sides of the civil law, both those who draft agreements providing for the use of expert determination and those litigators like myself who advise on the interpretation of expert clauses and on the conduct of the references themselves. For those readers who are not litigators I have included a glossary of terms connected with expert determination which derive mainly from the way the courts have approached the subject and from allied questions arising from litigation and arbitration.

I have drawn on the experience of specialists from every department of my firm. I am very grateful in particular to the following colleagues: Deborah Adams, Martin Bates, Paul Bedford, Kate Buckley, Doran Doeh, Ian Elder, Richard Everett, Ian Ferguson, Judith Gill, Jonathan Hitchin, Rupert Jones, Sarah Jones, Don McGown, William Norris, John Rink, Sara Robinson, Jeremy Sharman, Derek Sloan and Allan Tyrer. Malek Ali, Sally Brooks, Antony Fobel, Jason Hambury and Brian Rook, who were trainee solicitors at the time, and my secretary Carol Carder, all did very useful research and checking. Outside Allen & Overy I have to thank Stewart Boyd, Malcolm Clarke, Stephen Coleman, John Dick, Andrew Dobson, Brian Granger, Mark McGaw, Peter McMahon, Robert Morgan, Michael Renshall, Shaun Stewart, Christopher Thomas and John Uff. Lastly I must thank my wife Jenny for all her help in getting this book ready for publication.

Having had so much help, I am responsible for any errors that remain: and the expressions of opinion are my own.

I apologise for having found it easier to keep to the sexist tradition of referring to parties and experts has "he" and the colonialist tradition of referring to Wales as "England", and hope this will not offend readers. I have tried to state the law as at October 31, 1991.

PREFACE TO THE SECOND EDITION

In the current crisis in civil dispute resolution, expert determination is often chosen as a private system offering distinct savings of time, cost and complexity. It is found in commercial contracts of all kinds, both for resolving specific and general disputes; and the construction industry has adopted adjudication, a species of expert determination as first stage dispute resolution in many construction contracts.

A number of developments in the law and commercial practice led me to write this second edition. In 1992, when the first edition came out, the most outstanding feature of the law was the new robustness of the courts in limiting challenges to experts' decisions. Since then there has been a series of cases about the right of one of the parties to ask the court to intervene before the expert has made the decision, with two being heard by the Court of Appeal and one (*Mercury*) being heard by the House of Lords. The new Chapter 12 of this second edition is devoted to these jurisdiction battles.

I owe a considerable debt of gratitude to the Centre of Construction Law and Management at King's College London and to its director John Uff. I was a student on the Centre's postgraduate course on construction law and arbitration in the late 1980s and, as part of the course, wrote a short dissertation on an allied subject for which I had the privilege of being supervised by the late Donald Keating. Without that, I doubt this book would have been written.

In addition to those who helped with the first edition, many of whom helped with the second edition, I must thank the following in particular for their help and encouragement: from Allen & Overy; all my fellow litigation partners; Michael Conlon, Jas Gillar, Gillian Holgate, Lawrence Jacobs and John Scriven; and, from outside the firm, David Ashton, Hugh Aldous, Tony Blackler, Thayne Forbes, Clive Freedman, Richard Freeman, Robert Hughes, Hugh Jackson, Neil Kaplan, Karl Mackie, Keith Pickavance, David Sarre, Brian Totterdill and Christopher Vigrass.

I am very grateful also to my secretary Emma Fell and trainee solicitors Simon Irvine, Tom Pauk, Jonathan Swain and Nick Swiss for typing and proof-reading.

Last, I must thank my wife Jenny for tolerating an obsessive author as a husband.

I have tried to state the law as at August 31, 1996, and on the basis that the Arbitration Act 1996 and the Housing Grants, Construction and Regeneration Act 1996 will have been brought into force. At the time of writing the forecast commencement dates are April 1997 for both statutes.

John Kendall
One New Change
London EC4M 9QQ

PREFACE TO THE THIRD EDITION

Five years have gone by since the second edition, and during that time civil dispute resolution has gone through a massive upheaval with the Woolf reforms. Those reforms focus attention on alternative forms of dispute resolution, which includes expert determination. Commercial lawyers, other professionals working for business, and business executives all need to have a greater understanding of these alternatives.

Apart from the impact of the new Civil Procedure Rules, the last five years have seen a number of interesting developments in the law about expert determination. There has been further controversy about challenges to the court before the decision, and some help in understanding how serious an expert's mistake has to be for a court to refuse to enforce it. More (apparently unsuccessful) attempts have been made to sue experts for professional negligence. The arrival of statutory construction adjudication, a system very similar to expert determination, has provided useful material, in particular about what standard of fairness applies.

This suggests a great deal of controversy about expert determination. Much of the time the system is used without controversy in a wide range of commercial contracts, and, so far as one can tell, on a wider basis than before.

In 1998 I decided to cease practising as a solicitor in the City of London, and started to work as a dispute resolver and a trainer rather than an adviser and representative. Part of my new portfolio career has included training days with CEDR, dealing with the use of expert determination in specific industries. My colleagues for those training days, Michael Turner, Tony Waring, and Richard Byrom, and those who attended the training days have all helped me a great deal. They have drawn my attention, without any infringement of client confidentiality, to issues I would not otherwise have considered at all, or at least not in the same way. They have expressed their views about the process from their own experience. That help cannot be acknowledged specifically in the text, and too many individuals have been involved to name here; hence this general expression of thanks.

I owe a great debt of gratitude to Clive Freedman. I asked him originally to find me a junior tenant in his chambers to help me with the book. His response was to offer to do the job himself. He has made a very substantial contribution to the treatment of the subject, in particular by widening the ambit of the source material to include construction contract certification cases. As a result of his involvement, many improvements to the text have been made. I take full responsibility for any errors that remain.

I am also very grateful to my wife Jenny who has acted as proof-reader. Anyone who writes books will know how much time it robs from the family, so being able to work with my wife on some aspects has softened that feeling of being robbed.

I have changed from my practice in previous editions, and have tried to avoid the sexist pronoun "he" and words derived from it. However I have not found a way of dealing with another aspect of political correctness. Although I now live 200 metres on the Welsh side of the border, I still think it is too cumbersome to refer to Wales whenever there is a reference to English law. So the prefaces are the only part of the book where Wales is mentioned.

I have tried to state the law as at January 31, 2001.

John Kendall
The Manor House
St David's Street
Presteigne
Powys LD8 2BP
Wales
e-mail: jkendall@btinternet.com

CONTENTS

	Page
Foreword to the Second Edition	*v*
Preface to the First Edition	*vii*
Preface to the Second Edition	*ix*
Preface to the Third Edition	*xi*
Contents	*xiii*
Abbreviations	*xix*
Table of Cases	*xxi*
Table of Statutes	*xxvii*
Table of Statutory Instruments	*xxxix*
Table of Civil Procedure Rules	*xl*
Table of International Conventions	*xli*

1.	Introduction	1
	1.1 General remarks	1
	1.2 Sources of law and information	4
	1.3 Method	6
	1.4 Overview	8
	1.5 The predominant issues	9
	1.6 The context of modern dispute resolution	12
2.	Land	18
	2.1 Summary	18
	2.2 Freeholds	18
	2.3 Rent Review	19
	2.4 Other leasehold valuations	24
	2.5 Fittings, products, machinery and furniture	24
	2.6 Certificates triggering obligations	25
	2.7 Mortgage portfolios	26
	2.8 Development agreements	26
	2.9 Boundary disputes	26
	2.10 Dispute resolution	26
3.	Shares in Private Companies	28
	3.1 Summary	28
	3.2 Private companies	28
	3.3 Procedure depends on articles or shareholder agreements	29

	3.4	Appointment of a company's auditors	30
	3.5	Fair value and open market value	31
	3.6	Specific valuation instructions	32
	3.7	Unfair prejudice	33
	3.8	An alternative to winding-up on the just and equitable ground	34
	3.9	Liability of valuers	34
	3.10	Limitation of liability	35
4.		Sale and Purchase of Businesses and Companies	36
	4.1	Summary	36
	4.2	Certificates of items in accounts	36
	4.3	Pension schemes	39
	4.4	Tax liabilities	40
5.		Other Commercial Applications	41
	5.1	Summary	41
	5.2	Employee remuneration and share options	41
	5.3	Partnership agreements	42
	5.4	Finance leasing	42
	5.5	Capital markets	43
	5.6	Convertible preference shares	43
	5.7	Commodities	44
	5.8	Shipping	46
	5.9	Insurance	46
	5.10	Banking: "conclusive evidence" clauses	47
	5.11	Investment	47
	5.12	Insolvency	48
	5.13	Broadcasting	49
	5.14	Auctions	49
	5.15	Sports tribunals	49
	5.16	Intellectual property	49
6.		From Valuer to Expert	50
	6.1	Summary	50
	6.2	Use of the word "expert"	50
	6.3	New fields for experts	51
	6.4	Energy and mining	51
	6.5	Shipbuilding	55
	6.6	Computers	55
	6.7	Engineering	55
	6.8	Telecoms contracts	56
7.		Construction Contracts and Interim Determinations	57
	7.1	Summary	57
	7.2	Interim determinations	57
	7.3	Construction contracts and other potential applications of interim determination	58

	7.4	Certification	59
	7.5	Adjudication	62
	7.6	Dispute review boards	67
	7.7	Policy and management issues in joint ventures	68
	7.8	Final determination of specific issues	68
	7.9	Final determination of all issues	69
8.	Dispute Resolution		71
	8.1	Summary	71
	8.2	Experts closer to dispute resolution than valuers	71
	8.3	Contrasting use of experts as witnesses	72
	8.4	Litigation stayed?	73
	8.5	Multi-party disputes	75
	8.6	Multi-tier dispute resolution	75
	8.7	Clauses referring all disputes to an expert	77
	8.8	Lawyers as experts	80
	8.9	Why choose expert determination for dispute resolution?	82
	8.10	Proposing expert determination after a dispute has arisen	84
9.	The Expert Clause		87
	9.1	Summary	87
	9.2	Need to specify expert determination, and the effect	87
	9.3	Essential elements of an expert clause and implied terms	91
	9.4	The issue to be determined	93
	9.5	The expert's qualifications	94
	9.6	To act as an expert and not as an arbitrator	94
	9.7	How the expert is to be appointed	94
	9.8	That the decision will be final and binding	96
	9.9	The due date for payment of the amount determined	97
	9.10	That the expert has the power to award interest	98
	9.11	Provision for interest to run for late payment of the amount determined	99
	9.12	How the expert is to be paid	99
	9.13	Provision for awarding costs between the parties	100
	9.14	Provision where one party does not pay the expert's fees	100
	9.15	The procedure to be followed in the reference	100
	9.16	No applications to the court	103
	9.17	Expert to be immune	104
	9.18	Time bars	104
10.	Qualifications of an Expert		106
	10.1	Summary	106
	10.2	Person, firm or company	106

	10.3	A named individual, firm or company	107
	10.4	An individual, firm or company holding a particular position	108
	10.5	Qualification by profession or experience	108
	10.6	Criteria for an expert's suitability	109
	10.7	Independence	111
	10.8	Umpires	112
11.	Appointing an Expert	114
	11.1	Summary	114
	11.2	Appointment by the parties	114
	11.3	Absence of effective appointment machinery	115
	11.4	Validity of appointment	117
	11.5	Appointing authorities	119
	11.6	Application to the appointing authority	121
	11.7	Attempts to prevent appointments	121
	11.8	Conflicts of interest	122
	11.9	Accepting an appointment	123
12.	Jurisdiction of the Expert	124
	12.1	Summary	124
	12.2	Jurisdiction and how to establish it	124
	12.3	Disputes on jurisdiction issues	126
	12.4	The law should give effect to contracts	127
	12.5	Ouster of the court's jurisdiction	128
	12.6	The extent of the expert's jurisdiction	132
	12.7	Applications to the court	138
	12.8	Rules of construction	141
13.	Procedure for the Reference	143
	13.1	Summary	143
	13.2	Starting a determination does not stop the limitation period running	143
	13.3	No set procedure except the contract	144
	13.4	Where no procedure is laid down in the contract	145
	13.5	Terms of reference	146
	13.6	Procedural directions	146
	13.7	Conduct of the investigation	150
	13.8	The decision	153
	13.9	Procedures for specific applications	154
	13.10	Breakdown of the procedural machinery	155
14.	Enforcing the decision	157
	14.1	Summary	157
	14.2	Enforcement procedures	157
	14.3	Court action	158
	14.4	Effect of arbitration clause	159

	14.5	Insolvency	160
	14.6	Set-off	160
	14.7	Enforcement abroad	160
	14.8	Limitation	162
15.	Challenging the decision		163
	15.1	Summary	163
	15.2	Court proceedings	163
	15.3	Grounds for challenge	165
	15.4	Fraud, collusion and partiality	165
	15.5	Lack of independence	168
	15.6	Unfairness in the procedure	170
	15.7	Due process—express or implied	172
	15.8	Unfairness in the decision itself	173
	15.9	Grounds of challenge other than fraud, partiality, unfairness and mistake	175
	15.10	Mistake: earlier history	178
	15.11	Mistake: more recent developments	179
	15.12	Mistake: the present position	182
	15.13	Speaking and non-speaking decisions	186
	15.14	Questions of interpretation of the words in the agreement	190
	15.15	Other points of law	191
	15.16	Specific instructions for the expert	191
	15.17	"In the absence of manifest error"	192
	15.18	Consequence of an ineffective decision	193
	15.19	Evidence from the expert	194
	15.20	The prospects for challenges in the future	195
16.	Rights and Duties of Experts		197
	16.1	Summary	197
	16.2	Fees and expenses	197
	16.3	Arbitral immunity for experts until 1975	199
	16.4	*Sutcliffe v. Thackrah*	201
	16.5	*Arenson v. Casson Beckman*	202
	16.6	Quasi-arbitrators	204
	16.7	Liability for breach of contract and negligence	207
	16.8	A duty to make independent investigations	212
	16.9	A duty to act fairly	213
	16.10	A duty to apply the law	215
	16.11	A duty to reach a final and binding decision	216
	16.12	A duty of confidentiality	216
	16.13	Tortious liability	217
17.	Arbitration is Different		221
	17.1	Summary	221
	17.2	Is the reference to an expert or an arbitrator?	221

	17.3	Express words	222
	17.4	Key indicators	225
	17.5	A formulated dispute	225
	17.6	A judicial function	230
	17.7	Evidence and submissions	234
	17.8	Agreement to accept the decision	237
	17.9	Review of the indicators	239
	17.10	Procedural differences	240
	17.11	The different consequences of an expert's decision and an arbitration award	242
18.	A Third Category		244
	18.1	Summary	244
	18.2	The range of systems	244
	18.3	Decisions by one party (or its agent) only	245
	18.4	Decisions by reference to a document or a formula	248
	18.5	Competitions and wagers	249
	18.6	Decisions concerning membership of associations	250
	18.7	Statutory systems	251
	18.8	Public administration	252
	18.9	Conclusion	253

APPENDICES

A:	Precedents for an accountancy expert	255
B:	Appointment of Arbitrators (and Experts) by the President of the Law Society: guidance notes and application form	260
C:	Precedent for share valuation	265
D:	RICS application form	266
E:	Precedent for expert determination of all disputes under a construction contract	269
F:	Precedent for *ad hoc* reference of construction dispute with formal hearing	270
G:	Precedent for reference to panel of experts: Channel Tunnel	272
H:	Precedent for claims tribunal for company voluntary arrangement	274
I:	CEDR's brochure on expert determination	277

List of Appointing Authorities	*281*
Glossary	*285*
Further Reading	*288*
Index	*291*

ABBREVIATIONS

ADR	Alternative Dispute Resolution
CEDR	Centre for Dispute Resolution
CIArb	Chartered Institute of Arbitrators
CIC	Construction Industry Council
CPR	Civil Procedure Rules
FIDIC	Fédération Internationale des Ingénieurs-Conseils, and the international engineering contract they publish under those initials
IBA SBL	International Bar Association Section on Business Law
ICC	International Chamber of Commerce
ICE	Institute of Civil Engineers and the engineering contract they publish under those same initials
ICAEW	Institute of Chartered Accountants in England & Wales
LCIA	London Court of International Arbitration
RICS	Royal Institution of Chartered Surveyors
RSC	Rules of the Supreme Court
TCC	Technology and Construction Court
TECBAR	Technology and Construction Bar Association
TECSA	Technology and Construction Solicitors Association
UNCITRAL	United Nations Committee on International Trade Law, and the Model Law on Arbitration and the Arbitration Rules they publish under those initials

TABLE OF CASES

(All references are to paragraph numbers except for those prefixed "App." which refer to the appendices.)

A&D Maintenance and Construction Ltd v. Pagehurst Construction Services Ltd (2000) 16 Const. L.J. 199, QBD (T&CC) 9.2.6
AT&T Corp v. Saudi Cable Co. [2000] 2 All E.R. (Comm) 625; [2000] 2 Lloyd's Rep. 127; [2000] C.L.C. 1309; [2000] B.L.R. 743; *The Times*, May 23, 2000, CA; affirming [2000] 1 All E.R. (Comm) 201; [2000] 1 Lloyd's Rep. 22; [2000] C.L.C. 220, QBD (Comm Ct) 15.4.4
Abbey Leisure, Re; *sub nom.* Virdi v. Abbey Leisure [1990] B.C.L.C. 342; [1990] B.C.C. 60; *The Times*, December 19, 1989,CA; reversing [1989] B.C.L.C. 619; (1989) 5 B.C.C. 183 ....3.7.1
Agroexport Entreprise D'Etat pour le Commerce Exterieur v. Goorden Import Cy SA NV [1956] 1 Lloyd's Rep. 319, QBD 5.7.3
Agroment Motoimport Ltd v. Marlden Engineering Co. (Beds) Ltd [1985] 1 W.L.R. 762; [1985] 2 All E.R. 436, QBD 14.8.1
Alfred C Toepfer v. Continental Grain Co. [1974] 1 Lloyd's Rep. 11; (1973) 117 S.J. 649, CA; affirming [1973] 1 Lloyd's Rep. 289, QBD (Comm Ct) 5.7.2, 5.7.3, 15.11.3
Amalgamated Investment & Property Co. Ltd (In Liquidation) v. Texas Commerce International Bank Ltd [1982] Q.B. 84; [1981] 3 W.L.R. 565; [1981] 3 All E.R. 577; [1982] 1 Lloyd's Rep. 27; [1981] Com. L.R. 236; 125 S.J. 623, CA; affirming [1981] 2 W.L.R. 554; [1981] 1 All E.R. 923; [1981] Com. L.R. 37; 125 S.J. 133, QBD (Comm Ct) 12.2.4
Amec Building Ltd v. Cadmus Investment Co Ltd 51 Con. L.R. 105; (1997) 13 Const. L.J. 50, QBD (OR) 9.10.1
Amoco (UK) Exploration Co v. Amerada Hess Ltd [1994] 1 Lloyd's Rep. 330, Ch D 6.4.6, 12.5.5, 12.7.2
Amoco (UK) Exploration Co. v. Shell (UK) Ltd, unreported, December 21, 1989, Commercial Ct 6.4.6
Arbitration between Gregson and Armstrong, Re (1894) 70 L.T. 196 ....17.6.8
Arco British v. Sun Oil Britain; *The Financial Times*, December 20, 1988, CA 6.4.6
Arenson v. Casson Beckman Rutley & Co; *sub nom.* Arenson v. Arenson [1977] A.C. 405; [1975] 3 W.L.R. 815; [1975] 3 All E.R. 901; [1976] 1 Lloyd's Rep. 179; 119 S.J. 810, HL; reversing [1973] Ch. 346; [1973] 2 W.L.R. 553; [1973] 2 All E.R. 235; [1973] 2 Lloyd's Rep. 104; 117 S.J. 247, CA; affirming [1972] 1 W.L.R. 1196; [1972] 2 All E.R. 939, Ch D 3.2.2, 3.9, 7.4.1, 7.4.2, 15.3, 15.11.4, 16.5, 16.5.1, 16.5.3, 16.5.4, 16.6.5, 16.7.1, 16.13.1, 17.4.1
Arthur JS Hall & Co v. Simons; Barratt v. Woolf Seddon; Cockbone v Atkinson Dacre & Slack; Harris v Scholfield Roberts & Hill; *sub nom.* Harris v. Scholfield Roberts & Hall; Hall & Co v. Simons; Barratt v. Ansell (t/a as Woolf Seddon) [2000] 3 W.L.R. 543; [2000] 3 All E.R.

Table of Cases

673; [2000] B.L.R. 407; [2000] E.C.C. 487; [2000] 2 F.L.R. 545; [2000] 2 F.C.R. 673; [2000] Fam. Law 806; [2000] E.G.C.S. 99; (2000) 97(32) L.S.G. 38; (2000) 150 N.L.J. 1147; (2000) 144 S.J.L.B. 238; [2000] N.P.C. 87; *The Times*, July 21, 2000; *The Independent*, July 25, 2000, HL; affirming [1999] 3 W.L.R. 873; [1999] 1 F.L.R. 536; [1999] 2 F.C.R. 193; [1999] Lloyd's Rep. P.N. 47; [1999] P.N.L.R. 374; [1999] Fam. Law 215; [1998] N.P.C. 162; *The Times*, December 18, 1998; *The Independent*, December 18, 1998, CA; affirming [1998] 2 F.L.R. 679; [1999] P.N.L.R. 208; [1998] Fam. Law 524, QBD 16.5.4

B.P. Chemicals Ltd v. Kingdom Engineering (Fife) Ltd [1994] 2 Lloyd's Rep. 373; 69 B.L.R. 113; 38 Con. L.R. 14; (1994) 10 Const. L.J. 116, QBD (OR) 9.10.1
Babbage v. Coulbourn (1882) 9 Q.B. 235 ....2.5
Baber v. Kenwood Manufacturing Co. and Whinney Murray & Co. [1978] 1 Lloyd's Rep. 175; 121 S.J. 606, CA 3.5.2, 9.3.3, 9.8.3, 15.11.5, 17.8.2
Bache & Co (London) Ltd v. Banque Vernes et Commerciale de Paris SA [1973] 2 Lloyd's Rep. 437; (1973) 117 S.J. 483, CA ...5.10, 18.3.4
Balfour Beatty Civil Engineering Ltd v. Docklands Light Railway Ltd [1996] C.L.C. 1435; 78 B.L.R. 42; 49 Con. L.R. 1; (1996) 12 Const. L.J. 259,CA 7.4.1, 7.4.3, 15.8.2, 18.3.7
Baulderstone Hornibrook Engineering Pty Ltd v. Kayah Holdings Pty Ltd, unreported, December 2, 1997, Supreme Court of Western Australia 7.9.1, 8.7.2
Beaufort Developments (NI) Ltd v. Gilbert-Ash (NI) Ltd [1999] 1 A.C. 266; [1998] 2 W.L.R. 860; [1998] 2 All E.R. 778; [1998] N.I. 144; [1998] C.L.C. 830; 88 B.L.R. 1; 59 Con. L.R. 66; (1998) 14 Const. L.J. 280; [1998] E.G.C.S. 85; (1998) 95(24) L.S.G. 33; (1998) 95(31) L.S.G. 34; (1998) 148 N.L.J. 869; (1998) 142 S.J.L.B. 172; [1998] N.P.C. 91; [1998] N.P.C. 93; *The Times*, June 8, 1998, HL (NI); reversing [1997] N.I. 142; 83 B.L.R. 1; (1997) 13 Const. L.J. 321, CA (NI) 7.4.3, 12.2.3, 15.8.2, 18.3.7
Belchier v. Reynolds (1754) 3 Keny. 87 ....1.2.1, 15.10.1
Belvedere Motors v. King [1981] 2 E.G.L.R. 131; (1981) 260 E.G. 813 ....16.7.10
Benfield Greig Group plc, Re. See Nugent v. Benfield Greig Group plc
Bernhard's Rugby Landscapes Ltd v. Stockley Park Consortium Ltd (1998) 14 Const. L.J. 329 QBD (OR) .....7.4.3, 8.4.2, 9.2.9, 12.5.2, ...12.6.4, 13.10.2, 13.10.3
Bloor Construction (UK) Ltd v. Bowmer & Kirkland (London) Ltd [2000] B.L.R. 764; (2000) 2 T.C.L.R. 914, QBD (T&CC) ..7.5.5, 9.3.3, 15.9.10
Blundell v. Brettargh (1810) 17 Ves. 232 ....15.9.3
Bolam v. Friern Hospital Management Committee [1957] 1 W.L.R. 582; [1957] 2 All E.R. 118; [1955-95] P.N.L.R. 7; 101 S.J. 357, QBD 16.7.8
Bos v. Helsham (1866) L.R. 2 Exch. 72 ....17.5.1
Boswell (Steels), Re (1989) 5 B.C.C. 145 ....15.5.4
Bottomley v. Ambler (1878) 38 L.T. 545 ....6.2.2, 17.7.2
Bouygues UK Ltd v. Dahl-Jensen UK Ltd [2000] B.L.R. 522; (2000) 7(35) L.S.G. 36; *The Times*, August 17, 2000, CA; affirming [2000] B.L.R.

TABLE OF CASES

49; (2000) 2 T.C.L.R. 308; 70 Con. L.R. 41; *The Independent*, February 7, 2000 (C.S.) QBD (T&CC) 7.5.2, 7.5.5, 15.9.10, 15.12.9, 15.12.10, 15.13.5, 15.20, 18.7.4
Bow Cedar, The. *See* Bunge NV v. Compagnie Noga d'Importation et d'Exportation SA, (Bow Cedar, The) Boyd v. Emmerson (1834) 2 A.D. & E. 183 . . . . .8.8.1
Boynton v. Richardson [1924] W.N. 262 .16.3.6
Bridger Properties Ltd v. Dovey Holdings (South Wales) Ltd, unreported, June 25, 1991, ChD 2.6.1
British Shipbuilders v. VSEL Consortium plc [1997] 1 Lloyd's Rep. 106; *The Times*, February 14, 1996, Ch D 1.1.1, 4.2.4, 9.2.7, 9.15.9, 12.2.3, 12.6.1, 12.6.6, 12.6.8, 12.7.1, 13.3.2, 15.12.8
Brutus v. Cozens [1973] A.C. 854; [1972] 3 W.L.R. 521; [1972] 2 All E.R. 1297; (1972) 56 Cr. App. R. 799; [1973] Crim. L.R. 56; 116 S.J. 647, HL; reversing [1972] 1 W.L.R. 484; [1972] 2 All E.R. 1; 116 S.J. 217; [1972] 3 W.L.R. 521; [1972] 2 All E.R. 1297, QBD 12.6.2, 15.14.1
Bunge NV v. Compagnie Noga d'Importation et d'Exportation SA (The Bow Cedar) [1980] 2 Lloyd's Rep. 601; [1981] Com. L.R. 92, QBD (Comm Ct) 5.7.2
Burgess v. Purchase & Sons (Farms) Ltd [1983] Ch. 216; [1983] 2 W.L.R. 361; [1983] 2 All E.R. 4, Ch D 15.13.3, 15.13.4

Camden L.B.C. v. Thomas McInerney & Sons Ltd 9 Con. L.R. 99; (1986) 2 Const. L.J. 293, QBD (OR) 13.8.2
Cameron (A) v. John Mowlem & Co. plc 52 B.L.R. 24; 25 Con. L.R. 11; *The Financial Times*, December 12, 1990, CA 7.5.5, 14.2.3
Campbell v. Edwards [1976] 1 W.L.R. 403; [1976] 1 All E.R. 785; [1976] 1 Lloyd's Rep. 522; 119 S.J. 845, CA 2.4, 15.2.2, 15.2.4, 15.4.1, 15.11.4, 15.11.5, 15.12.6, 15.19.1, 16.7.14
Campbell and Palmer v. Crest Homes (Wessex) Ltd, unreported, November 13, 1989 . . . . .2.2.2, 15.11.7, 15.13.7
Canterbury Pipelines Ltd v. Christchurch Drainage Board [1979] 2 N.Z.L.R. 347 . . . . .15.4.2
Caparo Industries plc v. Dickman [1990] 2 A.C. 605; [1990] 2 W.L.R. 358; [1990] 1 All E.R. 568; [1990] B.C.L.C. 273; [1990] B.C.C. 164; [1990] E.C.C. 313; [1955-95] P.N.L.R. 523; (1990) 87(12) L.S.G. 42; (1990) 140 N.L.J. 248; (1990) 134 S.J. 494; (1990) L.S.G. March 28, 42; (1990) L.S.G. September 26, 28; *The Times*, February 12, 1990; *The Independent*, February 16, 1990; *The Financial Times*, February 13, 1990;The Guardian, February 15, 1990; *The Daily Telegraph*, February 15, 1990, HL; reversing [1989] Q.B. 653; [1989] 2 W.L.R. 316; [1989] 1 All E.R. 798; [1989] B.C.L.C. 154; (1989) 5 B.C.C. 105; [1989] P.C.C. 125; (1988) 138 N.L.J. 289; (1989) 133 S.J. 221; *The Times*, August 8, 1988; *The Independent*, August 10, 1988; *The Financial Times*, August 5, 1988; *The Daily Telegraph*, August 26, 1988, CA; reversing in part [1988] B.C.L.C. 387; (1988) 4 B.C.C. 144, QBD 16.13.1, 16.13.2
Cape Durasteel Ltd v. Rosser and Russell Building Services Ltd 46 Con. L.R. 75, QBD 7.5.1, 17.3.2, 17.3.6
Capricorn Inks Pty Ltd v. Lawter International (Australasia) Pty Ltd [1989] 1 Qd. R. 8 . . . . .8.3, 9.2.4, 13.6.1, 15.6.2, 17.5.8

TABLE OF CASES

Carus Wilson & Greene, Re (1886) L.R. 18 Q.B.D. 7, CA 1.6.6,
  10.8.1, 17.5.1, 17.5.3, 17.5.8
Chambers v. Goldthorpe [1901] 1 Q.B. 624 . . . . . .16.3.5, 16.4.1, 17.5.4
Channel Tunnel Group Ltd v. Balfour Beatty Construction Ltd; France
  Manche SA v. Balfour Beatty Construction Ltd [1993] A.C. 334;
  [1993] 2 W.L.R. 262; [1993] 1 All E.R. 664; [1993] 1 Lloyd's Rep. 291;
  61 B.L.R. 1; 32 Con. L.R. 1; [1993] I.L.Pr. 607; (1993) 137 S.J.L.B.
  36; [1993] N.P.C. 8; *The Times*, January 25, 1993, HL; affirming
  [1992] Q.B. 656; [1992] 2 W.L.R. 741; [1992] 2 All E.R. 609; [1992] 2
  Lloyd's Rep. 7; 56 B.L.R. 23; (1992) 8 Const. L.J. 150; (1992) 136
  S.J.L.B. 54; [1992] N.P.C. 7; *The Times*, January 23, 1992; *The
  Financial Times*, January 29, 1992, CA 1.5.3,
  7.5.6 8.4.1, 12.5.4, App. G
Charles E Ford Ltd v. AFEC Inc. [1986] 2 Lloyd's Rep. 307, QBD
  (Comm Ct) 5.7.3
Chartered Society of Physiotherapy v. Simmonds Church Smiles
  73 B.L.R. 130; [1995] 14 E.G. 145; [1995] E.G.C.S. 25,
  QBD 18.7.2
Chelsea Man plc v. Vivat Holdings plc, unreported, August 24,
  1989, CA 4.2.4, 12.3.1, 12.7.4, 13.6.4
Christopher Brown Ltd v. Genossenschaft Oesterreichischer
  Waldbesitzer Holzwirtschaftsbetriebe GessmbH [1954] 1 Q.B. 8;
  [1953] 3 W.L.R. 689; [1953] 2 All E.R. 1039; [1953] 2 Lloyd's
  Rep. 373; 97 S.J. 744, QBD 12.3.1
Coastal (Bermuda) Ltd v. Esso Petroleum Co Ltd [1984] 1 Lloyd's Rep.
  11; *The Times*, October 21, 1983, CA .5.7.3
Collier v. Mason (1858) 25 Beav. 200 . . . . .2.4, 15.10.2
Collins v. Collins (1858) 26 Beav. 306 . . . . .11.3.1, 17.5.1
Company (No.000330 of 1991) ex p. Holden, Re [1991] B.C.L.C. 597;
  [1991] B.C.C. 241 . . . . .3.7.1
Compton Group Ltd v. Estates Gazette Ltd (1978) 36 P. & C.R. 148;
  (1977) 244 E.G. 799; [1977] 2 E.G.L.R. 73,CA 2.3.4
Concorde Graphics v. Andromeda Investments SA (1983) 265 E.G. 386;
  [1983] 1 E.G.L.R. 53 . . . . .2.4, 10.7.1, 15.5.2
Conoco (UK) Ltd v. Philips Petroleum [1998] A.D.R.L.J. 55 . . . . . .6.4.6,
  12.6.8, 15.13.5, 15.17, 15.18.2
Cooper v. Shutterworth (1856) 25 L.J. Exch. 114 . . . . .6.4.8, 10.8.1
Cott UK Ltd v. FE Barber Ltd [1997] 3 All E.R. 540, QBD . . .1.5.3, 7.9.2,
  8.4.2, 8.7.2, 9.8.3, 9.15.7, 10.5.2, 11.2.3, 13.3.3, 17.3.5
Cozens v. Brutus. *See* Brutus v. Cozens
Credit Suisse First Boston (Europe) Ltd v. Seagate Trading Co. Ltd
  [1999] 1 All E.R. (Comm.) 261; [1999] 1 Lloyd's Rep. 784; [1999]
  C.L.C. 600, QBD (Comm Ct) 9.2.6
Croudace v. Lambeth L.B.C. (1986) 33 B.L.R. 20, CA; (1984) 1 Const.
  L.J. 128; [1984] C.I.L.L. 136, QBD (OR) 9.7.5, 11.3.5
Cruden Construction Ltd v. Commission for the New Towns [1995] 2
  Lloyd's Rep. 387; (1994) 75 B.L.R. 134 QBD 17.5.2
Crusader Resources NL v. Santos Ltd (1991) 58 S.A.S.R. 74 . . . .6.4.5,
  15.4.5
Currys Group plc v. Martin [1999] 3 E.G.L.R. 165; [1999] E.G.C.S. 115;
  (1999) 96(39) L.S.G. 40; [1999] N.P.C. 116, QBD 16.7.10

TABLE OF CASES

Cygnet Healthcare plc v. Higgins City Ltd (2000) 16 Const. L.J. 394,
  QBD (T&CC) 7.5.5
Czarnikow Ltd v. Roth Schmidt & Co.[1922] 2 K.B. 478; (1922)
  12 Ll. L. Rep. 195, CA; affirming (1922) 10 Ll. L. Rep. 687, KBD
  ....12.5.1, 12.5.5

D (A Child) v. Walker; *sub nom.* Walker v. D (A Child) [2000] 1 W.L.R.
  1382; [2000] C.P.L.R. 462; [2000] U.K.H.R.R. 648; [2000] P.I.Q.R.
  P193; (2000) 97(22) L.S.G. 44; *The Times*, May 17, 2000; *The
  Independent*, June 12, 2000 (C.S) CA 8.3
Damond Lock Grabowski v. Laing Investments (Bracknell) Ltd 60 B.L.R.
  112, QBD 8.8.6
Daniels v. Walker. *See* D (A Child) v. Walker.
Darlington B.C. v. Waring & Gillow (Holdings) [1988] 45 E.G. 102, DC
  ....11.4.4, 16.2.6
Daudruy van Cauwenberghe & Fils SA v. Tropical Product Sales SA;
  Tropical Product Sales SA v. Saudi Sabah Palm Oil Corp.[1986] 1
  Lloyd's Rep. 535, QBD (Comm Ct) 5.7.2
David Wilson Homes Ltd v. Surrey Services Ltd (in liquidation), & anr.
  See Wilson (David) Homes Ltd v. Surrey Services Ltd (in
  liquidation)
Davies Middleton & Davies Ltd v. Toyo Engineering Corp.85 B.L.R. 59,
  CA 1.1.7, 9.8.1
Davstone Estates Ltd's Leases, Re; *sub nom.* Manprop Ltd v. O'Dell
  [1969] 2 Ch. 378; [1969] 2 W.L.R. 1287; [1969] 2 All E.R. 849;
  (1969) 20 P. & C.R. 395; 113 S.J. 366, Ch D 2.4, 12.5.3,
                                                            12.5.4, 12.5.5
Dean v. Prince [1954] Ch. 409; [1954] 2 W.L.R. 538; [1954] 1
  All E.R. 749; 47 R. & I.T. 494; 98 S.J. 215, CA; reversing [1953]
  Ch. 590; [1953] 3 W.L.R. 271; [1953] 2 All E.R. 636; 97 S.J. 490,
  Ch D 6.2.3, 15.11.1, 15.13.5
Dinham v. Bradford (1867) L.R. 5 Ch. App. 519 ....5.3.1
Discain Project Services Ltd v. Opecprime Development Ltd [2000]
  B.L.R. 402, QBD (T&CC) 7.5.5, 15.6.4
Dixons Group plc v. Murray-Oboynski 86 B.L.R.16, QBD (OR) 4.2.4,
                                                    12.6.8, 15.17, 15.19.1
Doleman & Sons v. Ossett Corp. [1912] 3 K.B. 257, CA 12.5.1
Drake & Scull Engineering Ltd v. McLaughlin & Harvey plc 60 B.L.R.
  102, QBD 7.5.5, 14.3.2, 14.4

Eads v. Williams (1854) 24 L.J.Ch. 531 ....6.2.1
Elanay Contracts Ltd v, Vestry, The, unreported, August 30, 2000 ..7.5.5
Emery v. Wase (1803) 8 Ves. 506 ....15.10.2
Equitable Trust Co. of New York v. Dawson Partners Ltd (1927) 27 Ll. L.
  Rep. 49, HL; affirming (1926) 25 Ll. L. Rep. 90, CA; reversing (1926)
  24 Ll. L. Rep. 261, KBD 5.7.2, 11.4.3
Ess v. Truscott (1837) 2 M. & W. 385 ....15.9.6, 16.7.4
Esso Australia Resources Ltd v. Plowman [1994] 1 V.R. 1 ......9.15.10

FR Absalom Ltd v. Great Western (London) Garden Village Society Ltd
  [1933] A.C. 592, HL 12.5.4

Table of Cases

Finchbourne Ltd v. Rodrigues [1976] 3 All E.R. 581, CA 2.4, 10.7.1, 15.5.2
Finnegan v. Allen [1943] K.B. 425; [1943] 1 All E.R. 493, CA 16.3.7, 16.6.2, 17.6.6
Firth v. Midland Railway Company (1875) L.R. 20 Eq. 100 . . . . .9.7.5, 10.3.1
Fisher v. P.G. Wellfair Ltd (In Liquidation); Fox v. P.G. Wellfair Ltd [1981] 2 Lloyd's Rep. 514; [1981] Com. L.R. 140; 19 B.L.R. 52; (1982) 263 E.G. 589; (1982) 263 E.G. 657; 125 S.J. 413, CA [1979] I.C.R. 834, EAT 17.6.3
Fordgate Bingley Ltd v. Argyll Stores Ltd [1994] 2 E.G.L.R. 84 . . .17.3.4
Fordgate (Bingley) Ltd v. National Westminster Bank plc [1994] 39 E.G. 135; [1995] E.G.C.S. 97; [1994] 2 E.G.L.R. 84, Ch D 2.3.7
Fox v. P.G. Wellfair. See Fisher v. P.G. Wellfair Ltd (In Liquidation)
Frank H Wright (Constructions) Ltd v. Frodoor Ltd [1967] 1 W.L.R. 506; [1967] 1 All E.R. 433; 111 S.J. 210, QBD 15.18.2
Fraser Pipestock Ltd v. Gloucester City Council (1996) 71 P. & C.R. 123; [1995] 2 E.G.L.R. 90; [1995] 36 E.G. 141; [1995] N.P.C. 26, Ch D 2.3.5
Fuller v. Cyracuse Ltd, unreported, June 6, 2000, ChD 3.8, 8.10.3
Fulmar case. See Amoco (UK) Exploration Co. v. Shell (UK) Ltd
George v. Roach (1942) 67 C.L.R. 253 . . . . .10.3.1

Gill & Duffus SA v. Berger & Co Inc; sub nom. Berger & Co v. Gill & Duffus SA [1984] A.C. 382; [1984] 2 W.L.R. 95; [1984] 1 All E.R. 438; [1984] 1 Lloyd's Rep. 227; (1984) 81 L.S.G. 429; (1984) 128 S.J. 47,HL; reversing [1983] 1 Lloyd's Rep. 622; [1983] Com. L.R. 122, CA; reversing [1981] 2 Lloyd's Rep. 233; [1981] Com. L.R. 253, QBD (Comm Ct) 5.7.2, 15.11.3
Gillatt v. Sky Television Ltd (formerly Sky Television plc) [2000] 1 All E.R. (Comm) 461; [2000] 2 B.C.L.C. 103, CA 3.4.2, 3.5.2, 9.2.8, 9.2.9, 10.3.1, 11.3.5, 13.10.4
Glacier Bay, The. See West of England Shipowners Mutual Insurance Association (Luxembourg) v. Cristal Ltd
Gordon v. Whitehouse (1856) 18 C.B. 747 . . . . .16.11
Gosden v. Funnell (1899) 15 T.L.R. 547 . . . . .15.9.10
Government of Kelantan v. Duff Development Co. See Kelantan v. Duff Development Co. Ltd

Habib Bank Ltd v. Habib Bank AG [1981] 1 W.L.R. 1265; [1981] 2 All E.R. 650; [1982] R.P.C. 1; 125 S.J. 512, CA 15.2.4
Hammond & Waterton, Re (1890) 62 L.T. 808 . . . . .8.8.1, 17.3.2
Harben Style Ltd v. Rhodes Trust; Thomas Cook Group v. Rhodes Trust [1995] 1 E.G.L.R. 118; [1995] 17 E.G. 125; [1994] N.P.C. 99, Ch D 11.3.4
Harrison v. Thompson [1989] 1 W.L.R. 1325; (1989) 86(42) L.S.G. 41; (1989) 133 S.J. 1545, Ch D 3.4.2
Healds Foods Ltd v. Hyde Daries, unreported, December 6, 1996, CA 4.2.6, 15.13.4, 15.17, 15.19.1, 15.19.2
Hedley Byrne & Co. Ltd v. Heller & Partners Ltd [1964] A.C. 465; [1963] 3 W.L.R. 101; [1963] 2 All E.R. 575; [1963] 1 Lloyd's

Rep. 485; 107 S.J. 454; (1963) 107 S.J. 454, HL; affirming
[1962] 1 Q.B. 396; [1961] 3 W.L.R. 1225; [1961] 3 All E.R. 891;
105 S.J. 910; (1961) 105 S.J. 910, CA; affirming; *The Times*,
December 21, 1960 . . . . .16.5.2, 16.7.11, 16.13.1
Henderson v. Merrett Syndicates Ltd; Hallam-Eames v. Merrett
Syndicates Ltd; Hughes v. Merrett Syndicates Ltd; Arbuthnott v.
Fagan and Feltrim Underwriting Agencies; Deeny v. Gooda Walker
Ltd [1995] 2 A.C. 145; [1994] 3 W.L.R. 761; [1994] 3 All E.R. 506;
[1994] 2 Lloyd's Rep. 468; (1994) 144 N.L.J. 1204; *The Times*, July
26, 1994; Independent, August 3, 1994, HL; affirming *The Times*,
December 30, 1993; *The Independent*, December 14, 1993, CA;
affirming [1994] 2 Lloyd's Rep. 193; *The Times*, October 20, 1993,
QBD (Comm Ct) 16.13.2
Herschel Engineering Ltd v. Breen Property Ltd [2000] B.L.R. 272;
(2000) 2 T.C.L.R. 473; 70 Con. L.R. 1; (2000) 16 Const. L.J. 366;
The Times, May 10, 2000, QBD (T&CC) 7.5.5
Heyes v. Earl of Derby (1984) 272 E.G. 939; [1984] 2 E.G.L.R. 87, CA . . .2.4
Hickman v. Roberts [1913] A.C. 229, HL 7.4.2, 15.4.2, 16.9.1
Highway Contract Hire Ltd v. NWS Bank plc, unreported, April 17, 1996,
CA 4.2.1, 18.4
Hillsbridge Investments Ltd v. Moresfield Ltd, unreported, March 15,
2000, ChD 4.2.4, 12.2.1
Holt v. Payne Skillington 77 B.L.R. 51; 49 Con. L.R. 99; [1996] P.N.L.R. 179;
[1995] E.G.C.S. 201; (1996) 93(2) L.S.G. 29; (1996) 140 S.J.L.B. 30;
[1995] N.P.C. 202; *The Times*, December 22, 1995, CA 16.13.2
Homer Burgess Ltd v. Chirex (Annan) Ltd 2000 S.L.T. 277; [2000]
B.L.R. 124; (2000) 16 Constr. L.J. 242; *The Times*, January 25,
2000 . . . . .7.5.5
Hooper, Re (1867) L.R. 2 Q.B. 367 . . . . .17.6.2, 17.7.2
Hopcraft v. Hickman (1842) 2 Sim. & St. 130 . . . . .15.9.1
Hounslow L.B.C. v. Twickenham Garden Developments Ltd [1971] Ch.
233; [1970] 3 W.L.R. 538; [1970] 3 All E.R. 326; 7 B.L.R. 81; 69 L.G.R.
109; 114 S.J. 603, Ch D 15.6.1
Howe Richardson Scale Co. v. Polimex-Cekop [1978] 1 Lloyd's Rep. 161,
CA 5.10
Hudson (A) v. Legal & General Life of Australia [1986] 2 E.G.L.R. 130;
(1986) 280 E.G. 1434, PC 2.3.4, 15.11.6

Imperial Foods Ltd Pension Scheme, Re [1986] 1 W.L.R. 717;
[1986] 2 All E.R. 802; (1986) 83 L.S.G. 1641; (1986) 130 S.J. 447,
Ch D 4.3.3, 15.11.4
Insurance Co. v. Lloyd's Syndicate [1995] 1 Lloyd's Rep. 272; [1994] C.L.C.
1303; *The Times*, November 11, 1994; *The Independent*, November 8,
1994; Lloyd's List, February 1, 1995, QBD (Comm Ct) 8.9.7
International Semitech Microelectronics Ltd v. Scholl plc, unreported,
May 27, 1994 . . . . .4.2.2, 12.2.2
Ipswich B.C. v. Fisons plc [1990] Ch. 709; [1990] 2 W.L.R. 108; [1990] 1
All E.R. 730; [1990] 04 E.G. 127; (1990) 87(7) L.S.G. 32; (1990) 134
S.J. 517, CA; affirming [1989] 3 W.L.R. 818; [1989] 2 All E.R. 737;
(1989) 133 S.J. 1090, Ch D 17.5.7
Irwin v. Campbell (1915) 23 D.L.R. 279 .15.18.3

Table of Cases

Jenkins v. Betham (1855) 15 C.B. 32 .... 16.3.2, 16.3.4
John Barker Construction Ltd v. London Portman Hotel Ltd 83 B.L.R. 31;
  50 Con. L.R. 43; (1996) 12 Const. L.J. 277 QBD (OR) 7.4.3,
  .... 9.3.3, 15.6.1, 15.8.2, 15.18.3, 15.20, 16.6.7, 16.10, 18.3.7
John Holland Construction and Engineering Ltd v. Majorca Products
  (2000) 16 Const. L.J. 114, Sup Ct (Vic) 15.6.3, 16.9.1,
                                                    16.9.2, 16.13.2, 16.13.4
Johnston v. Chestergate Hat Manufacturing Co Ltd [1915] 2 Ch. 338,
  Ch D 5.2.1, 15.13.2, 15.13.3
Jones v. Sherwood Computer Services plc [1992] 1 W.L.R. 277; [1992] 2
  All E.R. 170; *The Times*, December 14, 1989, CA 1.2.3,
          10.8.2, 12.6.1, 12.6.3, 12.6.4, 12.6.8, 12.7.3,
          13.8.3, 15.8.2, 15.11.4, 15.12.1, 15.12.2, 15.12.7,
          15.12.8, 15.12.10, 15.13.2, 15.13.4, 15.13.5,
                 15.14.2, 5.14.3, 15.17, 15.19.1, 15.20
Jones (M) v. Jones (RR) [1971] 1 W.L.R. 840; [1971] 2 All E.R. 676; 115
  S.J. 424, Ch D 2.5, 9.2.1, 11.4.5, 15.9.5, 15.11.2,
                                  15.12.6, 15.12.8, 15.18.1, 15.18.2
Jordan v Norfolk C.C. [1994] 1 W.L.R. 1353; [1994] 4 All E.R. 218;
  93 L.G.R. 50; (1994) 91(30) L.S.G. 31; [1994] N.P.C. 69;
  The Times, May 25, 1994; *The Independent*, June 20, 1994
  (C.S.) Ch D 1.1.6, 9.2.1

Karenlee Nominees Pty Ltd v. Gollin & Co. Ltd [1983] V.R. 657 ..10.8.2,
                                                                    11.4.2
Kelantan v. Duff Development Co.Ltd [1923] A.C. 395, HL 12.5.4
Kemp v. Rose (1858) 1 Giff. 258 .... 10.7.1, 15.5.3
Killick v. PricewaterhouseCoopers, unreported, July 5, 2000 .... 3.9.
                                                      3.10, 16.7.11, 16.13.1
Kimberley v. Dick (1871) L.R. 13 Eq. 1 .... 15.5.3
King v. Thomas McKenna Ltd [1991] 2 Q.B. 480; [1991] 2 W.L.R. 1234;
  [1991] 1 All E.R. 653; 54 B.L.R. 48; *The Times*, January 30, 1991,
  CA 15.9.10
Knibb v. National Coal Board [1987] Q.B. 906; [1986] 3 W.L.R. 895;
  [1986] 3 All E.R. 644; (1986) 52 P. & C.R. 354; [1986] 2 E.G.L.R. 11;
  (1986) 280 E.G. 92; [1986] R.V.R. 123; (1986) 83 L.S.G. 3340; (1986)
  130 S.J. 840, CA; affirming in part (1985) 49 P. & C.R. 426; [1985] 1
  E.G.L.R. 182; (1985) 273 E.G. 307; [1984] R.V.R. 220; [1985] J.P.L.
  263, Lands Tr 9.10.1
Kollerich & Cie SA v. State Trading Corp. of India Ltd [1980] 2
  Lloyd's Rep. 32, CA; affirming [1979] 2 Lloyd's Rep. 442, QBD
  (Comm Ct) 5.7.2, 11.4.3, 15.9.6, 16.7.4

Laidlaw and Campbellford Lake Ontario and Western Railway Company,
  Re (1914) 19 D.L.R. 481 .... 17.3.1
Land Securities plc v. Westminster City Council [1993] 1 W.L.R. 286;
  [1993] 4 All E.R. 124; (1992) 65 P. C. & R. 387 .... 17.10.3
Langham House Developments v. Brompton Securities [1980] 2 E.G.L.R.
  117; (1980) 256 E.G. 719 .... 17.3.4
Lee v. Showmen's Guild of Great Britain [1952] 2 Q.B. 329; [1952] 1
  All E.R. 1175; [1952] 1 T.L.R. 1115; 96 S.J. 296, CA 12.5.3, 15.7,
                                                            15.11.1, 18.6

TABLE OF CASES

Leeds v. Burrows (1810) 12 East 1 ....2.5
Leigh v. English Property Corp. Ltd [1976] 2 Lloyd's Rep. 298; (1975)
  120 S.J. 64, CA 3.4.2, 17.5.5
Lewisham Investment Partnership Ltd v. Morgan [1997] 2 E.G.L.R. 150;
  [1997] 51 E.G. 75; [1997] N.P.C. 155; *The Times*, November 25, 1997,
  Ch D 16.7.10, 16.10
Lex Services v. Oriel House BV [1991] 2 E.G.L.R. 126; [1991] 39
  E.G. 139 ....17.6.3
Lishman v. Christie & Co. (1887) 19 Q.B.D. 333 ....5.8
Liverpool City Council v. Irwin [1977] A.C. 239; [1976] 2 W.L.R. 562;
  [1976] 2 All E.R. 39; (1984) 13 H.L.R. 38; 74 L.G.R. 392; (1976)
  32 P. & C.R. 43; (1976) 238 E.G. 879; [1976] J.P.L. 427; 120 S.J.
  267, HL; affirming in part [1976] Q.B. 319; [1975] 3 W.L.R. 663;
  [1975] 3 All E.R. 658; 74 L.G.R. 21; (1976) 31 P. & C.R. 34; 119
  S.J. 612, CA 9.3.2
Locabail (UK) Ltd v. Bayfield Properties Ltd (Leave to Appeal); Locabail
  (UK) Ltd v. Waldorf Investment Corp (Leave to Appeal); Timmins v.
  Gormley; Williams v. Inspector of Taxes; R. v. Bristol Betting and
  Gaming Licensing Committee, ex p. O'Callaghan [2000] Q.B. 451;
  [2000] 2 W.L.R. 870; [2000] 1 All E.R. 65; [2000] I.R.L.R. 96; [2000]
  H.R.L.R. 290; [2000] U.K.H.R.R. 300; 7 B.H.R.C. 583; (1999) 149
  N.L.J. 1793; [1999] N.P.C. 143; *The Times*, November 19, 1999;
  The Independent, November 23, 1999, CA 15.4.4
Lubenham Fidelities and Investment Co Ltd v. South Pembrokeshire
  D.C. and Wigley Fox Partnership 33 B.L.R. 39; 6 Con. L.R. 85; (1986)
  2 Const. L.J. 111; *The Times*, April 8, 1986, CA; affirming [1985]
  C.I.L.L. 214 ....7.4.4, 15.13.4
Ludlam v. Wilson [1901] 2 Ont.L.R. 549 (Canada) 10.7.1, 15.5.3

Macob Civil Engineering Ltd v. Morrison Construction Ltd [1999] C.L.C.
  739; [1999] B.L.R. 93; (1999) 1 T.C.L.R. 113; 64 Con. L.R. 1; [1999]
  3 E.G.L.R. 7; [1999] 37 E.G. 173; (1999) 15 Const. L.J. 300; (1999)
  96(10) L.S.G. 28; *The Times*, March 11, 1999; *The Independent*,
  March 1, 1999 (C.S.) QBD (T&CC) 7.5.2, 7.5.5, 14.4
Macro v. Thompson (No.3) [1997] 2 B.C.L.C. 36,
  Ch D 3.2.2, 3.3.2, 3.4.3, 3.5.2, 10.7.1, 11.3.3, 11.8.1,
              13.10.2, 13.10.3, 15.4.3, 15.4.3, 15.6.1, 15.6.2,
                   15.9.6, 15.12.10, 15.18.3, 15.20, 16.9.1
Macro (Ipswich) Ltd, Re (1994); *sub nom.* Earliba Finance Co Ltd, Re;
  Macro v. Thompson [1994] 2 B.C.L.C. 354; [1994] B.C.C. 781; *The
  Independent*, April 4, 1994 (C.S.) Ch D 15.4.3
Malpass (Deceased), Re; *sub nom.* Lloyds Bank plc v. Malpass [1985]
  Ch. 42; [1984] 3 W.L.R. 372; [1984] 2 All E.R. 313; (1984) 81 L.S.G.
  1916; (1984) 128 S.J. 334, Ch D 9.2.8, 11.3.5, 18.8.2
Mayers v. Dlugash [1994] 1 H.K.C. 755 ....17.5.1, 17.6.4
Mayne Nickless Ltd v. Solomon [1980] Qd.R. 171 ....15.13.5
Mediterranean and Eastern Export Co. Ltd v. Fortress Fabrics
  (Manchester) Ltd [1948] 2 All E.R. 186; (1947-48) 81 Ll. L.
  Rep. 401; 64 T.L.R. 337; [1948] W.N. 244; [1948] L.J.R. 1536;
  92 S.J. 362, KBD 17.6.6
Mercury Communications Ltd v. Director General of Telecommunications
  [1996] 1 W.L.R. 48; [1996] 1 All E.R. 575; [1998] Masons C.L.R. Rep.

39; *The Times*, February 10, 1995; *The Independent*, February 16, 1995, HL; reversing [1995] Masons C.L.R. Rep. 2; (1994) 91(36) L.S.G. 36; (1994) 138 S.J.L.B. 183; *The Times*, August 3, 1994; *The Independent*, August 19, 1994, CA 1.1.5, 6.8, 12.5.4, 12.6.2, 12.6.4, 12.6.6, 12.7.1, 12.7.4, 12.8.2, 15.14.3, 15.20, 18.8.3
Michael Salliss & Co. Ltd v. Calil 13 Con. L.R. 68; (1988) 4 Const. L.J. 125, QBD (OR) 16.9.2, 16.13.2
Mid-Kent Water v. Batchelor [1994] 1 E.G.L.R. 185; [1994] 07 E.G. 197; [1993] E.G.C.S. 103 ....2.2.1, 11.2.2, 12.3.2
Midland Montagu Leasing (UK) Ltd v. Tyne & Wear Passenger Transport Executive and Ernst & Whinney, unreported, February 23, 1990, Ch D 5.4.4, 13.7.2, 15.4.4, 15.6.2, 15.13.6
Mills v. Bayley (1863) 2 H. & C. 36 ....15.9.2
Milnes v. Gery (1807) 14 Ves. 400 ....11.3.3
Minster Trust, Ltd v. Traps Tractors Ltd [1954] 1 W.L.R. 963; [1954] 3 All E.R. 136; 98 S.J. 456, QBD 9.3.3, 15.4.2, 18.3.2
Monmouthshire C.C. v. Costelloe & Kemple Ltd; *sub nom.* Monmouth C.C. v. Costelloe & Kemple Ltd 5 B.L.R. 83; 63 L.G.R. 429, CA; reversing 63 L.G.R. 131 ....17.5.2
Moorcock, The (1889) L.R. 14 P.D. 64; [1886-90] All E.R. Rep. 530, CA 9.3.2
Morgan Sindall plc v. Sawston Farms (Cambs) Ltd [1999] 1 E.G.L.R. 90; [1999] 07 E.G. 135; [1998] E.G.C.S. 177; [1998] N.P.C. 159, CA; affirming [1997] E.G.C.S. 118, Ch D 15.12.10, 15.13.4, 15.20
Morse v. Merest (1821) 6 Madd. 26 ....13.6.3
Mutual Shipping Corp. of New York v. Bayshore Shipping Co. of Monrovia, Montan, The [1985] 1 W.L.R. 625; [1985] 1 All E.R. 520; [1985] 1 Lloyd's Rep. 189; (1985) 82 L.S.G. 1329; (1985) 129 S.J. 219, CA; affirming [1984] 1 Lloyd's Rep. 389, QBD (Comm Ct) 15.9.10

National Grid plc v. M25 Group Ltd , CA, unreported, August 28, 1998 ....12.6.5, 12.7.1, 12.7.3, 12.7.4
National Grid Co. plc v. M25 Group Ltd (No.1) [1999] 1 E.G.L.R. 65; [1999] 08 E.G. 169, CA; reversing [1998] 2 E.G.L.R. 85; [1998] 32 E.G. 90; [1998] N.P.C. 172,
  Ch D 2.3.4, 12.5.4, 12.6.1, 12.6.5, 12.6.6, 12.6.7, 12.7.1, 12.7.3, 12.7.4, 15.14.3, 15.20
Nelson Carlton Construction Company v. A.C. Hatrick (NZ) Ltd [1965] N.Z.L.R.144 ....15.6.3
Neste Production v. Shell UK[1994] 1 Lloyd's Rep. 447, Ch D 6.4.6, 12.6.8, 15.9.9
Nikko Hotels (UK) Ltd v. MEPC plc [1991] 2 E.G.L.R. 103; [1991] 28 E.G. 86 ....1.2.3, 2.3.4, 2.3.5, 12.3.1, 12.5.4, ...12.6.6, 12.6.7, 12.8.1, 13.6.4, 15.8.2, 15.12.1, 15.12.9, 15.12.10
North Eastern Cooperative Society v. Newcastle Upon Tyne City Council [1987] 1 E.G.L.R. 142; (1987) 282 E.G. 1409 ...10.7.2, 16.6.6, 17.5.6
Northern R.H.A. v. Derek Crouch Construction Co. Ltd [1984] Q.B. 644; [1984] 2 W.L.R. 676; [1984] 2 All E.R. 175; 26 B.L.R. 1; [1986] C.I.L.L. 244; (1984) 128 S.J. 279, CA; affirming 24 B.L.R. 60, DC 7.4.3, 12.2.3, 16.9.2, 18.3.7
Norwich Union Life Insurance Society v. P&O Property Holdings Ltd. *See* P&O Property Holdings Ltd v. Norwich Union Life Insurance Society

Nugent v. Benfield Greig Group plc; *sub nom.* Benfield Greig
  Group plc, Re [2000] 2 B.C.L.C. 488, Ch D (Companies Ct)
  ....3.7.2, 9.8.3, 15.19.1

O'Brien v. Perry & Daw (1941) 85 S.J. 142 ....16.3.6
Odebrecht Oil & Gas Services Ltd v. North Sea Production Co Ltd
  [1999] 2 All E.R. (Comm) 405, QBD (T&CC) . . .5.9.4, 7.2, 7.9.2, 9.8.4

P&O Property Holdings Ltd v. Norwich Union Life Insurance Society;
  sub nom. Norwich Union Life Insurance Society v. P&O Property
  Holdings Ltd (1994) 68 P. & C.R. 261, HL; affirming [1993] 1 E.G.L.R.
  164; [1993] 13 E.G. 108; [1993] E.G.C.S. 69; [1993] N.P.C. 1,
  CA 2.6.2, 12.2.4, 12.3.2, 12.5.4, 12.6.1,
                          12.6.2, 12.6.3, 12.6.5, 12.6.6, 12.6.7,
                      12.7.1, 12.7.3, 12.7.4, 15.14.1, 15.14.3, 17.3.5
Pacific Associates v. Baxter [1990] 1 Q.B. 993; [1989] 3 W.L.R. 1150;
  [1989] 2 All E.R. 159; 44 B.L.R. 33; 16 Con. L.R. 90; (1989) 139
  N.L.J. 41; (1989) 133 S.J. 123; [1993] 1 E.G.L.R. 164; 1989; *The
  Times*, December 28, 1988; *The Independent*, January 6, 1989,
  CA; affirming 1989 13 Con. L.R. 80 ....7.4.2, 16.7.11,
                                           16.9.2, 16.13.2, 16.13.4
Page v. Llandaff and Dinas Powis R.D.C. (1901) H.B.C. (4th Ed.) Vol.2,
  para. 316 ....15.6.3
Palacath Ltd v. Flanagan [1985] 2 All E.R. 161; [1985] 1 E.G.L.R. 86;
  (1985) 274 E.G. 143; (1985) 135 N.L.J. 364, QBD 16.5.3, 16.6.6,
                                            17.3.3, 17.6.4, 17.9.2
Pan Atlantic Group v. Hassneh Insurance Co. of Israel Ltd [1992]
  2 Lloyd's Rep. 120; *The Financial Times*, November 8, 1991,
  CA 10.6.1
Panamena Europea Navegacion Compania Limitada v. Frederick
  Leyland & Co. Ltd; *sub nom.* Compania Panamena Europea
  Navigacion Limitada v. Frederick Leyland & Co Ltd; Frederick Leyland
  & Co Ltd v. Compania Panamena Europea Navegacion Limitada
  [1947] A.C. 428; (1947) 80 Ll. L. Rep. 205; [1947] L.J.R 716; 176
  L.T. 524, HL; affirming (1943) 76 Ll. L. Rep. 113, CA; affirming (1942)
  74 Ll. L. Rep. 108, KBD 9.3.3, 13.10.2, 16.6.3
Pando Compania Naviera SA v. Filmo SAS [1975] Q.B. 742; [1975] 2
  W.L.R. 636; [1975] 2 All E.R. 515; [1975] 1 Lloyd's Rep. 560; 119 S.J.
  253, QBD (Comm Ct) 10.6.1
Pappa v. Rose (1872) L.R. 7 C.P. 525
  ....5.7.1, 5.9.1, 16.3.1, 16.3.2, 16.3.3
Parken v. Whitby (1823) Turn. & R. 367 ....15.9.4, 15.10.2
Parrott v. Shellard (1868) 16 W.R. 928 ....15.2.4
Pattison v. Cosgrove, unreported, November 27, 2000 ....8.3
Photo Production Ltd v. Securicor Transport Ltd [1980] A.C. 827; [1980]
  2 W.L.R. 283; [1980] 1 All E.R. 556; [1980] 1 Lloyd's Rep. 545; 124
  S.J. 147, HL; reversing [1978] 1 W.L.R. 856; [1978] 3 All E.R. 146;
  [1978] 2 Lloyd's Rep. 172; 122 S.J. 315, CA 12.4.1
Pioneer Shipping Ltd v. BTP Tioxide Ltd, Nema, The (No.2); BTP Tioxide
  Ltd v. Armada Marine SA; *sub nom.* BTP Tioxide Ltd v. Pioneer
  Shipping Ltd [1982] A.C. 724; [1981] 3 W.L.R. 292; [1981] 2 All E.R.

TABLE OF CASES

1030; [1981] 2 Lloyd's Rep. 239; [1981] Com. L.R. 197; 125 S.J. 542, HL; affirming [1980] Q.B. 547; [1980] 3 W.L.R. 326; [1980] 3 All E.R. 117; [1980] 2 Lloyd's Rep. 339; [1980] E.C.C. 467, CA; reversing [1980] 2 Lloyd's Rep. 83, QBD (Comm Ct) 12.6.2, 15.14.1

Pittalis v. Sherefettin [1986] Q.B. 868; [1986] 2 W.L.R. 1003; [1986] 2 All E.R. 227; [1986] 1 E.G.L.R. 130; (1986) 278 E.G. 153, CA 11.3.4

Pontsarn Investments v. Kansallis-Osake-Pankki [1992] 1 E.G.L.R. 148; [1992] 22 E.G. 103; (1992) 89(28) L.S.G. 33; [1992] N.P.C. 56, Ch D 2.3.4, 12.5.4, 12.6.7, 15.12.9, 15.17, 18.8.1

Porter v. Webb, unreported, February 22, 1996 .... 3.7.1

Postel Properties Ltd and Daichi Lire (London) Ltd v. Greenwell (1993) 65 P. & C.R. 239; [1992] 47 E.G. 106; [1992] E.G.C.S. 105; [1992] N.P.C. 97, [1992] 2 E.G.L.R. 130, Ch D 2.3.4, 12.6.3, 12.6.7

Public Authorities Superannuation Board v. Southern International Developments Corp. Pty Ltd, Decision No.17986 of 1987, 19 October 1987, Common Law Division of Supreme Court of New South Wales 1.6.13, 7.9.1, 8.7.2

R. v. Bow Street Metropolitan Stipendiary Magistrate, ex p. Pinochet Ugarte (No.2); *sub nom.* Pinochet Ugarte (No.2), Re; R. v. Evans, ex p. Pinochet Ugarte (No.2); R. v. Bartle, ex p. Pinochet Ugarte (No.2) [2000] 1 A.C. 119; [1999] 2 W.L.R. 272; [1999] 1 All E.R. 577; 6 B.H.R.C. 1; (1999) 11 Admin. L.R. 57; (1999) 96(6) L.S.G. 33; (1999) 149 N.L.J. 88; *The Times*, January 18, 1999; *The Independent*, January 19, 1999, HL 15.4.4

R. v. Disciplinary Committee of the Jockey Club, ex p. The Aga Khan [1993] 1 W.L.R. 909; [1993] 2 All E.R. 853; [1993] C.O.D. 234; (1993) 143 N.L.J. 163; *The Times*, December 9, 1992; *The Independent*, December 22, 1992, CA; affirming [1992] C.O.D. 51; *The Independent*, July 29, 1991 (C.S.) QBD 1.6.10, 5.15, 15.7, 18.5.1, 18.8.3

R. v. Football Association, ex p. Football League; Football Association v. Football League [1993] 2 All E.R. 833; [1992] C.O.D. 52; (1992) 4 Admin. L.R. 623; *The Times* August 22, 1991 .... 18.8.3

R. v. Gough (Robert) [1993] A.C. 646; [1993] 2 W.L.R. 883; [1993] 2 All E.R. 724; (1993) 97 Cr. App. R. 188; (1993) 157 J.P. 612; [1993] Crim. L.R. 886; (1993) 157 J.P.N. 394; (1993) 143 N.L.J. 775; (1993) 137 S.J.L.B. 168; *The Times*, May 24, 1993; *The Independent*, May 26, 1993; The Guardian, May 22, 1993, HL; affirming [1992] 4 All E.R. 481; (1992) 95 Cr. App. R. 433; (1993) 157 J.P. 612; [1992] Crim. L.R. 895; (1993) 157 J.P.N. 249; (1992) 142 N.L.J. 787; (1992) 136 S.J.L.B. 197; *The Times*, June 3, 1992; *The Independent*, June 3, 1992; The Guardian, May 27, 1992, CA (Crim Div) 15.4.4

R. v. Kidderminster District Valuer, West Midlands Police Authority and Secretary of State for the Home Department, ex p. Powell and West Midlands Branch of the Police Federation of England and Wales [1992] C.O.D. 381; [1991] R.V.R. 197; (1991) 135 S.J.L.B. 108; (1991) *The Times*, July 23, 1991 .... 18.8.2

R. v. Monopolies and Mergers Commission, ex p. South Yorkshire Transport; R. v. Monopolies and Mergers Commission, ex p. South Yorkshire Passenger Transport Authority; *sub nom.* South Yorkshire Transport v. Monopolies and Mergers Commission [1993] 1 W.L.R. 23;

TABLE OF CASES

[1993] 1 All E.R. 289; [1993] B.C.C. 111; [1994] E.C.C. 231; (1993) 143 N.L.J. 128; *The Times*, December 17, 1992, HL; reversing [1992] 1 W.L.R. 291; [1992] 1 All E.R. 257; [1992] B.C.C. 340; [1992] E.C.C. 432; (1992) 4 Admin. L.R. 385; [1992] C.O.D. 259; (1992) 156 L.G. Rev. 741; *The Times*, December 9, 1991; *The Financial Times*, December 6, 1991, CA; affirming [1991] B.C.C. 347; [1992] E.C.C. 1; [1991] C.O.D. 432; *The Times*, April 9, 1991; *The Daily Telegraph*, April 25, 1991, QBD 12.8.3
R. v. Simbodyal, *The Times*, October 10, 1991, CA 17.6.1
RD Harbottle (Mercantile) Ltd v. National Westminster Bank Ltd; Harbottle (Mercantile) Ltd v. National Westminster Bank Ltd [1978] Q.B. 146; [1977] 3 W.L.R. 752; [1977] 2 All E.R. 862; 121 S.J. 745,QBD 5.10
Rajdev v. Becketts (a firm) [1989] 35 E.G. 107; [1989] 2 E.G.L.R. 144 ....13.6.7, 17.6.4
Ranger v. G.W.R. (1854) 5 H.L.C. 72 ....10.7.1
Redmond v. Wynne (1892) 13 N.S.W.R. 39 ....12.5.5
Ridge v. Baldwin (No.1) [1964] A.C. 40; [1963] 2 W.L.R. 935; [1963] 2 All E.R. 66; 127 J.P. 251; 127 J.P. 295; 61 L.G.R. 369; 37 A.L.J. 140; 234 L.T. 423; 113 L.J. 716; 107 S.J. 313, HL; reversing [1963] 1 Q.B. 539; [1962] 2 W.L.R. 716; [1962] 1 All E.R. 834; 126 J.P. 196; 60 L.G.R. 229; 106 S.J. 111, CA; affirming [1961] 2 W.L.R. 1054; [1961] 2 All E.R. 523; 125 J.P. 422; 59 L.G.R. 327; 105 S.J. 384, QBD 15.7
Ripley v. Lordan (1860) 2 L.T. 154 ....12.2.3, 12.3.1
Robor Cartons Ltd, unreported, March 13, 2000 ....3.7.2
Rotheray (E) & Sons Ltd v. Carlo Bedarida & Co. [1961] 1 Lloyd's Rep. 220, QBD 15.19.2
Rourke v. Short (1856) 5 E. & B. 904 ....15.9.4, 18.5.2
Royal Bank of Scotland plc v. Jennings (1998) 75 P. & C.R. 458; [1997] 1 E.G.L.R. 101; [1997] 19 E.G. 152; [1996] E.G.C.S. 168; [1996] N.P.C. 145, CA; affirming (1995) 70 P. & C.R. 459; [1995] 2 E.G.L.R. 87; [1995] 35 E.G. 140, Ch D 11.3.4
Royal Trust International Ltd v. Nordbanken, unreported, October 13, 1989, ChD 4.4, 12.6.3, 12.6.6, 12.7.1

SB Property Co Ltd v. Chelsea Football & Athletic Co. Ltd; *sub nom.* Chelsea Football & Athletic Co Ltd v. SB Property Co. Ltd (1992) 64 P. & C.R. 440; [1992] N.P.C. 51; *The Times*, April 8, 1992; *The Independent*, April 28, 1992, CA 2.3.4
Safeway Food Stores v. Banderway (1983) 267 E.G. 850 .10.8.3, 17.3.4
Scott v. Avery (1856) 5 H.L. Cas. 811; (1855) 5 H.L.C. 809, HL 12.5.2, 12.5.3
Shearson Lehman Hutton Inc. v. Maclaine Watson & Co. Ltd [1988] 1 W.L.R. 496; [1988] 138 New L.J. 185 ....8.9.7
Shell UK Ltd v. Enterprise Oil plc [1999] 2 All E.R. (Comm) 87; [1999] 2 Lloyd's Rep. 456; *The Times*, June 17, 1999,Ch D 6.4.6, 15.12.8, 15.13.5, 15.16.2, 15.20
Shirlaw v. Southern Foundries (1926) Ltd. *See* Southern Foundries (1926) Ltd v. Shirlaw
Shorrock v. Meggitt [1991] B.C.C. 471; *The Times*, June 4, 1991, CA 4.2.4, 15.13.5, 15.13.6

Shui On Construction Co. v. Shui Kay Co. Ltd (1985) 1 Const. L.J. 305,
    HC (HK) 16.9.2, 16.13.2
Singer & Friedlander Ltd v. John D Wood & Co. [1955-95] P.N.L.R. 70;
    [1977] 2 E.G.L.R. 84; (1977) 243 E.G. 212, QBD 16.7.10
Sirros v. Moore [1975] Q.B. 118; [1974] 3 W.L.R. 459; [1974] 3 All E.R.
    776; 118 S.J. 661, CA 8.9.6
Smith v. Gale [1994] 1 W.L.R. 9; [1974] 1 All E.R. 401; (1973) 117 S.J.
    854, Ch D 5.3.1
Smith v. Peters (1875) L.R. 20 Eq. 511 ....2.5, 13.3.3, 13.4.2, 13.6.3, 13.6.7
Soules CAF v. Louis Dreyfus Negoce SA [2000] 2 All E.R. (Comm) 154;
    [2000] 2 Lloyd's Rep. 307, QBD (Comm Ct) 5.7.3
Southern Foundries (1926) Ltd v. Shirlaw [1940] A.C. 701, HL [1939] 2
    K.B. 206, CA 9.3.2
Staines Warehousing Co. v. Montagu Executor & Trustee Co. (1987) 54
    P. & C.R. 302; (1987) 283 E.G. 458, CA; affirming (1986) 51 P. & C.R.
    211; [1986] 1 E.G.L.R. 101; (1985) 277 E.G. 305, Ch D 11.6.3
Stanton v. Callaghan [2000] 1 Q.B. 75; [1999] 2 W.L.R. 745; [1998] 4 All
    E.R. 961; [1999] C.P.L.R. 31; [1999] B.L.R. 172; (1999) 1 T.C.L.R. 50;
    62 Con. L.R. 1; [1999] P.N.L.R. 116; [1998] 3 E.G.L.R. 165; [1999] 15
    Const. L.J. 50; [1998] E.G.C.S. 115; (1998) 95(28) L.S.G. 32; (1998)
    95(33) L.S.G. 33; (1998) 148 N.L.J. 1355; (1998) 142 S.J.L.B. 220;
    [1998] N.P.C. 113; *The Times*, July 25, 1998; *The Independent*, July
    16, 1998, CA 16.5.4
Stevenson v. Watson (1879) 4 C.P. 148 ....16.3.5
Street v. Mountford [1985] A.C. 809; [1985] 2 W.L.R. 877; [1985] 2
    All E.R. 289; (1985) 17 H.L.R. 402; (1985) 50 P. & C.R. 258; [1985] 1
    E.G.L.R. 128; (1985) 274 E.G. 821; (1985) 82 L.S.G. 2087; (1985) 135
    N.L.J. 460; (1985) 129 S.J. 348, HL; reversing (1984) 16 H.L.R. 27;
    (1985) 49 P. & C.R. 324; (1984) 271 E.G. 1153; (1984) 271 E.G. 1261;
    (1984) 81 L.S.G. 1844; (1984) 128 S.J. 483, CA 17.3.2
Sudbrook Trading Estate Ltd v. Eggleton [1983] 1 A.C. 444; [1982]
    3 W.L.R. 315; [1982] 3 All E.R. 1; (1982) 44 P. & C.R. 153; (1983) 265
    E.G. 215; (1982) 79 L.S.G. 1175; 126 S.J. 512, HL; reversing [1981] 3
    W.L.R. 361; [1981] 3 All E.R. 105; (1981) 260 E.G. 1033; 125 S.J. 513,
    CA 2.4, 9.2.8, 10.3.1, 11.3.3, 11.3.5, 15.18.3
Superior Overseas Development Corp and Phillips Petroleum (UK) Co. v.
    British Gas Corp. [1982] 1 Lloyd's Rep. 262, CA 6.4.2
Sutcliffe v. Thackrah [1974] A.C. 727; [1974] 2 W.L.R. 295; [1974] 1 All
    E.R. 859; [1974] 1 Lloyd's Rep. 318; 118 S.J. 148, HL; reversing [1973]
    1 W.L.R. 888; [1973] 2 All E.R. 1047; [1973] 2 Lloyd's Rep. 115; 117
    S.J. 509, CA 5.9.1, 7.4.2, 15.6.1, 16.4, 16.4.1, 16.5.1, 16.6.1,
           16.6.4, 16.6.5, 16.13.4, 17.4.1, 17.5.2, 17.5.4, 17.6.2

Tarmac Construction Ltd v. Esso Petroleum Co. Ltd 83 B.L.R. 65; 51
    Con. L.R. 187, QBD (OR) 7.4.3
Taylor v. Yielding (1912) 56 S.J. 253 ....17.3.2, 17.3.3
Temloc Ltd v. Errill Properties Ltd 39 B.L.R. 30; 12 Con. L.R. 109; (1988)
    4 Const. L.J. 63, CA 12.4.1
Tesco Stores Ltd v. Norman Hitchcox Partnership Ltd; Clark Care Group
    Ltd v. Norman Hitchcox Partnership Ltd; Maidstone Grove Ltd v. Norman
    Hitchcox Partnership Ltd 56 Con. L.R. 42, QBD (OR) 16.13.2

TABLE OF CASES

Tew(or Dew) v. Harris (1847) 11 Q.B. 7 ....11.4.1
Tharsis Sulphur & Copper Co. v. Loftus (1872)
  L.R. 8 C.P.1 ....5.9.1, 16.3.3, 17.5.2
Thomson v. Anderson (1870) L.R. 9 Eq. 523 ....15.9.2
Token Construction Co. Ltd v. Charlton Estates Ltd 1 B.L.R. 48,
  CA 13.8.2
Top Shop Estates v. Danino (C); Top Shop Estates v. Tandy Corp. [1985]
  1 E.G.L.R. 9; (1985) 273 E.G. 197 ....17.6.3
Town & City Properties (Development) v. Wiltshier Southern and Gilbert
  Powell 44 B.L.R. 109 ....8.8.6, 17.7.3
Tradax Export SA v. Volkswagenwerk AG [1970] 1 Q.B. 537; [1970] 2
  W.L.R. 339; [1970] 1 All E.R. 420; [1970] 1 Lloyd's Rep. 62; 113 S.J.
  978; *The Times*, November 21 1969, CA; affirming [1969] 2 Q.B. 599;
  [1969] 2 W.L.R. 498; [1969] 2 All E.R. 144; [1969] 1 Lloyd's Rep. 494,
  QBD (Comm Ct) 11.4.1
Triarno Pty Ltd v. Triden Contractors Ltd, unreported, July 22, 1992,
  Supreme Court of New South Wales 7.9.2, 8.7.2
Trollope & Colls Ltd v. North West Metropolitan Regional Hospital Board
  [1973] 1 W.L.R. 601; [1973] 2 All E.R. 260; 9 B.L.R. 60; 117 S.J. 355,
  HL 9.3.2
Trusthouse Forte Albany Hotels v. Daejan Investments Ltd (1980) 256
  E.G. 915 ....9.10.1
Trusthouse Forte Albany Hotels v. Daejan Investments Ltd (No.2) [1989]
  1 E.G.L.R. 133; [1989] 30 E.G. 87, CA 2.3.4
Tullis v. Jacson [1892] 3 Ch.441 ....12.5.5
Turner v. Goulden (1873) L.R. 9 C,P.D. 57 ....16.3.4

United Co-Operatives v. Sun Alliance and London Assurance Co. [1987]
  1 E.G.L.R. 126; (1987) 282 E.G. 91 ....11.7.1, 11.7.2
Universal Petroleum Co. v. Handels und Transport GmbH [1987] 1
  W.L.R. 1178; [1987] 2 All E.R. 737; [1987] 1 Lloyd's Rep. 517; [1987] 1
  F.T.L.R. 429; (1987) 84 L.S.G. 1238, CA 15.13.7

Venaglass Ltd v. Banque Paribas [1994] E.G.C.S. 18 ....2.8, 7.8,
                                                        7.9.2, 12.3.2
Vickers v. Vickers (1867) L.R. Eq. 529 ....5.3.1
Viney v. Bignold (1887) 20 Q.B.D. 172 ....12.5.2

Wallshire v. Aarons [1989] 1 E.G.L.R. 147; [1989] 2 E.G. 81,
  DC 16.7.10, 16.8.3
Weekes v. Gallard (1869) 21 L.T. 655 ....15.10.2
West of England Shipowners Mutual Insurance Association
  (Luxembourg) v. Cristal Ltd, Glacier Bay, The [1996] 1 Lloyd's Rep.
  370; [1996] C.L.C. 240; *The Times*, October 26, 1995; *The
  Independent*, November 1, 1995, CA; reversing [1995] 1 Lloyd's Rep.
  560; Lloyd's List, March 15, 1995, QBD (Comm Ct) ...12.5.4, 12.6.8,
                                                         15.20, 18.3.7
West Wake Price & Co v. Ching [1957] 1 W.L.R. 45; [1956] 3 All E.R.
  821; [1956] 2 Lloyd's Rep. 618; 101 S.J. 64, QBD 8.8.3
Westminster Chemicals & Produce Ltd v. Eichholz & Loeser [1954] 1
  Lloyd's Rep. 99, QBD 12.2.4

TABLE OF CASES

Whiteoak v. Walker (1988) 4 B.C.C. 122 . . . . .16.7.8, 16.7.9
Whitworth Street Estates (Manchester) Ltd v. James Miller & Partners Ltd; *sub nom.* James Miller & Partners Ltd v Whitworth Street Estates (Manchester) Ltd [1970] A.C. 583; [1970] 2 W.L.R. 728; [1970] 1 All E.R. 796; [1970] 1 Lloyd's Rep. 269; 114 S.J. 225, HL; reversing [1969] 1 W.L.R. 377; [1969] 2 All E.R. 210; 113 S.J. 126, CA 12.8.1
Wilander v. Tobin (No.2) [1997] 2 Lloyd's Rep. 293; [1997] 2 C.M.L.R. 346; [1997] Eu. L.R. 265; *The Independent*, January 24, 1997, CA 15.7, 18.5.1, 18.8.3
Wilsher v. Essex A.H.A. [1988] A.C. 1074; [1988] 2 W.L.R. 557; [1988] 1 All E.R. 871; (1988) 138 N.L.J. 78; (1988) 132 S.J. 418, HL; affirming [1987] Q.B. 730; [1987] 2 W.L.R. 425; [1986] 3 All E.R. 801; (1986) 83 L.S.G. 2661; (1986) 136 N.L.J. 1061; (1986) 130 S.J. 749; *The Times*, August 6, 1986, CA 16.7.8
Wilson (David) Homes Ltd v. Surrey Services Ltd (in liquidation) & anr [2001] E.W.C.A. Civ. 34—Court of Appeal (Civil Division), January 18, 2001 . . . . .17.3.4, 17.5.1
Woodley v. Robert Newman & Son [1950] W.N. 141, CA 18.8.2
Woods Hardwick Ltd v. Chiltern Air Conditioning, unreported, October 2, 2000 . . . . .7.5.5, 15.4.4, 15.6.4

Zubaida (t/a Elley's Enterprises) v. Hargreaves [2000] Lloyd's Rep. P.N. 771; [1955-95] P.N.L.R. 665; [1995] 1 E.G.L.R. 127; [1995] 09 E.G. 320, CA [1993] 43 E.G. 111, QBD 16.7.10

TABLE OF STATUTES

All references are to paragraph numbers.

1920	Administration of Justice Act (10 & 11 Geo. 5,c.81) 14.7.1	1984	Telecommunications Act (c.12) 12.6.4
1933	Foreign Judgments (Reciprocal Enforcement) Act (23 & 24 Geo.5,c.13) 14.7.1	1985	Companies Act (c.6) s.14 ....3.3.1 s.459 ....3.7.1, 15.2.1, ...15.5.4
1939	London Building Acts (Amendment) Act (2 & 3 Geo.6,c.xcvii) 18.7.2	1986	Agricultural Holdings Act (c.5) s.12 ....18.7.3
1950	Arbitration Act (14 Geo. 6,c.27)...12.5.1, 17.8.3	1986	Insolvency Act (c.45) s.123 ....14.5.1 s.125(2) ....3.8 s.268 ....14.5.1
1954	Landlord and Tenant Act (2 & 3 Eliz.2, c.56) ...2.3.8	1991	Civil Jurisdiction and Judgments Act (c.12) 14.7.1
1975	Arbitration Act (c.3) 14.7.1, ...17.8.3	1996	Arbitration Act (c.23) 3.5.2, ...8.9.5, 16.6.4, 16.6.5 Pt III ....14.7.1 s.7 ....9.2.6 s.8 ....15.9.3 s.9 ..1.5.3, 7.5.5, 8.4.1, ...14.4 s.12 ....9.18.4 s.13 (1) ....13.2 s.18 ....11.3.1 s.19 ....11.3.1 s.23 ....15.9.2 s.25 ....16.2.8 s.26 (1) ....17.5.5 s.29 .....8.9.6, 17.11.5 s.29 (1) .16.3.1, 16.7.11 s.30 ....12.3.1 s.32 ....13.6.4 s.33 .....17.6.4, 17.6.8 s.33 (1) (b) ......17.7.3 s.34 ....17.7.3 s.34 (2) (f) .....17.10.3 s.34 (2) (g) ......17.6.4 s.34 (2) (h) .....17.10.5 s.43 ....17.10.2 s.45 .....8.9.4, 13.6.4 s.46 ....16.10 s.49 ....9.10.1 s.49 (3) 9.10.1
1977	Unfair Contract Terms Act (c.50) .....3.10, 12.5.5 s.2 .....9.18.3, 16.7.11 s.3 .....9.18.3, 16.7.11		
1979	Arbitration Act (c.42) .3.5.2 s.1(1) ....12.5.1, 17.8.3 s.1(5) ....15.13.7 s.3 ......12.5.1, 12.5.4		
1979	Sale of Goods Act (c.54) s.9 ......5.7.5, 10.3.1		
1980	Limitation Act (c.58) s.5 .....9.18.7, 14.8.1, 15.2.3, 16.2.9, 16.7.15 s.7 ......14.8.1, 15.2.3 s.8 .....9.18.7, 14.8.1, 15.2.3, 16.2.9, 16.7.15 s.14A ....16.13.5 s.32 ....15.2.4		
1981	Supreme Court Act (c.54) s.49(3) 1.5.3, 8.4.1		
1982	Civil Jurisdiction and Judgments Act (c.27) .. 14.7.1		
1982	Supply of Goods and Services (c.29) s.13 ....16.7.8 s.14 ....16.7.5		

Table of Statutes

1996	Arbitration Act – *contd*		1996	Party Wall etc. Act (c.40)
	s.57 (3) 15.9.10			. . . . .18.7.2
	s.60 . . . . . . .8.9.2, 9.12		1996	Housing, Construction and Regeneration Act (c.53)
	s.63 . . . . .9.13.3			. . .9.2.6, 15.6.4, 15.7,
	s.64 . . . . .16.2.4			. . . . .15.9.10
	s.66 . . . . .14.2.3			Pt II 1.6.11
	s.67 . . . .12.5.1, 12.5.5,			s.104 . . . . .7.5.4
	. . . . . . .17.8.3, 17.11.4			s.108 . . . . .7.5.1
	ss.67–71 . . . . . . .12.5.1			s.108 (1) 7.5.4
	s.68 . . . . . .15.7, 17.6.3,			s.108 (2) (a)–(f) . . .7.5.4
	. . . . . . .17.7.3, 17.8.3,			s.108 (3) 7.5.4
	. . . . .17.10.2, 17.10.6,			s.108 (4) 7.5.4
	. . . . .17.11.4			s.108 (5) 7.5.4
	s.68 (3) (a) 17.8.3		1998	Human Rights Act (c.42)
	s.69 . . . .12.5.1, 12.5.5,			. . . . .1.6.11, 15.7
	. . . . . . .17.8.3, 17.11.4			Sched.1, Art.6 . . .7.5.5,
	s.69 (1) 12.5.4			. . . . .15.7
	s.69 (7) (c) 17.8.3		1999	Contracts (Rights of Third Parties) Act (c.31)
	s.70 (4) 15.13.7			
	s.74 . . . . .10.6.3			
	s.87 . . . . .12.5.1, 17.8.3			s.1 . . . . .8.5
	s.91 (1) 17.7.6			
	s.107 (2) 12.5.1			

TABLE OF STATUTORY INSTRUMENTS

All references are to paragraph numbers.

1965	Rules of Supreme Court (S.I.1965 No. 1776) Ord.18, r.19	15.13.1
1985	Supply of Goods and Services Regulations (S.I. 1985 No.1)	16.7.11
1986	Insolvency Rules (S.I.1986 No.1925)	5.12.1
1988	Scheme for Construction Contracts (England & Wales) Regulation (S.I. 1998 No.649)	7.5.4
1999	Unfair Terms in Consumer Contracts Regulations (S.I 1999 No. 2083) Sched.2, para.1	8.4.2

TABLE OF CIVIL PROCEDURE RULES

All references are to paragraph numbers.

1998 Civil Procedure Rules (S.I. 1998 No.3132) . . .2.3.8, 3.8	r.24.2 (a) (ii) 12.7.4
r.1.1 . . . . .8.10.3	r.26.4 . . . . .8.10.3
r.1.4 (2) (e) 12.5.4	r.35.3 . . . . .17.10.4
r.3.1 (2) (b) 12.7.4	r.35.7 . . . . .1.1.6, 1.6.3, 8.3
r.3.4 . . . . .15.2.1, 15.13.3	r.35.10 . . . . .17.10.4
Pt 8 . . . . .12.7.4	r.35.15 . . . . .1.6.3
Pt 11 . . . . .8.4.1	Pt 35 PD 17.10.4
Pt 24 . . . . .14.3.1	Sched.1, Ord.53 . . .15.7, 18.8.2

TABLE OF INTERNATIONAL CONVENTIONS
All references are to paragraph numbers.

1958	New York Convention	14.7.1, 14.7.2
	Art.1.2	14.7.4
1986	Brussels Convention	14.7.1
1988	Lugano Convention	14.7.1

Chapter 1

INTRODUCTION

General remarks 1.1

A simple procedure

Expert determination is a means by which the parties to a contract 1.1.1
jointly instruct a third party to decide an issue. The third party is now commonly known as an expert, and is a person who has been chosen for expertise in the issue between the parties. Expert determination is found in a wide range of commercial applications, from rent reviews to breach of warranty claims, from construction disputes to pension scheme transfers, and from computer disputes to oilfield exploration: it is simple, informal and contract-based. Expert determination had its origin in non-contentious valuation: it is increasingly being used for technical as well as valuation issues, and for general dispute resolution. Expert determination is quick, cheap and private. It is used to resolve issues about both small and large sums: the amounts at stake sometimes run into tens of millions of pounds. Expert determination is found in some of the largest construction projects,[1] and in some of the largest corporate acquisitions.[2] Television and sport provided the most high-profile single expert determination yet: the dispute about the BSkyB contract for the televising of rugby championship matches.[3] The continuing adaptation and development of expert determination into new areas show that its usefulness is appreciated by lawyers, other professionals and business executives.

Arbitration is different

The study of expert determination has traditionally been attached 1.1.2
to the study of arbitration. Both expert determination and arbitration

---

[1] For example, the panel of experts in the Channel Tunnel project: see 7.5.6.
[2] Here are two examples. First, in *British Shipbuilders v. VSEL Consortium plc* [1997] I Lloyd's Rep. 106, £60 million of the purchase price had already been paid, and the expert accountant could increase it by up to a further £40 million. Secondly, the adjustment of the price in the dispute between Brent Walker and Grand Metropolitan about the value of William Hill and Mecca bookmakers business was £117.5 million, according to *Legal Business,* November 1996, p.72.
[3] *The Times*, January 20, 1999, sports pages. The contract for the Five Nations matches was worth £87.5 million over five years.

are private systems of dispute resolution leading to a binding result. They are often confused with each other.[4] While the systems have many similarities, there are important differences. This has created a great deal of confusion, and it is for this reason that the whole of Chapter 17 is devoted to an explanation of the distinction between arbitration and expert determination. Experts are often loosely described as being some kind of arbitrator. The fact is that they are not. Experts are a distinct species of dispute resolver whose activities are subject to little or no control by the court, from whose decisions there is no appeal, but who may nevertheless be liable for negligence in performing these otherwise unreviewable functions. Arbitrators, by contrast, are subject to control by the court, some of their decisions are, at least in theory, subject to appeal, and they are immune from actions for negligence. A partnership or company can be an expert, whereas an arbitral tribunal always consists of readily identifiable individuals. The crucial difference between expert determination and arbitration lies in the procedure and the absence of remedies for procedural irregularity in expert determination. An arbitration award may be set aside because the procedure fails to conform to the statutory standard of fairness which is closely derived from the principles of natural justice: no such remedy is generally available to invalidate an expert's decision. An expert can adopt an inquisitorial, investigative approach, and need not refer the results to the parties before making the decision. An arbitrator needs the parties' permission to take the initiative, and must refer the results to the parties before making the award.

Enforcement and international contracts

1.1.3 Another important difference from arbitration is in the area of enforcement. Experts' decisions have a completely different status from arbitration awards or judgments of the court. Experts' decisions cannot generally be enforced without further court action wherever enforcement is sought, domestically or internationally. Particular care should be taken when using expert determination in international contracts, to ensure that enforcement by a local court will be available. This book describes only the English law and practice relating to expert determination, but the procedure is found in other jurisdictions: there have been some important Australian judgments on disputed expert determinations, and there are cases on the subject in the New Zealand law reports. The procedure has

---

[4] See the press reports of the *Texas Homecare* expert determination on February 4, 1997. *The Times*, *The Independent*, *The Daily Mail* and *Retail Week* all referred to the independent expert as an arbitrator: only *The Guardian* got it right.

been gaining ground in the United States.[5] Outside the common law there are comparable procedures in France, Germany, Italy, the Netherlands and the Scandinavian countries.[6]

From valuer to expert and dispute resolver

1.1.4 The development of the procedure from its origins in valuation to modern expert applications has led me to attempt to distinguish between these two types and to classify applications either as belonging to the traditional, valuation type, or as owing more to the concept of a technical expert. This distinction becomes clearer when one sees that it is mainly the technical applications which have developed into dispute resolution. The use of the label "expert" is now well recognised and more commonly encountered than "valuer". The clause in a contract which refers matters to an expert for determination is known in this book as the "expert clause".

Statutory valuers and adjudicators excluded

1.1.5 Some valuers, such as district valuers, and some adjudicators operate by statute, and numerous dispute resolvers, such as the Insurance Ombudsman, have been established by statute. This book does not deal with any of them, and is limited to the study of valuers and experts appointed under the terms of contracts. This contract-based private law does not apply to officials operating under a statute[7] unless those officials are appointed to act under private contracts.[8]

Court-appointed experts and expert witnesses excluded

1.1.6 The court may appoint an expert to facilitate the carrying out of a court order.[9] The law set out in this book does not apply to that kind of appointment, or to single joint experts appointed by the parties to litigation.[10]

---

[5] "Advantages and disadvantages of expert determination as compared to other methods of dispute resolution" by Osborne J. Dykes III, paper presented at the IBA SBL's 12th biennial conference at Paris in 1995.
[6] See John Kendall "Expert Determination: a European and American Survey" (November 1994) *International Business Lawyer*, Vol. 22, No. 10, pp. 433–80, and *Arbitrato irrituale: how should it be handled in a non-Italian jurisdiction? A discussion from a Swiss perspective* by Paolo Michele Patocchi and Giuseppe Schiavello, A.D.L.R.J. 1998 2 (Jun) 132–151.
[7] See 18.7 to 18.8.
[8] As in *Mercury Communications Ltd v. Director of Telecommunications and others* [1996] 1 W.L.R. 48: see 12.6.4, 18.8.3.
[9] As in *Jordan v. Norfolk County Council* [1994] 1 W.L.R. 1353.
[10] CPR 35.7.

1 : INTRODUCTION

Expert determination: a form of ADR?

1.1.7 The expression Alternative Dispute Resolution (ADR) was originally coined in the United States in the early 1980s to describe any means of resolving disputes other than the courts. Commercial litigants in the United States face years of expensive preparation culminating in a jury trial with unpredictable and sometimes very alarming results. Forms of arbitration have therefore become more popular in the United States, as an alternative to the court; but yet more radical solutions were sought, in non-binding systems chiefly consisting in forms of assisted negotiation. The two most important methods are mediation and the mini-trial. In the United States the expression ADR is used to refer to all systems other than the traditional procedures of courts. In England ADR is used generally to refer only to non-binding systems, but this has shifted to include binding systems other than the court, closer to the American usage.[11] Expert determination produces binding results.[12] Experts can, of course, be asked to give non-binding opinions or recommendations.[13] Large projects have produced expert systems for dealing with disputes during the works, some of which are non-binding and none of which produces a decision which is regarded as final until some later date. Contract provisions of this sort have to be carefully reviewed to see whether a decision is to be binding; and, if it is, whether the decision is to be made by a person (or persons) operating as an expert or an arbitrator, or perhaps in some other role.[14]

1.2 SOURCES OF LAW AND INFORMATION

Origins and options

1.2.1 There is nothing very new about expert determination.[15] It has been a feature of English commercial and legal practice for at least 250 years. The first reported case is found in 1754: *Belchier v. Reynolds*.[16] The procedure originated to deal with circumstances where parties wished to set up machinery for determining a price

---

[11] The Centre for Dispute Resolution, CEDR, whose chief interest is mediation, have published a Model Expert Determination Agreement, with guidance notes, which is reprinted at Appendix I.
[12] *Davies Middleton & Davies Ltd v. Toyo Engineering Corporation* (1997) 85 B.L.R. 59.
[13] For instance, the ICC DOCDEX system for recommendations to resolve banking disputes about letters of credit.
[14] See Chapters 7 and 18.
[15] See the account by Mark McGaw in *Travels In Alsatia*, in *Construction Law: Themes and Practice: Essays in honour of Ian Duncan Wallace* (Sweet & Maxwell, 1998) pp. 131–187.
[16] (1754) 3 Keny. 87.

without negotiations, often where the obligation to make a payment arises in the future, as with options. An option is, typically, a contract, a deed, or a will made by a party by which one party grants to the other the right to buy property from the first party at a future date. An option may say that the price for the purchase at that future date will be determined by a valuer acting as an expert if the parties cannot agree on the price at that time.

Contract law

Expert determination is usually found in contracts. When there are disputes about expert determination, the courts apply the law of contract, and the law of contract is the most important area of law for this subject. Thus, while all the usual contractual rules about offer and acceptance, consideration, intention to create legal relations, illegality, mistake, misrepresentation, repudiation, breach, discharge and so forth are relevant to understanding the contractual context of the reference to the expert, those rules may also have a direct bearing on whether a decision of an expert can be enforced.

1.2.2

The law reports

The most significant source of the law about expert determination is the law reports. This book does not cite all the cases on the subject, and does not cite a case where to do so would serve only to record the existence of that case, with no other purpose. The law reports provide information about the practical applications of expert determination, but the very fact that each of those cases resulted from a dispute which the parties could not settle by agreement and had to take to court may make them an unrepresentative sample of the applications of expert determination. Another random factor is the accident of reporting. The most important decision, *Jones v. Sherwood Computer Services plc*[17] was first published outside LEXIS 18 months after the judgment following a complaint from the judge in *Nikko Hotels (UK) Ltd v. MEPC plc*[18] that it had not been reported. Because *Nikko v. MEPC* was a property case, a full report of *Jones v. Sherwood* was published first[19] in the NPC (New Property Cases), a series of reports for property specialists. *Jones v. Sherwood* was not a property case, it was about the sale of a business. It also marked a major change in the law. It was eventually reported in two of the principal general series in 1992.[20]

1.2.3

---

[17] [1992] 1 W.L.R. 277,
[18] [1991] 2 E.G.L.R. 103.
[19] At [1991] N.P.C. 60.
[20] As well as the W.L.R. report cited above, it was also published at [1992] 2 All E.R. 170.

Practice

1.2.4 Although not a true source, in that it is not found in published material, the other main source of information about the applications of expert determination is provided by the instances encountered in the course of practice. Practice is, of course, even less representative than the law reports, but it does have the advantage of providing examples of the use of expert determination in areas where there are no reported disputes.

Statutes

1.2.5 No statute deals with the subject, and the citation of statutes in this book is necessary mainly because of the need to draw a distinction between expert determination and arbitration.

Confidentiality

1.2.6 The privacy of expert determination significantly reduces the volume of available information. References to experts are private in the same way that arbitrations are.[21] While this is an advantage for the parties and, for them, one of the principal attractions of expert determination, it does not facilitate studying the subject. There is no system at all for publishing information about individual determinations, or about the subject generally: and the parties themselves often agree to keep details of their cases confidential, and that agreement is a binding contractual obligation. So the capacity to make a thorough survey of the subject is inhibited by one of its most important characteristics.

Analogous systems in construction contracts

1.2.7 The study of certificates issued in construction contracts and adjudication decisions made in construction contracts is also helpful, as the court approaches disputes about them on a very similar basis, essentially applying contract law with the aim of fulfilling the presumed intentions of the parties. Thus the chapter on construction contracts, Chapter 7, compares expert determination with certification and adjudication, and sections of other chapters cite cases from these sources.

1.3 METHOD

Evolution through commercial practice

1.3.1 The study of expert determination is not just the study of a procedure for settling disputes. The subject is defined by its applications.

---

[21] See 9.15.10.

All the applications of expert determination have evolved through commercial practice. Chapters 2 to 7 look at the applications in detail.

Difference from studying litigation and arbitration

In this respect the study of expert determination is rather unusual. The study of litigation or arbitration does not depend on detailed study of the applications of those systems. Both arbitration and litigation have an independent existence beyond any specific application because they can be used very widely for all kinds of disputes. Expert determination has, until recently, been limited to the applications set out in Chapters 2 to 7. However, the trend is growing for expert determination to be used to resolve all aspects of a dispute arising under a contract, and not just one category of technical aspects. If this trend continues, the details of the applications may cease to matter, but that stage is still some way off. In the meantime, therefore, the applications are an integral part of a study of expert determination. 1.3.2

Different commercial applications, but one dispute system

As well as being the only textbook on expert determination, this book is the first study of all the different applications of expert determination alongside each other. Practitioners in one commercial area (for example, the oil industry) have tended to work from the cases on expert determination in that industry only, without considering cases from other areas. They are in fact all facets of the same system of dispute resolution, and should not be considered in isolation. Rent review experts operate in the same legal context as accountants adjusting the purchase prices of businesses, and information technology specialists assessing computer systems operate in the same legal context as geology experts assessing oilfields. 1.3.3

Different approaches to same subject-matter

The method adopted in this book tends to result in the same point being made in several different contexts. The only alternative to this is a probably unacceptable level of cross-referencing. In any event, the book is more likely to be consulted than read through, and few users will find the repetition tiresome. 1.3.4

Focus on traditional form

This book concentrates on expert determination where the expert is appointed by the parties to a contract to make a decision which is final and binding on them. To maintain this focus, the book does not dwell on the much rarer forms where the decision is not made 1.3.5

by a third party or where that third party is not jointly appointed.[22] The only significant instance of expert determination being used for interim (as opposed to final) decisions, adjudication in construction contracts, is discussed in its construction context: it could also be applied to computer disputes.[23]

1.4 OVERVIEW

The applications

1.4.1 Some issues have traditionally been seen as more suitable for expert determination than others. The principal application remains rent review, covered in Chapter 2. Chapter 3 considers another traditional application, the valuation of shares in private companies. Chapter 4 considers the use of expert determination for the valuation of assets or liabilities transferred by agreements for the sale and purchase of businesses and companies. Chapter 5 reviews the remaining commercial applications. The transition from valuation to expert determination, and some technical applications of expert determination, are considered in Chapter 6. Chapter 7 looks at construction contract applications and interim determinations.

Dispute resolution

1.4.2 Chapter 8 discusses how expert determination is used as a method of dispute resolution as a development from the applications reviewed in the earlier chapters. Expert determination is sometimes used alongside arbitration or litigation in the same contract, and there is a growing trend for the use of expert determination for general dispute resolution. Tactics in drafting agreements and conducting disputes are also considered.

Practice and procedure

1.4.3 The practical aspects of the subject, from drafting an expert clause[24] through to enforcing a decision, are discussed in Chapters 9 to 14. Chapter 9 analyses the essential elements of an expert clause, applying the rules of contract law. Chapter 10 considers who can act as an expert: as the answer is anyone whom the parties appoint, it is usual to build safeguards into the expert clause with a view to ensuring that a suitably qualified person acts as the expert. Chapter 11 looks at the procedures for appointing experts,

---

[22] See Chapter 18.
[23] See Chapter 7.
[24] See 1.1.4.

and in particular the role of professional bodies. Chapter 12, on the expert's jurisdiction, is interposed at this point. Chapter 13 considers appropriate procedures for conducting a reference and Chapter 14 looks at the means of enforcing experts' decisions. Appendix A contains a series of precedents whose use is explained in the text of these chapters.

Contentious aspects

The aspects of expert determination that have given rise to most court cases are covered in Chapters 12 and 15 to 17. Chapter 12 examines the jurisdiction of the expert and shows how challenges can be made by applying to the court. Chapter 15 explains the rule that the court does not set aside decisions of experts except in certain very limited circumstances. Chapter 16 deals with an expert's liability for professional negligence, and Chapter 17 explains the difference between experts and arbitrators. Chapter 18 then compares expert determination with other decisions by third parties under a contract.   **1.4.4**

THE PREDOMINANT ISSUES   **1.5**

How effective is expert determination?

The perennial questions are

- whether, after a dispute has arisen between parties to a contract containing an expert clause, parties have a choice whether to comply with the expert clause or to disregard it;   **1.5.1**
- what will be involved in the process, how much it will cost, and how much time it will take;
- what standard of fairness is applied to the process;
- whether expert determination guarantees a decision which will be final and binding;
- if not, on what grounds a challenge can be mounted;
- whether the expert can be sued.

Areas of contention remain

These issues continue to give rise to litigation. The desire of some parties for justice, or their overwhelming need not to lose at any cost, rather than finality, fuels challenges to references and to decisions; parties whose challenges fail wish to sue the expert; and the poorly defined boundary with arbitration provides material for disputes about disputes.   **1.5.2**

1 : INTRODUCTION

Attempts to bypass expert clauses

1.5.3 A party may attempt to bypass an expert clause by commencing proceedings in court. The court has jurisdiction to stay proceedings in these circumstances,[25] but this is subject to the discretion of the court to refuse a stay if the court considers that litigation through the courts would be more appropriate, and the burden is on the party seeking to litigate in breach of the expert clause to show grounds for refusing a stay.[26] The court also has jurisdiction to stay court proceedings under section 9 of the Arbitration Act 1996 where the contract requires the dispute to be referred to arbitration only after the exhaustion of "other dispute resolution procedures". The expression "other dispute resolution procedures" must include expert determination.

Sometimes litigation is commenced when an expert clause in a contract has not been invoked, for whatever reason, and there is either a strict time limit by which the machinery must be invoked, or it is on any view too late to invoke it. For a discussion of the issues arising from this, see 9.2.8, 9.18, and 11.3. There is as yet no doctrine of the separability of the expert clause, a concept found in arbitration law, which would allow the courts to enforce expert determination as the parties' chosen means of dispute resolution despite the invalidity or alleged invalidity of the rest of the contract containing the expert clause, but it could be applied in a future case.[27]

Disputing the expert's jurisdiction

1.5.4 One party may contend that particular disputed issues, such as the interpretation of words in the contract, do not fall within the matters required to be remitted to the determination of the expert. This will depend on the wording of the expert clause in each case. An application to the court for a ruling as to the extent of the expert's jurisdiction can be made before or during the reference and in some cases after the decision as well: see Chapter 12.

Challenging experts' decisions

1.5.5 Chapter 15 identifies two key concepts in the law of challenge to experts' decisions:

(a) the law of contract; and
(b) mistake.

---

[25] Under section 49(3) of the Supreme Court Act 1981 and the court's inherent jurisdiction: *Channel Tunnel Group Ltd and another v. Balfour Beatty Construction Ltd and others* [1993] A.C. 334. See 8.4.1.
[26] *Cott UK Ltd v. FE Barber Ltd* [1997] 3 All E.R. 540; see 8.4.2.
[27] See 9.2.6.

Primacy of contract law

1.5.6 As an expert determination is a contract, disputes between the parties as to its validity have to be determined on that basis. The clauses typically say that the decision of the expert is to be final and binding, and that is what the courts say it has to be, in the absence of fraud, partiality or mistake.[28]

Mistake and unfairness

1.5.7 Disallowing an expert's decision on the ground of fraud or partiality is uncontroversial. However, mistake and unfairness cause problems. A mistake has to be fundamental to constitute a sufficiently serious breach of contract, such as the expert making the decision about the wrong subject-matter. Anything less than a fundamental mistake is simply insufficient. Errors of fact or law will have to stand, provided the expert can be said to have considered the right question. Unfairness does not generally render a decision invalid.

Can you sue an expert?

1.5.8 Chapter 16 shows how experts used to have immunity on the ground that they were some kind of arbitrator, until that immunity was swept away in 1975, but that it is still difficult to sue an expert. One cannot always make a meaningful comparison, but it is likely to be easier to establish liability for professional negligence against an expert than to prove that an expert has made a mistake of sufficient gravity to invalidate the decision.

Arbitration

1.5.9 Disputes about whether a reference was to an expert or an arbitrator have, historically, produced many lawsuits. The boundary between the two procedures is traced in Chapter 17. Recent changes in arbitration law may have the effect of discouraging these disputes.

Enforcement

1.5.10 The effectiveness of expert determination depends on how easy it is to enforce experts' decisions. Chapter 14 notes some of the difficulties, some of which arise from the status of the expert's decision as a contractual event and not a judgment or arbitration award. Some types of decision cannot be enforced because of the nature of the issue referred to the expert. This arises, for instance, where an expert rules only on a technical question and is not required to go on to determine the financial consequences of that ruling.

---

[28] Thus the same rules apply when the parties decide an issue by reference to a document such as the accounts of a company: see 18.4.

1 : INTRODUCTION

1.6 THE CONTEXT OF MODERN DISPUTE RESOLUTION

Expert determination as dispute resolution

1.6.1 This book seeks to place expert determination in context with other forms of dispute resolution. There is no doubt that the current commercial practice is to use expert determination for dispute resolution, but it must be distinguished from other forms of dispute resolution.

Not legal proceedings

1.6.2 First, expert determinations are not legal proceedings. No court is involved unless there is a challenge. There is no statutory supervision by the court as there is with arbitration. A decision of an expert is not enforceable without court action.

Distinguish experts from expert witnesses

1.6.3 Secondly, expert determination should be distinguished from the use of expert witnesses in litigation and arbitration which is such a dominant feature of modern dispute resolution. In expert determination, the expert makes the decision and does not act as a witness. An expert witness is appointed by a party to assist in putting that party's case to a tribunal of either judge(s) or arbitrator(s), with other parties having the same right. In some European countries and in some international arbitrations, the tribunal appoints its own expert to advise on technical matters, and the parties' experts make their case to the tribunal's expert, and do not appear as witnesses before the tribunal. The court in England has recently acquired the power to direct that expert evidence in a lawsuit be given by a single joint expert, and appoints that expert when the parties cannot agree on the appointment.[29] While the evidence of a single joint expert witness or the advice of a tribunal-appointed assessor[30] may have a decisive influence, it is the tribunal of judge(s) or arbitrator(s) which makes the decision as part of its judgment or award, and not the expert.

Expert determination, traditionally not regarded as dispute resolution

1.6.4 The traditional view is that expert determination is not a form of dispute resolution at all. The argument depends on drawing a distinction between an "issue" and a "dispute"—or a "formulated dispute". It is said that experts settle issues on which the parties have not taken defined positions: where the parties have taken

---

[29] CPR 35.7.
[30] *Ibid.*, 35.15.

defined positions, which become disputes or (formulated) disputes, the referee is an arbitrator.[31]

Share valuation: expert determines even where no dispute

1.6.5 Perhaps the only commonly encountered instances of expert determination where there need be no dispute arise from the valuation of shares in private companies. The articles of association may say that the value will be fixed by the company's auditors acting as experts and not as arbitrators, and there is no other way to arrive at the figure which follows the requirements of the constitution of the company. Even if the parties are in complete agreement on the issue, the auditors have to fix the value. Similar considerations arise where auditors certify the adjustment rates of convertible shares and the price of shares for employees in share option schemes.

Artificial distinction between issues and disputes

1.6.6 In all other cases it is artificial to draw this distinction between

(a) issues where the parties have not taken defined positions; and
(b) disputes or formulated disputes where the parties have taken defined positions.

If people have gone to the trouble and expense of referring something to a third party for decision, they are most likely not to have agreed about it, and however one analyses their disagreement, they are in dispute. The distinction was recognised as inadequate over 100 years ago.[32] The choice of reference, whether it is to be to expert or arbitrator, is in any event usually made at the time of the original contract which precedes the time when the parties know whether they have an issue to settle or a formulated dispute, and they will be obliged to use whatever procedure was stipulated, unless they make some fresh agreement.

Development of expert determination into general dispute resolution

1.6.7 The fact is that parties to contracts do use expert determination for dispute resolution, and not only for certain types of disputes traditionally thought more suitable for experts: clauses referring all

---

[31] See 17.5.
[32] See the remarks of Lord Esher M.R. in *Re Carus-Wilson & Greene* (1886) 18 Q.B.D. 7 at 9: "... a person appointed to settle disputes ... still not bound to hear evidence and arguments ... [may] exercise some function other than that of an arbitrator ..."

disputes, both technical and otherwise, are beginning to be found in contracts as a substitute for litigation or arbitration. This is part of a general trend towards simpler, cheaper and quicker forms of dispute resolution. There is no overriding reason preventing expert determination being used to resolve a much wider range of disputes. The subject-matter of a dispute does not on its own make it more suitable for arbitration rather than expert determination. The choice of procedure may depend, not on the type of commercial dispute, but on its size and complexity.[33]

Classification of dispute resolution systems

1.6.8 One way of classifying systems of dispute resolution is to consider two fundamental issues about each system, whether the system is binding or non-binding and whether the procedure is "due process" or informal. The next sections consider how expert determination fits in alongside the other major systems.

Binding or non-binding?

1.6.9 Does a system of dispute resolution inevitably lead to a binding result? Once it has been initiated, the only means by which the parties can stop a binding system operating is to discontinue the use of the system on whatever terms are agreed. If only one party wishes to discontinue the use of the system, it cannot be forced to take an active role, but the dispute resolution process will continue, and that party will be bound by the result despite its failure to participate. A non-binding system can lead to a binding result, but that does not mean that it is a binding system, because either party can discontinue the use of the system without the other party's agreement.

Due process

1.6.10 Does the system require the observation of the rules of natural justice? By this is meant the second limb of the rules, the requirement that each party must be given a fair opportunity to be heard. (The first limb is that the tribunal must be unbiased and disinterested). As is argued later in this book,[34] the second limb of the rules of natural justice does not apply to expert determination unless the parties agree it should. This may at first sight seem somewhat shocking. However, consider the detailed implications of this rule as worked out in English law. The rule requires that all matters put to the tribunal by each party have to be disclosed to the other party

---

[33] For some views on rent review, see 2.3.7.
[34] See 15.6 to 15.7.

and that the other party must also have the opportunity of rebuttal. The rule also requires the tribunal to make known the result of its own investigations to the parties and to give them the same opportunity of rebuttal. This is a much more demanding standard than simple fairness, which applies in some form to every binding system.[35] The basic standard of fairness in expert determination is contractual, which does not mean due process. Some expert determination clauses incorporate due process rules into an expert determination. There seems little point in this. It leads to a procedure which is likely to be the same as the procedure in an arbitration, but with the risk of disputes, about the status of the reference, and about enforcement.[36]

Expert determination occupies a middle position

System	Binding?	Due process?
Litigation	Yes	Yes
Arbitration	Yes	Yes
Expert determination	Yes	No
Statutory adjudication of construction disputes	Yes	Uncertain
Early neutral evaluation	No	No
Conciliation	No	No
Mediation	No	No

1.6.11

From this chart one can see that litigation and arbitration have a great deal in common, both being binding systems where due process must be followed. Mediation, and other non-binding systems at the other end of the spectrum, cannot be made subject to due process because if they were they would not work. The grey area between the two extremes is occupied by expert determination and some forms of statutory adjudication of construction disputes.[37] Expert determination is a binding system, but at common law does not operate by due process. It is doubtful whether the

---

[35] See, *e.g. R. v. Disciplinary Committee of the Jockey Club, ex parte Aga Khan* [1993] 1 W.L.R. 909 at 933, discussed at 18.5.1.
[36] See, *e.g.* Lesley Webber in "Independent experts—Where has the law got to?", Blundell Memorial Lectures 1999.
[37] Housing Grants, Construction and Regeneration Act 1996, Part II.

1 : INTRODUCTION

Human Rights Act 1998 has made any difference to this proposition.[38] Statutory adjudication of construction disputes is a binding system, even if the result may be of only temporary effect, but the statute does not expressly require due process, and there are differing judicial views on the effect of a decision reached following non-compliance with the requirements of due process—the Human Rights Act 1998 may also have some impact on this issue.[39] The existence of binding systems without due process sometimes causes alarm, but the absence of due process is the essential difference in procedure between expert determination and adjudication on the one hand and arbitration on the other. If people want a simpler system, something of the formality of the more complex systems has to be jettisoned.

Appropriate dispute resolution

1.6.12 Means of dispute resolution now come under greater scrutiny than ever before in the drafting of commercial contracts, especially those used for large projects. In its use as adjudication and dispute review, expert determination has another advantage over arbitration: it can deter parties from pursuing disputes by providing immediate machinery for resolving them, in marked contrast to the months and years of preparation for a trial-type hearing. Expert determination rightly takes its place among the available systems both for large projects and more general use. This book can be consulted for examples of the use of expert determination for particular purposes in the context of particular industries, and should therefore be useful to commercial lawyers advising on new contracts as well as commercial lawyers dealing with disputes.

Public policy

1.6.13 The crucial stage may soon be reached when the English courts will have to decide whether to enforce a decision by an expert on all disputes arising under a contract, both general and technical. References of this type are becoming more common. A clause referring all disputes under a construction contract to an expert has been upheld in the Australian courts.[40] The extension of expert determination into general dispute resolution combined with this non-interventionist policy will produce a wider class of wrong and unchallengeable decisions. The law upholds experts' decisions because the parties have agreed to be bound, and not because of

---

[38] See 15.7.
[39] See 7.5.5.
[40] *Public Authorities Superannuation Board v. Southern International Developments Corporation Pty Ltd*, unreported, Smart J. in Common Law Division of Supreme Court of New South Wales, decision No 17986 of 1987, October 19, 1987, cited in [1990] I.C.L.R. 443: see 8.7.2.

any special factor deriving from the status of the expert, the quality of the decision or the manner in which it was reached. Until recently, the technical nature of the question put to the expert was a special factor, but this is ceasing to be the case with the extension of expert determination into general dispute resolution. If the courts accept this development, a new form of dispute resolution will have been created, allowing parties' legal rights to be determined without the procedures and safeguards that have always been thought essential. This is a major public policy issue on which the courts may soon have to make a judgment. On the analogy of the increasing number of unappealable arbitration awards, the courts are very likely to uphold the parties' original contract, not the second thoughts, after the result, of one of the parties only.

Chapter 2

LAND

2.1 Summary

This chapter deals with the use of expert determination in:

(a) the valuation of freehold land, including options (2.2);
(b) rent review (2.3);
(c) other leasehold valuations, including settling a price for long leases, compensation for surrender, options and service charges (2.4);
(d) the valuation of fittings, products and machinery associated with land (2.5);
(e) certificates triggering obligations (2.6);
(f) mortgage portfolios (2.7);
(g) development agreements (2.8);
(h) boundary disputes (2.9); and
(i) specific and general dispute resolution (2.10).

Land valuation is the most traditional application of expert determination, and rent review is now by far the most common instance of the procedure as applied to land valuation and, indeed, to any subject matter.

2.2 Freeholds

Freeholds with development potential

2.2.1 Developers are often granted an option on land which has development potential before obtaining planning permission. The purpose of the option is to lock up the land at minimum expense while the developer tries to get planning permission. Without the option the developer is at risk of making efforts for the sole benefit of the landowner. After obtaining a satisfactory planning permission, the developer can exercise the option; but the price has to be determined. Because conditions attached to planning permission may have a material effect on value, often the price is not settled when the option is granted but a formula is included in the option agreement, the usual intention being that the vendor receives a price which reflects at least part of the uplift in value due to the obtaining of planning permission. If the parties cannot agree that value, the option agreement should contain a provision that an expert will determine the value of the land having regard to the planning permission.[1]

Example of surveyor valuing development land in sale contract

Surveyors acting as experts sometimes decide the purchase price of land to be paid under contracts between vendor and purchaser. In *Campbell and Palmer v. Crest Homes (Wessex) Ltd*,[2] the claimant vendors agreed to sell some development land to the defendant purchasers at the price the property might reasonably be expected to fetch on the open market at the relevant date on a sale by a willing vendor to a willing purchaser; if the parties failed to agree the price within four weeks they were to refer to an independent surveyor to determine the price. The parties failed to agree and an independent surveyor, acting as an expert, determined the price. The purchasers failed in their challenge to the surveyor's valuation methods, and an order for specific performance of the expert's decision was made against them.

2.2.2

Options to purchase successive plots

Surveyors acting as experts also decide the purchase price of freehold land subject to option agreements. A common application of this is the sale and purchase of successive adjacent plots over a period of time.

2.2.3

Valuation on divorce

Surveyors acting as experts are appointed to value property owned by married couples on their divorce, sometimes under the terms of a court order.

2.2.4

RENT REVIEW 2.3

Purpose of rent review clauses

Rent review is a procedure enabling a landlord and tenant to revise the amount of the rent payable under the terms of their lease to reflect changes in rental levels or circumstances: if they do not agree on the rental, the revision is referred to a third party. Thus, in

2.3.1

---

[1] For an example, and a cautionary tale about drafting clauses of this type, see *Mid-Kent Water plc v. Batchelor* [1994] 1 E.G.L.R. 185.
[2] Unreported, Chancery Division, November 13, 1989. The case raised issues of general principle which are discussed at 15.5.6 and 15.7.9.

a typical example, a commercial lease for a term of 25 years contains a covenant by the tenant to pay the rent under the lease. That covenant specifies the rent payable for the first five years. For each of the four succeeding periods of five years the covenant brings into operation the rent review provisions of the lease. The rent review provisions state that in the absence of agreement the review is to be conducted by the third party according to certain assumptions. The purpose of these assumptions is almost invariably to ensure that the new rent is an "open market" rent, *i.e.* the rent which is commercially obtainable. The review is usually conducted by a surveyor acting either as an expert or as an arbitrator. The rent review procedure is a useful means of enabling landlord and tenant to establish a long-term commitment at a rental which continues, throughout that long term, to make commercial sense especially during periods of inflation (or recession). A rent review clause also reflects changes in the value of the property other than those caused by economic changes: there may be changes in the demand for a particular type of property, and the site of the property may become more or less valuable because of other changes in the neighbourhood.

Standard forms include provision for rent reviewer to act as expert

2.3.2 There is one main standard form of rent review clause from which most forms generally encountered derive. "Model Forms of Rent Review Clause" has been produced jointly by the Law Society and the RICS.[3] Precedent 1 provides for arbitration, precedent 2 for determination by an independent valuer (*i.e.* by an expert), and precedent 3 gives the landlord the right to choose whether the review is to be conducted by an expert or an arbitrator. In all cases, if the landlord and the tenant are unable to agree on the identity of the rent reviewer, the RICS will make the appointment. Many variants from the standard form are in circulation. One gives to the landlord only the right to apply for the appointment of a surveyor, with the tenant having no such right.[4]

Space and comparables

2.3.3 In deciding the right figure for the rent the surveyor has first to establish the size of the building by reference to the number of square feet of letting space which may be in a number of different categories, such as prime office space and storage. Both the measurement and the categorisation can be surprisingly controversial.

---

[3] *Handbook of Rent Review*, Ronald Bernstein and Kirk Reynolds, Sweet & Maxwell.
[4] See 11.3.4.

The surveyor then has to review comparable lettings to fix the market rent. A rent reviewer acting as an expert is not restricted as to the comparable evidence that can be considered in the same way that a rent reviewer is restricted when acting as an arbitrator. The expert can rely on his or her own expertise and can consider decisions and arbitration awards in other rent reviews: an arbitrator cannot.[5] This power can be restricted by the rent review clause or otherwise by agreement between the parties.[6]

Assumptions, disregards and construction arguments

2.3.4 The standard forms of rent review clauses contain certain "assumptions" and certain matters to be disregarded, known as "disregards". The principal assumption is an open market letting on the terms of the lease, and the principal disregard is the value of certain improvements. The interpretation of these provisions may provide material for one of the parties to ask the court for a ruling on the interpretation of the words used in the lease so that the rent review can proceed on the basis desired by the applicant.[7] In first instance decisions in 1991 and 1992[8] the court held that it was for the expert not only to assess the rent but also to decide, so far as it might be relevant to the task, how to interpret the words of the lease, and that the court should not give a ruling on the interpretation of contentious wording. However in *National Grid Co. plc v. M25 Group plc*[9] the Court of Appeal held, on the particular wording of the lease which was before the court, that questions of interpretation of the assumptions and disregards were a matter for the court to decide rather than the valuer appointed under the terms of the lease. They therefore allowed the application for a ruling by the court on the correct interpretation to proceed. The Court of Appeal reached this conclusion on the basis that each agreement must depend on its own terms, read in its own context, and that little assistance can be gained from previous cases which concerned different contract wording. Most rent review clauses are drafted in this way, which means that the vast majority of rent review determinations by an expert are open to unilateral application to the court for legal interpretation of the clause.

It has been said that the court will tell surveyors what to value in rent

---

[5] See 16.8, 17.6 and 17.10.3.
[6] See 16.8.6.
[7] See, for instance, *Trust House Forte Albany Hotel Ltd v. Daejan Investments (No 2)* [1989] 1 E.G.L.R. 133, [1989] E.G.L.R. 113 CA, *SB Property Co Ltd v. Chelsea Football and Athletic Company Ltd and Alexander Tatham and Co* [1992] N.P.C. 51, *Postel Properties Ltd v. Greenwell* [1992] 2 E.G.L.R. 130.
[8] *Nikko Hotels UK Ltd v. MEPC plc* [1991] 2 E.G.L.R. 103; *Pontsarn Investments Ltd v. Kansallis-Osake-Pankki* [1992] 1 E.G.L.R. 148.
[9] [1999] 1 E.G.L.R. 65; see 12.6.5.

review cases, but not how to value it, in the sense of what factors to take into account and what weight to give to them,[10] but this is subject to the court first having to decide whether there are issues of law which, applying the terms of the contract, are required to be decided by the court as opposed to the expert.[11] At the other extreme from *National Grid*, in another case[12] Lord Templeman delivered a robust rejection of forensic attacks on valuations by experts in rent reviews:

> "In general [we] consider that it would be a disservice to the law and to litigants to encourage forensic attacks on valuations by experts where those attacks are based on textual criticisms more appropriate to the measured analysis of fiscal legislation."

Accountants

2.3.5 In *Nikko Hotels (UK) Ltd v. MEPC plc*[13] an accountant acting as an expert determined the "average room rate" of an hotel as part of a rent review. The landlords said that the rate should be determined by reference to the published tariff. The tenants said that actual discounts given should be taken into account, this being the usual market practice with hotel rentals. In another case[14] the lease provided that the rental payable to the landlord was to be established by reference to a percentage of the rack rentals received by the tenant as certified by the tenant's accountants. There are some more specialised areas of accountancy expertise in rent review where accountants are appointed: one example is where figures, such as tax liability, in the tenant's accounts are at issue. The procedure can be for the tenant to produce an auditor's certificate, which, if not accepted by the landlord, is referred to expert determination by an accountant.

Interest

2.3.6 Old-fashioned rent review clauses resulted in there being no interest payable on the new rent except for the period after the date of the decision of the expert. Modern drafting ensures that interest is payable for the entire period covered by the revised rent as well.[15]

For rent review, expert determination is preferable to arbitration

2.3.7 *Bernstein and Reynolds* give a very full treatment of the subject, much of which turns on the interpretation of provisions in commer-

---

[10] *Compton Group Ltd v. Estates Gazette Ltd* [1977] 2 E.G.L.R. 73.
[11] In *Compton* itself, the Court of Appeal held that the court should decide the impact on the rent review of counter-inflation legislation.
[12] *Hudson (A) Pty Ltd v. Legal & General Life of Australia Ltd* [1986] 2 E.G.L.R. 130, PC; see 15.5.6 for a summary of the issues in this case.
[13] [1991] 2 E.G.L.R. 103.
[14] *Fraser Pipestock Ltd v. Gloucester City Council* [1995] 2 E.G.L.R. 90.
[15] See 9.10.

cial leases. *Bernstein and Reynolds* prefer rent reviews to be conducted as arbitrations and that appears also to be the preference of the property community where the rent is substantial. Some users prefer arbitration because it is easier to limit the evidence to the material the parties put before the arbitrator: an expert is not so constrained, unless the lease says so.[16] Some commercial leases give the landlord the right to decide, after the appointment of the independent surveyor as expert, that the surveyor is to act as an arbitrator. The preference for arbitration may result from the fact that market practice has made expert rent review clauses much more complicated, often incorporating the right to a hearing. This removes the advantages of expert determination (simplicity, speed and low cost) without conferring the benefits of arbitration. This author believes that expert determination, in its simple form, is better suited than arbitration to rent review[17] in cases where what is required is essentially a valuation exercise with clear comparables. Arbitration may be preferable for large-scale units with wide variation in specific lease terms for comparable properties. The formal adversarial nature of arbitration produces some strange effects. An exceptional feature of rent review arbitrations is that the law allows the parties to the rent review to use witness summonses to force other parties with no involvement in the affair to disclose the rental of buildings, even when that rental may be the subject of a commercial confidentiality agreement.[18]

Lease renewals—disputes about rent, other terms and drafting

The RICS and the Law Society have introduced a scheme providing the services of solicitors and surveyors for private determination of disputes about the terms for the renewal of business leases and the rent payable under them. The scheme is not recommended for use when renewal itself is opposed by the landlord. The scheme is known as Professional Arbitration on Court Terms ("PACT"),[19] but it uses expert determination as well as arbitration. The scheme provides various models. Those models include the appointee acting as an expert for some issues and as an arbitrator for others within the same dispute. The authors of the scheme evidently consider that arbitration is suitable for determining the interim rent and non-rental issues not related to drafting, and that expert determination is not, while expert determination is suitable for determining the

2.3.8

---

[16] See 16.8 and 17.6.3.
[17] Also the view of Nicholas Stewart Q.C., the deputy judge in *Fordgate Bingley Ltd v. Argyll Stores Ltd* [1994] 2 E.G.L.R. 84 at 89.
[18] Kendall and Dark "Countering Confidentiality Agreements" (1991) Law Society's Gazette, Vol. 31, p. 14.
[19] A booklet is available from the Law Society and the RICS. The second edition, compatible with the Civil Procedure Rules, was published in November 1999.

initial rent and drafting issues. Their reason for this is that the Landlord and Tenant Act 1954, which governs the parties' rights for renewal of business leases, requires the decision on the issue of interim rent to be on a basis which includes making a judgment of reasonableness between the parties. The authors extended this argument to exclude substantive non-rental points as well. This author's view is that an obligation to make a judgment of reasonableness could have been imposed by the scheme on experts appointed under it, which would have precluded the complexity of the dispute resolver taking on two different roles about the same renewal.

2.4 OTHER LEASEHOLD VALUATIONS

As well as rent review, other leasehold valuations include:

(a) the valuation of land held on long leases[20];
(b) compensation for surrender, payable by the tenant to the landlord, where the tenant wishes to end the tenancy before the expiry of the term in the lease, and compensation for quitting, payable by the landlord to the tenant, where the landlord wishes to buy the tenant out[21];
(c) options for tenants to purchase the freehold reversion[22];
(d) service charges payable by the tenant certified by the lessor's surveyor[23]; and
(e) compensation to tenants for damage to land caused by extraction of minerals.[24]

2.5 FITTINGS, PRODUCTS, MACHINERY AND FURNITURE

A number of cases have dealt with the valuation of fittings attached to or used in connection with land, whether freehold or leasehold, and associated products, machinery and furniture, whether in farms,[25] public houses,[26] factories[27] or private houses.[28]

---

[20] *Collier v. Mason* (1858) 25 Beav. 200.
[21] For a modern instance, see *Campbell v. Edwards* [1976] 1 W.L.R. 403.
[22] For an example, see *Sudbrook Trading Estate Ltd v. Eggleton* [1983] A.C. 444, discussed at 11.3.3.
[23] *Finchbourne Ltd v. Rodrigues* [1976] 3 All E.R. 581; *Concorde Graphics Ltd v. Andromeda Investments SA* [1983] 1 E.G.L.R. 53; *Re Davstone Estates Ltd's Leases, Manprop Ltd v. O'Dell* [1969] 2 Ch. 378; discussed at 12.5.3.
[24] *Heyes v. Earl of Derby (Pilkington Bros plc, third party)* [1984] 2 E.G.L.R. 87, CA.
[25] *Leeds v. Burrows* (1810) 12 East. 1.
[26] *Smith v. Peters* (1875) L.R. 20 Eq. 511.
[27] *Jones (M) v. Jones (R R)* [1971] 1 W.L.R. 840.
[28] *Babbage v. Coulbourn* (1882) 9 Q.B. 235.

CERTIFICATES TRIGGERING OBLIGATIONS   2.6

Agreements for lease or purchase of freehold

2.6.1 Where building or refurbishment work is being carried out, agreements for lease or the purchase of freehold sometimes provide that the tenant's obligation to start paying rent arises on the issue of the certificate of practical completion in the construction contract under which the building or refurbishment work is being carried out. Often there are parallel certification arrangements between the construction contract and the contract between the landlord and the tenant. There may be a requirement that the architect has to serve a different certificate to trigger the rent commencement obligation from that which is issued under the construction contract: the tenant is not usually a party to the construction contracts and therefore has no control over the issue of the certificate of practical completion. The certificate of practical completion is supposed to be issued when the building is in a fit state for occupation.[29] In practice there are often many matters still to be attended to,[30] and the building may not be in a state acceptable to the tenant. The issue of this certificate is said to "trigger" the tenant's obligation to pay rent or the purchaser's obligation to complete the purchase. In *Bridger Properties Ltd v. Dovey Holdings (South Wales) Ltd*,[31] there was a contract for the sale of land with a completion date 14 days after the issue of the certificate of practical completion. The purchaser did not accept that the building was in a state of practical completion and refused to complete. The contract did not say that the architect was acting as an expert or that the decision would be final and binding. The court said that nothing would be less commercial than to make the date for completion of a contract for sale and purchase of land turn upon the determination of an arbitrator. The decision was that it was irrelevant whether the architect issued the certificate mistakenly, because both parties had taken that risk.

Funding agreements

2.6.2 Agreements under which funding is being provided to developers may contain similar triggers of obligations to provide the next tranche of funds for the development. In one example[32] the arrangement was operated at one remove: the trigger was the certificate of a named third party[33] as to whether the building was practically

---

[29] See 7.4.5.
[30] A snagging list of what has still to be done is drawn up.
[31] Unreported, Chancery Division, June 25, 1991.
[32] *Norwich Union Life Insurance Society v. P&O Property Holdings Ltd* [1993] 1 E.G.L.R. 164.
[33] Who, misleadingly, was called an arbiter (the Latin and Scottish for arbitrator)—but acted as an expert.

complete and had been constructed in accordance with the design documents. The dispute was about the jurisdiction of the third party.[34]

2.7 MORTGAGE PORTFOLIOS

Sales of mortgage portfolios may contain a term providing that where there are disputes after completion of the transaction, the consideration may be adjusted by further evaluation by an accountant in the same way as other loan portfolios.[35]

2.8 DEVELOPMENT AGREEMENTS

Other real property valuation disputes arise in development agreements. One example is the extent of the available lettable space of a particular category or categories in a commercial building. Another example is of a development agreement with a provision for valuation by a quantity surveyor of the site on termination of the agreement.[36]

2.9 BOUNDARY DISPUTES

Surveyors acting as experts are appointed to resolve boundary disputes between neighbours.

2.10 DISPUTE RESOLUTION

Specific disputes

2.10.1 Expert clauses are sometimes found in agreements for leases and development contracts to resolve disputes about particular issues which arise. Between landlord and tenant, surveyors resolve whether defects in the building are inherent structural defects for the landlord to put right or whether they fall within the tenant's repairing obligation. Lawyers are sometimes appointed to resolve issues in contracts for the disposal of land, such as settling the terms of the conveyance.[37] In development contracts, one party may have an obligation to seek planning permission if a Q.C. advises there is a better than 50% chance of getting the permission.[38] A striking example of the extent of this type of application

---

[34] See 12.6.3.
[35] See 4.2.4.
[36] For an example, *Venaglass Ltd v. Banque Paribas* [1994] E.G.C.S. 18: see 7.8.
[37] See 8.8.2.
[38] See 8.8.3.

was found in a contract for the sale and purchase of a group of property companies. Disputes about undisclosed defects were thought to be the most likely to arise in the following areas: environment, title, planning, structure or condition. Depending on the classification of the dispute, disputes were to be resolved by either a lawyer, a valuation surveyor, an accountant, an architect or an engineer, with the President of the Law Society acting as an expert to resolve disputes about the classification of the dispute and which sort of expert should determine it.

General disputes

Expert clauses could be used to resolve all disputes under contracts for land in the same way as they have been used in some construction contracts.[39] One example encountered in practice is of management agreements in the property investment field.

2.10.2

---

[39] See 7.9.

CHAPTER 3

SHARES IN PRIVATE COMPANIES

3.1 SUMMARY

This chapter explains:

(a) the application of expert determination to the valuation of shares in private companies (3.2);
(b) that the application is usually prescribed by the company's articles of association (3.3);
(c) that the experts are usually the company's auditors (3.4);
(d) the effect of the auditors being obliged to determine the "fair value" of shares (3.5);
(e) the effect of specific valuation instructions (3.6);
(f) the special position where a minority shareholder petitions for winding-up (3.7);
(g) the use of expert determination as an alternative to winding-up on the "just and equitable" ground (3.8);
(h) the liability of valuers to parties with whom they do not have a contract (3.9); and
(i) limitation of liability by accountants (3.10).

3.2 PRIVATE COMPANIES

Shares not traded publicly

3.2.1 The valuation of shares in private companies is notoriously difficult, for the simple reason that the shares are not available for subscription by the public and their price is not quoted on a stock exchange. It is common commercial practice for the auditors of a private company to be called on to value the shares.

Occasions for transfer

3.2.2 Certain occasions, such as the resignation of a director[1] or other senior employee with a holding of the shares, dictate the com-

---

[1] See, e.g. *Arenson v. Casson Beckman Rutley & Co.* [1977] A.C. 405.

pulsory transfer of the shares in a private company. Sometimes there are pre-emption rights requiring a shareholder to offer shares to existing shareholders in a company before selling them to a third party. Shareholders may be ordered by the court to offer their shares to the other shareholders.[2] On these occasions it is usual to provide that the auditors fix the fair value of the shares. This method of valuation can be, and often is, also applied on the voluntary transfer of shares or transmission of shares on the death of a shareholder.

PROCEDURE DEPENDS ON ARTICLES OR SHAREHOLDER AGREEMENTS 3.3

Valuation may otherwise be invalid

The articles of association of each company or, in some cases, a shareholders' agreement, often lay down the procedures for share valuation. Articles of association are an agreement between the company and its members and between the members.[3] A shareholders' agreement is an agreement between all (or some) of the shareholders of a company, to which the company is sometimes also a party. The articles or the agreement may say that a reference to the auditors has to take place in every instance; in other cases a reference is necessary only if there is a dispute. If the articles or the agreement say that a reference is to take place in every instance, a reference there must be, even if there is no dispute about the value between the immediate parties to the valuation. If the immediate parties agree on a value, and do not refer the matter to the company's auditors, their agreement and the ensuing transaction may be invalid because the price of the shares has not been established in accordance with the company's rules; and as a practical matter it might be unfair to other shareholders. If the value is not to be determined by the auditors, there has to be unanimous agreement of the shareholders.

3.3.1

Usual wording

No standard forms for referring the valuation of shares in a private company to auditors as experts have been published. However, the relevant provisions usually specify that the price for the transfer is to be the fair price or fair value of the shares and that the auditors' task is to state that price or value.[4] A precedent is set out at Appendix C, showing typical provisions for valuations needed for a transfer. The fact that the valuer is usually required to certify a single value

3.3.2

---

[2] See, *e.g. Macro v. Thompson (No. 3)* [1997] 2 B.C.L.C. 36: but see 3.7.
[3] Companies Act 1985, s. 14.
[4] See 3.5.

for each share may give rise to complications where there are holders of shareholdings of different sizes: a sale of 15% of the share capital may be more attractive to a holder of 45% than to a holder of 5% of the share capital.[5]

No representations

3.3.3 These procedures are not framed in words which suggest that the determination is likely to be controversial. The parties are under no contractual obligation to allow each other to make representations to the auditor before he or she issues the certificate.[6]

3.4 APPOINTMENT OF A COMPANY'S AUDITORS

Atypical features

3.4.1 The words used say, almost invariably, that the auditors are to conduct the valuation, rather than an individual. This makes this form of reference atypical for two reasons:

(a) where, as is usually the case, the auditors are a partnership rather than a sole principal, the expert is a group of individuals rather than one individual; and
(b) the identity[7] of the expert is known immediately, because most companies must have auditors.

Experts and not arbitrators

3.4.2 The words used also usually say that the auditors are to act as experts and not as arbitrators. The precedents encountered do not contain arbitration clauses for share valuation. This commercial tradition is illustrated by two court decisions. In *Gillatt v. Sky Television Ltd*,[8] the clause said "as determined by an independent chartered accountant". Nowhere in the report is there any indication that anyone thought that this might be a reference to arbitration. In *Harrison v. Thompson*,[9] where the court had to review a share valuation dispute which had been referred to arbitration, the parties had made that choice of arbitration after the dispute had arisen.[10]

---

[5] *Macro v. Thompson (No. 3)* [1997] 2 B.C.L.C. 36, *per* Robert Walker J. at 70A.
[6] See 9.15.2.
[7] See 10.4.
[8] [2000] 1 All E.R. (Comm.) 461. Contrast *Leigh v. English Property Corporation* [1976] 2 Lloyd's Rep. 298, discussed at 17.5.5, where it was held to be arguable that the auditors were appointed as arbitrators.
[9] [1989] 1 W.L.R. 1325.
[10] See 9.2.4.

Reasons for appointing auditors

3.4.3 There are said to be two reasons for referring the valuation of a company's shares to its auditors. The first is that they should be sufficiently familiar with the company's affairs already not to need to take further time to acquaint themselves with its business in order to provide the valuation. The second reason is that a company's auditors are expected, because of their statutory duties and position under the Companies Acts, to be independent of the shareholders in the company. The auditor of a private company is in fact often very close to the principal shareholder[11]: it may be more advisable to appoint a valuer from a firm with no previous connection.

FAIR VALUE AND OPEN MARKET VALUE   3.5

Court review of these wordings

3.5.1 Questions have arisen as to whether the use of the word "fair" as a characterisation of the price of the shares to be determined by the auditors makes their task any different and whether a valuation can be challenged on the ground that the price is not fair. The expression "open market value" has also been considered by the courts.

Certainty preferred to risk

3.5.2 In *Baber v. Kenwood Manufacturing Co. Ltd and Whinney Murray & Co.*,[12] the auditors' task, following the wording of the company's articles of association, was to certify the fair selling value of shares. The claimants argued that the auditors had to use a basis of valuation which was capable of producing a figure which represented the fair selling value of the shares, and that if that basis were challenged, the court could decide whether the basis was adequate. Megaw L.J. said that each of the parties desired to avoid the possibility that the other might challenge the opinion of the valuer because the parties had stipulated that the auditors should act as experts, and by doing so they had shown that they wanted a measure of certainty, accepting the risk, which applied either way, that the expert might err. In other words, the fair selling value was to be assessed on whatever basis the auditors

---

[11] See, for instance, *Macro v. Thompson (No. 3)* [1997] 2 B.C.L.C. 36, where Robert Walker J. (at 66C) described the work done by the auditor as "a classic example of how not to conduct an articles valuation of shares in a private company", an allegation of partiality on the basis of proximity to the solicitor acting for the principal shareholder was not sustained: the case is summarised at 15.4.3.
[12] [1978] 1 Lloyd's Rep. 175.

considered to be appropriate. Despite the fact that the reason for the decision has been largely superseded,[13] the result would be the same today.

In a case about open market valuation, the court noted four different approaches: an earnings basis, an assets basis, a discounted cash flow basis, or a combination of these approaches[14]. For this reason it was seen to be a matter pre-eminently for the independent accountant entrusted with the task by the parties, who had agreed to accept the accountant's judgment as final and binding.

Challenges based on mistake

3.5.3   In dealing with claims that an expert's decision is not fair or that the valuation is not on an open market basis, the courts apply a doctrine of mistake which precludes all review of the expert's analysis, unless the expert values the wrong shares or considers entirely the wrong question.[15]

3.6 SPECIFIC VALUATION INSTRUCTIONS

Minority holdings and going concerns

3.6.1   Sometimes the auditors are given more specific instructions about how they are to conduct the valuation. For instance, they may be directed, when valuing a minority holding of shares in a company, to value the shares without regard to the fact that the holding is a minority holding. The auditors may also be directed to value the shares on the basis that the company's business is a going concern, as opposed to a break-up basis.

Challenges on this ground

3.6.2   A successful challenge could be mounted on the basis that the auditors have not followed these instructions,[16] but proving it may

---

[13] The argument depended on contrasting what would have happened if the auditors had been appointed as arbitrators. At that time (1978) there was a frequently used appeal procedure against arbitration awards known as "case stated" which sometimes resulted in an arbitration being followed by three further rounds of litigation in the High Court, the Court of Appeal and the House of Lords. The "case stated" procedure was abolished by the Arbitration Act 1979. The Arbitration Act 1996 has narrowed still further the opportunity for appeals. Arbitration awards now have almost as great a degree of finality as experts' decisions.
[14] *Gillatt v. Sky Television Ltd* [2000] 1 All E.R. (Comm.) 461, CA (see 9.2.8); see also *Macro v. Thompson (No. 3)*, above, at 70-71.
[15] See 15.12.
[16] For an example, see 15.11.2.

Specific Valuation Instructions

be difficult, especially where the auditors do not disclose their workings and calculations.[17]

Unfair Prejudice   3.7

Minority holdings

A minority shareholder may override the transfer provisions in a company's articles of association by a successful application for an order under section 459 of the Companies Act 1985. This has been considered in a number of winding-up cases, notably in *Re Abbey Leisure Ltd*,[18] where the Court of Appeal said that two grounds for preferring a winding-up order to the transfer notice procedure and valuation by a company's auditor were: 3.7.1

(a) that there was nothing unreasonable in a petitioner with a minority holding refusing to accept a discount being applied to the valuation of his interest in the company, where an auditor was likely to decide on that discount; and
(b) that there was machinery available in winding-up for the proper determination of claims, which was not available to an auditor.

In *Abbey Leisure* the transfer procedure was optional. In *Re a Company No. 00330 of 1991 ex parte Holden*,[19] the service of a transfer notice was a requirement imposed by the company's board under the articles of association. The judge in *Holden* upheld the petitioner's refusal to be bound by the transfer notice and granted his petition under section 459.

Thus, in this instance, unusually in the subject of expert determination, contract may be displaced by statute. A further explanation has been given by the Court of Appeal.[20]

> "The remedy (of valuation by the Company's auditor) may be tolerable to a member who genuinely wishes to leave the company and voluntarily sell his shares but which a member who is being forced out cannot be expected to accept. First, the valuation is to be carried out by the company's auditor who is likely to enjoy a close working relationship with the respondent. Secondly, the outgoing member is likely to be given no opportunity to put forward his case or evidence in support. Thirdly, it is left entirely to his discretion whether to value the shares subject to a discount for the fact that it is a minority shareholding . . ."

---

[17] See 15.13 on speaking and non-speaking decisions, and 15.19 on obtaining evidence from the valuer.
[18] [1990] B.C.C. 60.
[19] [1991] B.C.C. 241.
[20] In *Porter v. Webb*, unreported, February 22, 1996, Millett L.J.

Transfer provisions in articles of association

3.7.2 It has been held that there is nothing unfairly prejudicial in a shareholder being bound by the articles of association to transfer shares in accordance with the articles.[21] However an allegation that the auditors were not impartial may provide an arguable basis for an allegation of unfair prejudice.[22]

3.8 AN ALTERNATIVE TO WINDING-UP ON THE JUST AND EQUITABLE GROUND

A petition for winding up a company may be brought on the ground that it is just and equitable to do so on the basis that there has been a breakdown in trust and confidence between the parties. One of the orders that a court can make on the hearing of a winding-up petition of this kind is that one party buy the other party's shares. The legislation dealing with the conduct of winding-up petitions gives the court a discretion to strike out a winding-up petition if the court is of the opinion that some other remedy is available to petitioners and they are acting unreasonably in seeking to have the company wound up instead of pursuing that remedy.[23] In a case where the respondent made an offer to buy out the petitioner's shares in two companies at valuations by an independent accountant acting as an expert, the respondent sought to strike out the petitions on the basis that that offer was reasonable and should be accepted. The court found that the investigations necessary to conduct the valuation could be carried out equally well by an independent valuer, and at less expense than a court case.[24] The court then struck out the petitions.[25]

3.9 LIABILITY OF VALUERS

Sometimes there is no contractual relationship between the valuer and one or more of the shareholders whose shares are to be valued. This need not prevent a negligent valuer of shares being liable to the shareholder for damages.[26]

---

[21] *Re Benfield Greig Group plc, Nugent v. Benfield Greig Group plc*, [2000] 2 B.C.L.C. 488 at 512 para. 59, Arden J.
[22] *Re Robor Cartons Ltd*, unreported, March 31, 2000, David Mackie Q.C.
[23] Insolvency Act 1986, s. 125(2).
[24] See 8.10.3 on the relevance of the Civil Procedure Rules to this point.
[25] *Fuller v. Cyracuse Ltd*, Law Alert No. 0015801, Chancery Division, Companies Court, June 6, 2000, Deputy Judge P. Leaver Q.C.
[26] *Arenson v. Casson Beckman Rutley & Co.* [1977] A.C. 405; *Killick v. PricewaterhouseCoopers*, unreported, July 5, 2000, Neuberger J.; see 16.13.1.

LIMITATION OF LIABILITY 3.10

Accountants may agree to carry out the valuation on the basis that their liability for negligence should be limited. A limitation of liability of this kind is subject to the Unfair Contract Terms Act 1977. In *Killick v. PricewaterhouseCoopers*[27] the court held that a limitation of liability clause in the contract between the auditors and the company did not prevent a duty of care being owed by auditors to a shareholder who was unaware of the limitation of liability.

---

[27] Unreported, July 5, 2000, Neuberger J.; see 16.7.11 in relation to disclaimers generally.

CHAPTER 4

SALE AND PURCHASE OF BUSINESSES AND COMPANIES

4.1 SUMMARY

This chapter deals with the use of expert determination in agreements for the sale and purchase of businesses and companies,[1] and, in particular:

(a) the certification of figures in accounts and the determination of issues such as net asset value (4.2);
(b) the determination by actuaries of the values of pension rights transferred (4.3); and
(c) the determination of tax liabilities (4.4).

4.2 CERTIFICATES OF ITEMS IN ACCOUNTS

Establishing the amount of consideration

4.2.1 Agreements for the sale and purchase of shares in companies and the sale and purchase of businesses often provide that the amounts of the profits (or losses) or net assets of a company or business are to be certified by accountants[2] or by a reference to the company's accounts.[3] This may apply to all the assets transferred,[4] or just to certain items.
This is useful where, for instance:

(a) payment of part of the purchase price of a company or business is deferred pending determination of historic figures relating to the company or business, and

---

[1] For examples, see the corporate transactions cited in the footnote to 1.1.1, and the *Texas Homecare* determination in *The Times* on February 4, 1997, in which it was stated that the City had expected between £30 million and £70 million to be taken off the purchase price, but the expert reduced it by only £9.3 million.
[2] For a precedent, see Appendix A.
[3] *Highway Contract Hire Ltd v. NWS Bank plc*, unreported, April 17, 1996, CA. See 18.4.
[4] Exceptionally, this could mean re-performing the entire completion accounting exercise.

(b) the aggregate amount of the purchase price is itself dependent on the future performance of the company or the business over typically a one or two-year period; this arrangement is sometimes known as an earn-out; or
(c) payment for the company or business is to be based on the net asset value stated in what are known as completion accounts or a completion statement drawn up by accountants.

Sometimes these provisions are referred to as "escrow" arrangements.

A provision of this kind is also useful where shares in a company are the subject of put or call options which become effective after completion of the sale of that company.

Very substantial sums indeed can be at stake, and the amount adjusted by the determination can be the whole of the purchase price. The future livelihood of shareholders, directors and employees can depend on the result.

Breach of warranty

The expression "breach of warranty" is often used in disputes about consideration when the agreement contains a term providing that the vendors warrant that the profits reach a specified figure, and the purchasers seek a repayment from the vendors to compensate them for the loss occasioned by a breach of that warranty, often calculated by reference to a pre-agreed formula. If the profits exceed the specified figure, or the losses are less than the specified figure, the vendors may be entitled to additional consideration. Where, as is almost invariably the case, there are several warranties, it is important that clear drafting shows which warranties are covered by the expert determination process.[5]

4.2.2

Issues for accountants

Where the agreement provides for items to be certified by accountants, the issues which the accountants have to decide are the same whether the vendors are entitled to their deferred consideration or the purchasers to repayment of part of the purchase price. Very broadly, the accountants determine whether the right accounting methods have been used—for instance in dealing with such matters as rates of depreciation and work-in-progress. In certain cases, the accountants prepare the accounts of the company or business on predetermined bases or principles set out in the sale and purchase agreement. These principles can be quite complex, and there is no standard wording for

4.2.3

---

[5] See *International Semitech Microelectronics Ltd v. Scholl plc*, unreported, Garland J., May 27, 1994.

4 : SALE AND PURCHASE OF BUSINESSES AND COMPANIES

expressing them,[6] which can lead to ambiguity and dispute. If the issue is one of construction, it may be possible to apply to the court for a ruling on the correct interpretation. However, depending on the wording of the agreement, construction issues may be solely for the expert to decide.[7] The scope for challenging the determination on other grounds is very limited.[8] Often the vendors and the purchasers each appoint a firm of chartered accountants to act for them in determining the relevant amount. Reference to a third accountant occurs only if the two firms cannot agree on that amount. If the parties' accountants agree on the figures without recourse to the third accountant their decision is still likely to have the status of an independent decision, depending on the wording of the expert clause.[9]

Amounts commonly established

4.2.4 Amounts which are commonly established by accountants' certificates in sale and purchase of business agreements include:

(a) profits, losses and sales[10];
(b) the value of the stock[11];
(c) apportionments between vendor and purchaser;
(d) the turnover of service businesses and the value of service contracts;
(e) the valuation of loan portfolios of banks[12];
(f) net asset value[13];
(g) working capital[14];
(h) the amount of the indebtedness[15];
(i) the liabilities transferred on a privatisation[16];

---

[6] Commonly used references to GAAP and SSAPs are, unfortunately, themselves ambiguous. The Generally Accepted Accounting Principles define a range of acceptable alternatives, but rarely specify exactly what has to be done. The Statements of Standard Accounting Practice are constantly changing.
[7] See 12.6 and 12.7.
[8] See 15.12.6.
[9] See 10.8.2.
[10] See, for instance, *British Shipbuilders v. VSEL Consortium plc* [1996] I Lloyd's Rep. 106.
[11] Which may require specialist valuers familiar with the particular industry.
[12] See the case cited at 4.4.
[13] *Dixons Group plc v. Jan Andrew Murray-Oboynski* (1997) 86 B.L.R. 16; cf. *Shorrock Ltd v. Meggitt plc* [1991] B.C.C. 471 (the amount of the net deficit, i.e. liabilities less assets); *Chelsea Man plc v. Vivat Holdings plc*, unreported, CA, August 24, 1989.
[14] *Hillsbridge Investments Ltd v. Moresfield Ltd*, unreported, Law Alert No 0007501, Case no. HC 1999 03093, Chancery Division, Rimer J., March 15, 2000.
[15] *Hillsbridge Investments Ltd v. Moresfield Ltd*, above.
[16] For instance, the price paid by the U.K. government to Tarmac plc to take over PSA Projects with some of its liabilities, was reduced by £19,921,177 plus

(j)   the cost of repairing or replacing an asset also being transferred; and

(k)   the value of one party's interest in a joint venture on being bought out by the other party.

Complex drafting

4.2.5 Sale and purchase agreements often provide for complex procedures, including disclosure obligations, with detailed timetables, which are supposed to be followed before and during the reference to the expert.[17]

Effects of unreasoned determinations

4.2.6 The expert's task may be to deal with a number of items in dispute in a set of accounts. The determinations issued by accountants rarely, if ever, include reasons.[18] It may therefore be difficult to be sure that the expert has dealt with each item, particularly where the determination consists of one figure as the amount by which the price is to be adjusted.[19] In a case where it was alleged that the expert had failed to take the effect of tax into account, the expert's decision dealt with each disputed item but did not show detailed workings. The Court of Appeal refused to invalidate the decision, but did say that, if it could be proved that materials relevant to the tax issue had not been put before the expert, the determination might be questioned.[20]

PENSION SCHEMES   4.3

Transfer of pension rights

4.3.1 Sales of companies and businesses often include provision for the transfer of the pension rights of the employees concerned from the vendor's pension scheme to the purchaser's existing pension scheme or a new pension scheme to be set up by the purchaser. The transfer would, in a typical case, be achieved by a payment from the vendor's scheme to the purchaser's scheme and the

---

interest of £2,612,611.98, by the decision of an independent expert. This was announced in a Department of the Environment News Release, January 24, 1997.

[17] See further 9.2.7.
[18] Unreasoned determinations are sometimes known as "non-speaking decisions": see 15.13.
[19] In one case the expert accountant, surprisingly, admitted after the determination that he had failed to deal with tax. One of the parties wanted this issue to be referred back to the expert, or, failing that, to the court; the other did not. The dispute was resolved by mediation. See further 13.5.1, 15.12 and 15.13.
[20] *Healds Foods Ltd v. Hyde Dairies*, unreported, December 6, 1996, CA.

provision by the purchaser's scheme of benefits of equal value to those provided by the vendor's scheme.

Actuaries determine

4.3.2 It may be difficult or impossible to establish at the date of the sale the value of the pension rights to be transferred. Sale agreements commonly provide for the value of the pension rights to be calculated according to a formula set out in the agreement (or in an actuary's letter attached to the agreement) and for the detailed calculations to be agreed between the parties' actuaries, or, if they do not agree, to be determined by another actuary acting as an expert and not as an arbitrator. This application of expert determination is in fairly common usage.

The *Imperial Foods* case

4.3.3 A challenge was made to an actuary's determination in *Re Imperial Foods Ltd's Pension Scheme*.[21] A new pension scheme was to be set up after the sale of a business, and an actuary was to decide the portion of the funds from the old company's pension scheme to be set aside for the new company's scheme. The actuary had to choose between two different methods. The court upheld the actuary's choice. The court found that there was a wide division of opinion among actuaries as to the relative merits of both methods; that the method chosen by the actuary was a fair and proper method, and that the calculation based on that method was unobjectionable.

4.4 TAX LIABILITIES

Tax liabilities in sale and purchase agreements are often determined by accountants acting as experts. An example is found in *Royal Trust International Ltd v. Nordbanken*,[22] where there was an agreement for the sale and purchase of a bank. Among the bank's assets were some loans of doubtful recoverability. If the loans were found to have been sold at a loss, the vendor would make a repayment, dependent on whether there had been a reduction in the bank's tax liability or not. That issue was referred by the sale and purchase agreement to a named firm of chartered accountants to determine as experts.

---

[21] [1986] 1 W.L.R. 717.
[22] Unreported, Chancery Division, October 13, 1989: see 12.6.3.

CHAPTER 5

OTHER COMMERCIAL APPLICATIONS

SUMMARY 5.1

This chapter considers various other commercial applications of expert determination, namely:

(a) employee remuneration and share options (5.2);
(b) partnership agreements (5.3);
(c) finance leasing (5.4);
(d) capital markets (5.5);
(e) convertible preference shares (5.6);
(f) commodities (5.7);
(g) shipping (5.8);
(h) insurance (5.9);
(i) banking (5.10);
(j) investment (5.11);
(k) insolvency (5.12);
(l) broadcasting (5.13);
(m) auctions (5.14);
(n) sports tribunals (5.15); and
(o) intellectual property (5.16).

EMPLOYEE REMUNERATION AND SHARE OPTIONS 5.2

Remuneration

Under the provisions of a service agreement, an employee's salary, or a bonus, may be determined by the certificate of the company's auditors. This is quite common in practice and appeared as the subject matter of the dispute in *Johnston v. Chestergate Hat Manufacturing Co Ltd.*[1] In that case a clause in an agreement between a company and its manager stated that he should receive a fixed salary and, as soon as the profits for the year had been ascertained and certified by the company's auditors, a percentage of "the net profits (if any) of the company for the whole year". The dispute turned on the calculation of the net profits. 5.2.1

[1] [1915] 2 Ch. 338.

Share options

5.2.2 The auditors may also be called upon to certify the adjustment of the option prices which employees are required to pay to acquire shares in companies under employee share schemes: adjustment of the prices is necessary after capital reorganisation or certain share issues.

5.3 PARTNERSHIP AGREEMENTS

Use of auditors' certificates

5.3.1 Partnership agreements often use auditors' certificates. For an example, see *Smith v. Gale*[2] (solicitors).

Extent of valuation exercise

5.3.2 What auditors have to do to determine the value of a partnership share may, depending on the partnership agreement, be either:

(a) simply to certify what the accounts say; or
(b) to make a much more complex investigation of the financial affairs of the partnership.

5.4 FINANCE LEASING

Tax charges affecting rentals

5.4.1 Finance leases, which are similar to loans, often contain provisions for experts to determine variations in rental. Typically the customer selects the equipment from the supplier and the finance lessor buys it and leases it to the customer on rentals calculated to pay off the purchase price plus interest. Unlike a lender, however, the lessor can claim capital allowances on the purchase price, normally at 25% per annum of the reducing balance. Part of the lessor's cashflow benefit from the consequent reductions in his tax bill is passed on to the lessee by way of lower rentals, reducing the lessee's effective finance cost. A finance lease normally provides for rentals to vary should the lessor's cashflow not be as expected, for example if the lessor fails to obtain the expected allowances or there is a change in the rate of tax. Leases may also provide for rental variations by reference to changes in interest rate.

Midland Montagu v. Tyne & Wear

5.4.2 A recalculation of rentals after the 1984 reduction in corporation tax rates was considered in *Midland Montagu Leasing (UK) Ltd v. Tyne*

---

[2] [1974] 1 W.L.R. 9. For some earlier examples, see *Vickers v. Vickers* (1867) L.R. 4 Eq. 529 and *Dinham v. Bradford* (1869) L.R. 5 Ch. App. 519.

& Wear Passenger Transport Executive and Ernst & Whinney.[3] The court upheld the method (known as "net after tax rate of return") used by the expert accountant as being common in the finance leasing business and envisaged by the parties.

CAPITAL MARKETS 5.5

Trustee remuneration

Trustees for the stockholders and eurobond holders are appointed under trust deeds used for bond issues in the international capital markets. These trust deeds usually contain an expert clause dealing with the remuneration of the trustee appointed under the deed. If there is a dispute about the fees the matter is referred to a merchant bank to be resolved, with the President of the Law Society appointing the bank if the parties cannot agree on the choice of bank.   5.5.1

Swaps and derivatives

In some transactions in swaps and derivatives, technical questions of valuation and entitlement, such as the substitution of an appropriate bond, are sometimes referred to a "Calculation Agent", usually the bank issuing the instrument. Some of these contracts have provided for disputes about the decision of the Calculation Agent to be referred to final determination by a disinterested third party who is a dealer in similar instruments.[4]   5.5.2

Tax assumptions

Transactions may be subject to adjustment where there is a change in an assumption about the effect of taxation. The decision, about whether or not there has been a change, is made by a tax specialist acting as an expert.   5.5.3

CONVERTIBLE PREFERENCE SHARES 5.6

Expert determination is also used for the adjustment of the rate at which a convertible redeemable preference share is to be converted into, typically, an ordinary share, following a capital reorganisation or certain types of issue of the ordinary shares in the company. Under the relevant share rights the directors usually make the adjustment, and if there is any doubt or dispute arising in respect of the adjustment the matter is referred to the auditors to certify an adjustment which is fair and reasonable in their view, to be binding on all concerned.

---

[3] Unreported, Chancery Division, February 23, 1990.
[4] See 5.7.3, 8.6.1.and 18.3.6.

5.7 COMMODITIES

Arbitration preferred to expert determination

5.7.1 Disputes about the quality and price of commodities would seem to be natural applications for expert determination, but events have not borne out that assumption. In *Pappa v Rose*[5] there was a dispute about the assessment by a commodity broker of the quality of black Smyrna raisins. The defendant, who had acted as selling broker between the claimant purchaser and the seller of the raisins, stated that the raisins were "fair average quality of 1869 growth". The claimant said the raisins were not within that quality definition and that the broker had not exercised reasonable skill and proper care. The court held that the broker was in the position of an arbitrator, and therefore immune from liability.[6] Although expert determination would be entirely suitable, the tradition of the trade prefers arbitration and disputes of this sort are now generally referred to commodity arbitrations.[7]

Inspection certificates

5.7.2 Some commodity contracts state that certificates of inspection of certain commodities are final as to quality. The inspectors act as experts. The court has held that the certificates remain final even though the inspector has been negligent, on the basis that they are no different from experts' decisions.[8] However, to be valid, the certificate must relate to the contract goods, and not to a consignment which was not actually shipped.[9] Sometimes trade financing documents such as letters of credit require one of the parties to obtain the quality certificate of some internationally recognised body or otherwise acceptable authority or individuals.[10]

Public policy for international commodity contracts with a chain of sales

5.7.3 The court has stated that in international commodity contracts involving a chain of sales it is desirable that contractual provisions for the resolution of mistakes should not be open to challenge by

---

[5] (1872) L.R. 7 C.P. 525.
[6] See further 16.3.1.
[7] Discussed in 17.6.5.
[8] See 15.11.3.
[9] *Alfred C. Toepfer v. Continental Grain Co.* [1974] 1 Lloyd's Rep. 11, approved in *Gill & Duffus SA v. Berger & Co. Inc.* [1984] 1 A.C. 382: but see also *The Bow Cedar* [1980] 2 Lloyd's Rep. 601 and *Daudruy van Cauwenberghe & Fils SA v. Tropical Product Sales SA* [1986] 1 Lloyd's Rep. 535.
[10] *Equitable Trust Company of New York v. Dawson Partners Ltd* (1926) 27 Ll. Rep. 49; *Kollerich & Cie S A v. The State Trading Corporation of India* [1980] 2 Lloyd's Rep. 32.

the courts. In this case, the court said that the party alleging a clerical error should follow the contractually agreed procedure within the time limits. The court said that a contrary conclusion would not make commercial sense, since uncertainty would be created as to the extent of the inquiries that could be made into the nature of the possible mistake and the time within which those enquiries could be made.[11-12]

Price and volume

5.7.4 Some long-term commodity supply contracts contain provisions for the periodic redetermination of the price of the commodity and the minimum quantity obligations of the supplier. These are sometimes referred to expert determination,[13] and sometimes to arbitration.[14]

Statutory provision for fixing price

5.7.5 The Sale of Goods Act 1979, s. 9 makes provision for agreements for references to third parties to fix the price in sale of goods contracts.[15] However, in practice sale of goods contracts do not use expert determination except as set out above.

Price adjustments dependent on quality

5.7.6 Some contracts contain machinery for adjusting the price to be paid for a commodity supplied under the contract. If the quality varies by a measurable factor, the price is adjusted according to an agreed formula. The formula is usually one that the parties can operate without recourse to an expert.[16]

[11-12] *Soules CAF v. Louis Dreyfus Negate SA* [2000] All E.R. (Comm.) 154., citing *'Agroexport' Entreprise d'Etat pour le Commerce Exterieur v. NV Goorden Import Cy. S.A.* [1956] 1 Lloyd's Rep. 319, where a similar provision was upheld: *Alfred C. Toepfer v. Continental Grain Co.* [1974] 1 Lloyd's Rep. 11, in which the Court of Appeal decided construction issues about what the certificate covered in favour of the claimant and ruled that a mistake made by the certifier was binding even when afterward admitted by the certifier to be a mistake: *Coastal (Bermuda) Ltd v. Esso Petroleum Co. Ltd* [1984] 1 Lloyd's Rep 11 where a certificate produced by inspectors was upheld as the confirmation contemplated by the contract although the inspectors were alleged to have relied on the original suppliers of the cargo and had not given their own opinion; and *Charles E. Ford Ltd v. AFEC Inc.* [1986] 2 Lloyd's Rep 307, where the effect of there being no provision about sampling was considered. For the two-tier system, providing an appeal, see 5.5.2 and 8.6.1. For time limits, see 9.18. For mistake, see 15.10 to 15.15, and the earlier authority cited at 15.11.3.
[13] See further 6.4.
[14] Preferably so-called fast-track arbitration as described in I.C.C. Bulletin (November 1992) Vol. 3, No. 2.
[15] Benjamin's Sale of Goods, 5th edition, paras 2043 *et seq*. See also 10.3.1.
[16] See 18.4.

5 : OTHER COMMERCIAL APPLICATIONS

5.8 SHIPPING

Parties to a shipping contract sometimes agree that the statement of quantity in a bill of lading is to be conclusive. If so, the shipowners are bound by it unless they can show fraud, although the goods may not have been shipped and the ship's master may have made a mistake.[17] This is an interesting example of a provision for finality being upheld by the court.

5.9 INSURANCE

Tharsis Sulphur v. Loftus

5.9.1 Apportionment of cargo damage was referred to an average adjuster in *Tharsis Sulphur & Copper Co. Ltd v. Loftus*[18] in circumstances where the average adjuster appears to have determined the issue as an expert determination. However, the court decided following the recent authority of *Pappa v. Rose*,[19] that the average adjuster had the benefit of arbitral immunity. More recently, Lord Salmon made a trenchant criticism of the *Tharsis* decision.[20]

Legal questions

5.9.2 Insurance policies sometimes refer disputes about whether a claim should be defended to a Q.C.: see 8.8.3.

Technical questions

5.9.3 Where the insurer's liability turns on the outcome of a technical argument a solution sometimes considered is the appointment of a suitably qualified expert to decide the issue.

Performance bonds

5.9.4 Insurance companies issue performance bonds, under which parties to a contract can make claims against each other or third parties. One kind of performance bond requires reasons to be given to support a claim, and in one instance an expert was to determine liability and damages.[21]

---

[17] *Lishman v. Christie & Co.* (1887) 19 Q.B.D. 333.
[18] (1872) L.R. 8 C.P. 1.
[19] (1872) L.R. 7 C.P. 525.
[20] In *Sutcliffe v. Thackrah* [1974] A.C. 727 quoted at 17.5.2.
[21] *Odebrecht Oil and Gas Services Ltd v. North Sea Production Co. Ltd* [1999] 2 All E.R. (Comm.) 405 and see 7.9.2.

Insolvency

5.9.5 For an example of expert determination used to resolve disputes in a scheme of arrangement for a group of insurance companies, see 5.12.2.

BANKING: "CONCLUSIVE EVIDENCE" CLAUSES   5.10

Some loan agreements used to contain conclusive evidence clauses which said that the certificate of the lender was to be conclusive evidence of the borrower's default. These clauses have not found favour because the degree of subjectivity would be unacceptable to borrowers. Both borrowers and lenders prefer the jurisdiction of the High Court. Conclusive evidence clauses are used in current financing documents for the computation of debt including the setting of interest rates. They are also found in some bank guarantees and counter-indemnities,[22] where the clause may provide that a certificate or a demand by the lender is to be conclusive evidence of the amount owed by the principal debtor to the lender; the court gives effect to these clauses, provided that there are no exceptional circumstances, such as bad faith. Some letters of credit contain provisions requiring certificates as to quality.[23]

INVESTMENT   5.11

Investment disputes may turn on informed opinion rather than legal issues. Take the example of an investment agreement where the investor buys a minority shareholding in a private company. The majority shareholder has an obligation to float the company on a stock exchange in certain circumstances relating to financial and market conditions. If the parties are unable to agree on whether those circumstances had arisen the dispute could be referred to an investment banker to decide as an expert.[24]

An expert can also be used to resolve general disputes under investment contracts: for instance where a specialist provider of investment services manages an investment on behalf of another party.

---

[22] *Bache & Co. (London) Ltd v. Banque Vernes et Commerciale de Paris SA* [1973] 2 Lloyd's Rep. 437 (for a telling criticism of this judgment, see Lawrence Collins and Dorothy Livingston, "Aspects of Conclusive Evidence Clauses" [1974] Journal of Business Law, p. 212), *Howe Richardson Scale Co. Ltd v. Polimex-Cekop* [1978] 1 Lloyd's Rep. 161, *R D Harbottle (Mercantile) Ltd v. National Westminster Bank Ltd* [1978] Q.B. 146. Other cases are cited at *Halsbury's Laws of England* 4th edition, Volume 20, paragraph 182.

[23] See 5.7.

[24] The appropriate appointing authority would be the City Disputes Panel.

5 : OTHER COMMERCIAL APPLICATIONS

5.12 INSOLVENCY

Claims against insolvent companies

5.12.1 Insolvencies are subject to the supervision of the court, and the court can sanction schemes of arrangement. Unless special arrangements are made the procedure for resolving disputes about claims by creditors is proof of debt followed by litigation. Under a scheme of arrangement the mechanism may change from litigation to arbitration or expert determination. Expert determination was adopted in the administration of Olympia and York Canary Wharf group for claims by unsecured creditors. The tenant and construction claims totalled over £163 million: the assets available to meet them amounted to £27 million. Many of the claims were disputed. Without some arrangement dealing with these claims, the group would have been prevented from coming out of administration and could not have returned to solvency. The majority of the unsecured creditors voted for the scheme, known as a company voluntary arrangement, and it was approved by the court. The company voluntary arrangement included a mechanism for referring claims to a special tribunal which was to resolve disputed claims by applying the law on proof of debts against insolvent companies[25] by the means of expert determination. A panel was established with the Law Society as the appointing authority. The panel from which members of a tribunal to deal with a particular claim were to be chosen consisted of two solicitors or barristers, two surveyors and two accountants. Where a tribunal consisted of one person only, that person was to be a lawyer: where three, the chairman was to be a lawyer with a deciding vote.[26]

Claims between insolvent companies

5.12.2 Schemes of arrangement may also use expert determination for the resolution of disputes between one another. A group of companies (known by the acronym KWELM) operated a linked underwriting business. With "long tail" claims there was a run-off period of between 20 to 40 years and potential payouts of U.S. $500 million. Disputes are dealt with by an individual appointed under the scheme known as the Conflicts Administrator who decides which mechanism (arbitration or expert determination) is to be used in resolving the dispute. If expert determination is used, a chartered accountant fulfils the role.[27] Even where there is no scheme, two

---

[25] Insolvency Rules 1986.
[26] Relevant extracts from the company voluntary arrangement are at Appendix H.
[27] Many copies of the KWELM scheme have been distributed although it has not been formally published. The general provisions of the scheme, but not those relating to dispute resolution, have been discussed in a number of articles, notably in *The Scheme of Things—Scheme of Arrangement*, by John McKenna and Nigel Howcroft, Re Actions 9/94, p. 67.

insolvent companies may with the approval of creditors and/or the court refer a dispute between them to expert determination.

BROADCASTING 5.13

A number of contracts between independent television companies contain provisions for disputes between them to be settled by expert determination. The subject matter includes commercial disputes such as the apportionment of the cost of a networked programme, television rights to sports games,[28] as well as more technical questions.

AUCTIONS 5.14

Conditions of sale of auction houses sometimes provide that any dispute between bidders as to which is the buyer is settled by the auctioneer. A variant is for the conditions to provide that the auctioneer has absolute discretion to reject any bid.

SPORTS TRIBUNALS 5.15

A number of sporting bodies run tribunals of various kinds, some of which may be governed by the same legal principles as expert determination by an independent third party.[29]

INTELLECTUAL PROPERTY 5.16

Intellectual property agreements, such as know-how licences, sometimes contain provisions referring questions about the level of royalties to an accountant, unless the issues are technical in which case they are referred to a patent agent.

Intellectual property applications of expert determination thus straddle the divide between commercial applications and industrial applications discussed in the next chapter.

---

[28] The dispute about the BSkyB contract for the televising of the Five Nations rugby championship matches, *The Times,* January 20, 1999, sports pages.
[29] For example, *R. v. Disciplinary Committee of the Jockey Club, ex parte Aga Khan* [1993] 1 W.L.R. 909; discussed at 18.5.1.

CHAPTER 6

FROM VALUER TO EXPERT

6.1 SUMMARY

This chapter examines:

(a) how expert determination has been adapted and expanded by the notion that the referee is an expert rather than a valuer (6.2), leading to
(b) new applications (6.3) which are then set out in the remaining sections:
(c) energy and mining contracts (6.4);
(d) shipbuilding contracts (6.5);
(e) computer contracts (6.6);
(f) engineering contracts (6.7); and
(g) telecommunications contracts (6.8).

6.2 USE OF THE WORD "EXPERT"

Original labels "valuation" and "appraisement"

6.2.1 The earlier cases do not generally use the word "expert" to describe the dispute resolver. If any descriptive word is used at all, it is usually "valuer", and the procedure is called a "valuation" or an "appraisement", and not "expert determination" or a "reference to an expert". The word "experience" is used in some of the earlier cases to describe the necessary attribute of a valuer. For instance, in the 1854 case *Eads v. Williams*[1] arbitrators fixing the rent of a mine were said to be entrusted, from their *experience*[2] and observation, to form a judgment, and therefore not to need to examine witnesses.

Appearance of the label "expert"

6.2.2 The word "expert" appears in the law reports with this meaning in 1878 in *Bottomley v Ambler*[3] where the following are found: "... you

---

[1] (1854) 24 L.J. Ch. 531.
[2] Emphasis added.
[3] (1878) 38 L.T. 545.

refer the matter to a person who is an expert as an expert . . ." and, confusingly ". . . in such a case, arbitrators, being experts . . .". But "valuer" was much more common at that time.

Appearance of formula "as an expert and not as an arbitrator"

The first appearance in the law reports of the formula "as an expert and not as an arbitrator" is in *Dean v. Prince*[4] where an auditor was to certify the value of shares "and in so certifying . . . shall . . . act as an expert and not as an arbitrator." 6.2.3

NEW FIELDS FOR EXPERTS 6.3

The last hundred years have seen the growth of new technologies and of the power of organised professions. As a result, the role of the referee has expanded from valuer to expert. The energy and computer industries are obvious examples: applications of expert determination in the energy and computer industries are set out in the following sections. There are many new technologies, and expert determination may be appropriate to many more applications than these instances. The same changes in society have also been responsible for the parallel growth in the importance of experts acting as expert witnesses.

ENERGY AND MINING 6.4

Oil and gas agreements

Commercial agreements in the oil and gas industries use expert determination in the following three ways. The first relates to the pricing of oil and gas supplies; the second to apportioning costs and entitlements in unitised[5] oil and gas fields; and the third to the construction of facilities. This section looks at the first two of these applications. Construction applications are covered in Chapter 7. 6.4.1

Fixing the price

Gas supply agreements[6] often provide for the supply of gas over a long period, sometimes for a decade or more.[7] It used to be common for agreements for the supply of crude oil to do the same but these 6.4.2

---

[4] [1953] Ch. 590 at 591 (where it is misquoted) and, on appeal [1954] 1 Ch. 409 at 415.
[5] For an explanation of this, see 6.4.5.
[6] *United Kingdom Oil and Gas Law*, eds Daintith and Willoughby (Sweet & Maxwell) at 1–1183.
[7] *E.g.* 25 years in the agreement litigated in *Superior Overseas Development Corporation and Philips Petroleum (UK) Co. Ltd v. British Gas Corporation* [1982] 1 Lloyd's Rep. 262.

have gone out of fashion in recent years with the volatility of oil prices: they may reappear if the oil price settles down. In long-term supply agreements it is desirable to have some agreed method for fixing the price either on a quarterly or on a cargo by cargo basis. Agreements often specify market price. In some cases market price may be defined in relatively simple terms such as by reference to the price quoted in a recognised trade journal. In other cases, a formula may be spelled out in the agreement showing how the market price is to be established. This formula can be quite detailed. Sometimes the circumstances in which a change in price can be sought are more specific to the parties concerned: for instance in one case the trigger was "substantial change in the economic circumstances relating to this agreement such that either party feels that such change is causing it to suffer substantial economic hardship".[8] Thus the issues may be both technical and economic, and may involve judgments as to the efficacy of modification to the production platform and plant and as to the efficacy of extra drilling.[9] If the parties cannot agree on the formula or, as the case may be, on the changes and the resulting hardship, the matter is referred to an expert.

Establishing the quantity

6.4.3 As well as quality issues, some oil and gas supply contracts provide for expert determination if there are disputes about the measurement of the volume supplied: *i.e.* discrepancies between the amounts at the seller's end of the journey and at the buyer's end of the journey. Where the parties have complete confidence in the expert this is particularly useful for a long-term supply contract with a continuing commercial relationship.

Justifying termination on economic grounds

6.4.4 Expert determination is also applied to disputes about the right to terminate oil and gas supply contracts on economic grounds, for instance when a field is no longer economic.[10]

Unitised projects

6.4.5 Apportioning costs and entitlements in an oil or gas field is often necessary to settle matters between the participants in a unitised project.[11] In a unitised project, persons having differing interests in

---

[8] *Superior Overseas*, cited above.
[9] Paper presented to the IBA SBL 1995 Conference in Paris, ref PP253, by David Wilson.
[10] Also discussed in David Wilson's IBA paper cited above.
[11] See *United Kingdom Oil and Gas Law*, eds Daintith and Willoughby (Sweet & Maxwell) at 1–723 *et seq*.

two or more different areas or tracts agree that a field underlying their respective tracts should be developed and produced as one project. The exact proportions in which oil and/or gas is present in the respective tracts become fully apparent only as wells are drilled in the course of operations. Sometimes the issue is not the amount of oil but rather the amount of recoverable reserves, in which case prediction of costs and prices well into the future becomes necessary, and issues of economics are as important as those of geology. By a process known as re-determination of equities or equity determination, the interested parties agree that the proportion which their respective stakes bear to one another is to be reassessed after a certain period, or at periodic intervals.[12] When the final re-determination is made, the nature and extent of the oil and/or gas field and the amount of the oil and/or gas present in each of the tracts should be more apparent as a result of the drilling and production. The assessment of the relative equities of the parties depends on an understanding of the geology of the site and the engineering technicalities of extracting the oil and/or gas, and the application to that information of an agreed method of calculation with a prescribed specification of which computer software to use to make the calculations. If the parties are unable to agree on the precise application of the method of calculation to the information derived from the drilling and production, the dispute may be referred by the agreement to an expert to determine. In some cases the expert is appointed before there is a dispute, under the Guided Owner's method, where the expert monitors the determination process while it is carried out by the parties. As soon as a dispute arises, the expert (usually an organisation rather than an individual) is ready to act.[13] In one reported Australian case[14] the determination was made by one of the parties.[15]

Court review of re-determination disputes

The court has heard a series of cases on disputed re-determinations in recent years. In 1988/9 there were two cases[16] about completed re-determinations. In both these cases the method of re-determination employed by the experts was challenged on the ground of mistake as a matter of interpretation of the words of the agreement. The court's

6.4.6

---

[12] Apparently there have been as many as four different re-determinations under the same agreement.
[13] Papers presented to the IBA SBL 1995 Conference in Paris, refs PP252 and 253, by E. P. Greeno and David Wilson.
[14] *Crusader Resources NL v. Santos Ltd* (1991) 58 S.A.S.R. 74.
[15] See 18.3.
[16] *Arco British Ltd v. Sun Oil Britain Ltd* (1988) *Financial Times*, December 20, and *Amoco (UK) Exploration Company v. Shell (UK) Ltd*, unreported, Commercial Court, Potter J., December 21, 1989—this is known in the industry by the name of the second defendant as the *Fulmar* case.

investigations were very extensive in both these judgments, and the judgments contain much guidance on this very specialised type of expert clause. Reviews of this sort after the decision are unlikely to recur, because the courts have restricted the range of circumstances in which experts' decisions may be challenged. In 1993 there were two cases[17] about applications to the court before the re-determination decision.

For a discussion of the current law on the extent of the court's powers of review, see Chapter 12 for challenges before decision and Chapter 15 for challenges afterwards. The law of mistake has been applied and explained in two important cases in the industry, one about a gasfield[18] and the other about an oilfield.[19] In the first of these cases, the clause contained the words "save in the case of manifest error"; this wording is discussed in 15.17. These cases show that expert evidence may be relied on to assess whether the expert has made a mistake and how serious the mistake is.

Electricity

6.4.7 Expert determination is also used in electricity supply contracts, which are not strictly supply contracts but contracts for differences, because the electricity is supplied from a pool and the purpose of the contract is to cover price fluctuations. Experts are used in electricity contracts to determine technical issues and/or the price.

Mining

6.4.8 Mining contracts offer another application of expert determination.[20] Where there is no published market price, as with uranium, long-term contracts for the supply of concentrate have contained expert clauses for determining the price. Where there is a published market price, expert determination may be used to resolve disputes about other commercial terms such as the costs of treatment and refining.

Nuclear industries

6.4.9 As well as the price of uranium, expert clauses appear in agreements in the nuclear industry for other aspects of price review.

---

[17] *Amoco (UK) Exploration Co. v. Amerada Hess Ltd* [1994] I Lloyd's Rep. 330, and *Neste Production Ltd v. Shell UK Ltd* [1994] 1 Lloyd's Rep. 447.
[18] *Conoco (UK) Ltd v. Phillips Petroleum* [1998] A.D.R.L.J. 55. Morrison J. held that no error had been made and the re-determination was binding.
[19] *Shell (UK) Ltd v. Enterprise Oil plc* [1999] 2 Lloyd's Rep. 456.
[20] See *Cooper v. Shuttleworth* (1856) 25 L.J. Exch. 114; a dispute between landlord and tenant of a quarry about the ownership of stone.

Shipbuilding 6.5

Technical questions may be referred to an expert

Shipbuilding contracts often provide that technical disputes about the construction of a ship and the materials and workmanship are to be referred to an expert for determination. Sometimes the consent of both parties is necessary for the reference to take place. In other contracts, either party may refer a dispute to an expert. 6.5.1

Classification Societies

In practice, experts are rarely appointed to determine issues under shipbuilding contracts because of the role played by Classification Societies. The members of the International Association of Classification Societies are independent bodies of marine surveyors recognised by governments throughout the world as their agents for the implementation of the international maritime safety conventions. Shipbuilding contracts state that the ship must comply with the rules of the relevant Classification Society. Thus in practice the role of a Classification Society enables many disputes between a builder and an owner about the construction of a ship to be resolved without recourse to expert determination. 6.5.2

Computers 6.6

Computer contracts sometimes provide for experts to determine technical issues such as whether the computer equipment or software performs in accordance with its specification, or the interpretation of specifications or other related technical documentation.[21] No instance has yet reached a reported court case but one reached the trade press.[22] Interim determination, as found in the construction industry, might be useful in computer disputes.[23] Expert clauses are also found in some source code deposit agreements for the purpose of appointing a new custodian where the parties cannot agree who to appoint.[24]

Engineering 6.7

Engineering contracts offer many opportunities for specific issues to be settled by an engineering expert. Here are some examples:

---

[21] See *Computer Contracts*, by Richard Morgan and Graham Stedman, (5th ed., Sweet & Maxwell, 1995).
[22] *Computing*, March 26, 1992, a dispute between British Telecom and a supplier, involving the British Computer Society as (at that time) an unwilling appointing authority.
[23] See 7.3.2.
[24] See *Computer Contracts*, cited above, page 511.

disputes under engine lease agreements about maintenance costs; acceptance tests under aircraft contracts; technical issues in telecommunication contracts.

For the position where the engineering contract is effectively a construction contract, see Chapter 7.

6.8 TELECOMS CONTRACTS

Mercury Communications Ltd v. Director General of Telecommunications[25] is an example of a telecommunications contract in which the parties had agreed to refer to the industry regulator disputes as to the terms of contract which should apply to the parties' future dealings in the event of a fundamental change of circumstances. A telecommunications supply contract contained an expert clause for the resolution of all disputes arising.[26]

---

[25] [1996] 1 W.L.R. 48; see 12.6.4.
[26] See 8.7.2.

CHAPTER 7

CONSTRUCTION CONTRACTS AND INTERIM DETERMINATIONS

Summary 7.1

This chapter considers:

(a) various applications of expert determination where the decision is not final and binding (7.2);
(b) whether those applications could be used in other applications such as computer contracts (7.3);
(c) certification (7.4);
(d) adjudication (7.5);
(e) dispute review boards/panels of experts (7.6);
(f) policy and management issues in joint ventures (7.7);
(g) resolution of specific issues (7.8); and
(h) general dispute resolution (7.9).

Interim determinations

The principal subject of this book is expert determination where the determination is final and binding. Construction contracts contain instances of a different type of expert determination, where the determination made by the expert is usually not final or binding; or it may be binding but only final after the fulfilment of some later condition. As is the case for expert determination generally, the law approaches these systems by an examination of the words of the contract. It is (at least) convenient to treat interim but nevertheless binding determinations as a species of expert determination. However an expert determination which does not produce a binding result is probably not best included in any classification of expert determination: it is a form of ADR and should be called a review, case review, dispute review or early neutral evaluation. Non-binding systems are mentioned in this chapter because the systems are better understood when considered together, and because expressions like "Dispute Review Board" can be used to describe both binding and non-binding systems.[1] Another 7.2

[1] See 1.1.7.

variant combines interim and final determination: interim determinations are made at intervals during a project, with a final adjustment at the end.[2]

7.3 CONSTRUCTION CONTRACTS AND OTHER POTENTIAL APPLICATIONS OF INTERIM DETERMINATION

Why are these special forms found in construction contracts?

7.3.1 The variants of expert determination found in construction contracts are discussed in the sections which follow. They run from certification by the employer's agent, through interim decisions by a construction professional known as adjudication, to expert determination of specific issues or general issues. Certain factors seem to have caused construction contracts to make use of this wide range of systems. There is the traditional role of the contract administrator or certifier who issues certificates that work has been carried out and that payment should be made for it, and certificates relating to matters like extension of time. Other factors are technical subject-matter and the need for speedy interim resolution. Another feature, which has not so far played a significant role in this development, is the fact that most construction projects involve numerous parties because of the use of sub-contractors and consultants. This may promote wider use of expert determination for the general resolution of construction disputes because the procedure lends itself to multi-party disputes.[3] Perhaps for some or all of these reasons, draftsmen often use multi-tier dispute resolution in construction contracts.[4]

Could these forms be used elsewhere?

7.3.2 The special features identified above should be considered to see whether they could be used in other applications. Certification is sometimes used in banking and international capital market agreements to establish a default, where one of the parties, such as the trustee, may certify the default. The other forms discussed below are relevant to consideration of improvements in dispute resolution in any contract with a technical element where the works take a long period of time to complete, and the parties both wish to contain the dispute within the contractual framework.[5] Computer disputes are the most obvious contender for this.

---

[2] See *Odebrecht Oil and Gas Services Ltd v. North Sea Production Co. Ltd* [1999] 2 All E.R. (Comm.) 405 discussed at 7.9.2.
[3] See 8.5.
[4] See 8.6.
[5] See John Uff Q.C. "Control of disputes within the contract framework", (1992) *Future Directions in Construction Law*, pp. 197–220, published by the Centre of Construction Law and Management, King's College London.

CERTIFICATION   7.4

Administration and dispute resolution

7.4.1 A classic role for a construction professional or expert such as an architect, engineer or surveyor, is to act as a contract administrator or certifier. The task of the certifier, usually combined with the role of issuing instructions to the contractor, is to issue certificates which specify the sums to be paid to the contractor for work done under the contract, and to issue decisions on matters other than money such as extensions of time. The certifier is appointed by the employer and acts as the employer's agent. As a third party appointed by one of the parties only, a certifier does not fit into quite the same mould as most of the experts described in this book. The decisions of certifiers are binding but not usually final, as certificates of this kind can be reviewed and revised in arbitration, although in some cases summary judgment may be given by a judge to uphold certificates. The work of certifiers is administrative, but an important part of it is the making of decisions which resolve disputes: for example the certifier often has to accept or reject claims by the contractor as to what should be certified for payment. Where an architect's certificate is conclusive, the same general legal principles apply as those which apply to a binding certificate issued by an auditor or by another expert.[6]

Liability of certifiers

7.4.2 A certifier under a building contract must act impartially,[7] and the building-owner must not try to influence the certifier to act in a manner inconsistent with the position of certifier.[8] The courts used to see this certifying role as quasi-arbitral, giving the certifier a very similar status to that of an expert, with the result that a certifier could not be sued for negligence until 1974, when this line of authorities was overruled by the House of Lords.[9] In 1975 the Lords, in a case about auditors valuing shares in a private company, went on to abolish the immunity of experts as well.[10] An expert can be liable in contract or tort to both the parties who have referred an issue to the expert for decision.[11] However, a certifier is usually liable only to the employer-client and not to the contractor.

---

[6] *Arenson v. Casson, Beckman, Rutley & Co.* [1977] A.C. 405, *per* Lord Simon at 419H and 421G-H, *Keating on Building Contracts* 7th edition, 2001, paras 5–38 to 5–39, *Balfour Beatty Civil Engineering Ltd v. Docklands Light Railway Ltd* (1996) 78 B.L.R. 42. See 18.3.
[7] *Sutcliffe v. Thackrah* [1974] A.C. 727 at 737.
[8] *Hickman v. Roberts* [1913] A.C. 229.
[9] *Sutcliffe v. Thackrah* [1974] A.C. 727: see 16.4.
[10] *Arenson v. Casson Beckman Rutley & Co.* [1977] A.C. 405: see 16.5.
[11] See 16.7 to 16.13.

In the leading case[12] the contractor sought to sue the engineer for losses arising from alleged under-certification of the amounts due to the contractor but the contractor's claim was struck out.

Certification usually, but not always, interim and reviewable

7.4.3 Certificates issued by architects or engineers under construction contracts are decisions by the agent of the building-owner, and in contrast with decisions by independent third parties acting as experts, standard-form construction contracts usually provide that the certificates of architects and engineers are subject to review by an arbitrator.[13] Where certificates are reviewable their effect is provisional only.[14] The terms of the contract may expressly provide that a particular type of certificate is to be conclusive on certain matters, or that it is to be conclusive unless arbitration or other proceedings are commenced within a specified period of time after the issue of the certificate. Cases have occurred in which the parties have deleted the standard clause which provided for review of certificates. In one case the Court of Appeal held that certificates by the engineer (an employee of the building-owner) were unreviewable by the court, except on the ground of legal misdirection, dishonesty, unfairness or unreasonableness.[15] In a later case the House of Lords held that this decision was wrong, and that the court should be slow to find that a certificate by an architect is unreviewable.[16]

Certificates as condition precedent, and the exceptions to this requirement

7.4.4 Many of the standard contract forms for construction contracts have been interpreted by the court as making the certificate of

---

[12] *Pacific Associates Inc. v. Baxter* [1990] Q.B. 993; see Timothy Trotman, "*Pacific Associates v. Baxter*: Time for re-consideration" (1999) 15 Const. L.J. 449 for a criticism of this decision in the light of more recent authorities, and *Hudson's Building and Engineering Contracts*, 11th edition, Vol. 1 paragraph 1–304 for a commentary on the case. See 16.13.2 for other cases on this point.

[13] In some engineering contracts (*e.g.* ICE and FIDIC) it is a condition precedent to arbitration that the dispute first be referred to the engineer for decision. For the importance of contractual analysis of the effect of a certificate and whether it is reviewable, see *Tarmac Construction Ltd v. Esso Petroleum Company Ltd* (1996) 83 B.L.R. 65.

[14] See for example *Bernhard's Rugby Landscapes Ltd v. Stockley Park Consortium Ltd* (1998) 14 Const. L.J. 329 at 348.

[15] *Balfour Beatty Civil Engineering Ltd v. Docklands Light Railway Ltd* (1996) 78 B.L.R. 42. Another case where the arbitration clause was deleted was *John Barker Construction Ltd v. London Portman Hotel Ltd* (1996) 83 B.L.R. 31; discussed at 15.8.2.

[16] *Beaufort Developments (NI) Ltd v. Gilbert-Ash NI Ltd* [1999] A.C. 266 at 276, 281–2 and 292. The House of Lords overruled *Northern Regional Health Authority v. Derek Crouch Construction Co. Ltd* [1984] 1 Q.B. 644, where the Court of Appeal had held that the review powers of an arbitrator could not be exercised by the court.

the architect, engineer or contract administrator a condition precedent to recovery of payment by the building contractor.[17] Some exceptions to the requirement for a certificate are clearly established by authority; others are less clearly established by authority but have been put forward in the leading text-books on building contracts[18]:

- waiver
- disqualification of the certifier on the ground of fraud or collusion[19]
- prevention, interference or improper pressure by the employer[20]
- disqualification of the certifier on the ground of a disqualifying interest not known at the time the contract was made[21]
- death or incapacity of the certifier[22]
- unreasonable refusal by the certifier to give any consideration to the matters relevant to the certification[23]
- conduct of the certifier which, consistent with the certifier's other duties, falls short of a proper standard of fairness, independence and impartiality in relation to the issue of a certificate[24]
- taking into consideration by the certifier of matters extraneous to the certifier's proper jurisdiction under the contract or applying the wrong principles.[25]

Practical completion triggers

7.4.5 One application of expert determination where the expert is the agent of one party only is in land transactions between vendor and purchaser or landlord and tenant. The completion date for the purchase of the land or the date when rent starts to be payable by the tenant is triggered by the issue of the certificate of practical completion of the building being bought or leased.[26] The certificate of practical completion is issued by the architect (or other construction professional) who is the agent of the vendor and acting as certifier in the separate contract for the construction of the building

---

[17] *Lubenham Fidelities and Investment Co. Ltd v. South Pembrokeshire District Council* (1986) 33 B.L.R. 39 at 55 (May L.J.).
[18] *Hudson's Building and Engineering Contracts* 11th edition, paras 6–096 to 6–151 and *Keating on Building Contracts* 7th edition (2001) paras 5–18 to 5–46, where this topic is extensively discussed.
[19] See 15.4.2.
[20] *ibid.*
[21] See 15.5.3.
[22] See 9.7.5, 11.3.5, 13.10 and *Keating on Building Contracts* 7th edition (2001) para. 5–23.
[23] See 13.10.
[24] See 15.4.2 and 15.6.3.
[25] See 15.12.
[26] See the discussion at 2.6, and compare condition precedent and Q.C. clauses discussed at 8.8.3.

being sold or let. Would the issuer of a practical completion certificate be potentially liable in the tort of negligence to the purchaser? If the issuer did not know that the issue of the certificate triggered completion of the sale, or that it would be likely to do so, the issuer would probably not be liable.[27]

Confusion over the word "certificate'

7.4.6 The expression "certificate" and its cognates can cause confusion between the construction industry usage and the wordings found in expert accountant clauses where the word "certificate" means the decision of the expert. The context and the tradition are different. In the practical completion trigger cases the word "certificate" has both meanings simultaneously.

7.5 ADJUDICATION

Definition and context

7.5.1 The word "adjudication" is used in the construction industry to denote a system of interim determination of disputes arising during the course of a construction contract by a construction professional whose decision is usually binding and may become final if not subsequently challenged.[28] It has been used in some major projects, was recommended for wider use by the Latham Report[29] and is, by statute,[30] mandatory for most construction contracts. Each adjudication clause needs to be read carefully as there is no standard form. The use of the word "adjudication" is confusing to those outside the construction industry, since one would expect the word to be used to describe a judicial process, which is not how the industry sees or uses it[31] or how the courts see adjudicators' decisions. But, on the other hand, there is no magic in the word "adjudication", even in context: a clause in a sub-contractor's standard terms of business providing for adjudication of disputes has been held to be an arbi-

---

[27] See 16.13.
[28] For an excellent survey of contractual adjudication, if now slightly out of date, see Mark McGaw "Adjudicators, experts and keeping out of court" (1992) *Legal Obligations in Construction*, Centre of Construction Law and Management, Kings College London, p. 605. See also John Uff Q.C. "Control of disputes within the contract framework" (1992) *Future Directions in Construction Law*, Centre of Construction Law and Management, Kings College London, p. 197. On the statutory system, see *The Construction Act: Time for Review*, edited by Frances A. Paterson and Philip Britton, Centre of Construction Law and Management, Kings College London 2000.
[29] "Constructing the Team" by Sir Michael Latham, "Final Report of the Government/Industry Review of Procurement and Contractual Arrangements in the UK Construction Industry", HMSO 1995, at Chapter 9, para. 9.14.
[30] Housing Grants, Construction and Regeneration Act 1996, s. 108: see 7.5.7.
[31] If it were a judicial process, it would be arbitration: see 17.6.

tration clause because that was what the parties intended by the word.[32]

Is it a form of expert determination?

7.5.2

Some adjudication provisions in construction contracts say that the adjudicator is to act as an expert: some do not assign a status; and the Engineering and Construction Contract[33] states that the adjudicator settles the dispute as independent adjudicator.[34] In most contexts, it is reasonably clear that the adjudicator is not acting as an arbitrator. If the role is not that of an arbitrator, it is likely that it will be construed as similar to that of an expert, subject to the effect of all the special contractual words qualifying the usual aspects of that role in each specific application.[35] If there is concern that classifying an adjudicator as an expert would permit the adjudicator to make a decision outside the parties' submissions,[36] that can be prevented by appropriate words.[37] In the cases on statutory adjudication that have reached the courts so far, statutory adjudication has been treated similarly to expert determination.[38] However there is one very important difference: by statute, construction contracts have to provide for the adjudicator to be immune from liability, except where the act or omission of the adjudicator is in bad faith.[39]

Jurisdiction

7.5.3

Adjudication had its origins in the need to resolve interim disputes between contractors and sub-contractors about set-off. It therefore had a restricted role because of this limitation on the jurisdiction of the adjudicator. This was reflected in some of the standard forms. The Engineering and Construction Contract never had a restriction and all disputes have to go to adjudication first. Under the statutory regime jurisdiction is unlimited.

---

[32] *Cape Durasteel Ltd v. Rosser and Russell Building Services Ltd* (1996) 46 Con. L.R. 75; and see 17.3.
[33] The renamed second edition of the New Engineering Contract.
[34] Clause 92.1.
[35] See "Adjudication and Expert Determination", by John Kendall, in *Construction Law: Themes and Practice, Essays in Honour of Ian Duncan Wallace Q.C.*, Sweet & Maxwell 1998.
[36] A concern of Phillip Capper "The adjudicator under NEC 2nd edition: a new approach to disputes" (December 1995) *Engineering, Construction and Architectural Management*, Special issue on the New Engineering Contract, Vol. 2, No. 4, (published by Blackwell Science).
[37] See 16.8.6.
[38] See *e.g. Macob Civil Engineering Ltd v. Morrison Construction Ltd* [1999] B.L.R. 93, *Bouygues UK Ltd v. Dahl-Jensen UK Ltd* [2000] B.L.R. 522 (CA).
[39] See 7.5.4. The statute also provides that adjudicators must be impartial.

Statutory adjudication

7.5.4 The Housing Grants, Construction and Regeneration Act 1996 introduced a new system giving parties to construction contracts[40] the right to refer disputes to adjudication complying with certain requirements.[41] Contracts to which the Act applies must[42]:

(a) enable a party to give notice at any time of its intention to refer a dispute to adjudication;
(b) provide a timetable with the object of securing the appointment of the adjudicator and referral of the dispute to the adjudicator within seven days;
(c) require the adjudicator to reach a decision within 28 days or a longer period if agreed after the dispute arose;
(d) allow the adjudicator to extend that period of 28 days by up to 14 days with the consent of the referring party;
(e) impose a duty on the adjudicator to act impartially;
(f) enable the adjudicator to take the initiative in ascertaining the facts and the law.

Construction contracts also have to provide that the decision of the adjudicator is binding until the dispute is finally determined by legal proceedings, arbitration or agreement, but the parties may accept the decision as finally determining the dispute.[43] The adjudicator[44] must be given immunity for acts and omissions as adjudicator unless the act or omission is in bad faith.[45]

If these requirements are not met the provisions of the government's scheme apply,[46] which introduces a number of other issues not dealt with here. Several sets of adjudication rules have been published[47]. The level of activity, after a very slow start, has been high. The existence of the statutory scheme may itself be a factor which encourages parties to reach agreement rather than become locked in dispute.

---

[40] Widely defined: see Housing Grants, Construction and Regeneration Act 1996, s.104.
[41] Housing Grants, Construction and Regeneration Act 1996, s. 108(1).
[42] *ibid.*, s. 108(2)(a)–(f).
[43] *ibid.*, s. 108(3).
[44] And the adjudicator's employees and agents, if any.
[45] Housing Grants, Construction and Regeneration Act 1996, s. 108(4).
[46] *ibid.*, s. 108(5). The government's scheme is contained in The Scheme for Construction Contracts (England & Wales) Regulations 1998, S.I. 1998 No. 649.
[47] CEDR, CIC, ICE, RICS, TeCSA, TECBAR.

Procedure and enforcement

The adjudicator may be appointed at the time the contract is made or the appointment may be made when there is a dispute. An informal procedure is followed with written submissions within short time limits, and no provision for a hearing. Does the rule of natural justice, which requires that each party should be given a fair opportunity to be heard, and that there are to be no private communications between the tribunal and either party, referred to here as "due process", apply to a statutory adjudication? The answer may depend on the adjudication rules adopted; a requirement of due process is not expressly imposed by the statute.

7.5.5

However, in a case where a decision was challenged on the ground of procedural invalidity, the court seems to have assumed that the rule of natural justice requiring due process had to be followed, although the judgment did not turn on this point. The court nevertheless held that even if it was alleged that there had been a procedural error which might later be held to have been sufficient to invalidate the decision, the decision still had to be enforced in the meantime.[48] In a later case it was recognised that the requirements of due process did not apply with full force to adjudication of this kind: adjudicators had to work under pressure of time and circumstance which make it extremely difficult to comply with the rules of natural justice in the manner of a court or an arbitrator, and the statutory system can be made to work in practice only if some breaches of the rules of natural justice which had no demonstrable consequences are disregarded. However the court refused to enforce the adjudicator's decision on the ground that there had been non-compliance with the rules of natural justice with respect to communications between the adjudicator and one only of the parties, and that if those rules had been complied with there might have been a different decision.[49] In adjudications subject to the statutory scheme, there is a duty on the adjudicator to make available to the parties any information received and taken into consideration in reaching the decision. Failure to comply with this duty may prevent the decision being enforced.[50]

It has also been argued that the entitlement under the Human Rights Act 1998 to a fair and public hearing in the determination of

---

[48] *Macob Civil Engineering Ltd v. Morrison Construction Ltd* [1999] B.L.R. 93. See Ian Duncan Wallace Q.C., "HGCRA Adjudicators' Errors and Enforcement" (2000) 16 Const. L.J. 102, for trenchant criticism of the judgment, and the Scottish case of *Homer Burgess Ltd v. Chirex (Annan) Ltd* (2000) 16 Const. L.J. 242 at 257.

[49] *Discain Project Services Ltd and Opecprime Development Ltd* [2000] B.L.R. 402, H.H. Judge Bowsher Q.C., TCC.

[50] S.I. 1998 No. 649, The Scheme for Construction Contracts (England and Wales) Regulations 1998, para. 17, applied in *Woods Hardwick Ltd v. Chiltern Air Conditioning*, October 2, 2000, unreported, H.H. Judge Thornton Q.C., TCC.

one's civil rights and obligations applies to statutory adjudication: so far the court has disagreed, on the basis that the adjudicator's decision is only a temporary one.[51] Whether or not the Human Rights Act does apply to statutory adjudication, and to what extent, are outside the scope of this book. If due process is held to be a requirement, and/or the Human Rights Act entitlement to a fair and public hearing[52] is held to apply, much more caution will be needed in making analogies between statutory adjudication and expert determination.

Before the introduction of statutory adjudication, the courts held that an adjudicator's decision could not be enforced as an arbitration award,[53] but did enforce an adjudicator's decision by a mandatory injunction.[54] Statutory adjudication decisions are enforced by the courts in the same way as expert determination decisions. Where the contract contains an arbitration clause, the mandatory stay under Arbitration Act, s. 9 may not apply.[55] A party to a building contract may refer a dispute to adjudication after commencing proceedings in relation to the same dispute.[56] The adjudicator's decision may be enforced even in cases where there is an obvious error in the calculation.[57] However, in the absence of agreement to the contrary, there is an implied term of the contract referring the dispute to adjudication that the adjudicator might, within a reasonable time, correct an error arising from an accidental error or omission, so long as there is no prejudice to the other party.[58]

By late 2000, two and a half years after the introduction of statutory adjudication, commentators had already collected 50 cases on disputed adjudication decisions, most of them being about the enforceability of the decision[59]: but only one of the cases

---

[51] *Elanay Contracts Limited v. The Vestry*, unreported, August 30, 2000, H.H. Judge Richard Havery Q.C., TCC.
[52] Human Rights Act 1998, Schedule 1, Article 6.
[53] *A. Cameron Ltd v. John Mowlem & Co. plc* (1990) 52 B.L.R. 24.
[54] *Drake & Scull Engineering Ltd v. McLaughlin & Harvey plc* (1992) 60 B.L.R. 102. This was another case about an adjudicator's decision under DOM/1.
[55] *Macob Civil Engineering Ltd v. Morrison Construction Ltd* [1999] B.L.R. 93; and see 14.4.
[56] *Herschel v. Breen Property Ltd* [2000] B.L.R. 272; contrast *Cygnet Healthcare v. Higgins City Ltd* (2000) 16 Const. L.J. 394, where the parties had agreed to refer a particular dispute to arbitration before any question of adjudication arose.
[57] *Bouygues UK Ltd v. Dahl-Jensen UK Ltd* [2000] B.L.R. 522. In that case the effect of an error as to how retention moneys should be treated resulted in a net payment to one party instead of to the other party.
[58] *Bloor Construction (UK) Ltd v. Bowmer & Kirkland (London) Ltd* [2000] B.L.R. 764, Judge Toulmin Q.C. In this case the adjudicator admitted he had made an error.
[59] John Rushton and Marina Milner, in *The court's interpretation of the Act*, Chapter 19 of *The Construction Act, Time for Review*, edited by Frances A. Paterson and Philip Briton, Centre of Construction Law and Management, Kings College London, 2000.

had gone to the Court of Appeal.[60] More guidance from the Court of Appeal is clearly needed, particularly on the issue of due process.

The Channel Tunnel

The procedures for interim determination in the Channel Tunnel project have become well-known because of the high profile of the project and because of the dispute about the role of the English courts in the dispute procedures under the contract.[61] The Dispute Review Board in this case was called a Panel of Experts and consisted of four engineers, two appointed by each party, chaired by a French law professor. The board for each dispute consisted of two of the engineers, one appointed by each side, and the law professor. If their decisions were unanimous, they were binding pending final resolution in an international arbitration.[62]   7.5.6

FIDIC adjudication boards

Adjudication is found in the FIDIC contract, where clause 67.1 has been rewritten substituting adjudication for the decision of the engineer. The adjudication board is formed at the beginning of the contract: either named in the contract or selected by the parties within 28 days. The board consists of either one or three members: three if the contract price exceeds US$25 million. Board members are usually engineers, but sometimes lawyers. Board members have to be independent, impartial and benefit from immunity. The board has full power to establish the procedure to be applied in deciding a dispute. Board members are said to act as experts and not as arbitrators. Either party may notify its dissatisfaction with a decision, which otherwise becomes binding after 28 days.[63]   7.5.7

DISPUTE REVIEW BOARDS   7.6

Dispute Review Boards[64] (DRBs) have appeared in a number of major construction contracts, notably the Channel Tunnel and the Hong Kong Airport, and are being adopted in contracts financed by the World Bank. The wording of any DRB provision needs to be

---

[60] *Bouygues UK Ltd v. Dahl-Jensen UK Ltd* [2000] B.L.R. 522.
[61] *Channel Tunnel Group Ltd v. Balfour Beatty Construction Ltd* and others [1993] A.C. 334.
[62] The clause is set out at Appendix G.
[63] See "The New FIDIC provision for a Dispute Adjudication Board", by Christopher R. Seppala [1997] I.C.L.R. 443–462.
[64] See the following articles: Andrew Pike "Dispute Review Boards and Adjudicators" (1993) I.C.L.R. 157; Gordon L. Jaynes "Dispute Review Boards—Yes!" (1993) I.C.L.R. 452; Andrew Pike "Dispute Review Boards—Yes! A Review" (1993) I.C.L.R. 468; Burt Campbell "Dispute Review Boards" (1994)

studied carefully, as there is no standard form: what follows picks up the principal features of some of the better-publicised examples. As boards rather than as individuals, their constitution is usually at least three persons, one appointed by each party and a neutral chairman. DRB members are often appointed at the start of the project, not just when there is a dispute. This feature is said to influence parties either not to make claims at all or to settle them before they are taken to the DRB. The DRB makes regular visits to the site whether or not there is a dispute; receives submissions and may or may not hold hearings which are likely to be informal. The DRB does not usually have the power to issue binding decisions, but merely, as the word suggests, to review the project and take note of any disputes. The DRB may then consider representations made about a dispute and issue an opinion. The status of that opinion may be non-binding, but failure to observe it or comply with it may be the occasion of a costs penalty if the same matter is raised in a later arbitration under the contract.

7.7 POLICY AND MANAGEMENT ISSUES IN JOINT VENTURES

Joint venture contracts sometimes contain a provision for dealing with disputes about policy and management issues, by referring them to a third party for decision. This enables the joint venture to continue operating without the risk of deadlock. Arguably both parties have an interest in retaining control, and the existence of the provision may make agreement between the parties more likely, in preference to third party decision. Another example is where parties have to agree on a programme for the construction works, and, if they fail to agree, the programme is determined by an expert.

7.8 FINAL DETERMINATION OF SPECIFIC ISSUES

An example of the final determination by an expert of a specific issue in a construction contract appeared in a contract for the construction of offshore oil exploration facilities in the North Sea: technical disputes about whether the work or the facilities complied with the contract were to be referred to an expert. Other examples are of a quantity surveyor valuing a development where the freeholder of the site terminates the development agreement[65]; work method

---

Arbitration 17–18; Gordon L. Jaynes "Dispute resolution under standard form international construction contracts: the changes for the 1990s" and Peter H.J. Chapman "Dispute review boards for the construction industry" conference papers, I.C.C. conference on "International commercial disputes; new solutions?" Brussels, October 1995.

[65] *Venaglass Ltd v. Banque Paribas* [1994] E.G.C.S. 18, CA.

statements; and whether systems have been fully commissioned. Typically, contracts with provisions of this sort provide that all other disputes are referred to arbitration. If arbitration is not chosen, they will be litigated in court.

FINAL DETERMINATION OF ALL ISSUES 7.9

Australian cases

Not many examples of clauses providing for the final determination of all issues arising in connection with a contract can be found. The earliest available court decision about a clause of this type is an unreported Australian case. An engineer was to resolve all disputes about the construction of a shopping centre in Sydney, and the New South Wales court gave effect to the clause.[66] In two other Australian cases the New South Wales court and the Western Australian court declined to give effect to similar clauses.[67]   7.9.1

English examples

The English court has refused to grant a stay of litigation which would otherwise have been in breach of a clause providing for a soft drinks executive to resolve disputes under a contract for the bottling and packaging of soft drinks.[68] Another English case concerned the interpretation of an expert determination clause in a performance bond. The context was a contract for the conversion of a motor tanker into a floating production storage and off-take facility. Claims for breach of contract were to be referred by the employer to an expert. The expert was to make assessments of damages arising from breaches of contract. The assessments could be revised during the project, and the final amount due (from whichever of the two parties) adjusted accordingly. Expert determination would therefore be used for both interim and final decisions. The court case was about the interpretation of the   7.9.2

---

[66] *Public Authorities Superannuation Board v. Southern International Developments Corporation Pty Ltd*, unreported, Smart J. in Common Law Division of the Supreme Court of New South Wales, decision No. 17986 of 1987, October 19, 1987, cited by Burke and Chinkin in [1990] I.C.L.R. 443: see 8.7.2.

[67] *Triarno Pty Ltd v. Triden Contractors Ltd*, unreported, Supreme Court of New South Wales, Cole J., July 22, 1992, cited by Doug Jones in "Is expert determination a 'final and binding' alternative?" *Arbitration*, August 1997 Vol. 63, No. 3, p. 213; *Baulderstone Hornibrook Engineering Pty Ltd v. Kayah Holdings Pty Ltd*, unreported, Supreme Court of Western Australia, December 2, 1997, Heenan J.; discussed by A. A. de Fina in "Australian courts look at expert determination", A.D.L.R.J. 1999, 3 (September) 148–152; and see 8.7.2.

[68] *Cott UK Ltd v. FE Barber Ltd* [1997] 3 All E.R. 540: see 8.4.2.

clause, and not about its validity to deal with potentially very wide-ranging issues.[69]

Another example is found in standard conditions of contract for process plant,[70] which refer a number of potential areas of dispute to an expert, including disputes about variation, documentation, certificates, performance tests, defects and suspension. The contract states that the powers of the expert are not limited to *quantum* but are to include the determination of factual and legal issues.[71] Some development agreements and building leases encountered in practice provide that "any . . . dispute . . . in any way relating to the execution of the project shall be referred to the decision of an independent surveyor (acting as an expert and not as an arbitrator) . . .". This expert might have to deal with a wide variety of issues, including the builder's/lessor's obligations to obtain planning permission, as well as the design and construction obligations.[72]

---

[69] *Odebrecht Oil and Gas Services Ltd v. North Sea Production Co. Ltd* [1999] 2 All E.R. (Comm.) 405. The issues were whether a notice was valid; and whether the same ground could be revisited.

[70] Red Book, 3rd edition (Institute of Chemical Engineers 1995).

[71] Clause 45.4.

[72] The development agreement in *Venaglass* (cited above) contained a provision for expert determination of all issues by an expert surveyor (except valuation issues on termination which were to be determined by a quantity surveyor acting as an expert: see 7.8). This appears in the transcript of the judgment and not in the published report.

CHAPTER 8

DISPUTE RESOLUTION

SUMMARY 8.1

This chapter looks at how expert determination has come to be used as a means of dispute resolution rather than a means for just settling specific issues, not only with regard to specific valuation and technical disputes but also in the wider context of the resolution of all disputes arising in connection with a contract. The chapter tracks:

(a) the shift from deciding specific issues of expertise to resolving disputes (8.2);
(b) the contrast with expert witnesses (8.3);
(c) the approach of the court to legal proceedings commenced in breach of an expert clause (8.4);
(d) the greater ease with which multi-party disputes can be resolved by expert determination (8.5);
(e) the use of expert determination as one tier in clauses providing for several tiers of dispute resolution (8.6);
(f) the use of expert determination for the resolution of all disputes arising under a contract (8.7); which leads to
(g) consideration of the use of lawyers acting as experts (8.8).

The chapter ends by evaluating:

(h) expert determination as a dispute clause when negotiating a contract (8.9); and
(i) expert determination as a proposal for dispute resolution after a dispute has arisen (8.10).

EXPERTS CLOSER TO DISPUTE RESOLUTION THAN VALUERS 8.2

Along with the development of the concept of the expert described in Chapter 6 there has been a trend towards the role of the expert being that of a dispute resolver. Surveyors, accountants and actuaries making valuations are often resolving disputes but the disputes are generally limited to valuation issues. Leases and sales of business agreements often reserve specific issues to an expert; for instance, what the figure for sales should be in a particular set of accounts. In the more recently developed applications, some expert clauses are less specific in that they do not reserve individual issues such as sales figures for determination by an expert, but refer general types of disputes to experts: *e.g.*, "all disputes of a technical nature arising under this agreement". The traditional objection to the use of expert determination to resolve what are known as "formulated disputes"[1] is less frequently encountered.

8.3 Contrasting use of experts as witnesses

Dispute resolution now relies very heavily on expert witnesses for proof of technical issues. Expert witnesses should not be confused with expert determination[2] but there can be an overlap between the two. In a court case or arbitration where the only remaining issue is a matter of expertise the parties can agree to refer that issue to an expert for determination. In an Australian case,[3] the parties had settled the question of liability in their dispute and instructed a firm of accountants to act as experts to decide the amount of damages. Unfortunately one party increased its claim without notice to the other which led to the dispute reaching the court.[4] The parties had chosen to refer the damages issue to a firm of accountants acting as experts in preference to litigation or arbitration. In both litigation and arbitration the parties would, unless a single joint expert witness had been appointed, have had to use accountants as expert witnesses with the judge or arbitrator deciding between them on the basis of the expert witnesses' reports and their ability to withstand cross-examination. Either arbitration or litigation with expert witnesses on each side would have taken more time and cost more money than a successful expert determination. Under the Civil Procedure Rules introduced in April 1999[5] a single joint expert may be appointed, instead of expert witnesses on each side. The report of a single joint expert is strictly speaking not binding on the parties, but it might nevertheless be decisive unless the party dissatisfied with it persuades the court to give permission to allow other expert evidence to be adduced.[6]

---

[1] See 17.5.
[2] See 1.6.3.
[3] *Capricorn Inks Pty Ltd v. Lawter International (Australasia) Pty Ltd* [1989] 1 Qd R. 8.
[4] See 15.6.2.
[5] CPR 35.7.
[6] *Daniels v. Walker* [2000] 1 W.L.R. 1382, CA, *Pattison v. Cosgrove*, unreported, November 27, 2000, Neuberger J.

Litigation stayed? 8.4

Reasons for granting a stay

A key test of the recognition of expert clauses as a means of dispute resolution is whether the court will grant a stay of litigation in relation to a contract containing an expert clause. Where a party commences proceedings in relation to a dispute which the contract states should be determined by an expert, the court does have jurisdiction to stay the proceedings.[7] A stay was granted in *Channel Tunnel Group Ltd v. Balfour Beatty Construction Ltd*,[8] a case concerning the construction of the Channel Tunnel. The expert clause in that case[9] provided for disputes during the course of the works to be referred to a panel of three persons, acting as experts and not as arbitrators, who were to state their decision. Unanimous decisions were to be given immediate effect and the works to continue. Additionally, unanimous decisions were to be final and binding unless referred to arbitration. Lord Mustill in the House of Lords stated:

8.4.1

> "This is not a case of a jurisdiction clause, purporting to exclude an ordinary citizen from his access to a court and featuring inconspicuously in a standard printed form of contract. The parties here were large commercial enterprises, negotiating at arms length in the light of a long experience of construction contracts, of the types of disputes which typically arise under them, and of the various means which can be adopted to resolve such disputes . . . having promised to take their complaints to the experts . . . that is where the appellants should go[10]."

The court also has jurisdiction to stay court proceedings under section 9 of the Arbitration Act 1996 where the contract requires the dispute to be referred to arbitration only after the exhaustion of "other dispute resolution procedures", which must include expert determination.

Reasons for refusing a stay

The court has a discretion whether or not to grant a stay of proceedings, and a stay will be refused if the court considers that litigation through the courts would be more appropriate; the burden is on the party seeking to litigate in breach of the expert clause to show grounds for refusing a stay: *Cott UK Ltd v. FE Barber Ltd.*[11] That case concerned a contract for the bottling and packaging of

8.4.2

---

[7] Under section 49(3) of the Supreme Court Act 1981 and the court's inherent jurisdiction. The application is made under Part 11 of the Civil Procedure Rules.
[8] [1993] A.C. 334.
[9] See Appendix G.
[10] *Channel Tunnel* case at 353: Lord Mustill.
[11] [1997] 3 All E.R. 540.

soft drinks. Instead of a standard arbitration clause, the contract provided that all disputes should be referred to the determination of a person appointed by the Director General of the Soft Drinks Association. The dispute clause itself was drafted badly,[12] but it was construed as an expert clause. Judge Hegarty Q.C. decided that the court should exercise its discretion to refuse a stay on the ground that the procedure chosen by the parties was for a number of reasons unsatisfactory and might result in repeated problems and disputes during the course of the reference. First, the appointing authority had no rules governing any form of dispute resolution.[13] Secondly, the appointing authority's appointee had no experience in dispute resolution.[14] Thirdly, the expert clause laid down no principles or procedures pursuant to which the expert was to approach the dispute.[15] Fourthly, the appointed expert (a businessman from the soft drinks industry) would be dealing with questions of the construction of a legal agreement, and matters of *quantum* and compensation.[16] The judge said:

> ". . . any such ad hoc procedure involving decisions taken from time to time requiring the consent of all three parties, is likely to produce confusion and delay, rather than producing a short, speedy and cheap determination of the dispute."[17]

In another case[18] the contract required disputes to be referred to the decision of the construction manager and provided that the decision of the construction manager should be final and binding until completion of the works. Proceedings were commenced without the dispute having first been referred to the decision of the construction manager. The court declined to grant a stay of the action, on the ground that no purpose would be served as it was already very clear what decision the construction manager would reach.[19]

A further ground on which the court might decide that a stay should be refused would be that one of the parties to the contract is a consumer, who had no alternative but to accept the standard terms and conditions of the other party.[20] Other cases in which applications were made to stay proceedings are referred to in 8.7.2.

---

[12] See 9.6.2 and 17.3.
[13] See 11.5.
[14] See 10.6.
[15] See 13.4
[16] See 8.7.
[17] [1997] 3 All E.R. 540 at 549J.
[18] *Bernhard's Rugby Landscapes Ltd v. Stockley Park Consortium Ltd* (1998) 14 Const L.J. 329.
[19] See *ibid.* at 354.
[20] The Unfair Terms in Consumer Contracts Regulations 1999, S.I. 1999 No. 2083 would be relevant: see Schedule 2, paragraph 1, which gives as an example of an unfair term a term which excludes the right to take legal action.

Multi-party disputes 8.5

Expert determination can be used for multi-party disputes without the difficulties encountered in arbitration.[21] The main contract could refer all disputes to expert determination with a clause in all other associated contracts providing that the decision of the expert appointed under the main contract would be binding on all those other parties. Coupled with a provision that there would be no formal hearing, difficult procedural questions of the type that arise in consolidated arbitrations should not arise. There would be none of the problems about the order in which evidence was to be taken and cross-examination allowed. Expert determination would therefore be more adaptable to the needs of multi-party construction disputes than arbitration.[22] Many construction disputes are multi-party and all construction disputes are potentially multi-party. However, where expert determination has been provided as the dispute system for one contract in a set of contracts, it will not be possible for one party to arrange for all the allied disputes to be decided concurrently by the same expert unless all the other parties agree.[23]

Multi-tier dispute resolution 8.6

Getting the right forum

Commercial contracts often use various types of multi-tier dispute resolution. The dispute clauses found in these contracts may provide, initially, for various forms of alternative dispute resolution, such as reference to a meeting between senior management and/or mediation or mini-trial. Technical and/or interim disputes may be referred to an expert or experts, either with the label expert or adjudicator or Dispute Review Board, and all other kinds of disputes and all those which have not yet been resolved go to arbitration or litigation. Sometimes there are appeal systems where both levels of resolution are a form of expert determination.[24]   8.6.1

---

[21] *Russell on Arbitration*, by David Sutton, John Kendall and Judith Gill, 21st edition, Sweet & Maxwell 1997, at para. 3–027 *et seq*.
[22] For a precedent, see Appendix E.
[23] Whether third parties can use expert determination provisions depends on express words, or on whether rights have been conferred which can be enforced under section 1 of the Contracts (Rights of Third Parties) Act 1999. Section 8 of the Act applies to arbitration, and not to expert determination.
[24] For an example from a capital markets contract, see 5.5.2, and, for judgments upholding the finality of an appeal system in international commodity contracts, see 5.7.3.

8 : Dispute Resolution

Avoid disputes about the choice of forum

8.6.2 Multi-tier dispute clauses can lead to disputes about whether a dispute is a valuation/technical dispute to be referred to an expert or one that should be referred to an arbitral tribunal or the court. Some of these clauses have the further complication of saying that valuation disputes are to go to a valuation expert and technical disputes to a technical expert. Another occasional variant, encountered where expert determination is used for general dispute resolution, is for disputes up to a certain value to be referred to expert determination, with litigation or arbitration for disputes of higher value. These clauses raise issues of interpretation of the disputes clause and an investigation of the type and/or the value[25] of the dispute which, unless some other provision is made in the contract, can be resolved only by the court if it has jurisdiction, by arbitrators or a supervisory arbitral body, or possibly not at all. An awkward defendant could exploit this to the claimant's considerable disadvantage in both time and money.

Solutions to this problem

8.6.3 One solution is a clause which says that the question of categorising disputes in contracts where there are several different modes of dispute resolution is itself to be referred to the expert for final decision. Another solution would be for the clause to say that disputes which the parties could not agree to refer to expert determination should be referred to arbitration (or litigation) along with all other non-technical disputes.

Alternative Dispute Resolution (ADR)

8.6.4 A number of contracts now contain provisions for disputes to be referred to various forms of ADR before reference to binding systems. Clause 66 of the sixth edition of the ICE contract introduced a further tier of dispute resolution by interposing optional ADR between the decision of the engineer and arbitration. The claimant must first refer the dispute to the engineer. If it is not settled the dispute may then go to ADR when the conciliator makes a determination which becomes binding unless one of the parties serves notice of arbitration within one month. The expression "Med-Ex" has been coined to describe a system where the same neutral acts first as

---

[25] See Doug Jones, "Is expert determination a 'final and binding' alternative?'" in Arbitration (1997) Vol. 63, No. 3, p. 213 at 217, where he points out the potential for dispute about whether a claim encompasses one dispute of a large value or many disputes of small value. He also criticises the type of clause which provides that the determination will be final and binding only if the amount awarded is less than some maximum figure, which could prompt an expert to award less than the figure the expert actually believes is the right amount.

mediator and then as expert, and which avoids the problems associated with "Med-Arb".[26]

Adjudication

Similarly, in some modern construction contracts disputes are referred to adjudication under which a named individual designated to act as an expert makes a preliminary finding which is then subject to review by arbitration.[27] **8.6.5**

Pre-arbitral expertise

The International Chamber of Commerce (ICC) has published Rules for Technical Expertise. Under these rules parties can agree to refer technical questions to one or more experts and seek a determination on an issue. Unless otherwise agreed, the findings of the expert(s) are not binding on the parties: they may simply be recommendations for the future performance of the contract.[28] **8.6.6**

CLAUSES REFERRING ALL DISPUTES TO AN EXPERT **8.7**

General dispute resolution

Clauses referring all disputes under a contract to an expert are encountered from time to time in practice.[29] These clauses do not limit the exercise of the expert's judgment to valuation or technical questions but call on the expert to act more like a judge or arbitrator. They have been found so far mainly in construction disputes[30] but there is nothing to prevent their use in other contexts. In one unreported case[31] the contract provided for the appointment of an expert to determine all disputes under a telecommunications supply contract: the case did not proceed beyond the failure by one of the parties to obtain an injunction preventing the appointment of an expert. Clauses referring general disputes seem to choose **8.7.1**

---

[26] See 13.7.1.
[27] See 7.5.
[28] See Michael Buhler "Technical Expertise: an additional means for preventing or settling commercial disputes" (March 1989), *Journal of International Arbitration*, pp. 135–57; and Benjamin Davis "The ICC pre-arbitral referee procedure in context with technical expertise, conciliation and arbitration", (1992) I.C.L.R. 218–31.
[29] According to Doug Jones, "vast numbers" have taken up this option: see "Expert Determination in Commercial Contracts", in *The Expert in Litigation and Arbitration*, ed. D. Mark Cato, Lloyd's of London Press, 789. For a precedent, see Appendix E. See also "Australian courts look at expert determination" by A. A. de Fina 1999 A.D.L.R.J. 3 (Sep.) 148–152. Note the problem with a clause which provides for disputes up to a certain value to be referred to an expert, discussed at 8.6.2 .
[30] For some examples, see 7.9.
[31] See *Computing*, March 26, 1992.

individuals as experts rather than firms or companies. Where they are not contained in the original contract, they may be agreed between the parties in substitution for the chosen method, such as arbitration, for the particular dispute which has arisen.[32]

Do the courts give effect to these clauses?

8.7.2 Dispute clauses which refer questions of fact and law to a non-lawyer expert are likely to be considered by the court either on the application of one of the parties for a stay of litigation in breach of the clause or at the enforcement stage. There is only one fully reported English law authority, a first instance decision where a stay was refused.[33] One of the four grounds for the refusal was the unsuitability of the appointed expert to decide legal questions. The appointee was an executive in the soft drinks industry. The court found that this individual was not the most obvious person to determine questions of construction of a commercial agreement which would not be entirely straightforward. The court was even more concerned about this person determining questions as to the *quantum* of any compensation. The individual would be better suited to the function of expert witness in the dispute, the court thought. Other reasons why the court considered that the procedure specified in the contract was unsatisfactory are referred to above.[34]

The other available authorities are unreported. In the first of three Australian cases,[35] the contract referred all disputes about the construction of a Sydney shopping centre to an engineering expert. An attempt was made to stop a claim for extra costs being decided by an expert, on the grounds that the reference to a non-legal expert was inappropriate to a dispute about legal liability, and that despite the express words in the disputes clause in the contract, the parties could never have intended it: litigation was the only suitable system. The court refused to stop the reference, stating that the parties should have considered the potential difficulties of using what the court called "a single alternative dispute resolution process" for all disputes under the contract before making their contract. The court emphasised that it was upholding party autonomy and would not rewrite the contract to take account of subsequent concerns.

---

[32] For a precedent, see Appendix F.
[33] *Cott UK Ltd v. FE Barber Ltd* [1997] 3 All E.R. 540. See 8.4.2.
[34] See 8.4.2.
[35] *Public Authorities Superannuation Board v. Southern International Developments Corporation Pty Ltd*, unreported, Smart J. in Common Law Division of the Supreme Court of New South Wales, decision No. 17986 of 1987, October 19, 1987, cited by Burke and Chinkin in [1990] I.C.L.R. 443.

Two other unreported Australian decisions went the other way. In the first,[36] the court refused to uphold a clause referring disputes about liability under a bank guarantee to expert determination on the grounds that it made no provision for payment of the expert, for the procedures to be followed or for the rights and obligations of the parties in relation to the expert determination. In the second case,[36a] the court declined to give effect to a clause referring a construction dispute to a "referee" for a final and binding decision on the grounds that the dispute was not within the expertise of the person appointed referee, the court's jurisdiction was ousted, and an expert cannot deal properly with questions of mixed fact and law.

In another unreported English case,[37] the applicant objected to expert determination on the ground that legal aid would not be available. The court rejected this, and granted a stay.[38] Even if legal aid remains available at all, its availability is unlikely to be an issue in most instances of commercial dispute resolution where the parties are of equal bargaining power.

Objections to general clauses

The following objections are raised[39] to the use of expert determination for the resolution of general disputes:

8.7.3

- An expert does not act judicially in matters where the subject matter requires that the dispute resolver should do so. An expert can address issues and review evidence of which the parties have not been aware.
- Arbitration procedures are more flexible now and therefore more attractive.
- The machinery is more likely to break down irretrievably because the court cannot help as it can in arbitration.
- There are more remedies in arbitration.
- Expert determination decisions are much more difficult to enforce than arbitration awards or judgments.

---

[36] *Triarno Pty Ltd v. Triden Contractors Ltd*, unreported, Supreme Court of New South Wales, Cole J., July 22, 1992, cited by Doug Jones in "Is expert determination a 'final and binding' alternative?" *Arbitration*, August 1997 Vol 63, No. 3, p. 213.

[36a] *Baulderstone Hornibrook Engineering Pty Ltd v. Kayah Holdings Pty Ltd*, unreported, Supreme Court of Western Australia, December 2, 1997, Heenan J.; discussed by A.A. de Fina in "Australian courts look at expert determination", ADLRJ 1999, 3 (September) 148–152

[37] The telecommunications case at 8.7.1 was settled after the injunction proceedings, and so gives no guidance on the point.

[38] Information given to the author, but the case is not reported and no transcript is available.

[39] See Doug Jones, "Is expert determination a 'final and binding' alternative?" *Arbitration* August 1997 Vol. 63, No. 3, p. 213.

8 : Dispute Resolution

In answer to these points it can be said that:

- It is for parties, properly advised, to decide how their disputes should be settled, and people are free to have their dispute resolved non-judicially, in the same way as they may decide to refer the dispute to mediation.
- Whatever procedure is followed in arbitration, the fact that parties have the right to put their own case and rebut their opponent's case and the tribunal's investigations does require more cost and time to be spent.
- Good drafting reduces the likelihood of the dispute machinery in expert determination clauses breaking down.
- Good drafting can give the expert the power to grant the necessary remedies.
- Enforcement has been a problem, but this can be overcome[40].

Practical problems

8.7.4 There may be practical difficulties in finding an expert willing to accept an appointment to determine all disputes under a contract. Determining all disputes is very likely to take an expert into matters that are outside the expert's particular professional competence. An expert is (subject to contractual exception clauses) liable for negligence[41] and will face a greater risk of being sued when deciding matters which are not within his or her expertise. In one instance a party seeking to prevent expert determination of a dispute on a contract containing a clause referring all disputes under it to expert determination wrote letters to all the potential appointees explaining the risk of their being sued.

8.8 LAWYERS AS EXPERTS

The principle

8.8.1 There is no reason why a legal issue should not be determined by a legal expert. It is a matter for the parties to decide how the lawyer should determine the issue and this does not mean that the procedure has to be an arbitration—a lawyer can act as an expert. The practice does not seem to be very common but there is evidence from nineteenth century cases that it is not an altogether novel concept. A dispute about a cheque was referred to counsel in *Boyd v. Emmerson*[42] and the reference was held not to be an arbitration. In *Re Hammond & Waterton*[43] the court said that if a building dispute

---

[40] See 14.7.
[41] See 16.7.
[42] (1834) 2 A.D. & E. 183.
[43] (1890) 62 L.T. 808.

were referred to a barrister umpire the procedure would be more likely to be an arbitration but if the umpire were a quantity surveyor it would be more likely to be a valuation. This suggests that in 1890 it was thought that a barrister umpire could be appointed as a valuer. To restate the proposition in modern terms, a lawyer can act as an expert.

Leases to be settled by solicitor as expert 8.8.2

Property agreements sometimes state that the terms of conveyances or leases are to be agreed by the parties, or, if they fail to agree, will be settled by a solicitor of so many years' qualification specialising in real property and practising in a particular locality, such as the City of London. These provisions are references to an expert.

Q.C. clauses

Commercial agreements sometimes say that the opinion of a Queen's Counsel will determine whether, and if so how, a claim should proceed. Clauses of this type, often known as Q.C. clauses, are encountered where litigation may need to be conducted in the name of or at the expense of another party and that other party wants some assurance that the claim is sound.[44] These clauses are also found in insurance policies to resolve disputes between insurer and insured as to whether a claim should proceed.[45] 8.8.3

Another example of the use of Q.C. clauses is in development agreements where one party has an obligation to seek planning permission if a Q.C. advises that there is a better than 50% chance of getting the permission.[46] What both the insurance and the planning example have in common is the provision of machinery for ensuring the party charged with conducting a case or a contract partly on behalf of another party acts in accordance with the best available advice. These clauses in the forms usually encountered are more likely to be conditions precedent than true expert clauses but the status of the opinion is the same as that of an expert's decision.

Contractual interpretation

Contractual interpretation questions may be resolved by a legal expert. In an ad hoc reference, a Q.C. acting as an expert determined which of the parties to a petrol supply agreement should bear the financial loss resulting from a change in the method of calculating excise duty. 8.8.4

---

[44] See, for example, *West Wake Price & Co. v. Ching* [1957] 1 W.L.R. 45.
[45] *MacGilvray and Parkington on Insurance Law*, 8th edition (Sweet & Maxwell 1988) at 2033, 2042.
[46] See 2.10.1.

8 : Dispute Resolution

Conditional fee agreements

8.8.5 It has been suggested that lawyers, acting as experts, should settle disputes between solicitors and their clients about conditional fee agreements in litigation.[47]

Lawyer resolving general disputes

8.8.6 There may be considerable advantages in the appointment of a lawyer to act as a legal expert to decide all types of disputes arising under a contract. Proceedings can be tailored to suit the subject-matter of the dispute and the resources the parties are prepared to devote to it. Written submissions can save some or all of the time taken by a formal hearing with cross-examination. Where parties find an arbitration timetable and procedure too hasty they can apply to the court to set aside the award.[48] These tactics are not available if the parties have agreed to determination by an expert.

Expert tribunals

8.8.7 There may also be an advantage in appointing an expert tribunal with *e.g.* two members—a lawyer and a technical expert, with the lawyer having the final say. Thus a dispute about a computer contract could be referred to a tribunal consisting of a lawyer and an IT expert with the IT expert assisting the lawyer.[49]

8.9 WHY CHOOSE EXPERT DETERMINATION FOR DISPUTE RESOLUTION?

Speed

8.9.1 A properly conducted expert determination should take less time than an arbitration or court case. The fact that expert determinations sometimes do take a long time is usually the result of tactical court applications.

Cost

8.9.2 As cost is so much a function of time, litigation and arbitration will generally be considerably more expensive than expert determinations. The following considerations also apply:

(a) There is no statutory control over experts' fees as there is over the fees of arbitrators.[50] In litigation the costs of judges

---

[47] "A new vocation for lawyers", by Richard Harrison, [1998] N.L.J. 915.
[48] See, for example, *Town and City Properties (Developments) Ltd v. Wiltshier Southern Ltd and Gilbert Powell* (1988) 44 B.L.R. 109 and *Damond Lock Grabowski v. Laing Investments (Bracknell) Ltd* (1992) 60 B.L.R. 112.
[49] For another example of an expert tribunal see Appendix H.
[50] See 16.2.4.

are borne by the state and not charged to the parties. Expert clauses usually say that the experts' fees are to be shared equally between the parties irrespective of the result but other variations are found.[51] An agreement to the effect that one party is to pay the whole or part of the costs of an arbitration is only valid if made after the dispute has arisen.[52]

(b) The expert cannot order one party to pay the other's costs unless the power is specifically stipulated.[53]

(c) The proportion of irrecoverable costs in litigation and arbitration is about 35%, to be weighed against the potential damages and the costs that are recoverable.

Procedure

Is a formal, adversarial procedure appropriate for dealing with the issues? If formality is required, litigation is indicated, but in any arbitration a formal hearing is more usual,[54] with the result that arbitration usually is formal. By contrast, formal hearings can be, and generally are, avoided in expert determinations.[55] Witnesses can be ordered by the court to attend arbitration[56] and court hearings but there is no such right in expert determination. Litigation obliges both parties to disclose all their documents to each other and a similar process may be sought in arbitration. General disclosure obligations are not appropriate in expert determinations.[57]

8.9.3

Legal questions

Legal questions can be argued between lawyers before a judge who can decide them. An arbitrator may hear submissions but, if not qualified to decide on them, may seek outside help or recommend a reference to the court.[58] An expert can take outside help but not from the court.

8.9.4

Finality

The position used to be that if the parties wanted one final decision, even if it were wrong, they should choose expert determination

8.9.5

---

[51] See 9.12.
[52] Arbitration Act 1996, s. 60.
[53] See 9.13.
[54] See 17.10.5.
[55] See 13.6.5.
[56] See 17.10.2.
[57] See 13.6.5.
[58] Under Arbitration Act 1996, s. 45.

8 : Dispute Resolution

because it is difficult to challenge experts' decisions. However, since the Arbitration Act 1996 appeals from arbitration awards are unavailable for most purposes[59] and there is little now in the point. Litigation provides appeals as of right.

Recourse

8.9.6 It is possible, although difficult, to sue an expert for breach of duty.[60] Conversely, it is not possible to take similar action against an arbitrator or judge unless their conduct was shown to be in bad faith.[61]

Privacy

8.9.7 Expert determinations and arbitrations are both private whereas litigation is not. However, the precise extent of the privacy accorded to arbitration is uncertain[62] and arbitration can lose its privacy by applications to the court and by disclosure obligations in litigation on connected issues.[63] There is a much narrower range of opportunities for applications to the court about an expert determination. Special measures to ensure confidentiality between the parties can be taken in expert determinations.[64] Measures of that sort are rare in arbitration and unavailable in litigation.

Relationship of the parties

8.9.8 Is there a continuing relationship worth saving? Expert determination should be a less hostile way of settling disputes than arbitration or litigation, particularly where there is to be a long-term contract. Aggressive litigation procedures which are often used in arbitration as well as in litigation are not available in expert determination. That said, parties sometimes conduct expert determinations with a great deal of aggression.

Location of the parties

8.9.9 International enforcement of experts' decisions can be difficult whereas there are established means of enforcing judgments and arbitration awards internationally.[65]

---

[59] See 17.8.3.
[60] See 16.7.
[61] Arbitrators: Arbitration Act 1996, s. 29; judges: *Sirros v. Moore* [1975] 1 Q.B. 118.
[62] See, for instance, *Insurance Company v. Lloyd's Syndicate* [1995] 1 Lloyd's Rep. 272.
[63] *Shearson Lehman Hutton Incorporated v. Maclaine Watson and Co. Ltd (No.3)* [1988] 1 W.L.R. 946.
[64] See 9.15.10.
[65] See 14.7 for methods of facilitating enforcement.

Proposing expert determination after a dispute has arisen 8.10

The original choice of forum is part of the negotiations

8.10.1 The same checklist for choosing between means of dispute resolution applies after a dispute has arisen, but there is an additional factor. The parties' contract will provide a means of dispute resolution. Either a specific means of dispute resolution will have been chosen or court litigation will be implied where no particular choice has been made. Both parties will wish to obtain the best advantage from whatever means they have to use. Thus a badly drafted expert clause (or a badly drafted arbitration clause) may give a considerable advantage to a party wishing to postpone proceedings and avoid liability.

Ad hoc expert clauses

8.10.2 If the parties agree to refer an existing dispute to expert determination it may be advisable to review the procedure desired and to set it out at some length as terms of reference.[66] Care should be taken to provide for expert determination for the resolution of a specific dispute rather than amending the original contract. The original contract may contain terms inconsistent with the current position, for instance with regard to an issue such as timing. Uncertainty of that type could give rise to a court case.

The court may back the proposal

8.10.3 Where a dispute has arisen over a contract which does not contain an expert clause and one party proposes expert determination, the other party may see it as a sign of weakness because it signals an unwillingness and an inability to pursue the case through the courts or arbitration. The other party is likely to maintain this view unless that other party believes that it will ultimately be disadvantageous to insist on the dispute being litigated or arbitrated, where the costs risk cannot be justified. Where the dispute turns on one issue which could be determined by an expert quickly and decisively, the party refusing to agree to an expert determination may, conversely, be seen as showing weakness by postponing a decision and sheltering behind an unnecessarily long form of dispute resolution. It may help if the party suggesting expert determination does so in an open letter warning the other party that failure to agree to the proposal will be referred to the judge on the question of costs.

The Civil Procedure Rules have an impact here. The rules give judges a much greater role in case management. One of the management objectives is to deal with cases, so far as is practicable, in

---

[66] For a precedent, see Appendix F.

8 : DISPUTE RESOLUTION

ways which are proportionate to the amount at stake.[67] The court looks at systems of alternative dispute resolution whose use could achieve the objective. Expert determination is recognised as a system of alternative dispute resolution "suitable for purely technical or complex construction disputes where a speedy award is important".[68] The court may support a party's proposal to resolve a dispute by expert determination and order an adjournment to allow this to be done.[69] In some cases the court may be able to go further. For instance, a petition to wind up a company where the court's order would be for one party to purchase the other party's shares at a value has been struck out because of the unreasonable refusal of the petitioner to accept a valuation by an independent accountant acting as an expert.[70]

Expert determination as an aid to mediation

8.10.4 During mediations, the parties sometimes find there are serious stumbling blocks to progress, commonly issues on which both parties have very strong but opposing views. There is a temptation to press the mediator for a view in private session, and then to try to go further and to press the mediator to make that view known to the other party. This is not a desirable course for a mediator to take, as it will prejudice the mediator's neutrality. In these circumstances it may be helpful to adjourn the mediation and bring in another third party to act as expert, who can either resolve the issue or provide an authoritative opinion. The mediation can then resume in the light of the decision or opinion thus obtained.[71]

---

[67] CPR 1.1.
[68] Paragraph 21, Alternative Dispute Resolution, Summary of Responses to the Discussion Paper, May 2000, published by the Lord Chancellor's Department.
[69] CPR 26.4.
[70] *Fuller v. Cyracuse Ltd*, Law Alert No. 0015801, Chancery Division, Companies Court, June 6, 2000, Deputy Judge P. Leaver Q.C., and see 3.8.
[71] *CEDR Mediator Handbook*, CEDR, 2000, pp. 31–36.

CHAPTER 9

THE EXPERT CLAUSE

SUMMARY 9.1

This chapter looks at the expert clause in detail. The chapter:

(a) explains the need to specify expert determination, and the effect (9.2);
(b) identifies the essential elements of an expert clause, and considers how far the court may imply terms into the contract (9.3);
(c) analyses each of those elements (9.4 to 9.18).

The chapter should be read in conjunction with the precedent at Appendix A, I.

NEED TO SPECIFY EXPERT DETERMINATION, AND THE EFFECT 9.2

Prior agreement necessary

Every expert determination arises out of a contract and the agreement to refer disputes to expert determination must be expressly specified in the contract.[1] If the parties to a contract want to refer their disputes to an expert and to keep the dispute out of court they must say so specifically in the contract. Only that sort of provision can bind the parties in advance. 9.2.1

The expert clause

In every contract where expert determination is to be used, there is a clause which refers questions arising under the contract to an expert and which contains a number of ancillary provisions. In this book this clause is referred to as the expert clause. It may be very brief, for example "as certified by the auditor"; or it may be quite lengthy, at least as long as the precedent provided in 9.2.2

---

[1] In *Jones (M) v. Jones (R R)* [1971] 1 W.L.R. 840, a valuer was to be appointed under a court order but that order was a consent order and therefore a contract. For a court-appointed expert, see *Jordan v. Norfolk County Council* [1994] 1 W.L.R. 1353.

9 : The Expert Clause

this book[2] which itself runs to some 40 lines: and some much longer versions are encountered. Differences in drafting styles have a number of consequences, some quite fundamental,[3] which the parties are unlikely actually to have considered; but their intentions are ascertained objectively if there is a dispute about the clause.

Incorporation of expert determination

9.2.3 The manner in which expert determination is incorporated into the agreement depends on the type of reference contemplated. Here are some examples:

(a) Articles of association of a private company may say that the share price on a compulsory transfer is to be certified by the auditors.

(b) An agreement for the sale and purchase of a business may reserve a number of issues to expert determination, such as the profits figure for a company or the net asset value of a business.[4] Those issues appear in various parts of the agreement and expert determination is applied to those issues by one expert clause. The expert clause specifically refers to those other clauses and states that expert determination is to be applied to issues arising under them. It is more often the case that the expert clause does not specifically refer to those other clauses so a later review will therefore involve careful trawling through the agreement to make sure all the instances are noted.

(c) A construction contract may provide for the determination by an expert of technical issues in a disputes clause providing for arbitration of non-technical issues.[5]

(d) The disputes clause of a construction contract may refer general disputes to an expert for determination.[6]

(e) A commercial lease refers rent review disputes to an independent surveyor who is to act as an expert but gives the landlord the option to give notice that the surveyor is to act as an arbitrator. This operates as an expert clause unless the landlord exercises the option.

The expression "expert clause" refers to all of these types of clause.

---

[2] Appendix A, I
[3] See 9.2.8.
[4] See the full list at 4.2.4.
[5] See 7.8.
[6] See 7.9 and 8.7.

Agreements to refer after a dispute has arisen

9.2.4 There is nothing to stop the parties agreeing, after a dispute has arisen, to refer their dispute to expert determination and this is done from time to time in the same way as arbitration agreements entered into after a dispute has arisen. A dispute about damages was referred to accountants by an agreement entered into after the parties' dispute about liability had been settled by some other method although there had been no prior agreement in the original contract to refer to an expert.[7] The same law and the same rules of construction apply both to clauses in agreements entered into before a dispute has arisen and subsequent agreements to refer entered into after a dispute has arisen. The latter are sometimes known as *ad hoc* references.

Difficulties with oral agreements

9.2.5 An agreement to refer an issue to expert determination need not be in writing but modern commercial practice makes oral agreements for expert determination most unlikely. Parties are likely to create at least one piece of paper when making an agreement of sufficient complexity to incorporate expert determination. In any case, the problems of proving the terms of an oral agreement may be insurmountable.

A separate agreement?

9.2.6 Arbitration clauses are now understood as separate agreements capable of surviving breach of the agreement to which they provide the dispute mechanism. Thus if the main contract has been terminated or broken, or is alleged to be illegal or void, the arbitration clause survives to resolve disputes about that contract. This is known as the doctrine of separability.[8] The doctrine has not yet had to be applied to expert clauses but it is likely that the courts would apply it in order to give effect to the intention of the parties with regard to their choice of dispute resolution mechanism.[9]

---

[7] *Capricorn Inks Pty Ltd v. Lawter International (Australasia) Pty Ltd* [1989] 1 Qd R. 8.

[8] Arbitration Act 1996, s. 7.

[9] In *Credit Suisse v. Seagate Trading Co. Ltd* [1999] 1 Lloyd's Rep. 784 at 794 Rix J. was prepared to assume that the doctrine of separability applied, by analogy with arbitration clauses, to an exclusive jurisdiction clause. In *A & D Maintenance and Construction Ltd v. Pagehurst Construction Services Ltd* (2000) 16 Const. L.J. 199 Judge Wilcox Q.C. held that the adjudication provisions of the Housing Grants, Construction and Regeneration Act 1996 survive termination of the contract.

Steps to be taken before operation of the expert clause

9.2.7 Some contracts contain rather complex provisions describing the steps the parties are to take before the expert clause comes into operation. Inability to comply with them can give one of the parties a tactical advantage by obliging the other party to incur the much greater cost of litigation to achieve the result that could and should have been achieved by expert determination. For instance,[10] a sale and purchase agreement provides for expert determination by an accountant of disputes about the completion accounts, with an obligation on the purchaser to make the underlying documents available to the vendor. What is the position if the vendor fails to provide the documents? In one case, the court's interpretation of the contractual wording was that the court had jurisdiction to order production of the documents,[11] but under different wording the right to order that production might be within the expert's jurisdiction. The difficulty would then arise that the expert's order to disclose could be disobeyed and the expert would have no sanction to ensure compliance.

Contractual entitlement or dispute machinery?

9.2.8 A contractual provision for expert determination may be more than the expression of the parties' agreement about how to resolve disputes: it may define the essence of their contractual rights.[12] This is not a theoretical distinction in cases in which the passage of time prevents an expert clause from being invoked, because the entitlement may be barred as well as the remedy.[13] For example, a contract provides for a party to be paid "55% of the open market value of . . . shares . . . as determined by an independent chartered accountant". What is the contractual entitlement? The Court of Appeal in *Gillatt v. Sky Television Ltd*[14] held that the right answer was not simply "55% of the open market value of the shares", as one had to add the words "as determined by an independent chartered accountant". Therefore if there were no determination there could be no payment. The court relied principally on these factors:

- the contrast with another clause in the contract which contained detailed provisions for the procedure to be followed in the expert determination of other accounting issues; and

---

[10] Other contexts produce similar procedural complexities; *e.g.* re-determination provisions in oil unitisation agreements: see 6.4.
[11] *British Shipbuilders v. VSEL Consortium plc* [1997] 1 Lloyd's Rep. 106 at 112.
[12] *Sudbrook Trading Ltd v. Eggleton* [1983] A.C. 444 at 484. See 11.3.3.
[13] See 9.18.
[14] [2000] 1 All E.R. (Comm.) 461.

- the absence of objective criteria for determining open market value.[15]

Drafting traditions for expert determination, which often rely on precedent, need to be examined in view of the potential consequences where the expert machinery is not or cannot be invoked. In the case referred to above the result was that there could be no claim at all.[16]

Conditions precedent

Gillatt v. Sky Television Ltd provides an example of a case in which the determination of the expert amounted in effect to a condition precedent to recovery. Other examples are the certificate of the architect or engineer in certain types of construction contract[17] and Q.C. clauses in insurance policies and development agreements.[18] Outside construction contract certification, this form of wording is rarely encountered today. Whether an expert clause is in effect a condition precedent depends on the construction of the contract terms.[19] Even if it is held to be a condition precedent, there are established exceptions to the requirement that a certificate must be obtained. Most of the cases relate to certificates under construction contracts.

9.2.9

ESSENTIAL ELEMENTS OF AN EXPERT CLAUSE AND IMPLIED TERMS   9.3

Essential elements of an expert clause

Expert clauses should contain the items in this list, which also identifies where to find discussion in the text and wording in the precedent at Appendix A, I:

- the issue to be determined (9.4), (App. A, I.1);
- the expert's qualifications (9.5), (App. A, I.1);
- the duty to act as an expert and not as an arbitrator (9.6), (App. A, I.3);
- how the expert is to be appointed (9.7), (App. A, I.1);
- that the decision will be final and binding (9.8), (App. A, I.3);
- the due date for payment of the amount determined (9.9), (App. A, I.3);

9.3.1

---

[15] See 3.5.2.
[16] See also *Re Malpass* [1985] Ch. 42.
[17] See 7.4.4.
[18] See 8.8.3.
[19] See 7.4.4, and, for an example, *Bernhard's Rugby Landscapes Ltd v. Stockley Park Consortium* (1998) 14 Const. L.J. 329 at 349.

- that the expert has the power to award interest from the date the matter was referred (9.10), (App. A, I.3);
- provision for interest to run for late payment of the amount determined (9.11), (App. A, I.4) (sometimes found elsewhere in the agreement); and
- how the expert is to be paid (9.12), (App. A, I.3).

Sometimes the following are useful:

- provision for awarding costs between the parties (9.13);
- provision where one party does not pay the expert's fees (9.14);
- procedure for the actual reference (9.15), (App. A, I.1);
- a provision prohibiting court applications (9.16);
- a provision giving the expert immunity (9.17); and
- time bars (9.18).

Implied terms

9.3.2 Where the contract is silent on the consequences of an event which then occurs, the law of implied terms comes into play.[20] A term will be implied in a contract if it is necessary to imply the term in order to give business efficacy to the contract,[21] or if the term would have been accepted at once by both parties when making the contract and represents the obvious, necessary, but unexpressed intention of both parties.[22] A clause will not be implied merely because it would be reasonable.[23] Terms implied to make sense of a contract should be distinguished from terms implied by statute.[24]

Only the most basic terms implied in expert clause

9.3.3 As a contract law concept, implied terms underpin the law of expert determination,[25] because some basic terms are not spelled out: namely, that the parties would not accept a final decision intended to have binding effect when that decision was vitiated by dishonesty, partiality or mistake. Dishonesty and partiality are never mentioned in expert clauses as factors whose presence the parties agree would be sufficient to upset a decision as they are so obvious and a term may therefore be implied. Where the expert must act independently (which is almost invariably the case), there is an

---

[20] *Chitty on Contracts* 28th edition (Sweet & Maxwell 1999) 13–001.
[21] *The Moorcock* (1889) 14 P.D. 64 at 68.
[22] *Shirlaw v. Southern Foundries (1926) Ltd* [1939] 2 K.B. 206 at 227 (affirmed at [1940] A.C. 701), *Trollope & Colls Ltd v. North West Metropolitan Regional Hospital Board* [1973] 1 W.L.R. 601 at 609.
[23] *Liverpool City Council v. Irwin* [1977] A.C. 239.
[24] For an example of a term implied by statute, see 16.7.5.
[25] As can be seen from the remarks of Sir David Cairns in *Baber v. Kenwood Manufacturing Co. Ltd and Whinney Murray & Co.* [1978] 1 Lloyd's Rep. 175 at 181, quoted at 15.11.5.

implied term that the parties will not seek to interfere with the expert's independence.[26] In one case it was held to be an implied term that the expert should act lawfully and fairly, so that an unfair determination was invalid.[27] Where the wording of the contract suggests that this is what the parties intended, the court may imply a term that the expert's determination is to be final and binding on the parties.[28] Most contracts contain an implied term that the parties will co-operate with each other in the performance of the contract, and this will apply to a clause providing for expert determination[29]; the extent of co-operation required will vary from one contract to another. There is probably (by analogy with adjudication) an implied term that clerical errors in the decision can be corrected.[30]

However, the law of implied terms cannot be relied on except for the basic concepts applicable to expert determinations: it would not enable the elements of an expert clause dealt with below to be implied. Relying on implied terms cannot be recommended as it may take a great deal of time and money to obtain a satisfactory ruling from the court if the other party contests the implication.

Interpretation of the expert clause

The principles adopted by the court when interpreting clauses of a contract are discussed at 12.8.　　9.3.4

THE ISSUE TO BE DETERMINED　　9.4

Jurisdiction

The task of the expert, the issue to be determined and the manner in which it is to be performed are, obviously, central questions. Ambiguity and uncertainty about them can promote disputes which prevent the operation of the expert clause. Because of the importance of this topic and the number of recent court decisions on it, Chapter 12 is devoted to a full discussion.　　9.4.1

Permissive or mandatory referral

Some expert clauses say that disputes *may* be referred to expert determination, others that they *shall* be referred to expert determination. The latter is preferable.　　9.4.2

---

[26] *Minster Trust Ltd v. Traps Tractors Ltd* [1954] 1 W.L.R. 963 at 973–5.
[27] *John Barker Construction Ltd v. London Portman Hotel Ltd* (1996) 83 B.L.R. 31. It is questionable whether the same term would be implied in other cases: see 15.8.2, where this case is discussed more fully.
[28] See 9.8.2.
[29] See, for example, *Panamena Europea Navigacion (Compania Limitada) v. Frederick Leyland & Co. Ltd (J. Russell & Co.)* [1947] A.C. 428 at 436, and 13.6.7.
[30] *Bloor Construction (UK) Ltd v. Bowmer & Kirkland (London) Ltd*, [2000] B.L.R. 764 H.H. Judge Toulmin Q.C.; see 15.9.10.

9 : THE EXPERT CLAUSE

9.5 THE EXPERT'S QUALIFICATIONS

The clause establishes conclusively what qualifications[31] the expert is supposed to have. It is therefore most important to provide for this in the expert clause. This is usually taken care of by stipulating an appointing authority. Appointing authorities have reputations to keep and therefore have an incentive to maintain standards. It is also usual to specify a professional qualification.

9.6 TO ACT AS AN EXPERT AND NOT AS AN ARBITRATOR

The favourite wording

9.6.1 The most commonly encountered wording is that the referee is "to act as an expert and not as an arbitrator". That wording is much more common than one which merely says that the referee is to act as an expert, omitting "and not as an arbitrator". It is doubtful whether it makes any difference if those words are omitted. The extra words are probably left in by most draftsmen because of understandable caution.

Serious consequences of omitting these words

9.6.2 Failure to use words which make it clear that the referee is to act as an expert can lead to a lot of confusion, and provide opportunities for awkward parties to obstruct a reference by questioning the procedure used to arrive at a result which they expect to be unfavourable.[32]

9.7 HOW THE EXPERT IS TO BE APPOINTED

By agreement

9.7.1 If the expert's identity is not pre-determined by, for instance, being stated to be the company's auditors, the expert clause should say that the expert is to be appointed by agreement of the parties.[33]

By a professional body

9.7.2 The clause must also deal with how the expert is to be appointed if the parties cannot agree on the appointment, usually with the help of a professional body acting as an appointing authority.[34] If there is no appointing authority the clause may fail altogether as the court

---

[31] See Chapter 10.
[32] This can be seen from the cases reviewed in Chapter 17, in particular 17.3.
[33] See 11.2.
[34] *Ibid.*

does not appoint experts.[35] Some expert clauses have tried to cater for the risk of the selected appointing authority ceasing to exist by providing that references to one body include references to its successor.

Avoid the requirement for joint applications

Difficulties sometimes arise when one of the parties refuses to join the other party in applying to the designated appointing authority to appoint an expert. This can be solved by a provision enabling either one of the parties to apply on its own. Without that provision, either the appointing authority will have to be persuaded to act and the other party persuaded to drop its objections, or an application will have to be made to the court for a declaration as to whether the reference should proceed.

9.7.3

Where one party only can appoint

Some rent review clauses say that only the landlord can appoint an expert (in this case a surveyor). This is valid, and it would be valid in other commercial contexts as well.[36]

9.7.4

Replacement experts

Sometimes provision is made for appointing a replacement expert, to take account of the situation arising from the death, retirement or incapacity of an expert after appointment. It may be as well to provide for the eventuality. Case law provides some illustrations. In the case of death, a contract required an estimate to be approved by a specified person, in case of difference to be determined by another specified person. The first specified person died before he could be asked to give his approval. The court found that the requirement of his approval was an essential term of the agreement, and therefore refused to enforce performance.[37] In the case of retirement, the court has awarded damages for breach of contract to a building contractor where the employer had failed to appoint a new architect. The previous architect had retired, and the failure to appoint a successor prevented certificates being issued, leaving the contractor unpaid.[38] Generally, the court is likely to be disposed to assist, unless, as in the first case quoted above, the involvement of a specified person is an essential term.[39]

9.7.5

---

[35] See 11.3.1.
[36] For the effect of this, see 11.3.4.
[37] *Firth v. Midland Railway Company* (1875) L.R. 20 Eq. 100.
[38] *Croudace v. London Borough of Lambeth* (1986) 33 B.L.R. 20 (CA).
[39] See 11.3. and 13.10.

9.8 THAT THE DECISION WILL BE FINAL AND BINDING

Is the process bound to lead to a binding result?

9.8.1 Expert determination leads to a binding result. If a procedure set out in a contract does not necessarily lead to a binding result, the system is not expert determination. Some contract wordings need careful examination to see which side of the line they fall. For instance, a contract provided as follows:

> "Both parties agree to nominate a representative with the authority to address the speedy preparation and agreement of a final account package in 'QS' style, which will deliver a result which both parties will recognise . . . it is understood that no further payment(s) will be made by [one of the parties] until the final evaluation is agreed."

At first instance, this was held to be an expert determination clause, but the Court of Appeal disagreed, adopting contentions that the machinery might break down in various ways, including, critically, the contention that the representatives might fail to reach agreement. The Court of Appeal rejected the view taken by the judge at first instance that if the representatives did not reach agreement, the amount payable would be the lower of their two figures.[40]

Is there any difference between "final" and "binding"?

9.8.2 Expert clauses very commonly provide that the decision will be "final and binding", and it is clearly in the parties' interests that it should be so. Is there any difference between "final" and "binding"? "Final" means that the decision is not subject to review and "binding" means that the parties are obliged to comply with the decision. Therefore both words should be included in the clause to preclude arguments later, unless, of course, the intention is that the decision should be interim such as adjudication,[41] and therefore not final, or that it should not be binding as with some Dispute Review Boards[42] or other forms of ADR.

Would the court imply the term?

9.8.3 Where the wording of the contract suggests that this is what the parties intended, the court is likely to imply a term that the expert's determination is to be final and binding on the parties[43] but the

---

[40] *Davies Middleton & Davies v. Toyo Engineering Corporation* (1997) 85 B.L.R. 59.
[41] See 7.5.
[42] See 7.6.
[43] *Cott UK Ltd v. FE Barber Ltd* [1997] 3 All E.R. 540 at 549B, *Re Benfield Greig Group plc, Nugent v. Benfield Greig Group plc* [2000] 2 B.C.L.C. 488, Arden J. at 514, paras 61–63; in *Baber v. Kenwood Manufacturing Co. Ltd and Whinney Murray & Co.* [1978] 1 Lloyd's Rep. 175 the determination was treated as being final and binding without this being expressly stated: see Megaw L.J. at 179 and Lawton L.J. at 180–1.

Interim decisions in construction contracts

9.8.4 In some construction contracts the decision of the engineer or adjudicator may be that of an expert but still be reviewable by arbitration and therefore not final although it is binding unless and until reviewed by arbitration or affected by an agreed settlement of the dispute.[44]

Effect of certain qualifying words

9.8.5 Sometimes the finality of the decision is expressed to be subject to the qualification "save in the case of manifest error". These words enlarge the scope for challenge.[45]

Conclusiveness

9.8.6 An expert's decision may be invalid if it contains qualifying words which render it inconclusive.[46]

Form

9.8.7 It is unusual to specify a particular form for the decision, and not advisable. If a form is specified and not followed, the decision may invalid, depending on the nature and degree of the departure from the specified form.

9.9 THE DUE DATE FOR PAYMENT OF THE AMOUNT DETERMINED

It is useful to specify in the contract the due date for payment of the amount determined by the expert. A provision of this sort need not always be included because it may be implicit from the nature of the issue referred. The obvious example is rent review where the date for payment of the revised rent is found in the lease provided it has been properly drafted, but other expert clauses may well need this provision to prevent arguments about when the amount is payable: 14 days from the date of publication of the decision is the usual period.

---

[44] See Chapter 7. Note that expert determination can be used for both interim and binding decisions in the same contract: see *Odebrecht Oil and Gas Services Ltd v. North Sea Production Co. Ltd*, [1999] 2 All E.R. (Comm.) 405, discussed at 7.9.2.
[45] See 15.17.
[46] See 15.13.6.

9 : THE EXPERT CLAUSE

9.10 THAT THE EXPERT HAS THE POWER TO AWARD INTEREST

No implied power

9.10.1 The expert does not have the power to award interest unless the contract says so. There is a doctrine that an arbitrator whose task is to declare an amount payable rather than award damages, or an expert performing a similar role, does not have the power to award interest.[47] This still appears to be the case despite arbitrators having statutory power to award interest.[48] Thus, when a lease under which a rent reviewer was acting as an expert did not provide for interest to compensate the landlord for the tenant's delay in paying the increased rent, the court refused to imply the missing term.[49] There is conflicting authority on whether an arbitrator reviewing a certificate of an architect or an engineer can award interest in respect of the period between the date of the original certificate and the date of the arbitrator's award, and the court may also lack the power in these circumstances.[50]

Where an expert does have the power to award interest, the express or implied terms of the expert clause and/or other clauses in the contract will govern whether the interest may be simple or compound.

Cases where power is needed

9.10.2 The need to ensure that the expert has the power to award interest arises in the following circumstances:

(a) The issue referred to the expert includes a claim for damages arising from some breach of contract that has already occurred.

(b) The issue the expert is called on to determine is essentially what amount of money one party owes the other and when that sum is payable.

(c) There is likely to be a delay in obtaining the expert's decision on the amount payable.

At least one of these circumstances arises in the majority of instances of expert determination.

---

[47] *Knibb v. National Coal Board* [1987] Q.B. 906.
[48] Arbitration Act 1996, s. 49.
[49] *Trust House Forte Albany Hotels Ltd v. Daejan Investments Ltd (No. 1)* [1980] 256 E.G.L.R. 915.
[50] See *BP Chemicals v. Kingdom Engineering (Fife) Ltd* [1994] 2 Lloyd's Rep. 373 and *Amec Building Ltd v. Cadmus Investments Co. Ltd* [1996] Con. L.R. 105, at 124–5, and Arbitration Act 1996, s. 49(3).

Rent reviews

9.10.3 For rent reviews, commercial leases contain their own machinery for dealing with this problem because the new rental decided by the expert becomes the rent as defined in the lease and the landlord's rights to the rent and interest on late payment are generally as full as the law permits, with penal rates of interest for delay. However, many other agreements incorporating expert determination do not have this sort of machinery.

Interest to counteract delay by the party ultimately liable

9.10.4 The likelihood of delay should not be underestimated. The party ultimately having to make a payment will look for ways to postpone that event for as long as possible and will be able to do so without risk if there is no interest provision. As well as simple tactics like tardiness in dealing with correspondence, applications to the court can cause significant delay.[51] Interest should run from the date the matter was referred to expert determination, and an appropriate rate of interest should be specified. In some cases the parties may wish to provide that the expert has discretion to fix an earlier date from which interest runs, such as when the dispute arose.

9.11 PROVISION FOR INTEREST TO RUN FOR LATE PAYMENT OF THE AMOUNT DETERMINED

Clauses often provide that the amount determined by the expert is payable within 14 days of the publication of the decision. There needs to be some method of ensuring that interest compensates for delay after this date. Usually the expert clause does not give the expert the right to award this interest. It is provided elsewhere in the agreement as an obligation arising between the parties.

9.12 HOW THE EXPERT IS TO BE PAID

The clause may often say that the expert's fees are to be borne equally or in agreed proportions by the parties or wholly by one of the parties or as the expert may direct, or in the case of share valuation, that the fees are to be borne by the company. The clause may not say how the fees are to be paid, in which case this should be covered at the time of fixing the procedure. Sometimes clauses make similar provision for the expert's expenses as well as the expert's fees. By contrast, advance apportionment of costs before a dispute has arisen is illegal in arbitrations.[52]

---

[51] See 12.3.2.
[52] Arbitration Act 1996, s. 60.

9.13 Provision for awarding costs between the parties

Liability for costs could deter frivolous references

9.13.1 The expert does not have the power to award costs between the parties unless the clause says so. In arbitration as well as litigation the tribunal has a discretionary power to order the payment of costs between the parties; usually the loser has to pay the winner's costs. Giving the expert a similar power in the expert clause could be valuable in deterring frivolous references. It would almost certainly not be obtainable by negotiation later than this stage.

A special kind of power?

9.13.2 It has been suggested that an expert has to act as an arbitrator when awarding costs, because an expert is not qualified to decide questions of costs, whereas an arbitrator is qualified to do so.[53] There is no judicial authority for this proposition. Experts do other, more significant things that they may not be formally qualified to do, such as deciding issues between the parties. Experts are authorised to do what the parties' contract says they are to do.

No machinery available for assessment of costs

9.13.3 In litigation and arbitration, the amount of the costs is subject to the control of the court's taxation procedures,[54] but this procedure cannot be made available for expert determinations by any means, including a provision to that effect in the expert clause. A solution is to provide that the expert is to assess the costs or delegate the task to an independent costs draftsman.

9.14 Provision where one party does not pay the expert's fees

It may be useful to say what is to be done if one party does not pay its share of the expert's fees. Standard rent review clauses usually contain a provision entitling the other party to pay the expert's fees in full and then reclaim the balance from the non-paying party as a debt payable on demand.

9.15 The procedure to be followed in the reference

The right to make representations

9.15.1 Expert clauses take various approaches to the question of whether the procedure the expert is to follow in the reference should be set

---

[53] Bernstein & Reynolds, *Handbook of Rent Review*, Sweet and Maxwell, 8–72. For the practical implications, see 13.8.4.
[54] Made available for arbitration by Arbitration Act 1996, s. 63.

out in the expert clause. Some clauses say that the parties have the right to make representations or submissions, whereas others do not. These expressions do not mean that the parties have the right to be heard at a formal hearing; what they convey is that the parties can state their case in writing.

No right in certain company applications

9.15.2 Articles of association of a company do not specify a procedure but merely say that the auditors are to certify the value of the shares[55]; the same brevity is encountered in the share option[56] and convertible preference share examples.[57] This suggests that the draftsman did not expect there to be controversies; all that would happen would be the consideration of the issue by the expert and the publication of the determination. In the second and third examples, it also reflects the practical difficulties of the potentially very large number of parties affected who might want to make representations.

Sale of businesses

9.15.3 In cases where accountants determine matters such as the net asset value of a business which has been transferred,[58] the expert clauses sometimes, but not always, specify that the parties can make representations.

Rent reviews

9.15.4 Standard rent review clauses say that both the landlord and the tenant have the chance to make representations to the valuer.

Dispute resolution

9.15.5 However, in cases where all technical disputes are referred to an expert for determination and those where all disputes, technical and non-technical, are referred, it is uncommon to find provisions allowing the parties to make representations to the expert. Whether this reflects poor drafting or a more leisurely attitude to the question of the right to make representations is unclear. It may reflect the reality that an expert clause catering for all the needs of dispute resolution turns into a very long document.[59]

Right to make representations and to have them considered

9.15.6 Some expert clauses expressly give parties the right to make representations. In theory, if that right is not set out in the expert

---

[55] See 3.4.
[56] See 5.2.
[57] See 5.6.
[58] See 4.2.
[59] For an idea of what is entailed, see Appendix A, III and IV.

clause the agreement of the parties (and probably the agreement of the expert as well) is needed for it to become part of the reference. It is very unlikely that an expert would not receive representations from the parties. Some expert clauses also say that the expert is to take into account representations made by the parties. It would be odd if an expert did not do so and in any event very difficult to prove.

Should details of the procedure be set out in the expert clause?

9.15.7 Some expert clauses specify time limits by which representations have to be made, and whether representations are to be exchanged simultaneously between the parties or served consecutively like pleadings. This is unnecessary. If there is a clear road to the appointment of a suitable expert it should be safe to leave the details of the procedure to be settled after the appointment. In one case however, the court took a different view.[60]

It may be an advantage in some cases

9.15.8 There may be an advantage in laying down a procedure where the application is novel, and/or the parties believe that a particular approach is necessary and that if it is not stipulated an expert is likely to follow some other undesired procedure. If the parties do not want the expert to consider any evidence other than that contained in their submissions and do not want the expert to make independent investigations, they could stipulate to that effect in the expert clause.[61]

Obligation to provide information

9.15.9 The implied duty to co-operate[62] ought to make it unnecessary to stipulate that the parties are to provide the expert with all information and documents reasonably required, but difficulties can arise and sometimes expert clauses contain a specific provision to this effect. In some cases, notably sale and purchase agreements of the type discussed in Chapter 4, the agreement imposes an obligation on one of the parties to allow the other party access to its documents. In one case disputes about this obligation were held to be matters for the court and not for the expert[63] but different contract wordings might make it a matter within the expert's jurisdiction.[64]

---

[60] *Cott UK Ltd v. FE Barber Ltd* [1997] 3 All E.R. 540: see 8.4.2.
[61] See 16.8.6.
[62] See 9.3.3 and 13.6.2.
[63] *British Shipbuilders v. VSEL Consortium plc* [1997] 1 Lloyd's Rep. 106, Lightman J.
[64] See 9.2.7.

Duty of confidentiality

9.15.10
Some expert clauses impose on the expert an express duty of confidentiality in respect of all information, data and documents received in the course of the reference. The duty would probably be implied in order to keep the information confidential except as required by law, but it could be overridden by a valid witness summons.[65] Expert clauses sometimes also impose duties of confidentiality on the parties. Private systems of dispute resolution have always been thought to be private and confidential but this has been questioned for arbitration by an Australian court decision.[66] There are no recorded cases on the confidentiality of expert determination. Where it is regarded as critically important to impose duties of confidentiality on all the parties it may be wise to include an express term to this effect.

Party in default of directions

9.15.11
In some expert clauses, particularly those providing for dispute resolution, it may be desirable to include a provision that if either or both of the parties fail to comply with directions of the expert, or if the expert determines that the party is failing to pursue the proceedings with reasonable dispatch, the expert may proceed to a determination. In one case, the expert was given the power simply to reject the claim.[67]

Expert's right to take legal advice

9.15.12
The expert clause may give the expert the right to take legal advice, sometimes specifying that counsel is to be consulted. This is however more usually dealt with in terms of reference.

NO APPLICATIONS TO THE COURT 9.16

During the reference

9.16.1
Some expert clauses say that no application is to be made to the court about the subject matter of the reference until after the decision. The court gives effect to clauses of this kind, and this can improve the effectiveness of the expert clause. If the clause is silent on the matter, it is most likely to be interpreted as permitting court applications. Clauses expressly permitting court applications are not encountered. Failure to address this issue at the time of drafting the contract can lead to the parties having to spend much more

---

[65] See 16.12.
[66] *Esso Australia Resources Ltd v. Plowman* [1994] 1 V.R. 1.
[67] See Appendix H, tribunal provision 13.

9 : THE EXPERT CLAUSE

money and time on lawyers in resolving the dispute than is the case if the expert clause expressly excludes court applications.[68]

After the decision

9.16.2 Some expert clauses say that the parties cannot apply to the court after the decision. In an extreme case a clause of that type may not be effective to prevent a party contending that the expert has fundamentally departed from instructions, or has acted in bad faith. However a clause of that type would be a material factor in the court's decision as to what the parties intended should be the extent of the jurisdiction of the expert, and what they intended should be the extent of the jurisdiction of the court to intervene.[69]

9.17 EXPERT TO BE IMMUNE

Some expert clauses say that the expert is to be immune from suit and that there is to be no involvement of the expert in proceedings or correspondence after the decision.[70] Where these are not contained in the expert clause, an expert would be well advised to consider making these provisions a condition of accepting an appointment, in view of the obvious risk that one or other party will be convinced that the expert's decision was completely misconceived.

9.18 TIME BARS

Time bars may prevent references to an expert

9.18.1 Commercial contracts often contain time bars which seek to prevent references to an expert after a specified date, or the passage of time may simply make it impossible to invoke the expert machinery. Where reliance on the time bar or the passage of time is successful, it may be impossible for a determination to take place at all; or, in some cases an existing determination which has been made by or on behalf of one of the parties, but not accepted by the other, may stand as the binding determination.

Effect of time bar

9.18.2 Failure to refer a matter to an expert in time (or at all) may have the effect of there being no other means of establishing a contractual

---

[68] See 12.3.2, 12.6 and 12.7.2.
[69] See 12.5.5, 12.6 and 12.7.3, and CEDR's *Model Expert Determination Agreement*, clause 12. The brochure is reprinted at Appendix I.
[70] See CEDR's *Model Expert Determination Agreement*, clauses 13 and 16: Appendix I.

right. This depends on whether the contract wording expresses the essence of the entitlement or mere dispute machinery.[71]

Time bars are enforced

Time bars are enforced but the benefit of any doubt is usually given to the party adversely affected.[72] Time bars may in some circumstances be subject to the requirement of reasonableness.[73] Where, however, they are found in a specially negotiated contract between two companies the court is unlikely to have sympathy with the party who has missed the deadline.

9.18.3

No machinery for extending time

There is no machinery for extending the period for claims as there is with late notices of arbitration.[74]

9.18.4

Rent reviews

There are special problems with time provisions in the rent review clauses in leases. These can turn on whether there has been an effective indication of intention to appoint an expert.[75]

9.18.5

Time limits for the expert

Some expert clauses say that the expert is to make a decision by a particular date. These provisions are inserted to encourage speed in the reference, which is generally desirable. However the effect of the expert failing to comply could seriously weaken the value of using expert determination at all, as it would be open to one of the parties to try to resist enforcement on the grounds that the decision was outside the terms of the contract.

9.18.6

Limitation

There is a statutory time limit of six years for claims under contracts under hand and 12 years if the contract is under seal.[76–77]

9.18.7

---

[71] See 9.2.8 to 9.2.9 and 11.3.3.
[72] This rule is known as the *contra proferentem* rule, which is that ambiguous wording should be construed against the party which put forward the document containing the ambiguous wording: *Chitty on Contracts*, 28th edition (Sweet & Maxwell 1999), 12–081.
[73] Unfair Contract Terms Act 1977, ss. 2 and 3.
[74] Arbitration Act 1996, s. 12.
[75] See Bernstein and Reynolds, *Handbook of Rent Review*, Sweet & Maxwell, para. 3–66.
[76–77] Limitation Act 1980, ss. 5 and 8, and see 14.8.

CHAPTER 10

QUALIFICATIONS OF AN EXPERT

10.1 SUMMARY

This chapter explains:

(a) that the identity and qualifications of an expert are established by the parties, usually in the expert clause, and that an expert need not be an individual (10.2);
(b) the practice of referring disputes to a named individual, firm or company (10.3);
(c) the practice of referring disputes to the individual, firm or company holding a particular position (10.4);
(d) the practice of referring disputes to members of a particular profession (10.5);
(e) the effect of stipulating criteria for an expert's eligibility (10.6);
(f) the effect of a requirement that an expert be independent (10.7); and
(g) the practice relating to umpires (10.8).

10.2 PERSON, FIRM OR COMPANY

A firm or company can act as expert

10.2.1 An expert need not be an individual person. A firm, such as a firm of accountants which has been appointed auditors to a company, can be an expert.[1] Even a company can be an expert. It is usual, for instance, in trust deeds used in the capital markets to provide that disputes about remuneration of the trustee are to be resolved by a merchant bank acting as an expert.[2]

Appointment of a firm or company more common in commercial application

10.2.2 Clauses which provide for the expert to be a firm or company are usually found in commercial applications of the type considered in

---
[1] See 3.4.
[2] See 5.5.

Chapters 2 to 5. Technical questions of the type considered in Chapters 6 and 7 could be determined by a firm or company but the practice is rare. Rarer still is an agreement to refer general disputes under a contract[3] to a firm or company as expert.

Expert determination need not be a personal process

10.2.3 The courts do not appear to have been troubled by the notion of an issue being determined by an expert other than an individual. This may demonstrate one of the essential features of expert determination, namely that it need not be a personal process. It certainly underlines the court's policy of giving effect to the contract between the parties rather than seeking to establish general rules about who is qualified to act as an expert.

Expert clause must designate the expert

10.2.4 It is therefore essential to examine the expert clause which should state who the expert is to be, whether the expert is to be:

(a) a named individual (see 10.3);
(b) a named firm or company (see 10.3);
(c) the individual, firm or company holding a particular position (see 10.4); or
(d) a member of a particular profession or a holder of a particular academic or professional qualification (see 10.5);

and to see whether

(e) there are any special criteria for the expert's suitability (see 10.6).

Each of these is examined in the sections which follow.

A NAMED INDIVIDUAL, FIRM OR COMPANY 10.3

A named individual may not be available when needed

10.3.1 Generally, referring issues to a named individual is not advisable unless a dispute has already arisen. The reason for this is that some time may pass after the making of the original contract containing the reference to the specifically named individual. By the time a dispute arises that individual may have died, retired, become ill, have a conflict of interest or be otherwise unavailable or unsuitable. The nominee may simply refuse[4] to conduct the reference.

---

[3] See 8.7.
[4] As in the Australian case of *George v. Roach* (1942) 67 C.L.R. 253.

10 : Qualifications of an Expert

In these circumstances the expert clause is almost certain to fail completely, and the parties may have no remedy at all, by expert determination or any other means.[5] However where any dispute that does arise is likely to arise quite soon there may be some merit in nominating a named individual.

Similarly with a firm or company

10.3.2 Referring issues to a named firm or company can run into similar problems but, again, it is appropriate when a dispute has already arisen.[6]

Potential deadlock

10.3.3 Naming specific experts in the expert clause may allow an awkward party to create intractable deadlock.[7]

10.4 AN INDIVIDUAL, FIRM OR COMPANY HOLDING A PARTICULAR POSITION

Referring issues to the firm holding a particular position is especially popular in share valuation and other functions entrusted to the firm of auditors for the time being of the company in question.

10.5 QUALIFICATION BY PROFESSION OR EXPERIENCE

Professional qualifications are usually stipulated

10.5.1 Referring issues to a member of a particular profession has become more and more prevalent in parallel with the growth of the importance of the professions and the diversity of technologies. As has already been seen in the earlier chapters, the professions most often specified are surveyors, accountants, actuaries and engineers. The qualification may be membership of a particular professional body or the holding of a professional certificate or academic degree. Academic degrees are rarely stipulated. In fields where there are no professional or academic qualifications, the expert may be required to have relevant experience. This may be contentious, as it less easy to prove than membership of a professional body.

---

[5] *Sudbrook Trading Ltd v. Eggleton* [1983] A.C. 444 at 484; see 11.3.3. *Firth v. Midland Railway Company* (1875) L.R. 20 Eq. 100 supports this proposition; the estimate was to be made by the engineer, who died. See also *Gillatt v. Sky Television Ltd* [2000] 1 All E.R. (Comm.) 461; see 9.2.8. See also 9.7.5 and section 9 of the Sale of Goods Act 1979, which provides that where the price of goods is to be fixed by a third party, the contract is avoided if the third party does not make the valuation: if one party is at fault the other party may maintain an action for damages.
[6] See 9.2.4.
[7] See 11.3.

No qualifications necessary unless expert clause says so

10.5.2 However, unless the expert clause says so, or unless it is agreed by the parties before the appointment is made, the expert need have no particular qualifications at all. This is illustrated by what at first sight is the odd proposition that clauses where one of the parties, or an agent of one of the parties, is to make the decision are subject to the same general principles as clauses requiring a decision to be made by an independent third party.[8] In one case[9] in which the expert appointed by the appointing authority[10] had no relevant experience, the court relied on this as one of a number of reasons why the proposed expert determination procedure was unsatisfactory, and the court declined to stay proceedings commenced in breach of the expert clause.

CRITERIA FOR AN EXPERT'S SUITABILITY 10.6

Need to be specific, but not so as to limit the availability of experts

10.6.1 The expert clause may lay down criteria for the expert's suitability. Where this is a matter of education, training and experience it is best to specify an academic degree, professional certificate or membership of a professional body. A clause which says no more than that the expert is to be "suitably qualified" can provide material for a wasteful argument if a dispute arises subsequently. The available pool of people eligible to be appointed as expert may in any event be small,[11] and being too specific about the requisite qualifications may reduce the size of the pool to vanishing point. This results in the expert clause defeating its own object, with no expert appointed. In arbitrations, whole court cases have been devoted to whether potential appointees qualify as "commercial men",[12] and whether a disinterested executive official of an insurance or reinsurance company could continue to act as arbitrator after he had retired from his executive post.[13] The consequence of the purported appointee's qualifications not being in accordance with the clause is that the appointment is invalid.[14]

---

[8] See 7.4.1 and 18.3.
[9] *Cott UK Ltd v. FE Barber Ltd* [1997] 3 All ER 540; see 8.4.2.
[10] It was a separate ground that the appointing authority also had no experience of dispute resolution.
[11] See, in an arbitration context, the remarks of the Court of Appeal in *Pan Atlantic Group Inc v. Hassneh Insurance Co. of Israel* [1992] 2 Lloyd's Rep. 120, Leggatt L.J. at 126.
[12] For example, *Pando Compania Naviera SA v. Filmo SAS* [1975] 1 Q.B. 742.
[13] *Pan Atlantic v. Hassneh*, cited above: the arbitrator was allowed to stay on.
[14] See 11.4.

Liability of appointing authority

10.6.2 Some expert clauses seek to make the appointing authority (or its President) responsible for ensuring that the expert has suitable qualifications. A clause of this type could be relied on in an action against an appointing authority for failing to appoint a suitably qualified person. The argument would run that the appointing authority would have seen the clause (as they always ask to do) before making the appointment; would have taken a fee for making the appointment; that the arrangement was therefore a contract incorporating the clause about suitability, and that an aggrieved party could sue for breach of that term of the contract. Some appointing authorities seek to exclude their potential liability.[15] In 1993 the Royal Institution of Chartered Surveyors (RICS) removed a number of surveyors from its list of experts and arbitrators.[16] In 1995 the RICS published its Criteria for Arbitrator and Independent Expert Appointments.[17] The criteria state that the President has an absolute discretion on who is included in, and who is removed from, the President's Pool. Among the requirements are: (generally) being under 65 years of age; attendance on courses in the law and practice of arbitration; experience; competence; satisfactory, monitored, performance; and attendance at continuing professional development courses. In the case of experts only, the criteria extend to regular involvement in the market-place appropriate to the declared area of expertise; attendance at a training course which deals with setting up an expert appointment and conducting it to a conclusion; and a working knowledge of rent review case law and the way case law has dealt with points of construction.

An implied term

10.6.3 Where there is no clause of this type, the aggrieved party would have to argue that there was an implied term[18] in the appointment contract that the authority would appoint a suitably qualified person.

Tortious liability

10.6.4 Where there is no fee charged by the appointing authority for the appointment there would be no consideration and therefore no

---

[15] For example, CEDR's liability is excluded by clause 13 of its *Model Expert Determination Agreement*: see Appendix I. There are several examples from the world of arbitration. The LCIA and CIArb rules exclude their respective liability. In any case, arbitral institutions have statutory immunity for acts or omissions done in good faith: Arbitration Act 1996, s. 74.

[16] *Estates Gazette*, February 12, 1994, 28.

[17] *Arbitrations Newsletter* (December 1995), No. 5.

[18] See 9.3.2–3. When they appoint arbitrators, appointing authorities have statutory immunity unless their conduct is in bad faith: Arbitration Act 1996, s. 74.

contract. It may be arguable that the appointing authority owes a duty of care in tort.[19]

INDEPENDENCE 10.7

Meaning

Independence is clearly a desirable quality in an expert: no one would be against it, but the courts do not necessarily imply independence[20] as one of the essential qualities of any expert. Thus an expert's decision is not held to be invalid on the ground of conflict of interest, unless 10.7.1

(a) the expert clause used the word "independent", or, as construed by the court, showed that the parties intended to exclude decisions made by persons with conflicts of interest,[21] or
(b) the expert had a conflict of interest which was unknown to one of the parties at the time of appointment.[22]

Thus there is generally no objection to the appointment of auditors to value shares in an unquoted company despite their close association with one of the shareholders,[23] or to the appointment of an employee of the building-owner as the certifier under a construction contract.[24] The same general legal principles apply to the appointment of one of the parties as the decision-maker as to the appointment of an independent third party.[25]

Where an expert has been properly appointed notwithstanding a close association with one of the parties, actual partiality has to be shown in order to impugn the expert's decision.[26]

Drafting traditions

Draftsmen often use the word "independent", as in phrases like "an independent valuer" or "an independent accountant": the latter is 10.7.2

---

[19] See 16.13.
[20] See 15.5 and 11.8.
[21] See, *e.g. Finchbourne Ltd v. Rodrigues* [1976] 3 All E.R. 581 and *Concorde Graphics Ltd v. Andromeda Investments SA* [1983] 1 E.G.L.R. 53, discussed at 15.5.2.
[22] *Kemp v. Rose* (1858) 1 Giff. 258, *Kimberley v. Dick* (1871) L.R. 13 Eq. 1, *Ludlam v. Wilson* [1901] 2 Ont.L.R. 549 (Canada); see *Hudson's Building and Engineering Contracts* 11th edition, Vol. 1, paras 6–099 to 6–105 and 6–140 for summaries of cases on this point.
[23] *Macro v. Thompson (No. 3)* [1997] 2 B.C.L.C. 36 at 65G.
[24] See 7.4.1, and the opinion of Lord Cranworth L.C. in *Ranger v. GWR* (1854) 5 H.L.C. 72.
[25] See 18.3.
[26] See 15.4.4.

used in the precedents in Appendix A. Sometimes this wording seems to have been intended to draw a distinction between expert determination and arbitration. In one disputed lease[27] the parties were supposed to agree on an independent surveyor and if they could not agree, the RICS was to appoint an arbitrator. Other leases contain wording which says that the *arbitrator* must be an independent surveyor but, ultimately, the wording of each clause has to be considered to determine whether the word "independent" carries any particular message about the status of the referee.

Specific exclusions

10.7.3 Some expert clauses say that a person appointed as expert shall not have certain types of connection with either party, such as being a director or shareholder in the previous five years. These specific exclusions, depending on their exact interpretation, are likely to be effective to prevent a person with those connections from being appointed, and to invalidate any decision the expert may make if appointed. Like some arbitration rules,[28] clauses of this type may also impose on the expert a duty to disclose the occurrence, after appointment, of events which would have prevented the appointment; and some expert clauses include a challenge procedure enabling either party to object to the continuation in office of the expert on the grounds that some disqualifying event has occurred and has been newly discovered. The challenge procedure works only if a third party such as the appointing authority is willing to operate it, and it may refuse to do so. The court is unlikely to assist in cases where the appointing authority will not do so.

10.8 UMPIRES

Nineteenth century procedure

10.8.1 Some expert clauses have referred the issue not just to one expert but to two experts, one appointed by each party, or if the two party-appointed experts could not agree, to the two experts and an umpire. From the cases, this seems to have been common practice in the nineteenth century.[29] A typical procedure is that each party appoints a valuer; the two party-appointed valuers meet and try to agree the valuation, and, if they are unable to agree, the matter is referred to an umpire appointed by them. This procedure is open to sabotage by an awkward party who declines to appoint a valuer,

---

[27] *North Eastern Co-operative Society Ltd v. Newcastle Upon Tyne City Council* [1987] 1 E.G.L.R. 142.
[28] *E.g.* UNCITRAL Arbitration Rules, arts 9-12.
[29] See, for instance, *Cooper v. Shuttleworth* (1856) 25 L.J. Exch. 114 and *Re Carus-Wilson & Greene* (1886) 18 Q.B.D. 7.

but the court may be able to break the deadlock by giving directions for the determination of the value by the court.[30]

Similar modern practice

10.8.2 Modern practice has moved away from express reference to two experts and an umpire described above, but the procedures are sometimes somewhat similar in practice. For instance, in *Jones v. w*,[31] the sale and purchase agreement said that a sales statement prepared by the purchasers was to be reviewed by the vendors' and the purchasers' accountants. Those accountants were to seek to approve the statement or agree on an adjusted version and only if they could not agree would the matter then be referred to an expert. The agreement also said, unnecessarily, that all the accountants concerned were acting as experts. An Australian case shows the practice, not encountered in England, of the determination being ascertained by taking the average of the two valuations made by each party's valuer.[32]

Umpires can be either experts or arbitrators

10.8.3 The umpire procedure has often been relied on as an argument for a reference being an arbitration rather than an instance of expert determination (or, in the older cases, a valuation) but the courts have not seen the umpire procedure as an important factor, and the involvement of an umpire does not turn an expert determination into an arbitration. In one case where this was argued[33] the judge said that the word "umpire" was quite neutral and did not cast any light on the nature of the reference.

---

[30] See 11.3.3.
[31] [1992] 1 W.L.R. 277.
[32] *Karenlee Nominees Pty Ltd v. Gollin & Co. Ltd* [1983] V.R. 657.
[33] *Safeway Food Stores Ltd v. Banderway Ltd* (1983) 267 E.G. 850.

CHAPTER 11

APPOINTING AN EXPERT

11.1 SUMMARY

This chapter:

(a) describes how an expert is appointed, either by the parties or by a professional body (11.2);
(b) explains the problems created by the absence of effective appointment machinery independent of the parties (11.3);
(c) shows how an appointment may be invalid (11.4);
(d) provides a list of appointing authorities with some figures showing the number of appointments (11.5);
(e) outlines procedures for making an application to an appointing authority (11.6);
(f) shows that the court does not help parties to obstruct appointments (11.7); and
(g) considers issues raised by conflicts of interest (11.8) and immunity (11.9).

11.2 APPOINTMENT BY THE PARTIES

Identity determined in advance

11.2.1 Where the expert clause establishes the identity of the expert conclusively it is not necessary to provide for the selection and appointment of the expert. However these cases are rare and probably the only exception encountered with any frequency is the appointment of a company's auditors to value its shares. Naming a particular individual, firm or company in the expert clause can cause problems.[1]

All other cases

11.2.2 Many expert clauses provide that the parties should, in the first instance, try to agree on the expert to whom the issue will be referred. This usually involves informal discussions about various

---
[1] See 10.3.

candidates. This method of appointment has the merit of being quick and cheap, but without the sanction of a clause dealing with appointment where the parties cannot agree: it is no use at all where one party makes a policy decision to wreck the expert determination by rejecting every nominee proposed by the other party.[2] More formal methods of appointment by agreement have been devised, such as the "list" system: parties exchange lists, sometimes with points systems, with a view to appointing a name (or names) appearing on both lists.[3] But that could also fail to produce an appointment. The parties therefore need to have agreed that, where they cannot agree on the identity of an expert, the appointment may be made by a third party.

Appointing authorities

A well-drafted clause must state that, if the parties cannot agree on who is to be the expert, a specified body will make the appointment on the application of either party. That body, almost always a professional association, then becomes known as the appointing authority.[4] The function of the appointing authority is simply to appoint the expert, not to supervise the subsequent conduct of the reference, as is the case for some arbitrations which are supervised by arbitration bodies such as the International Chamber of Commerce or the London Court of International Arbitration. A professional body acting as an appointing authority should have some understanding of its functions; this might be illustrated by publishing rules for one of the systems of private dispute resolution.[5]   **11.2.3**

ABSENCE OF EFFECTIVE APPOINTMENT MACHINERY   **11.3**

The court cannot appoint experts

Where an appointment provision is necessary but the clause does not include one there can be difficulties. Without the appointing authority, there is no means by which an expert can be appointed. The court does not have the power to appoint experts.[6] Its power to appoint arbitrators arises under statute,[7] and there is no similar statutory provision for experts, and no inherent power.   **11.3.1**

---

[2] For an example of a contract which contained both a reference to a specified firm and some other agreed appointee, see *Mid-Kent Water Plc v. Batchelor* [1994] 1 E.G.L.R. 185, although in that case it was a different issue which provoked the court application.
[3] This system is used in oil and gasfield re-determinations.
[4] See Appendix A, precedent I.1.
[5] *Cott UK Ltd v. FE Barber Ltd* [1997] 1 All E.R. 540; see 8.4.2.
[6] *Collins v. Collins* (1858) 26 Beav. 306 at 314, but going no further than interpreting the then current statute.
[7] Arbitration Act 1996, ss. 18 and 19.

11 : APPOINTING AN EXPERT

Particular difficulty with umpire procedure

11.3.2 There used to be a particular difficulty in clauses providing for the appointment of valuers by each party who would then refer the matter to an umpire.[8] Draftsmen found an answer by providing that, if either party neglected to appoint a valuer, the valuation provided by the other party's valuer would be binding. But, where the clause did not contain that useful provision an awkward party ran no risk in simply refusing to appoint a valuer, with the result that the reference could not go ahead and there was no way of obtaining a valuation.

Sudbrook v. Eggleton breaks the deadlock

11.3.3 For many years the court refused to help, but the House of Lords overturned the old authorities in *Sudbrook Trading Estate Ltd v. Eggleton*.[9] Under the lease in *Sudbrook* the valuers appointed were to refer the matter to an umpire but the lessors had refused to appoint their valuer to discuss and seek to agree the value of the reversions with a valuer appointed by the lessees. The result was that the procedure was deadlocked and no umpire could be appointed, because that could be achieved only by an act of the two valuers after they had both been appointed. The House of Lords broke the deadlock by ordering an inquiry to be conducted by the court into the value of the reversions: it did not order the lessors to appoint a valuer. The court cannot supply the valuation if provisions in the contract for ascertaining the value are an essential element of the contract, *e.g.* where the valuation is to be carried out by a named individual who has special knowledge relevant to the valuation.[10]

Where only one party can appoint an expert

11.3.4 Some expert clauses (like some arbitration clauses) provide that in default of agreement only one party can apply to have the dispute resolved. This is quite lawful. There is no rule that the right to appoint has to be mutual in arbitration[11] and no reason why the same should not apply to expert determination. In long-term contracts where the expert clause is applied to price review, such as rent review clauses in commercial leases, the practical effect of the landlord having the sole right to appoint an expert and not exercising that right is that the price/rent cannot be revised downwards. In a rent review case where this occurred[12] tenants applied to the court for an inquiry as

---

[8] See 10.8.
[9] [1983] A.C. 444. The line of precedent went back to *Milnes v. Gery* (1807) 14 Ves. 400.
[10] See *Sudbrook* at 483–4; applied in *Macro v. Thompson (No. 3)* [1997] 2 B.C.L.C. 36.
[11] *Pittalis v. Sherefettin* [1986] Q.B. 868.
[12] *Harben Style Ltd v. The Rhodes Trust; The Thomas Cook Group Ltd v. The Rhodes Trust* [1994] N.P.C. 99.

to the rent payable, which would have led to the court determining the market rent. The court refused to do so, distinguishing *Sudbrook* on the ground that the landlord was under no express obligation to appoint an expert and the contractual machinery had not broken down. In another case in similar circumstances,[13] but with slightly different wording, another judge reached the opposite decision and made a declaration that the landlord was bound to apply to the appointing body for a valuer to be nominated. The Court of Appeal agreed with the judge that it was right for the court to make an order to prevent the landlord frustrating the contractual machinery, but expressed doubt as to whether it was correct for the landlord to be forced to apply to the appointing body. An alternative would have been for the court to substitute its own machinery, such as ordering an inquiry as to the appropriate revised rent.

Other types of deadlock

Sudbrook is likely to apply to other similar situations of deadlock. Badly drafted clauses sometimes encountered say that the expert must be acceptable to both parties, or that the expert is to be appointed by some person or institution acceptable to both parties. An awkward party could block the procedure by declaring unacceptable every expert or appointing individual or authority put forward by the other party. This is likely to be viewed as a breach of the implied duty to co-operate, so that the court can substitute its own machinery for determining the value.[14] But the court does not assist a party who simply fails to invoke the expert determination procedure at all, nor where the machinery for dispute resolution is an essential term of the contract,[15] except where the other party has obstructed the procedures.[16]

11.3.5

VALIDITY OF APPOINTMENT 11.4

When is an appointment complete?

The following three requirements may be necessary: **11.4.1**

  (a) informing the appointee;

---

[13] *Royal Bank of Scotland plc v. Jennings* [1995] 2 E.G.L.R. 87, Evans-Lombe J.; on appeal, [1997] 1 E.G.L.R. 152.
[14] *Sudbrook* at 484.
[15] *Gillatt v. Sky Television Ltd* [2000] 1 All E.R. (Comm.) 461; *Sudbrook* at 483–4 (11.3.3 above); *In re Malpass Dec'd, Lloyds Bank plc v. Malpass* [1983] 1 Ch. 42.
[16] See the construction contract certification case of *Croudace v. London Borough of Lambeth* (1986) 33 B.L.R. 20, CA; the certifier retired and the employer did not appoint a replacement. The court held this to be a breach of contract for which damages could be recovered.

(b) acceptance by the proposed appointee; and
(c) notification of the appointment to the other party.[17]

The need for these requirements to be met has been distinguished in an Australian case.[18] It is obviously desirable to take all the steps but it may not always be necessary to secure the completeness of the appointment as a matter of law. The issue appears to have arisen only in cases where one party's valuer/expert or arbitrator was entitled by the contract to act as sole referee to decide the issue if the other party defaulted in making a parallel appointment by a particular date, a system which does not form part of current practice for expert determination in England.

What does the validity depend on?

11.4.2 Whether a completed appointment is valid depends on the interpretation of the expert clause, correspondence between the parties about the appointment, and the acts of an appointing authority.

The wording of the expert clause

11.4.3 Provisions in the expert clause have to be adhered to strictly. Thus, a certificate for a letter of credit was under the contract to be signed by "experts who are sworn brokers". It was signed by only one expert sworn broker and was held invalid.[19] In another example certificates of the quality of cement were under the contract to be issued by one of two named agencies. Certificates were in fact issued by a third party and stated, falsely, that one of the named agencies had attended and inspected. The certificates were declared invalid.[20] There are more examples of this from the law of arbitration.[21]

Conditional agreements

11.4.4 The effects of correspondence between the parties were considered in *Darlington Borough Council v. Waring & Gillow (Holdings) Ltd.*[22] In that case there had been a failure to make an application to appoint an independent surveyor within the time limit in the lease.

---

[17] *Tew or Dew v. Harris* (1847) 11 Q.B. 7, and by analogy from the arbitration case *Tradax Export SA v. Volkswagenwerk AG* [1970] 1 Lloyd's Rep. 62 at 64.

[18] *Karenlee Nominees Pty Ltd v. Gollin & Co. Ltd* [1983] V.R. 657, itself unusual in that the determination was to be the average of the valuations made by the parties' representatives.

[19] *Equitable Trust Company of New York v. Dawson Partners Ltd* (1926) 27 Ll. L. Rep. 49.

[20] *Kollerich & Cie SA v. The State Trading Corporation of India* [1980] 2 Lloyd's Rep. 32.

[21] Some are noted at 10.6.1.

[22] [1988] 45 E.G. 102.

The parties then wrote letters to each other about a proposed appointment of a surveyor to review the rent. Both parties marked their letters with a variety of combinations of expressions like "without prejudice", "subject to contract", and "subject to approval by ...". The court held that the effect of these conditions was that no agreement to appoint the expert had taken place and the whole procedure was invalid.

Appointor cannot appoint himself or herself

The court has held that a person charged with making an appointment cannot validly appoint himself or herself as the expert.[23] This would not apply if the expert clause expressly allowed the appointor to do this.

11.4.5

APPOINTING AUTHORITIES 11.5

Advantages of appointing authorities

The provision in the expert clause of a person or institution to make the appointment where the parties cannot agree avoids the risk of deadlock and should also help to ensure that a suitable person is appointed.

11.5.1

Appointing authorities tend to be fairly permanent institutions and therefore likely to be still in existence when the need arises to apply to them to make the appointment. Some expert clauses try to cater for the possibility that an appointing authority may not then still be in existence.[24]

Is the appointing authority willing to act?

Care should be taken to ensure that the person or institution designated by the expert clause to take on this role is willing to do so. There are some precedents of expert clauses in circulation naming as appointing authorities certain bodies which do not undertake that function. If the person or institution is not willing the clause may be ineffective because the contract is not binding on that person or institution, and the court will not make the appointment instead.[25]

11.5.2

List of appointing authorities

The following institutions state that they act as appointing authorities. They share the characteristic of being established recognised professional bodies. It is important to refer to them by the correct name. Failure to do so may prevent the appointment taking place

11.5.3

---

[23] *Jones (M) v. Jones (R R)* [1971] 1 W.L.R. 840.
[24] See 9.7.2.
[25] See 11.3.1.

either because the appointing authority refuses to accept the role or because one of the parties takes the point.

- The Academy of Experts
- The British Computer Society
- The Centre for Dispute Resolution
- The Chartered Institute of Arbitrators
- The Chartered Institute of Management Accountants
- The City Disputes Panel
- The General Council of the Bar of England and Wales
- The Electricity Arbitration Association
- The Institute of Actuaries
- The Institute of Chartered Accountants in England and Wales
- The Institute of Petroleum
- The Institution of Chemical Engineers
- The International Centre for Expertise of the International Chamber of Commerce
- The Law Society of England and Wales
- The Royal Institute of British Architects
- The Royal Institution of Chartered Surveyors.

(a) The RICS appointed 8,547 surveyors in 1993 with 3,924 as experts, and 4,527 as arbitrators; 6,359 in 1994 with 2,809 as experts and 3,471 as arbitrators; and 5,381 in 1995 with 2,239 as experts and 3,070 as arbitrators. The RICS have not kept these statistics for more recent years. They estimate an annual rate of 8,000–9,000 appointments split roughly equally between experts and arbitrators.

(b) The ICAEW appointed 69 accountants in the year 2000 of whom 16 were arbitrators and 53 were experts.

(c) The Law Society makes an average of 50 appointments each year of which no more than about five are experts, the remainder being arbitrators.

(d) The number of experts appointed by the other bodies is very small.

(e) A list of the addresses and telephone numbers of these bodies appears after the Appendices.

Appointment by a President

11.5.4 In many cases the clause provides that the appointment is to be by the President (for the time being) of the body concerned. This causes difficulty if the institution does not appoint a President. It is probably unnecessary to specify the President as the relevant institution's procedures can be followed even if the President is not specified. The Law Society has published its procedure. Where the President of the Law Society is to make an appointment, the

President's staff draw up a short list and the President places the names in the order of preference.[26] The ICAEW arranges for the Deputy or Vice-President to appoint in the absence of the President.

APPLICATION TO THE APPOINTING AUTHORITY 11.6

By letter

With most of these bodies an application by letter is sufficient but the letter should take care to set out the request in a convenient way. The letter should specify the parties, the contract, the expert clause and the issue to be resolved at the very least and further details may be useful. 11.6.1

Application forms and fees

No doubt because of the large volume of applications in connection with rent reviews the RICS has established more formal procedures. The RICS publishes application forms recommended for use when applying to that body for the appointment of experts or arbitrators.[27] There is usually a fee to be paid. In 2001 the rates are as follows: the RICS charges £275 including VAT; the ICAEW charges £387.75 including VAT, which is based on an average of three and a half hours of the Institute's time spent on each application. Flat fees used to be the rule, but the Law Society's charges are on a sliding scale up to £1,000. 11.6.2

Effect of formal procedures

Where a lease provides that an application to appoint a surveyor is to be made to a specified appointing body like the RICS, the application must follow the procedures laid down by that appointing body.[28] Application should be in writing and preferably on the RICS form. No application is processed until the appropriate non-refundable fee has been received together with a copy of the lease or other document conferring power on the RICS President to make the appointment. This rule is likely to be applied to other similar procedures. 11.6.3

ATTEMPTS TO PREVENT APPOINTMENTS 11.7

Can an appointment be prevented?

Will the court prevent an appointing authority from making an appointment because one of the parties objects to the reference 11.7.1

---

[26] See Appendix B.
[27] See Appendix D.
[28] *Staines Warehousing Co. Ltd v. Montagu Executor & Trustee Co. Ltd* [1987] 2 E.G.L.R. 130.

proceeding? This question was raised in *United Cooperatives Ltd v. Sun Alliance & London Assurance Co. Ltd*.[29] Tenants tried to injunct the President of the RICS from appointing an independent surveyor to act as an expert in a rent review. They said the appointment would be premature because they were contemplating proceedings for rectification of the lease and the expert could not determine the rent until after those proceedings. There were also arguments about the interpretation of notice periods relating to the rent review.

The court refused to grant an injunction

11.7.2 The President of the RICS at the time of the *United Cooperatives* case filed evidence about his practice for dealing with the very large number of applications for appointments of rent review experts and arbitrators.[30] The RICS checks each lease to make sure there is a power of appointment. Other than that, the President did not consider it his function to determine any legal questions which might arise in the course of a rent review. The judge refused to grant an injunction. He said it was for the valuer to decide whether to proceed or not and that the President of the RICS owed no duty to the parties not to make an appointment. It is likely that the court would take a similar attitude to attempts to stop appointments by other bodies. That said, it might be difficult for an appointing authority to find an expert prepared to accept such a controversial appointment.

11.8 CONFLICTS OF INTEREST

Other commercial relationships

11.8.1 Appointing authorities sometimes get drawn into arguments about whether members of certain professional firms can be independent in a dispute because of their firm's relationship with one of the parties. This delays the appointment and adds to the work of the appointing authority. If a party wishes to object to an expert on this ground, it is clearly advisable to take the point early. However a conflict of interest does not automatically disqualify an expert from being appointed.[31]

RICS policy statement

11.8.2 The RICS has issued a policy statement on alleged conflicts of interest.[32] This states that the result of objections has sometimes

---

[29] [1987] 1 E.G.L.R. 126.
[30] 7,664 in 1985. It rose to 14,450 in 1990. See 11.5.3 for more recent figures.
[31] *Macro v. Thompson (No. 3)* [1997] 2 B.C.L.C. 36 at 65, quoted at 15.4.3., *e.g.* a company's auditors may be appointed.
[32] RICS publication April 1992, PAGA/S (92)1.

been an attempt to exclude every specialist in a given field. The statement says that the President of the RICS will give "careful weight to objections but then reach his own decision". The RICS appointment procedures include asking potential appointees to disclose matters which would compromise independence.

Accountancy firms

Accountants have similar though less well-publicised problems. Clauses often say that the accountant appointed as an expert must be a partner in an international firm, which has been interpreted to mean one of what used to be the big eight firms and has now become the big six. Mergers between these firms have had the effect of reducing the number of accountants who do not have a conflict of interest simply because there are fewer firms. Also, different departments of the chief accountancy firms often have client relationships with the other party to the dispute, as many clients prefer not to give all their work to one firm. The result can be that all the experts who would otherwise be suitable are conflicted out, in today's inelegant but pithy expression. The ICAEW resolves the problem by choosing an expert from amongst the next 20 to 30 firms after the big six. **11.8.3**

Generally insufficient to justify a challenge

Conflicts of interest giving rise to concerns about lack of independence are likely to be insufficient to justify a challenge to an expert. However the courts have taken a sterner line, where the wording of the expert clause makes this possible, in cases where the appointed expert is the agent of one of the parties, and that agent is either a company controlled by one of the parties or a firm frequently instructed by that party.[33] **11.8.4**

ACCEPTING AN APPOINTMENT **11.9**

An expert should consider the terms on which to accept an appointment before losing a good bargaining position, and should make an agreement on important issues like immunity from suit and fee rates a condition of acceptance.[34]

---

[33] See 15.5.2.
[34] See 9.17, 16.2 and 16.7.

CHAPTER 12

JURISDICTION OF THE EXPERT

12.1 SUMMARY

This chapter deals with how the nature and extent of the expert's task is established. The chapter considers:

(a) which part of the contract defines the jurisdiction of the expert (12.2);
(b) challenges on jurisdiction issues (12.3);
(c) whether the court's jurisdiction is ousted by the expert clause (12.4-5);
(d) the extent of the expert's jurisdiction (12.6);
(e) applications to the court (12.7); and
(f) the rules of construction (12.8).

12.2 JURISDICTION AND HOW TO ESTABLISH IT

Central issue

12.2.1 The word "jurisdiction" is used to describe the nature and scope of the expert's task. It is, therefore, a central issue in the determination process. Unless the expert is determining all disputes under a contract,[1] a definition is necessary. If there is uncertainty about what the expert is supposed to do and how the expert is to do it, the determination process may be confused and ultimately ineffective. To justify application to the court on an issue of construction, the uncertainty must be sufficient to make the expert's task incapable of definition because of ambiguity in the language. It is important to distinguish between genuine ambiguity and imprecision. Imprecision usually has the effect of widening the expert's discretion[2]; it does not make it incapable of

---

[1] See 8.7. There may still be room for argument about wordings, based on analogies with arbitration law: see *Russell on Arbitration*, David Sutton, John Kendall and Judith Gill, 21st edition, Sweet & Maxwell, 1997, para. 2–067 *et seq*.

[2] A wide meaning was given to "the matter" in *Hillsbridge Investments Ltd v. Moresfield Ltd*, unreported, Law Alert No. 00087501, Case No. H.C. 1999 03093, Chancery Division, Rimer J., March 15, 2000.

definition.³ Application to the court has two serious consequences. The first is that there will be delay and increased expense. The second is that the court may take over the decision-making process from the expert: the parties had agreed that an expert would make the decision.

Expert clause, other clauses in the contract and terms of reference

12.2.2

The expert clause is the first part of a contract to look at to find out what the expert's task is, but the expert clause has to be read in the context of the whole contract to discover its full meaning. It may in fact not be intelligible or complete without referring to other parts of the contract. An expert clause should not be read in isolation from the performance obligations of the parties and the commercial purpose of the contract. Expert clauses often refer to other clauses in the contract by stating that expert determination is to apply to disputes under any other clause of the contract which says expert determination is to apply. Reference must be made to the clauses referred to. When that has been done, it may still not be possible to define the expert's task because of conflicts between different parts of the contract.⁴

If terms of reference⁵ are agreed between the parties, they may refine the expert's task and provide more detail than is found in the contract.

Limitations on the powers of the expert

12.2.3

The wording of an expert clause is always likely to be scrutinised in court applications for opportunities to defeat its effectiveness.⁶ The expert clause should be clear about the expert's status as an expert.⁷ There is no longer any need for a judge, and therefore an expert likewise, in construction disputes to be given the powers of an arbitrator to review certificates issued under the contract by the architect or engineer.⁸ In one case the court rejected a submission that there could only be one decision by the expert, and that the expert had no power to reach interim determinations to facilitate the final decision or save unnecessary areas of work.⁹

---

³ See 12.8.2.
⁴ See *International Semitech Microelectronics Ltd v. Scholl plc*, unreported, Garland J., May 27, 1994.
⁵ See 13.5.1.
⁶ See *Ripley v. Lordan* (1860) 2 L.T. 154 discussed at 12.3.1.
⁷ See 9.6.
⁸ *Northern Regional Health Authority v. Crouch (Derek) Construction Co. Ltd* [1984] 1 Q.B. 644 was overruled by the House of Lords in *Beaufort Developments (NI) Ltd v. Gilbert-Ash NI Ltd* [1999] 1 A.C. 266.
⁹ *British Shipbuilders v. VSEL Consortium plc* [1997] I Lloyd's Rep. 106.

Implied submission

12.2.4 Arbitration law has expanded the concept of implied submission to the jurisdiction of an arbitrator or to extension of that jurisdiction.[10] A party who takes part in an arbitration cannot later deny the power of the tribunal to decide issues argued by both parties before it. This line of argument could be used as a defence to a challenge to an expert's jurisdiction.[11] The other party may be able to argue that because both parties have acted on the assumption that the expert does have jurisdiction, the party disputing jurisdiction is precluded from denying that the expert has jurisdiction.[12]

12.3 DISPUTES ON JURISDICTION ISSUES

Expert should deal with issue first

12.3.1 Unless no expert has yet been appointed the issue of the expert's jurisdiction may well be raised by one of the parties with the expert as well as with the other party. The expert may independently decide that there is a question about jurisdiction which should be raised with the parties. The expert is certainly not precluded from ruling on jurisdiction and, on the analogy of arbitration, the expert is encouraged to do so,[13] but the decision is always subject to review by the court. The expert may seek legal advice to help in making the ruling.[14] Application of the rules of construction shows the importance of careful drafting. A contract for the manufacture of a glue-cutting machine stated that it was to be constructed with strong and sound workmanship to the approval of a specified person. The court held that the approval of that specified person was limited to questions of whether the machine was of strong and sound workmanship, not whether it was efficient in cutting glue.[15]

Application to the court

12.3.2 Whatever view the expert may take about it, either party may apply to the court for a ruling as to the extent of the expert's jurisdiction,

---

[10] Arbitration Act 1996, s. 73 (see, for instance, *Westminster Chemicals & Produce Ltd v. Eichholz and Loeser* [1954] 1 Lloyd's Rep. 99 for the similar position at common law). See also *Russell on Arbitration,* by David Sutton, John Kendall and Judith Gill, 21st edition, Sweet & Maxwell, 1997, at para. 2–023.

[11] *Norwich Union Life Insurance Society v. P&O Property Holdings Ltd* [1993] 1 E.G.L.R. 164, *per* Sir Donald Nicholls V.-C. at 166M (referring to a submission by counsel).

[12] Relying on the principle of estoppel by convention (*Amalgamated Investment and Property Co. v. Texas Commercial International Bank* [1982] Q.B. 84, CA).

[13] *Brown (Christopher) Ltd v. Genossenschaft Oesterreichischer Waldbesitzer R GmbH* [1954] 1 Q.B. 8, and Arbitration Act 1996, s. 30.

[14] As in *Chelsea Man plc v. Vivat Holdings plc*, unreported, Court of Appeal, August 24, 1989 and *Nikko Hotels (UK) Ltd v. MEPC plc* [1991] 2 E.G.L.R. 103.

[15] *Ripley v. Lordan* (1860) 2 L.T. 154.

if the expert has not yet made the determination, or as to whether in making the determination the expert has exceeded his or her jurisdiction. Moreover, if both parties agree to this course being followed, a party may seek a ruling from the court on issues of law which strictly speaking fall within the jurisdiction of the expert.[16] Where one party applies unilaterally to the court, without the agreement of the other party, the effect is to take to the court a dispute which the parties had agreed to refer to an expert.[17] This can have considerable tactical significance because the consequences of extra costs and delay are inevitable whatever the outcome.

THE LAW SHOULD GIVE EFFECT TO CONTRACTS 12.4

Primacy of contract law

Agreements to refer disputes to expert determination are contracts, and contracts are to be enforced according to their terms. For example, in *Photo Production Ltd v. Securicor Transport Ltd*[18] Lord Diplock said: "A basic principle of [contract law] is that the parties are free to determine for themselves what primary obligations they will accept". In that case, an exclusion clause allowed Securicor to escape all liability for the burning down of a factory which had been caused by their employee's negligence. Another graphic reminder of this policy is to be found in *Temloc Ltd v. Errill Properties Ltd*,[19] appropriately a case about another private system of dispute resolution, namely liquidated damages. The Court of Appeal refused to allow the owner any claim for damages in a building contract where the word "nil" had been written in as the amount of liquidated damages. The choice of liquidated damages precluded a claim for damages at large, and the writing in of "nil" was said to be "an exhaustive agreement as to damages . . . payable by the contractor in the event of his failure to complete the works on time".[20] The natural corollary of being able to make whatever contract you like is that the court will enforce whatever contract is made. If a contract is technically valid, the only reason for not enforcing it is that to do so would offend some principle of public policy[21]: that is, a principle of public policy other than that contracts should be enforced.

12.4.1

---

[16] As, for example, in *Mid-Kent Water plc v. Batchelor* [1993] 1 E.G.L.R. 185 and *Venaglass Ltd v. Banque Paribas* [1994] E.G.C.S. 18; see also *Norwich Union* at 169F.
[17] *Norwich Union Life Insurance Society v. P&O Property Holdings Ltd* [1993] 1 E.G.L.R. 164.
[18] [1980] A.C. 827 at 848.
[19] (1989) 39 B.L.R. 30.
[20] Nourse L.J. at 39.
[21] See 12.5.1.

But what is the parties' contract?

12.4.2 Enforcing a private system of dispute resolution still begs many questions. Was it agreed that one party cannot apply to the court when the agreed decision-maker is alleged to have gone beyond the bounds of the authority? Did the parties agree that a decision alleged to be outside the terms of the contract would be enforced? Because the answer to these questions is generally no, disputes in court about these jurisdiction issues are allowed.

12.5 OUSTER OF THE COURT'S JURISDICTION

The principle

12.5.1 The public policy objection to upholding experts' decisions would be that the procedure ousts the jurisdiction of the court. Prior to the Arbitration Act 1979, the courts applied in arbitration cases the general principle that no provision purporting to exclude a right to sue in court would be recognised.[22] In *Czarnikow v. Roth, Schmidt & Co.*[23] the Court of Appeal applied this principle in deciding that the then current arbitration rules of the Refined Sugar Association were an ouster of the court's jurisdiction in that they prevented applications to the court under the case stated procedure[24]; the right to appeal to the court by case stated could not be excluded. Parliament abolished the case stated procedure and permitted parties to agree in certain cases to exclude all rights of appeal.[25] Parliament is sovereign and decides when the jurisdiction of the court can be ousted.

Scott v. Avery clauses

12.5.2 All arbitration clauses by definition result in the court's jurisdiction being ousted to some extent. The *Scott v. Avery* type of arbitration clause[26] states that an arbitration award is a condition precedent to the enforcement of rights under the contract. If one of the parties starts court proceedings, the clause does not invalidate the action,

---

[22] *Doleman and Sons v. Osset Corporation* [1912] 3 K.B. 257.
[23] [1922] 2 K.B. 478.
[24] A system of appeal against arbitration awards to the High Court, abolished by the Arbitration Act 1979.
[25] Arbitration Act 1979, ss. 1(1) and 3; although that statute has been repealed by Arbitration Act 1996, s. 107(2), case stated remains firmly abolished with the repeal of the substantive parts of the Arbitration Act 1950 by the same section, and the court's powers on appeal have been further restricted: Arbitration Act 1996, ss. 67–71. For exclusion agreements, see Arbitration Act 1996, s 87. Although the arbitrator has jurisdiction to decide whether an issue is within his or her jurisdiction, the parties cannot contract out of the right to appeal to the court on a jurisdiction point: contrast section 67 of the Arbitration Act 1996 with section 69 of the Arbitration Act 1996.
[26] Named after the case of *Scott v. Avery* (1855) 5 H.L.C. 809.

but provides a defence and postpones enforcement.[27] A similar provision making expert determination a condition precedent to the enforcement of rights under a contract would be very likely to be enforced by the courts in the same way,[28] but it is necessary to analyse the terms of the contract to determine whether the provision for reference to expert determination has been made a condition precedent.[29]

Re Davstone

In *Re Davstone Estates Ltd's Leases, Manprop Ltd v. O'Dell and Others*,[30] leases provided that the certificate by the surveyor to the lessor of the lessor's expenses was to be "final and not subject to challenge in any manner whatsoever". Ungoed-Thomas J. held:

12.5.3

(a) that the question of what expenses were within the ambit of the clause was a question of interpretation of the agreement and therefore a question of law; and
(b) that the clause was void as contrary to public policy, since it purported to oust the jurisdiction of the courts on questions of law.

He relied on the dictum of Denning L.J. in *Lee v. Showmen's Guild of Great Britain*[31]:

"... parties cannot by contract oust the ordinary courts from their jurisdiction [citing *Scott v. Avery* see 12.5.2]. They can, of course, agree to leave questions of law, as well as questions of fact, to the decision of the domestic tribunal. They can, indeed, make the tribunal the final arbiter on questions of fact, but they cannot make it the final arbiter on questions of law. They cannot prevent its decisions being examined by the courts. If parties should seek, by agreement, to take the law out of the hands of the courts and put it into the hands of a private tribunal, without any recourse at all to the courts in case of error of law, then the agreement is to that extent contrary to public policy and void."

The judge rejected the suggestion that Denning L.J.'s dictum was confined to arbitrations and tribunals as opposed to experts. He went on to hold that the objectionable part of the clause was not separately expressed so as to be severable, leaving the unobjectionable parts unaffected, because the words making the certificate final on questions of law made it final on all other questions, including

---

[27] See, for instance, *Viney v. Bignold* (1887) 20 Q.B.D. 172.
[28] See 9.2.8, 9.2.9, and 11.3.3.
[29] See for example *Bernhard's Rugby Landscapes Ltd v. Stockley Park Consortium Ltd* (1998) 14 Const. L.J. 329, at 349.
[30] [1969] 2 Ch. 378.
[31] [1952] 2 Q.B. 329 at 342.

those on which its finality was free from objection; the objectionable parts could only be separated by re-moulding the agreement between the parties, which was not within the province of the courts.

Re Davstone not followed

12.5.4 The approach to interpretation issues taken by Ungoed-Thomas J. in *Re Davstone* has not been followed in more recent cases.[32] In *Nikko Hotels (UK) Ltd v. MEPC plc*[33] Knox J. was referred to *Re Davstone* in support of the proposition that the courts lean against excluding the courts from deciding questions of law. Knox J. referred to the opinion of Lord Wright in *F R Absalom Ltd v. Great Western (London) Garden Village Society Ltd*[34] as negativing any suggestion that there is a rule of public policy that prevents parties from agreeing to remit to the exclusive and final jurisdiction of an expert a pure question of law. He referred also to the legislative change in section 3 of the Arbitration Act 1979,[35] allowing parties to agree to exclude the right to appeal from an arbitrator's award on a question of law, as showing that Parliament no longer considered it improper for citizens to exclude resort to the court in particular circumstances. He went on:

> "I do not accept that there should be in today's climate any [leaning against excluding the court from deciding questions of law]. It seems to me that if there is a leaning to be discerned, it is in favour of allowing the parties to do what they wish and keeping the parties to their agreement, if they make one, that an expert, as opposed to the courts, should decide particular issues. The parties may very well have all sorts of very justifiable reasons for preferring an expert's decision in such a matter over the decision that might be reached in the courts, and I do not, myself, discern any particular policy of the law as being likely to lead to any different result in that regard."

The judge therefore decided that the question of the interpretation of the words said to have been misconstrued was within the remit of the expert, and his decision was binding on the parties.

In *The Glacier Bay*[36] Neill L.J. referred to *Nikko* as showing that expert determination has become established as a "partial exception" to the rule against ouster of the jurisdiction of the court. The opinion of Lord Mustill in the House of Lords in *Channel Tunnel Group Ltd v. Balfour Beatty Construction Ltd*[37] also provides strong

---

[32] John Kendall "Ousting the Jurisdiction" (1993) 109 L.Q.R. 385.
[33] [1991] 2 E.G.L.R. 103.
[34] [1933] A.C. 592 at 615, relying on and quoting *Government of Kelantan v. Duff Development Co.* [1923] A.C. 395 at 409.
[35] The equivalent provision now is Arbitration Act 1996, s. 69(1).
[36] *West of England Shipowners Mutual Insurance Association (Luxembourg) v. Cristal Ltd (The Glacier Bay)* [1996] 1 Lloyd's Rep. 370 at 377, CA.
[37] See 8.4.1.

support for Knox J.'s approach that parties should be required to comply with their own agreement. Courts are now expressly required to encourage the parties to use an alternative dispute resolution procedure if the court considers that appropriate.[38] It is now clear that a clause empowering a third party expert to decide a question of law will not be held to be void as being contrary to public policy.[39] The position where a provision of a contract empowers one of the parties to the contract (as opposed to a third party) to reach a conclusive decision on issues of law might be different. The judgment of Neill L.J. in *The Glacier Bay* provides a basis for arguing that a provision to that effect is unenforceable.[40]

The jurisdiction of the court cannot be *totally* excluded

If the wording of the clause in *Re Davstone* were encountered today, the court would be likely to hold that the clause was effective to confer on the expert exclusive jurisdiction to decide the matters remitted to the expert for decision, including questions of construction which it was necessary for the expert to determine in order to arrive at the final decision. However it need not follow that, however wide the language of the clause, *all* decisions by the expert would be unchallengeable on any basis, including decisions outside the expert's jurisdiction or decisions obtained as a result of fraud or collusion. Thus the principle that the jurisdiction of the court cannot be *totally* ousted would still apply. Except perhaps in extreme cases which are unlikely to occur, the clause would not be void, so that a properly reached decision by the expert would be held to be ineffective, but the court would still, despite the apparent width of the wording of the clause, retain jurisdiction to decide whether the expert has exceeded jurisdiction and whether the expert has followed the instructions set out in the expert clause.[41] It would not be necessary to "sever" the

12.5.5

---

[38] CPR 1.4(2)(e).
[39] A similar decision to that of Knox J. in *Nikko* was reached by Judge Paul Baker Q.C. in *Pontsarn Investments Ltd v. Kansallis-Osake-Pankki* [1992] 1 E.G.L.R. 148. At first instance in *Norwich Union Life Assurance Society v. P&O Property Holdings Ltd* [1993] 1 E.G.L.R. 164 Sir Donald Nicholls V.-C. distinguished *Re Davstone* as turning on very different facts, stating that parties were "not readily to be taken to have intended that any necessary prerequisite to [the expert's] determination, which raises a question of law, is to be outside the matter so remitted" (this passage was approved by Dillon L.J. in the Court of Appeal at 169E). The decisions of the Court of Appeal in *Norwich Union* and *National Grid plc v. M25 Group Ltd* [1999] 1 E.G.L.R. 65 are inconsistent with there being any governing principle that the jurisdiction of the court on issues of law cannot be excluded, and the existence of a principle to that effect does not appear to have been suggested in *Mercury Communications Ltd v. Director General of Telecommunications* [1996] 1 W.L.R. 48.
[40] See 18.3.7.
[41] In the case of arbitration clauses, while the arbitrator has jurisdiction to decide whether an issue is within his or her jurisdiction, the parties cannot contract

clause, in the manner rejected by Ungoed-Thomas J. in *Re Davstone*, as the court can decide as a matter of construction that the only decisions which cannot be challenged are those properly made by the expert within the limits of the expert's decision-making authority. It is likely that a clause stating that the certificate cannot be set aside even on the ground of fraud or collusion would be ineffective.[42] On the other hand a clause prohibiting applications to the court until after the expert determination process is complete will be enforced.[43]

12.6 THE EXTENT OF THE EXPERT'S JURISDICTION

The contract defines the scope of the expert's jurisdiction

12.6.1 Where the parties have entrusted the power of decision to an expert, the extent of the expert's jurisdiction depends on the construction of the terms of the contract between the parties.[44] Each agreement depends on its own terms, read in its own context, and little assistance can be gained from other cases decided in relation to different agreements.[45]

Determinations which involve questions of interpretation of the words of the contract

12.6.2 In some cases the determination to be made by the expert may depend on a question of interpretation of the words of the contract on which the parties hold opposing views. These questions are traditionally treated by the courts as questions of law,[46] though as Dillon L.J. explained in *Norwich Union*,[47] what is in dispute may be not so much a bare point of law as a question of the meaning of an ordinary word in the English language, which may not be a question of law.[48]

---

out of the right to appeal to the court on a jurisdiction point: contrast section 67 of the Arbitration Act 1996 with section 69 of the Arbitration Act 1996.

[42] *Czarnikow v. Roth, Schmidt* [1922] 2 K.B. 478, *per* Scrutton L.J. at 488, and *Re Davstone Estates Ltd's Leases* [1969] 2 Ch. 378 at 386, doubting *Tullis v. Jacson* [1892] 3 Ch. 441, where a clause of this type was held to be effective. See also *Redmond v. Wynne* (1892) 13 N.S.W.R. 39, where an agreement to this effect was held void as contrary to public policy. The Unfair Contract Terms Act 1977 might also defeat a clause of this type.

[43] *Amoco (UK) Exploration Co. v. Amerada Hess Ltd* [1994] 1 Lloyd's Rep. 300; see 12.7.2.

[44] *Jones v. Sherwood Computer Services plc* [1992] 1 W.L.R. 277, *Norwich Union Life Assurance Society v. P&O Property Holdings Ltd* [1993] 1 E.G.L.R. 164, *National Grid plc v. M25 Group Ltd* [1999] 1 E.G.L.R. 65, *British Shipbuilders v. VSEL Consortium plc* [1997] 1 Lloyd's Rep. 106.

[45] *National Grid plc v. M25 Group Ltd* [1999] 1 E.G.L.R. 65, at 67H.

[46] *Pioneer Shipping Ltd v. BTP Tioxide Ltd (The Nema)* [1982] A.C. 724, *per* Lord Diplock at 736.

[47] Cited above, at 168.

[48] See *per* Lord Reid in *Cozens v. Brutus* [1973] A.C. 854 at 861.

In his dissenting judgment in the Court of Appeal in *Mercury Communications Ltd v. Director General of Telecommunications*,[49] Hoffmann L.J. explained that questions of interpretation of the words in a contract do not necessarily fall within the decision-making authority of the expert:

> "One must be careful about what is meant by 'the decision-making authority'. By 'the decision-making authority' I mean the power to make the wrong decision, in the sense of a decision different to that which the court would have made. Where the decision-maker is asked to decide in accordance with certain principles, he must obviously inform himself of these principles and this may mean having, in a trivial sense, to 'decide' what they mean. It does not follow that the question of what the principles mean is a matter within his decision-making authority in the sense that the parties have agreed to be bound by his views. Even if the language used by the parties is ambiguous, it must (unless void for uncertainty) have a meaning. Accordingly, if the decision-maker has acted upon what in the court's view was the wrong meaning, he has gone outside his decision-making authority."

Jones v. Sherwood Computer Services plc and *Norwich Union Life Assurance Society v. P&O Property Holdings Ltd*

12.6.3 *Jones v. Sherwood Computer Services plc*[50] concerned the determination of the amount of "sales" by expert accountants for the purpose of calculating the consideration in a share sale agreement. The Court of Appeal held that questions of construction could be decided by the expert accountants:

> "Any number of issues could arise under the various sub-paragraphs of paragraph 2 of appendix 1 as to the application of the wording of those sub-paragraphs to particular facts. All these issues are capable of being described as issues of law or mixed fact and law, in that they all involve issues as to the true meaning or application of wording in paragraph 2. I cannot read the categorical wording of paragraph 7 as meaning that the determination of the accountants or of the expert shall be conclusive, final and binding for all purposes unless it involves a determination of an issue of law or mixed fact and law in which case it shall only be binding if the court agrees with it."[51]

In *Norwich Union Life Assurance Society v. P&O Property Holdings Ltd*[52] a funding agreement provided that the date of completion of a development should, in the absence of agreement, be

---

[49] Unreported, July 22, 1994, transcript p. 10; reversed at [1996] 1 W.L.R. 48, the House of Lords agreeing with Hoffmann L.J.
[50] [1992] 1 W.L.R. 277; see 15.12.
[51] *Per* Dillon L.J. at 287.
[52] [1993] 1 E.G.L.R. 164.

determined by a "nominated arbiter", acting as expert. A dispute arose (amongst other points) as to whether "completed" bore the same meaning as the expression "practical completion" in the building contract between the building owner and the building contractor, and the building owner contended that this was a question of law which had to be decided by the court rather than the expert. At first instance Sir Donald Nicholls V.-C. held:

(a) that the ambit of the matters remitted to the expert turned on the interpretation of the funding agreement;
(b) that even if some of the matters in dispute were questions of law or questions of mixed fact and law, these questions had all been remitted to the expert ; and
(c) that since the questions had been remitted to the expert, the jurisdiction of the court to decide these questions, whether before or after the expert had reached the decision, had been excluded.

The Court of Appeal dismissed the building owner's appeal, Dillon L.J. citing with approval the following passage in the judgment of Sir Donald Nicholls V.-C. at first instance[53]:

"[The parties] are not readily to be taken to have intended that any necessary prerequisite to [the expert's] determination, which raises a question of law, is to be outside the matter so remitted. On the contrary, they are unlikely to have intended that fine and nice distinctions were to be drawn between factual matters which fall within the expert's remit and questions of law or questions of mixed law and fact which do not."

Earlier cases in which the court proceeded on the basis that it had a discretion to decide questions of law which fell within the jurisdiction of the expert were distinguished or not followed.[54]

Mercury Communications Ltd v. Director General of Telecommunications

12.6.4 In *Mercury Communications Ltd v. Director General of Telecommunications,*[55] a contract between Mercury and British Telecom contained a clause providing for review of the terms if either party reasonably considered that a fundamental change in circumstances had occurred. Reference was to be made to the Director General of Telecommunications for the determination of any terms

---

[53] [1993] 1 E.G.L.R. at 169E.
[54] *Royal Trust International Ltd v. Nordbanken*, unreported, October 13, 1989, Hoffmann J. *Postel Properties Ltd v. Greenwell* [1992] 2 E.G.L.R. 130, Timothy Lloyd Q.C.
[55] [1996] 1 W.L.R. 48.

which could not be agreed. The Director General's determination was required to be made in accordance with specified criteria. Mercury sought a declaration as to the correct interpretation of the phrases "fully allocated costs attributable to the services to be provided" and "relevant overheads". One of the grounds on which the Director General and BT applied to strike out the application was that this issue could be raised only, if at all, on an application for judicial review. At first instance, Longmore J. dismissed the application to strike out.[56] The Court of Appeal allowed the appeal,[57] and struck out Mercury's application. Dillon L.J. held that the parties had left these matters to the determination of the expert and that the court had no jurisdiction. Saville L.J. held that the court did have jurisdiction to decide the issues, but that the parties should be held to their bargain. Hoffmann L.J. dissented, holding that the court should determine the proper interpretation of the words at issue. In the House of Lords, Lord Slynn, with whom the other members of the House of Lords agreed, reached the same conclusion as Hoffmann L.J.:

> ". . . [in] *Jones v. Sherwood* . . . the Court of Appeal held that in a case where the parties had agreed to be bound by the report of an expert the report could not be challenged in the courts unless it could be shown that the expert had departed from the instructions given to him in a material respect. In that case the experts had done exactly what they were asked to do [Referring to the instant case] . . . if [the expert] misinterprets these phrases and makes a determination on the basis of an incorrect interpretation, he does not do what he was asked to do."[58]

Counsel for the Director General had conceded that if the Director General misconstrued the principles he was required to apply by the terms of the contract, the court could set aside his award.[59] This concession would have been made in the light of the fact that the dispute arose against the background of the statutory licensing regime under the Telecommunications Act 1984 and public law powers under that Act. The contract was not a freely-bargained agreement between commercial organisations but an arrangement made in a public law context. This supported the view that the contract should be construed as requiring matters of interpretation to be decided by the courts.

---

[56] Unreported, February 28, 1994.
[57] Unreported, July 22, 1994: passages from the judgments of Hoffman and Saville L.JJ. are cited in *Bernhard's Rugby Landscapes v. Stockley Park Consortium Ltd* (1998) 14 Const L.J. 329 at 343-6.
[58] *Per* Lord Slynn at 273B–E.
[59] See page 13 of the transcript of the judgment of Hoffmann L.J.

National Grid plc v. M25 Group Ltd

12.6.5 *National Grid plc v. M25 Group Ltd*[60] concerned a rent review clause in a lease which contained definitions and limitations as to how the expert should go about the task. The Court of Appeal held, reversing the judge at first instance, that the question of whether the rent review provisions in the lease excluded the jurisdiction of the court to construe the lease turned on the construction of the terms of the particular lease: the parties had placed limitations on how the valuer should determine the new rent, and the lease did not confer on the valuer the sole and exclusive power to construe the lease. The Court of Appeal referred to *Norwich Union* and stated that it was following the guidance of Sir Donald Nicholls V.-C. at first instance in that case. Adopting the same approach as Nicholls V.-C., it reached a different conclusion, having regard to the particular wording of the lease in question, and allowed the application for a ruling by the court on the disputed construction issues to proceed.

In an earlier unreported decision in the same action[61] the Court of Appeal rejected an application for the hearing of the appeal to be expedited, so that the court could decide the construction issues before the valuer reached the decision. The Court of Appeal held (agreeing with Sir Donald Nicholls V.-C. at first instance in *Norwich Union*[62]) that it was immaterial whether the valuer reached the decision before the court ruled on the construction issues. A decision of the valuer outside the remit would not be binding.

No general principle that court can decide questions of interpretation

12.6.6 It might have appeared from the *Nikko Hotels* and *Norwich Union* cases, decided in 1991 and 1993, that the court would usually not intervene where an expert had to decide questions as to the meaning of the words of the contract. On the other hand, it is possible to interpret the House of Lords' decision in *Mercury* as laying down a principle that the court always has jurisdiction to decide these questions, and as implicitly over-ruling the decision of the Court of Appeal in *Norwich Union*. However in *Mercury* Lord Slynn referred to *Norwich Union* without any disapproval, and Hoffmann L.J. in the Court of Appeal contrasted the facts in *Mercury* with those in *Norwich Union*. Both Pumfrey J. at first instance and the Court of Appeal in *National Grid*[63] confirmed that in *Mercury* the House of Lords did not overrule *Norwich Union*.

---

[60] [1999] 1 E.G.L.R. 65.
[61] August 28, 1998.
[62] See 12.6.3 above.
[63] *National Grid plc v. M25 Group Ltd* [1998] 2 E.G.L.R. 85 at 89M, [1999] 1 E.G.L.R. 65 at 66M; also *British Shipbuilders v. VSEL Consortium plc* [1997] 1 Lloyd's Rep. 106 at 110.

What *National Grid* made clear is that there is no general principle either that the expert *always* has exclusive jurisdiction to decide the meaning of the terms of the contract, or that the expert *never* has exclusive jurisdiction to do so. In each case it is necessary to examine the contract itself in order to decide what the parties intended should be a matter for the exclusive decision of the expert, and little assistance can be gained from previous cases involving different contract wording.[64] Each of the cases referred to above involved different contract wording and arose in a different context, and in each case the court reached the decision it considered to be most appropriate on the facts of the case it was dealing with. In the absence of both parties' consent the court generally has no discretion to decide interpretation issues which the expert has jurisdiction to decide.[65]

The *Mercury* and *National Grid* cases do however demonstrate that in cases where the contract gives no clear indication either way (and other judges have reached a different conclusion on the scope of the issues to be decided by the expert), the courts may be prepared to infer from the other terms of the contract and from the circumstances that the parties did not intend to refer questions of interpretation to the expert.

Rent review clauses

As stated above, in *National Grid plc v. M25 Group Ltd*[66] the Court of Appeal held that where the rent review clause contained definitions and limitations the lease did not exclude court applications on issues of construction. Earlier cases involving rent review clauses where the court held that questions of construction were for the exclusive decision of the expert were *Nikko Hotels UK Ltd v. MEPC plc*[67] and *Pontsarn Investments Ltd v. Kansallis-Osake-Pankki*.[68] In *Postel Properties Ltd v. Greenwell*[69] on the other hand Timothy Lloyd Q.C. held that the court could determine an issue of interpretation arising in relation to a rent review clause, at any rate before the expert reached the decision. Each of these cases must be

12.6.7

---

[64] *Norwich Union Life Assurance Society v. P&O Property Holdings Ltd* [1993] 1 E.G.L.R. 164, *National Grid plc v. M25 Group Ltd* [1999] 1 E.G.L.R. 65.

[65] *Norwich Union Life Assurance Society v. P & O Property Holdings Ltd* [1993] 1 E.G.L.R. 164 at 167E–F and 169F (disapproving *Royal Trust International Ltd v. Nordbanken*, unreported, October 13, 1989, Hoffmann J., *British Shipbuilders v. VSEL Consortium plc* [1997] 1 Lloyd's Rep. 106.

[66] [1999] 1 E.G.L.R. 65.

[67] [1991] 2 E.G.L.R. 103.

[68] [1992] 1 E.G.L.R. 148.

[69] [1992] 2 E.G.L.R. 130. In *Norwich Union* at first instance Sir Donald Nicholls V.-C. distinguished this case on the basis that it appeared not to have been argued that the court had no power to determine the construction of the contentious words.

treated with caution in the light of the decisions of the Court of Appeal in *Norwich Union* and *National Grid*. Rent review clauses are usually in a form similar to the clause in *National Grid*, and it is therefore possible for one party to require disputes about the interpretation of rent review clauses to be decided by the court rather than by the expert.

Other cases

12.6.8 There have been further cases in which it has been held on the one hand that questions of interpretation of the language of the contract were to be decided by the expert,[70] and on the other hand that particular issues were not within the jurisdiction of the expert.[71] Where the contract empowers one of the parties to reach decisions on matters arising under the contract, the court is more likely to decide that the court has jurisdiction to decide issues of law.[72]

12.7 APPLICATIONS TO THE COURT

Applications to the court before or during the reference

12.7.1 Where an application is made to the court before or during the reference the court will not intervene to decide matters which the parties have agreed should be decided by the expert: if the issue has been referred to the expert, this excludes the jurisdiction of the court to decide the issue and the court has no discretion to decide the issue itself.[73]

---

[70] *Conoco (UK) Ltd v. Phillips Petroleum* [1998] A.D.R.L.J. 55 (gasfield redetermination—see 6.4.6; Morrison J. referred to *West of England Shipowners Mutual Insurance Association (Luxembourg) v. Cristal Ltd (The Glacier Bay)* [1996] 1 Lloyd's Rep. 370, CA (discussed at 18.3.7), and *Jones v. Sherwood Computer Services plc* [1992] 1 W.L.R. 277 (see 12.6.3)); *Dixons Group plc v. Jan Andrew Murray-Oboynski* (1997) 86 B.L.R. 16, at 291 (share sale agreement—calculation of price based on net assets).

[71] *British Shipbuilders v. VSEL Consortium plc* [1997] 1 Lloyd's Rep. 106 (sale of shares and loan capital—see 4.2.4); *Neste Production Ltd v. Shell UK Ltd* [1994] 1 Lloyd's Rep. 447 (oil and gas exploration joint venture, dispute as to whether the parties had agreed to vary the contract was not within the jurisdiction of the expert).

[72] *West of England Shipowners Mutual Insurance Association (Luxembourg) v. Cristal Ltd (The Glacier Bay)* [1996] 1 Lloyd's Rep. 370 at 377, CA, discussed at 18.3.7.

[73] *Norwich Union Life Assurance Society v. P&O Property Holdings Ltd* [1993] 1 E.G.L.R. 164 at 167E–F and 169F (disapproving *Royal Trust International Ltd v Nordbanken*, unreported, October 13, 1989, Hoffmann J), *British Shipbuilders v. VSEL Consortium plc* [1997] 1 Lloyd's Rep 106. It is theoretically possible for a contract to provide that both the expert and the court should have jurisdiction to decide an issue. This is very unlikely and would require clear language: *Norwich Union per* Sir Donald Nicholls V.-C. at first instance at 167E, *National Grid plc v. M25 Group Ltd*, unreported, August 28, 1998, at pp. 8–9 of the transcript (12.6.5 above).

In *Mercury* Hoffmann L.J.[74] in the Court of Appeal and Lord Slynn[75] in the House of Lords referred to cases in which it had been held that the court normally will not give a ruling as to the meaning of words to be applied by another decision-maker before that other decision-maker has had a chance to express his or her own views about it, and will not answer questions which are wholly academic and hypothetical. Hoffmann L.J. referred to a further reason why the court may be reluctant to give a pre-emptive ruling on the interpretation of the principles according to which the decision-maker is required to decide[76]:

> "A party may be attempting to secure a ruling in advance because he fears that if the decision-maker departs from what he considers to be the correct meaning of those principles, he may have evidential difficulties in proving that he has done so. The terms of the valuation may not provide enough material to enable the court to say that the decision-maker has gone outside his authority. But this is not usually a legitimate reason for seeking a pre-emptive ruling. The party has agreed to submit to a particular form of decision-making with whatever evidential difficulties that might entail."

In *British Shipbuilders v. VSEL Consortium plc*[77] Lightman J. stated (referring to the judgment of Hoffmann L.J. and the speech of Lord Slynn in *Mercury*) that the court will normally decline to rule in advance of the expert's determination on the limits of the expert's remit or the conditions which the expert must comply with in making the determination. This was because the question is ordinarily a hypothetical one which would only prove live if one party considers that the expert has got it wrong. An application to the court in anticipation of the expert's decision, and before it was clear that the expert had got it wrong, was likely to prove wasteful of time and costs. However, a number of cases have been decided in which the courts have ruled in advance of the expert's decision (see 12.6), including *British Shipbuilders* itself.[78] So far as the limits of the expert's remit are concerned, this is often the more convenient course to follow.

Specific prohibition from court application

12.7.2 In one of the recent cases there was an express prohibition against applications to the court in advance of the determination. *Amoco*

---

[74] Transcript pp. 11–12.
[75] At p. 59.
[76] Transcript at p. 11.
[77] Per Lightman J. in *British Shipbuilders v. VSEL Consortium plc* [1997] 1 Lloyd's Rep. 106 at 109, following *Norwich Union*.
[78] In *National Grid Co. plc v. M25 Group plc* [1999] 1 E.G.L.R. 65, Mummery L.J. at 68 agreed with the view of Pumfrey J. at first instance, [1998] 2 E.G.L.R. 85, that if the issues were issues which the court had jurisdiction to decide, the discretion should be exercised in favour of determining the issues of construction in advance of the expert's determination.

12 : JURISDICTION OF THE EXPERT

(UK) Exploration Co. and others v. Amerada Hess Ltd[79] concerned an oilfield re-determination,[80] and the relevant clause said:

> ". . . [the parties] agree that no action or other legal proceedings should be brought in respect of any matters in dispute which may be referred to the expert for a decision in the course of the redetermination or in respect of or arising out of any decision of an expert on any key step or the reason therefor, until all the key steps[81] in that re-determination have been completed . . .".

In a submission to the expert, the defendants referred to data which were not on an agreed database and the claimants applied to the court for a declaration as to whether this was permissible. The court found that the prohibition was in the widest possible terms and that the parties had agreed that the dispute about the database should be remitted to the expert. A similar result might be achieved by the expert clause giving the expert the exclusive right to rule on issues concerning the interpretation of the contract.

Applications to the court after the decision

12.7.3 After the expert has reached the decision, it is possible for a party to seek a ruling from the court that the expert has gone beyond the limits of his or her jurisdiction, so that the expert's determination is null and void.[82] But it is not possible to ask the court for a ruling on questions of law which the expert has necessarily had to decide in order to make the determination if these questions fall within the expert's jurisdiction.[83]

The power of the court to decide interpretation issues is not affected by whether the expert has or has not already issued the decision,[84] provided that the party challenging the decision is not precluded from doing so by having allowed the determination to proceed without raising any objection.[85]

Attempts to exclude the jurisdiction of the court are discussed at 12.5.5 above.

Machinery for challenge

12.7.4 Before or during a reference, the most likely procedure for challenging jurisdiction will be an application under part 8 of the Civil Procedure Rules for a decision of the court on the proper

---

[79] [1994] 1 Lloyd's Rep. 330.
[80] See 6.4.
[81] Of which there were 21.
[82] *Jones v. Sherwood Computer Services plc* [1992] 1 W.L.R. 277, CA.
[83] *Norwich Union, National Grid.*
[84] *Norwich Union, per* Sir Donald Nicholls V.-C. at first instance at 166M (12.6.3 above), *National Grid*, unreported, August 28, 1998 (12.6.5 above).
[85] See 12.2.4.

interpretation of the expert clause. Consideration may also have to be given to seeking an injunction to stop the reference,[86] though it may be difficult to establish that any prejudice would be suffered if the expert's decision is given before the court has ruled on interpretation issues. The parties' potential remedies in the courts would not be restricted simply as a result of the expert giving the decision,[87] and the argument that it may be impossible after the expert's decision has been given to tell whether the expert misapplied the terms of the contract will not usually be considered a reason for the court to give a pre-emptive ruling.[88]

The court has power to direct that there should be an early hearing of the application[89]: however in *National Grid*[90] it was held to be more appropriate that the expert's determination should be deferred until after the court has given its decision. The defendant might apply for summary judgment against the claimant, contending that the claimant has no realistic prospect of success.[91] A party who wishes to make a challenge after the publication of the expert's decision could apply to the court for a ruling that the decision is not binding, but may also use defence to enforcement procedures as an occasion on which to raise the question. The question of whether that party has left it too late to complain may need to be considered.[92]

Rules of construction 12.8

Contract basis

The expert clause is a clause in a contract and it is therefore subject to the same rules of interpretation as a contract. This means that express terms are interpreted according to what are known as the rules of construction of contracts, and these contractual rules apply when attempts are made to imply terms which are needed to 12.8.1

---

[86] *Norwich Union, per* Sir Donald Nicholls V.-C. at first instance at 166C (referred to by the Court of Appeal in *National Grid* at [1999] 1 E.G.L.R. 68B), and *National Grid*, unreported, August 28, 1998 (see 12.6.5.).
[87] See 12.7.3.
[88] See *per* Hoffmann L.J. in *Mercury*, cited at 12.6.4 above. In *Chelsea Man plc v. Vivat Holdings plc*, unreported, August 24, 1989, the Court of Appeal declined to grant an injunction to a party which relied on this argument – the parties had chosen to have the matter determined by the expert, and were bound to follow this course.
[89] CPR 3.1(2)(b).
[90] Unreported, August 28, 1998 (12.6.5). The reasons for the decision were (1) that there was little prospect of an expedited hearing resulting in a decision before the expert's decision had been given, and (2) the disruption to the Court Lists (and prejudice to other litigants) should not be accepted where the party applying for an expedited hearing had been dilatory.
[91] CPR 24.2(a)(ii).
[92] See 12.2.4.

12 : Jurisdiction of the Expert

make sense of a contract. The same rules are also applied to terms of reference, the procedure and the decision of an expert, all discussed in Chapter 13. Parties may discuss the expert's task in correspondence after the dispute arises but the court gives more weight to provisions in the original agreement than to the subsequent exchanges, which may be inadmissible.[93]

Resolving ambiguities, not mere imprecision

12.8.2 The rules of construction applied to contracts generally may be found in textbooks on the law of contract, such as *Chitty on Contracts*.[94] *Chitty* states that the object of all construction is to discover the intentions of the parties and that the cardinal presumption is that parties have intended what they have in fact said. The court will read the words of a contract by understanding the words used in their ordinary meaning, except where that would be absurd in the context. The contract should be read as a whole, rejecting those parts which are inconsistent. Rules have developed restricting the admissibility of evidence other than the written words of the contract. The rules do not prevent the use of extrinsic evidence in interpreting genuine ambiguities in the words of the contract. In some cases it may be appropriate to distinguish ambiguity from imprecision, as the court may be more willing to decide that the parties did not intend to remit to the expert disputes as to the interpretation of ambiguous wording in the contract.[95]

Implied terms

12.8.3 Where the contract is silent on the consequences of an event which then occurs, it may be necessary for the court to imply further terms into the contract.[96]

---

[93] *Nikko Hotels (UK) Ltd v. MEPC plc* [1991] 2 E.G.L.R. 103 at 108F, *James Miller & Partners Ltd v. Whitworth Street Estates (Manchester) Ltd* [1970] 572 at 603, HL.
[94] 28th edition, 1999, Vol. 1, paras 12-041 *et seq.*
[95] See for example Hoffmann L.J. in *Mercury* in the Court of Appeal, unreported, July 22, 1994, citing Mustill L.J. in *R. v. Monopolies and Mergers Commission, ex parte South Yorkshire Transport Ltd* [1993] 1 W.L.R. 23 at 32.
[96] See 9.3.2.

Chapter 13

PROCEDURE FOR THE REFERENCE

Summary **13.1**

This chapter examines the progress in a reference after the expert has been appointed, and explains:

(a) the limitation trap (13.2);
(b) that there is no set procedure outside the contract (13.3);
(c) that there may be nothing in the contract about the procedure (13.4);
(d) terms of reference (13.5);
(e) procedural directions (13.6);
(f) conduct of the investigation (13.7);
(g) the form of the decision (13.8);
(h) specific applications procedures (13.9); and
(i) consequences of the procedure failing (13.10).

This chapter should be read in conjunction with the precedents in Appendix A.

Starting a determination does not stop the limitation period running **13.2**

It may be crucial to the success of an expert determination that a statutory limitation period is no longer running. This is particularly the case if expert determination is being used to resolve all disputes under a contract in place of arbitration or litigation. The commencement of an arbitration stops time running against a claimant for the purpose of the statutory limitation period or contractual time bars.[1] This principle does not apply to expert determination, therefore the parties must enter into an agreement to extend the limitation period (a "tolling" or "standstill" agreement); otherwise the period may expire during a reference, making the decision unenforceable.

---
[1] Arbitration Act 1996, s. 13(1).

13 : Procedure for the reference

13.3 No set procedure except the contract

Expert clause: the only decisive document

13.3.1 The law lays down no set procedure for the manner in which an expert should conduct a reference. Expert determination is not a type of legal proceeding like litigation which has a formal and highly regulated structure, nor does it have machinery for its supervision by judges as does arbitration. The expert clause in the parties' contract is the only document likely to have a decisive effect and then only if it lays down the procedure in detail, which many do not. Setting out the procedure in detail might help in special or novel applications.

The court may help

13.3.2 Depending on the wording of the expert clause, the court may have jurisdiction to decide issues of the construction of expert clauses; in cases where it has that jurisdiction, it may decide construction issues before, during, and after a reference.[2] The court may also grant an injunction to stop a reference being conducted on the wrong basis. The issues before the court are usually limited to the interpretation of the words of the expert clause or other relevant parts of the original contract, or of terms of reference or other agreed procedure. Questions of fairness of the procedure are decided by interpreting the contract and determining what standard of fairness is required in the particular circumstances rather than by reference to an external standard.[3] Thus if an expert and the parties are faced with an ambiguous or impossible procedure laid down by contract, the parties may be able to obtain guidance from the court.[4] The court may also make an order requiring a party to a reference to cooperate in the arrangements for the reference.[5]

But in an extreme case, the expert clause may not be enforced

13.3.3 In one case in which the contract provided that the expert was to resolve all disputes under the contract, the court refused to grant a stay on the ground that there was too much uncertainty as to the procedure to be followed in the reference.[6] The appointed expert was a non-lawyer with no experience in dispute resolution. The judge exercised his discretion to refuse a stay on the ground that the procedure chosen by the parties was for a number of reasons

---

[2] See Chapter 12.
[3] See 15.6 to 15.7.
[4] See Chapter 12. An example is *British Shipbuilders v. VSEL Consortium plc* [1997] 1 Lloyd's Rep 99.
[5] *Smith v. Peters* (1875) L.R. 20 Eq. 511; see 13.6.3.
[6] *Cott UK Ltd v. FE Barber Ltd* [1997] 1 All E.R. 540; see 8.4.2.

unsatisfactory and might result in repeated problems and disputes during the course of the reference. He was concerned that the expert was not qualified to deal with questions of construction, questions as to whether one of the parties was in breach of contract and what damages to award. The expert might wish to obtain legal or accounting advice and the parties might not be prepared to pay for it. There might be difficulties about access to documents. The parties and the (unqualified) expert would have to make up the rules as they went along:

> ". . . any such ad hoc procedure involving decisions taken from time to time requiring the consent of all three parties, is likely to produce confusion and delay, rather than producing a short, speedy and cheap determination of the dispute."[7]

Taken together, the unsatisfactory aspects led to the conclusion that it was inappropriate to grant a stay of the action.

Procedure set out in expert clauses

Expert clauses set out either: **13.3.4**

(a) no guidance at all;
(b) the right to make submissions; or even
(c) full details of the procedure with time limits.[8]

WHERE NO PROCEDURE IS LAID DOWN IN THE CONTRACT   **13.4**

General

Where the contract does not lay down a procedure the expert will have to do so. The expert may receive suggestions from the parties on which the parties agree and which the expert can adopt. Suggestions for procedure which have evolved in practice and are commonly accepted are considered in 13.6.   **13.4.1**

Settled between expert and parties

Procedure is usually discussed between the expert and the parties. This may be achieved by correspondence but a meeting may be necessary and is almost always desirable. If the parties agree on a procedure and the expert does not, the parties should appoint another expert. If one of the parties agrees with the expert and the other does not, that other party may, depending on the circumstances, be in breach of its obligation to cooperate in the reference.[9] The expert is not obliged to secure the agreement of   **13.4.2**

---

[7] [1997] 3 All E.R. 540 at 549J.
[8] See 9.15.
[9] *Smith v. Peters* (1875) L.R. 20 Eq. 511; see 13.6.3 and 9.3.3.

13 : Procedure for the reference

each party to every step and it is unwise for the expert to attempt to operate on that basis.

13.5 Terms of reference

Ensuring the right basis

13.5.1 Whatever procedure is followed it must be ensured that the expert has a copy of the contract incorporating the expert clause and the basic information about the issue the expert is to decide and between whom it is to be decided. These points should present no difficulty, particularly if the expert has been appointed by an appointing authority. They are sometimes called terms of reference. Terms of reference can also describe the documents leading up to the expert's investigation of the issue. These could be, for example:

(a) the original contract;
(b) the letter of appointment; and
(c) a summary of the issues to be determined.

Other matters can be covered

13.5.2 Terms of reference that go beyond these matters result from discussions between the parties, and probably the expert as well, where it is convenient to have terms of reference separate from procedural directions. Jurisdiction may well be an issue. The parties and the expert should take the opportunity to secure a precise definition of the issue the expert is to decide. The definition should keep the issue within the framework of the parties' original contract: precision within that framework may save costs and time. If there is no agreement between the parties about jurisdiction the expert should make a ruling.[10] Terms of reference should also address the question of the expert's fees and expenses. The expert clause may say how the fees and expenses are to be apportioned: if not this must be decided. The rate or amount of the fee can be settled at this stage. Any other matters not covered in the expert clause can also be dealt with in terms of reference.[11]

13.6 Procedural directions

Representations

13.6.1 Even though some expert clauses do not specifically reserve the right of the parties to make submissions or representations to the

---

[10] See 12.3.1.
[11] See the list at 9.3.

expert,[12] it is unlikely that this right will be lost through its omission because the expert will usually want to receive submissions or representations of some kind to help to understand the issue that has to be determined. The expert will in most cases want each party to send in a written submission accompanied by copies of the documents referred to or relied on in the submission. Views differ as to whether submissions should be exchanged simultaneously or whether one party's submission should follow the other's.

It is usual and desirable to provide that each party is to be sent a copy of the other party's submission. In some cases the parties may wish to keep their respective submissions confidential from each other and there is nothing inherently objectionable in that, provided it is clearly agreed between the parties and the expert. However if one of the parties objects to confidential representations being submitted to the expert by the other party, or is unaware of representations which have been made by the other party, there would be a risk of the court deciding that there had been improper collusion between the other party and the expert, rendering the decision liable to be set aside.[13] In one case decided in Australia, a claim was set out in one letter agreed by both parties and a later increased claim was not copied to the other party: the resulting decision was held invalid.[14]

Sometimes one of the parties makes no representations, in which case the expert should ensure that that party does know that it has the right to make them and has full copies of the other side's representations. The RICS Guidance Notes[15] say that an expert who receives representations from one party only should check those representations. A party who is aware of the right to make representations and decides not to do so runs the risk that the decision will be more adverse than if the right had been exercised. An action for negligence against the expert by the silent party might be met by a defence of contributory negligence.

Timing

Procedural directions should include provision for the publication of the expert's decision, and whether it should give reasons. It is obviously desirable to set a timetable for submissions and a decision. However, difficulties may arise if a strict time limit is set for the publication of the decision and the decision is published after it has expired. It may suit one of the parties to refuse to accept it

13.6.2

---

[12] See 9.15.1 to 9.15.6.
[13] See 15.4.
[14] *Capricorn Inks Pty Ltd v. Lawter International (Australia) Pty Ltd* [1989] 1 Qd R. 8; see 15.6.2 and 15.6.3 for this and other cases where communications have taken place between one party and the expert.
[15] *Guidance Notes for Surveyors acting as Arbitrators or as Independent Experts in Commercial Property Rent Reviews*, 7th edition (RICS Books), at 4.3.7.

13 : Procedure for the reference

on that ground. The expert does, in any case, have an implied statutory duty to deliver a decision within a reasonable time[16].

Inspections

13.6.3 The expert may need to do more than receive submissions, and directions should be given about the arrangements for physical inspections, site visits and the like. Where these arrangements need the co-operation of one or other of the parties, the court, if necessary, makes an order to enforce that co-operation. In *Smith v. Peters*[17] there was an agreement for the sale of fixtures and fittings of a public house at a valuation by a person named by both parties. The vendor refused to let that person into the public house. The court made a mandatory order compelling the vendor to allow the person to enter so that the valuation could proceed.

Legal advice

13.6.4 Consideration should be given to whether the expert will need outside assistance such as legal advice in order to complete the work. The expert must seek the parties' agreement to the principle and the cost of obtaining that outside assistance. Usually the need for legal advice is for help in interpreting the expert's task.[18] In *Nikko v. MEPC*[19] the expert arranged for the point of law to be decided as a preliminary issue at a formal hearing. The expert was addressed by counsel on behalf of the parties and was assisted by a Queen's Counsel as legal adviser.

An expert cannot seek this sort of help from the court in the way that an arbitrator can.[20]

Litigation-type procedures

13.6.5 The remaining question is the extent to which the expert and the parties allow the reference to resemble arbitration (or even litigation). This depends on the nature of the dispute and the extent of the part played by lawyers in the proceedings but, for the reasons set out below, lawyers serve their clients' interests better if they refrain from imposing too many legal formalities on the procedure. For instance, should the parties be ordered to disclose documents on a wide-ranging basis similar to the disclosure procedures of the court? Should the parties be allowed to examine and cross-examine witnesses? Should they be allowed to conduct a formal

---

[16] See 16.7.5.
[17] (1875) L.R. 20 Eq. 511. See also *Morse v. Merest* (1821) 6 Madd. 26.
[18] See Chapter 12.
[19] [1991] 2 E.G.L.R. 103. In *Chelsea Man plc v. Vivat Holdings plc,* unreported, Court of Appeal, August 24, 1989, the expert informed the parties that he intended to obtain legal advice.
[20] Arbitration Act 1996, ss. 32, 45.

hearing? All of these features have appeared in expert determinations. Their intrinsic value has to be weighed against the extra cost and time taken. As is explained in the next section, informal arrangements may be preferable. One ploy which is definitely not available (unless included in the expert clause) is the right of one party to require the other party to provide security for the costs of the reference.

Inquisitorial procedure

The procedure adopted by an expert may be less like the adversarial, party-driven mechanisms of arbitration and litigation and more like an inquisitorial investigation. By these words is meant a freedom for the expert to initiate lines of enquiry with or without the involvement of the parties. The expert clause and/or the parties may preclude the expert from making independent investigations without involving the parties.[21]

13.6.6

Default

What should the expert do if a party fails to comply with the directions? The expert can and should proceed to make the determination. Some expert clauses provide for this[22] expressly, but it is an implied term of the procedure that both parties will cooperate in bringing the determination to a conclusion[23] and is probably unnecessary in most cases. Consider the following example. In a rent review, an expert gave a two-month time limit for representations: not ungenerous but geared to a provision in the lease. A surveyor representing the tenant wished to object to the expert on the grounds of the expert's conflict of interest but failed to send representations by the deadline or to take any action. The court held that the surveyor should have sent in representations by the deadline without prejudice to the contentions that the expert should withdraw, and that the expert acted properly in proceeding to make the determination without having received representations from both parties; if one side only had put in late representations, it would also have been proper for those to be disregarded.[24] It may nonetheless be desirable that an expert, before proceeding to the next stage, gives the defaulting party clear warning that that is what he or she proposes to do. If the expert does not proceed, there are only two other possible outcomes: either the whole process goes into limbo or the expert resigns. Neither is at all attractive. Where one party refuses to comply with a procedural direction made by the expert, the court is likely to make an order

13.6.7

---

[21] See 9.15.8 and 16.8.6.
[22] See 9.15.11.
[23] See 9.4.3 and 13.6.3.
[24] *Rajdev v. Becketts (a firm)* [1989] 2 E.G.L.R. 144, especially 147L.

requiring compliance,[25] though there is no other reported instance of an order being made. Non-compliance is often a breach of the implied duty to cooperate in the reference.[26] It can be made an express term. One provision empowers the expert tribunal, in its discretion, to reject the claim in the event of non-compliance.[27]

Parties with unequal bargaining power

13.6.8 Should an expert adjust the directions to take account of the fact that the parties are of unequal bargaining power? The RICS Guidance Notes suggest that, if the weaker party does not wish to incur the expense of a professional valuation, it might be justifiable for the expert to invite factual submissions only. But the RICS Guidance Notes go on to say that, whether or not either or both parties submit valuations for consideration, the expert is still under a duty to make his own valuation.[28] That must be right, as an expert's professional duty in respect of the subject matter comes first.

13.7 CONDUCT OF THE INVESTIGATION

Informality preferred

13.7.1 With what degree of formality should the investigation be conducted? The anecdotal evidence is that parties often want informal, non-legalistic meetings where the expert can hear what the parties' non-legal representatives have to say without any lawyers being present. Meetings of this type are not hearings in the litigation sense. The expert needs to be sure of understanding both points of view, and in doing so, may decide to try to persuade one or both of the parties to agree with the other's position. The expert may also wish to find the common ground shared by the parties and build on it. The expert is not precluded from taking this role unless the parties agree to prohibit it. It is important that the expert and the parties are clear about the expert's role and that, once the expert has adopted a style, it is consistently maintained. The style adopted by individual experts may share some of the characteristics of mediation. An arbitrator who meets the parties separately breaks one of the rules of natural justice but, as those rules do not apply to expert determinations,[29] an expert can hold separate meetings. Thus the same individual might be able to act first as a mediator and subsequently

---

[25] *Cf. Smith v. Peters*, 13.6.3.
[26] See 9.3.3.
[27] See Appendix I, clause 13.
[28] *Guidance Notes for Surveyors acting as Arbitrators or as Independent Experts in Commercial Property Rent Reviews*, 7th edition (RICS Books), at 4–34.
[29] See 15.6 to 15.7.

as an expert in the same case[30] without some, at least, of the difficulties of the procedure known as med-arb.[31]

Avoid suggestions of partiality

13.7.2

In these discussions the prudent expert avoids conduct which might be thought to cast doubt on his or her impartiality. In a finance leasing case[32] the expert had separate discussions with the parties about the form of the certificate. The expert also attended a meeting at which the lessors and their solicitors discussed tactics for dealing with the lessees. The court said that the expert should have remained aloof from the tactical discussions. However, that did not invalidate the expert's decision, and there was nothing wrong in the expert meeting the parties separately to discuss the certificate. The expert refused to do what the lessors wanted him to do, namely to rewrite the certificate in a way which the expert thought would make the certificate conclusive, contrary to the lessees' interests. Ironically, the court found the certificate conclusive anyway.[33] Other cases involving communications between the expert and one of the parties are referred to at 15.4 and 15.6.

Expert pursuing independent investigations

13.7.3

An expert can pursue independent investigations into the issue for decision, and traditionally that is one of the functions which differentiates the expert's role from that of an arbitrator.[34] The expert does not, however, have to pursue independent investigations if the parties have provided the expert with sufficient evidence, or the expert has agreed with the parties to consider only the evidence submitted by the parties.[35] There is nothing to stop the parties acting together, specifically preventing the expert from pursuing independent investigations and limiting consideration of evidence to the material submitted by the parties. This can be attended to at this stage if it has not been already provided for in the expert clause.[36]

---

[30] See "'Med-Ex': An interesting variation on the ADR theme", by John Fordham, in *Resolutions*, issue 26, summer 2000, at page 6. and CEDR's *Model Expert Determination Agreement*, clause 7: the brochure is reprinted at Appendix J. "Med-arb" is a procedure where the same person acts as both mediator and arbitrator.
[31] The mediator/expert would still require the parties to enter into an agreement expressly excluding all their rights of action against him or her.
[32] *Midland Montagu Leasing (UK) Ltd v. Tyne & Wear Passenger Transport Executive and Ernst & Whinney*, unreported, Chancery Division, February 23, 1990.
[33] See 15.13.6.
[34] See 17.6.3.
[35] See 16.8.
[36] See 9.15.8.

Disclosure of documents

13.7.4 Parties usually wish to provide the expert with documents supporting their respective cases. Difficulties can arise if one party refuses to disclose a document which the other party wishes the expert to see. Unless there is a specific provision about this in the expert clause, the expert has no power to impose disclosure on an unwilling party. But the expert can draw adverse inferences from the failure to disclose. General disclosure directions such as those used in litigation[37] are not likely to be either welcome or appropriate.

Conduct of hearings

13.7.5 If formal hearings take place, no law governs the way they should be conducted. The expert clause may set out some rules but this is very unusual. It is for the expert and the parties to decide how hearings should be run. Thus there are no rules of evidence as are applied to court trials and some arbitration hearings. The rules of natural justice do not apply to expert determinations[38] but the expert will be wise to ensure that the procedure adopted is fair.[39] It is of course always open to the parties to agree to the application of, for instance, rules of evidence: but it is difficult to see why expert determination is being used if that is done as the process might just as well be an arbitration.

Defamation

13.7.6 Can an expert or the parties be sued for defamation for remarks made in the course of a reference? There is no direct authority. Some parts of an expert determination are likely to be seen as protected by qualified privilege, so that a claimant can succeed in a defamation action only by proving malice on the part of the defendant. The privilege would be absolute, which means that nothing, including evidence of malice, could rebut it, if the court found that the expert determination closely resembled judicial proceedings. This should not be used as an excuse for making references more legalistic.

Negotiations and without prejudice correspondence

13.7.7 The expert should not be told about the progress of negotiations unless both parties agree. The purpose of the without prejudice privilege is to prevent one party from disclosing the other party's negotiating position to the tribunal. Accordingly the expert should not be sent copies of without prejudice correspondence between the parties, unless both parties agree on the disclosure.

---

[37] See 13.6.5.
[38] See 15.3.4 to 15.3.5.
[39] See 13.7.2.

The Decision 13.8

The decision-making process

The process by which the expert comes to a decision depends on the sort of information provided and reviewed and on whether the expert possesses and has applied the intellectual skills necessary in the particular area of expertise. In reviewing the material and making the decision the expert should have regard to the contractual task and provide no more and no less than the parties expect. **13.8.1**

Form of the decision

The decision, which is usually in the form of a letter from the expert, should set out: **13.8.2**

- the name of the expert;
- the names of the parties;
- the issue they asked the expert to determine;
- the relevant contract and expert clause;
- the manner by which the expert was appointed;
- the terms of reference;
- the procedural directions;
- compliance (or otherwise) by the parties with those directions;
- the decision itself;
- any reasons;
- the principal amount of money to be transferred from one party to another (if any);
- interest (if any);
- the fees and expenses;
- any other costs dispositions;
- whatever its form, the decision should be signed, dated and sent to the parties.

Some guidance is available from the law relating to certificates issued under construction contracts. The courts have held that it must be obvious that the document is the physical expression of the certifying process, that it must be clear and unambiguous,[40] and that a certificate is ineffective until issued or delivered.[41]

Reasons

The decision itself is likely to be a brief answer to the question put. For a one-line example see the decision in *Jones v. Sherwood Computer Services plc*[42]: "We determine that the sales amount to **13.8.3**

---

[40] *Token Construction v. Charlton Estates* (1973) 1 B.L.R. 48.
[41] *London Borough of Camden v. Thomas McInerney* (1986) 2 Const. L.J. 293.
[42] [1992] 1 W.L.R. 277.

£2,527,135." The provision of reasons for decisions has become unpopular because reasons give more ammunition for challenge and negligence claims.[43] An earlier agreement obliging the expert to give reasons should be enforceable. If the expert has not agreed beforehand to give reasons, the court will not compel the expert to do so.[44]

Financial provisions

13.8.4 To the extent they are part of the expert's jurisdiction, and necessary to complete the specific task, the decision should also state the principal amount of money to be transferred from one party to another and deal with interest, the expert's fees and expenses and the parties' costs.[45] There is no authority on how an expert should exercise the power to award costs awarded by the expert clause[46]: clearly it is sensible to ask for submissions from the parties first.[47]

Draft submitted for comments

13.8.5 Sometimes the expert circulates the decision in draft first. This enables any factual errors to be corrected. However it can seriously weaken the effectiveness of expert determination by giving the parties an opportunity they would not otherwise have to challenge the decision before it is final. It may be useful in some cases to issue a reasoned decision in two parts: the first part, setting out non-contentious matters, can be circulated for approval by the parties, before the expert issues the second part of the decision.

13.9 PROCEDURES FOR SPECIFIC APPLICATIONS

Rent review

13.9.1 The RICS Guidance Notes[48] deal with recommended procedures for the independent expert conducting a rent review. The Guidance Notes recommend that the expert calls a preliminary meeting to establish the terms of the appointment and the procedure for the reference. The Guidance Notes also set out a number of matters specific to rent review as well as the more general principles.[49]

---

[43] See 16.7.12.
[44] See 15.7.7.
[45] See 9.10 to 9.13.
[46] See 9.13.2.
[47] *Handbook of Rent Review*, by Bernstein & Reynolds, Sweet & Maxwell, 1–97.
[48] *Guidance Notes for Surveyors acting as Arbitrators or as Independent Experts in Commercial Property Rent Reviews*, 7th edition (RICS Books) at 4.3.
[49] Some of which are referred to and discussed at the appropriate places in this book.

PROCEDURES FOR SPECIFIC APPLICATIONS

Adjudication of construction disputes

Numerous forms have been published.[50]   **13.9.2**

Institution of Chemical Engineers

The Conditions of Contract for Process Plant published by the Institution of Chemical Engineers provide for expert determination of general disputes.[51] They have published an accompanying brochure, "Expert Procedures", which gives guidance, not only on the procedure to be followed by the expert, but on many other aspects as well. As regards the procedure to be followed, their recommendation is that the expert has wide discretion.   **13.9.3**

Other applications

There are no published guides for other applications. Appendix A contains precedents which can be adapted to suit the occasion.   **13.9.4**

BREAKDOWN OF THE PROCEDURAL MACHINERY   13.10

What happens if the reference cannot be completed?

Difficulties can arise during expert determinations which result in their not being completed. Sometimes these difficulties arise at the appointment stage.[52] Where the difficulties occur later, during the reference, the problem may be that the expert has sought the agreement of the parties to the procedure and failed to get it from at least one of the parties,[53] or one of the parties does not co-operate in some other way,[54] and that, faced with this sort of problem, the expert fails to act. The legal effect of this type of event depends on whether the machinery is found to have broken down.   **13.10.1**

Has the machinery broken down?

The courts have held that a breakdown in the contractual machinery occurs when without material default or interference by a party to the contract the machinery is not followed by the person appointed to administer and operate it and as a result its purpose is not achieved and is no longer capable of being achieved.   **13.10.2**

---

[50] See 7.5.4.
[51] See 7.9.2.
[52] See 9.7.5 and 11.3.
[53] See 13.3.2.
[54] See 13.6.7.

"Non-compliance with the machinery by the administrator is not in itself sufficient: the effect must be that either or both of the parties to the contract do not in consequence of the breakdown truly know their position or cannot or are unlikely to know it."[55]

One example of machinery having broken down is a case where the court described the procedure that had been followed by an auditor as a "classic example of how not to conduct a valuation".[56] Another is a case where the expert, who was the agent of one of the parties, refused to act.[57]

Consequences of breakdown

13.10.3 If the machinery has broken down, "either [party] is then free to have its position established by the appropriate means available: litigation or arbitration (preceded, if the contract so requires, by recourse to adjudication or the like)".[58] This is not possible where the provision for expert determination is held to be an essential term of the contract.[59]

Machinery not broken down

13.10.4 If the machinery has not broken down, and there is no agreement between the parties to use other appropriate means, the parties must either, to the extent it is still possible to do so, continue to seek to make it work or abandon the matter.[60]

Default by one party

13.10.5 Cases where the reference cannot proceed because of default by one of the parties have been considered above.[61]

---

[55] *Per* Judge Humphrey Lloyd Q.C. in *Bernhard's Rugby Landscapes Ltd v. Stockley Park Consortium Ltd* (1998) 14 Const. L.J. 329 at 357, itself relying on Goddard L.J.'s judgment in *Panamena Europea Navigacion v. Frederick Leyland & Company Ltd* (1943) 76 Lloyd's Rep. 113 at 127, approved by the House of Lords at [1947] A.C. 428.
[56] *Macro v. Thompson (No. 3)* [1997] 2 B.C.L.C. 36 at 66.
[57] *Panamena Europea Navigacion v. Frederick Leyland & Company Ltd* [1947] A.C. 428, HL
[58] *Per* Judge Humphrey Lloyd Q.C. in *Bernhard's Rugby Landscapes Ltd v. Stockley Park Consortium Ltd* (1998) 14 Const. L.J. 329 at 357. See also *Macro v. Thompson (No. 3)* [1997] 2 B.C.L.C. 36 at 69.
[59] See 11.3.3.
[60] See, in the context of failure to invoke a clause and appoint an expert, *Gillatt v. Sky Television Ltd* [2000] 1 All E.R. (Comm) 461; see 9.2.8.
[61] See 11.3.3, 13.6.3, and 13.6.7.

CHAPTER 14

ENFORCING THE DECISION

SUMMARY   **14.1**

This chapter explains whether, and if so how, an expert's decision may be enforced, and explains:

(a) the nature of enforcement procedures (14.2);
(b) the use of court action to enforce experts' decisions (14.3);
(c) the effect of an arbitration clause (14.4);
(d) the use of the threat of insolvency (14.5);
(e) enforcement by the use of set-off (14.6);
(f) difficulties with enforcement abroad (14.7); and
(g) time limitation on enforcement (14.8).

ENFORCEMENT PROCEDURES   **14.2**

Securing compliance with an expert's decision

Enforcement usually involves sanctions for non-compliance, of which a range are available against those who disobey judgments and orders of the court. An example of enforcement is execution, which means seizure and removal of the defendant's goods to the value of the unsatisfied judgment plus interest and costs. The threat of enforcement is often sufficient to secure payment.   **14.2.1**

Is the expert's decision on technical issues only?

The decision may not be readily enforceable if the jurisdiction of the expert is limited to technical issues without their financial consequences. Thus if an IT expert decides that a computer system has not been supplied in accordance with the specification, and the contract provides that all other disputes are to be decided by arbitration, arbitration will have to be used to resolve the dispute about the financial consequences and there will be nothing to enforce until that stage is reached.   **14.2.2**

An expert's decision cannot be enforced as if it were an arbitration award

14.2.3 A decision of an expert is not the result of a judicial examination of a dispute and no statute has been enacted providing enforcement machinery. An arbitration award can be enforced by application to the court,[1] which allows enforcement of the award in the same way as if it were a court judgment. Can an expert's decision be enforced as an arbitration award? There is no direct authority on this point, although the differences between arbitration and expert determination would be sufficient to ensure that enforcement of experts' decisions under the section would not be permitted. At first sight *A Cameron Ltd v. John Mowlem & Co. plc*[2] provides guidance, but the case was decided on rather different grounds. The Court of Appeal considered whether an adjudicator's decision in a construction contract[3] was enforceable as an arbitration award and decided that it was not, but their judgment was based on the interim nature of the adjudicator's decision pending arbitration to which the decision would be subject, and not on any of the usual characteristics of experts' decisions: the interim nature of adjudicators' decisions is itself untypical of experts' decisions. The absence of straightforward systems for international enforcement of experts' decisions weakens their effectiveness in international disputes, although some solutions can be found.[4]

Insolvency

14.2.4 The threat of insolvency can be used to enforce experts' decisions without court proceedings as a necessary preliminary.[5]

Leases

14.2.5 Leases contain their own procedures for defaulting tenants who do not pay the increased rental determined by an expert.

14.3 COURT ACTION

Summary judgment

14.3.1 Unless the threat of insolvency can be used successfully,[6] court action will be necessary. Refusal by a party to comply with the decision is a breach of contract so the claimant should plead the

---

[1] Arbitration Act 1996, s. 66.
[2] (1990) 52 B.L.R. 24.
[3] See 7.5.
[4] See 14.7.
[5] See 14.5.
[6] *Ibid.*

contractual background, the determination by the expert and the default. The claimant will probably wish to seek summary judgment,[7] *i.e.* a decision made at an early stage in the action without a full trial attended by witnesses giving oral evidence. The court action of course gives the defendant the opportunity to challenge the decision of the expert. Chapter 15 sets out the grounds on which challenge is allowed. If the claimant succeeds the court gives judgment for the claimant with costs. This is a final judgment but is subject to the defendant's right to appeal. If the defendant succeeds the court may make various orders, including allowing the defendant to defend the claim. This means that the claimant's next opportunity to obtain judgment against the defendant is unlikely to arise before the end of a full trial. An order allowing the defendant to continue to defend the action may have conditions attached to it, such as the defendant paying into court part, or all, of the amount claimed.

Mandatory injunction

One form of expert determination, an adjudicator's decision,[8] has been enforced by mandatory injunction.[9] An injunction is appropriate to enforce an adjudicator's decision because of the commercial importance of proceeding with construction works without a deadlock between the parties. Similar considerations might make it appropriate to enforce other types of expert decisions by this remedy.

14.3.2

EFFECT OF ARBITRATION CLAUSE

14.4

Contracts which include an expert clause often use arbitration as the final system of review. Under section 9 of the Arbitration Act 1996, court proceedings are stayed as a breach of the arbitration clause. Thus in a contract containing an applicable arbitration clause, an action brought to enforce an expert's decision must be stayed and an arbitration award obtained before enforcement by the court.[10] A solution would be to exclude from the ambit of the arbitration clause all matters relating to the enforcement of experts' decisions. An injunction enforcing the decision of the adjudicator may be granted despite the presence in the contract of an arbitration clause.[11]

---

[7] CPR part 24.
[8] See 7.5.
[9] *Drake & Scull v. McLaughlin & Harvey* (1992) 60 B.L.R. 102.
[10] In *Macob Civil Engineering Ltd v. Morrison Construction Ltd* [1999] B.L.R. 93 at 99, the court held, on the facts, that the decision of the adjudicator should be enforced by the court despite the presence of an arbitration clause.
[11] *Drake & Scull Engineering Ltd v. McLaughlin & Harvey plc* (1992) 60 B.L.R. 102.

14 : ENFORCING THE DECISION

14.5 INSOLVENCY

Demands

14.5.1 If the party obliged to make a payment as the result of an expert's decision does not do so the defaulting party may, if an individual, be served with a statutory demand[12] or, if the defaulting party is a company, it may be served with a written demand.[13] The effect of both these procedures is that the defaulting party has 21 days in which to make the payment following which the party making the demand can present a bankruptcy petition against an individual or a winding-up petition against a company.

An effective means of enforcement

14.5.2 If there is a defence to liability for the amount determined, the demand will be set aside and the party seeking the bankruptcy or winding-up order may be ordered to pay the costs of the insolvency proceedings. If there is no defence, however, this may be a very effective means of enforcement.

14.6 SET-OFF

Enforcement without court action

14.6.1 If the potential claimant has other dealings with the potential defendant, these may offer the opportunity to exercise rights of set-off. In other words, the potential claimant may withhold payment of money which is due to the potential defendant as an alternative way of obtaining the benefit of the expert's decision. This may provide a means of enforcement without immediate court action.

Court action may result

14.6.2 This kind of self-help may provoke an action from the other party to recover the payment that has been withheld or, if the other party is a defendant in proceedings with the same claimant, withholding the payment may provoke a counterclaim.

14.7 ENFORCEMENT ABROAD

Reciprocal enforcement of judgments and arbitration awards

14.7.1 Court judgments and arbitration awards may be enforced in countries other than England under various treaties. For court judgments there are for the European Community the Brussels and

---

[12] Insolvency Act 1986, s. 268.
[13] *ibid.*, s. 123.

the Lugano Conventions[14] and reciprocal enforcement treaties with various other countries.[15] Arbitration awards are enforced under the 1958 New York Convention.[16]

No such machinery for experts' decisions

14.7.2 Careful thought should be given before using expert determination in international contracts, because decisions by experts cannot be enforced abroad in this way: they are not judgments or arbitration awards.[17] There are two possible solutions to this problem. The first is to turn the expert's decision into a judgment, and the second is to use the framework of an arbitration.

Court judgment

14.7.3 Under the first route, it will be necessary either to take court action in England to turn the decision into a judgment which may then be enforced abroad through a treaty, or to take court action in the country where enforcement is desired. It may be an advantage for the expert's decision to be accompanied by reasons, because the foreign court is likely to be more sympathetic to enforcing it in that form.

Arbitration framework

14.7.4 The second route is as follows. The issue for expert determination is referred, by agreement, to arbitration and a tribunal appointed. Next the parties agree to stay the arbitration pending expert determination, and the expert determination takes place. Then the arbitration is revived solely for the purpose of turning the decision in the expert determination into a final arbitration award, by consent, and the arbitration is brought to an end.[18] Drafting will be needed to provide for this arbitration framework in the dispute

---

[14] Made part of English law by the Civil Jurisdiction and Judgments Acts of 1982 and 1991 respectively.
[15] Under the Administration of Justice Act 1920 and the Foreign Judgments (Reciprocal Enforcement) Act 1933.
[16] Originally incorporated into English law by the Arbitration Act 1975, now repealed and re-enacted in Arbitration Act 1996, Part III.
[17] The Italian *arbitrato irrituale* is a form of expert determination: see John Kendall, "Expert Determination: a European and American Survey" (1994) International Business Lawyer Vol. 22, p. 458. The Italian Supreme Court held that an *arbitrato irrituale* was enforceable under the New York Convention in 1978: a German court (in Hamburg) refused enforcement of an *arbitrato irrituale* under the New York Convention in 1979: see Albert Jahn van den Berg "The New York Arbitration Convention of 1958" 1981 Kluwer, art. 1–1.7.
[18] This process has not been tested yet. It is an adaptation of the ingenious and practical suggestion, for mediation, of Christopher Newmark and Richard Hill, *Can a Mediated Settlement Become an Enforceable Arbitration Award?* in (2000) Arbitration International, Vol. 16, No. 1, at pp. 81–7.

clause, to prevent a party taking advantage of the enforcement issue: perhaps a safeguard would be that, if there were any difficulty, the dispute would be referred to arbitration and the expert determination provisions would fall away. It is insufficient simply for the contract to provide that the expert's decision is to be treated for all purposes as an arbitration award, as that would not make the decision qualify as an arbitral award under article 1.2 of the New York Convention.

14.8 LIMITATION

General six-year period

14.8.1 The time limit for enforcing an expert's decision is the same as that for enforcing other contracts: six years if the contract to refer to the expert is under hand, 12 years in the very much less common case of its being under seal.[19] Time runs from the date of the breach, which is usually the date of non-compliance with the decision.[20] An expert's decision is probably not an "award" for the purpose of section 7 of the Limitation Act 1980, as an "award" is the word used to refer to a decision by an arbitrator as opposed to a decision by an expert.[21]

Limitation period not stopped by a reference to expert determination

14.8.2 Starting an expert determination does not stop the original limitation period running.[22] Thus, if a dispute under a contract is referred to expert determination rather than arbitration or litigation, claims may become barred by limitation regardless of what happens in the expert determination. The solution is an agreement that time does not run pending the expert determination.

---

[19] Limitation Act 1980, ss. 5 and 8.
[20] Compare the arbitration case *Agroment Motoimport Ltd v. Marlden Engineering Co. (Beds) Ltd* [1985] 1 W.L.R. 762.
[21] See 14.2.3.
[22] See 13.2.

CHAPTER 15

CHALLENGING THE DECISION

Summary 15.1

This chapter looks at the limited right of challenge to the validity of an expert's decision, and explains:

(a) the types of proceedings in which parties may challenge the decision of the expert (15.2);
(b) the grounds for challenge (15.3);
(c) fraud, collusion and partiality (15.4);
(d) lack of independence (15.5);
(e) unfairness in the procedure (15.6);
(f) due process (15.7);
(g) unfairness in the decision itself (15.8);
(h) other grounds of challenge (15.9);
(i) mistake: earlier history (15.10);
(j) mistake: more recent developments (15.11);
(k) mistake: the current position (15.12);
(l) speaking and non-speaking decisions (15.13);
(m) interpretation of words in the agreement (15.14);
(n) points of law (15.15);
(o) various other matters where decisions are challenged (15.16–15.19); and
(p) the prospects for challenges in the future (15.20).

Court proceedings 15.2

Court proceedings used for challenging decisions

Challenges to decisions are made in court proceedings between the parties such as the following: 15.2.1

(a) An application for an injunction which, as well as being a court order stopping the reference, can also be used to stop further performance of the contract following the decision.
(b) An application for an order for specific performance which is a court order that the decision be put into effect, *e.g.* a sale of property at an expert's valuation.

15 : CHALLENGING THE DECISION

(c) Defence to court proceedings, typically an application for summary judgment, brought to enforce the decision.
(d) An application to strike out either side's claim.[1]
(e) An application to the court for a ruling on an allegedly ambiguous document.[2]
(f) A petition under Companies Act 1985, s. 459.[3]

An application for a declaration can accompany any of the above.

Bringing a claim against the expert

15.2.2   Bringing a claim against the expert by suing for negligence, where it is the expert, rather than the decision, which is being challenged, is dealt with in Chapter 16. An attempt to join the expert in challenge proceedings as a co-defendant with the other party to the determination was disapproved in *Campbell v. Edwards*.[4] There were two possible outcomes to the challenge to the decision. Investigations might show that the expert had not been negligent, in which case the action against the expert would fail; alternatively, investigations might show that the expert had been negligent, in which case it would be possible to set the determination aside, and the claimant would have suffered no loss. That was in 1975 when it was easier to set aside a determination. Since the early 1990s setting aside a determination has become much more difficult and a claimant does not succeed simply by showing that the expert was negligent.[5] There has to have been a material departure from instructions. On this basis there is no reason why joinder should not now be allowed in an appropriate case. However the most likely course is for a party dissatisfied with a determination to consider challenging it first, and then proceeding to sue the expert in the light of either:

(a) the unavailability of that remedy; or
(b) the unsuccessful result in an action challenging the award; or
(c) a successful result in that action if loss has still been suffered.

If it is expected that a claim may be made against the expert, it is prudent to keep the expert informed as to the course being followed.

Limitation

15.2.3   An action to challenge a decision must, generally, be brought within six years of the decision where the contract to refer issues to the

---

[1] CPR 3.4.
[2] See Chapter 12.
[3] See 3.7.
[4] [1976] 1 W.L.R. 403 at 409.
[5] See 15.12.6.

expert is under hand and 12 years in the less common case of its being under seal.[6] Time runs from the date of the breach, probably no later than the date of the publication of the decision. Where the decision has been obtained by fraud the limitation period may be extended.[7]

Delay and acquiescence

Delay in bringing an action may prejudice a challenge because it is evidence of acquiescence.[8] This may disentitle the claimant to obtain equitable remedies such as specific performance or an injunction, and it may in certain circumstances prevent the claimant from obtaining relief on the ground of estoppel.[9]

15.2.4

GROUNDS FOR CHALLENGE **15.3**

Fraud (or dishonesty) and partiality have always been valid reasons for refusing to uphold an expert's decision[10]: they are discussed in 15.4. Much more controversy has however been generated by the question of whether a mistake qualifies as a reason, and, more particularly, how serious the mistake has to be. The court approaches the question by looking at the wording of the contract and whether the expert has materially departed from the parties' instructions in carrying out the determination. The court's decision is reached by reference to the terms of the contract between the parties and the presumed intentions of the parties, rather than by reference to any general principle of law that mistaken decisions by experts can be over-turned by the courts. This is discussed in 15.10 to 15.17. Similarly, to the extent that there is a requirement that the expert should act fairly in the decision-making process, this is decided by reference to the contracts between the parties rather than by reference to any objective standard of fairness. This is discussed at 15.5 to 15.8.

FRAUD, COLLUSION AND PARTIALITY **15.4**

Fraud unravels everything

A number of the cases where the courts have held that parties are bound by the decision of the expert contain general statements to

15.4.1

---

[6] Limitation Act 1980, ss. 5 and 8. An expert's decision is probably not an award within section 7 of the Limitation Act 1980. See 14.2.3.and 14.8.1.
[7] Limitation Act 1980, s. 32.
[8] As it did in *Parrott v. Shellard* (1868) 16 W.R. 928: the claimant had signed a receipt for the amount decided on, adding the words "under protest", and then brought proceedings nine months later.
[9] See for example *Habib Bank Ltd v. Habib Bank AG Zurich* [1981] 1 W.L.R. 1265 at 1283–4.
[10] *Arenson v. Casson Beckman Rutley & Co.* [1977] AC 405 at 442, *Campbell v. Edwards* [1976] 1 W.L.R. 403 at 407, CA.

the effect that the decision would not be binding in the event of fraud or collusion. An example is *Campbell v. Edwards*,[11] where Lord Denning M.R. said: "If there were fraud or collusion, of course, it would be very different. Fraud or collusion unravels everything."

Construction contract certification cases

15.4.2 Most of the cases which deal with collusion, improper attempts to influence the expert and partiality are construction contract certification cases, and usually the issue has been whether the contractor can recover without the necessary certificate from the architect or engineer.[12] However the same legal principles are applied to cases where the contractor has sought to overturn a certificate which is alleged to be unduly favourable to the building-owner. The leading case is *Hickman v. Roberts*,[13] where it was held that the building-owner could not rely on the absence of a certificate where the architect had allowed himself to be influenced by the building-owner in a manner which was inconsistent with his position as certifier.[14] A certificate was held to be ineffective[15] where the court found that, although there had been no improper attempt to influence the engineer, he had appeared to assume the role of adversary more than that of a professional man holding the scales. Where the expert must act independently (which is almost invariably the case), there is an implied term that the parties will not seek to interfere with the expert's independence.[16]

Macro v. Thompson

15.4.3 There is always a risk of allegations of improper interference or partiality where meetings take place between the expert and one only of the parties. In *Macro v. Thompson (No. 3)*[17] an auditor who had been appointed to value the shares of two companies under the articles of association had a series of dealings with the solicitor to the principal shareholder. The solicitor had recently been conducting hostile litigation on behalf of that shareholder about the value of the shares. During the valuation, a meeting took place between the solicitor and the auditor. The auditor disclosed his rough working figures to the solicitor. The solicitor told the auditor that the figures were adrift, and the auditor responded by throwing away his notes. At that meeting, the solicitor had a copy of a judgment in an earlier

---

[11] [1976] 1 W.L.R. 403 at 407.
[12] See 7.4.4.
[13] [1913] A.C. 229, HL.
[14] See also the other cases cited in *Hudson's Building and Engineering Contracts* 11th edition, Sweet & Maxwell, 1995, Vol. 1, paras 6–106 to 6–145.
[15] *Canterbury Pipelines Ltd v. Christchurch Drainage Board* [1979] 2 N.Z.L.R. 347.
[16] *Minster Trust Ltd v. Traps Tractors Ltd* [1954] 1 W.L.R. 963 at 973–5.
[17] [1997] 2 B.C.L.C. 36.

stage of the dispute[18] in front of him, but maintained his position that the auditor should not see it. The auditor did then see a copy of the judgment, and sought legal advice from the solicitor, but the meeting did not result in any advice being given: the auditor said he wished he hadn't seen the judgment, and the solicitor called him a "bloody fool". At an earlier stage the auditor wrote letters about the valuation from the office of the company, where he was spending a lot of time in connection with the audits, under the letterhead of the company.

Robert Walker J. found the dealings extremely imprudent, and described the entire episode as a classic example of how not to conduct an articles valuation of shares in a private company. However, he found that the auditor had not yielded sufficiently to the solicitor's influence for the valuation to be invalidated on the ground of partiality. The court reached this conclusion on the balance of probability, and also bearing in mind the seriousness of a finding of partiality against a professional man, even if the finding went to liability between third parties and did not result in any liability being imposed on the professional himself.[19]

Robert Walker J. considered the test for partiality in this type of case[20]:

"... when the court is considering a decision reached by an expert valuer who is not an arbitrator performing a quasi-judicial function, it is actual partiality, rather than the appearance of partiality, that is the crucial test. Otherwise auditors (like architects and actuaries) with a long-standing relationship with one of the parties (or persons associated with one party) to a contract might be unduly inhibited, in continuing to discharge their professional duty to their client, by too high an insistence on avoiding even an impression of partiality."

The test for partiality

Thus partiality in this context generally requires actual bias or a real danger of injustice resulting from the alleged bias and not just conflicts of interest or apparent lack of independence. However in other circumstances the appearance of partiality, from an objective standpoint, can be enough to disqualify.[21] In another case the expert attended a meeting with one of the parties and tactics for dealing with the other party were discussed. The court said that the

15.4.4

---

[18] *Re Macro (Ipswich) Ltd* [1994] 2 B.C.L.C. 354.
[19] This arose because the claimants agreed that their claim against the auditor should be dismissed.
[20] *Macro v. Thompson (No. 3)* [1997] 2 B.C.L.C. 36 at 65G.
[21] *R. v. Gough* [1993] A.C. 646, *R. v. Bow Street Magistrate, ex parte Pinochet (No. 2)* [2000] 1 A.C. 119 (HL), *Locabail (UK) Ltd v. Bayfield Properties Ltd* [2000] 2 W.L.R. 870 (CA), *A T & T Corporation v. Saudi Cable Co.* [2000] 2 Lloyd's Rep. 127 (CA), (a case concerning alleged bias on the part of an arbitrator).

15 : CHALLENGING THE DECISION

expert should have remained aloof from the discussions but did not invalidate the decision on the grounds of partiality.[22]

In a construction adjudication case, the adjudicator decided to shut out further comments from a party in the belief that any further comments, particularly from the other party, would not affect the view the adjudicator had taken as to that party's position. The adjudicator had attempted to act in an impartial manner and had shown no conscious bias or hostility, but the court found that the statutory requirement to act impartially required the adjudicator to act in a way that did not lead to a perception of partiality by one party which might objectively be held by that party. Matters became worse when the adjudicator subsequently gave a witness statement in support of the other party's case. The enforcement proceedings were dismissed.[23]

Fraud claims rare

15.4.5 Cases where fraud has been alleged are rare. Deceptive conduct was alleged in an Australian case arising from a dispute in connection with a joint venture for exploiting gas reserves. The contract provided that the participations should be determined by one of the parties to the contract. That party made changes to the input data on which the decision was to be based without the other party's knowledge. The court held the determination to be invalid, and that there had been a breach of fiduciary obligation, but the judgment was based on the breach of contract in altering the input data.[24]

15.5 LACK OF INDEPENDENCE

Conflict of interest not determinative

15.5.1 A distinction must be drawn between being independent on the one hand, and reaching an independent decision on the other hand. The fact that the proposed expert has a conflict of interest does not usually provide grounds for objection,[25] nor grounds for challenge if that expert is in fact appointed. Whilst it is not an essential requirement that an expert should be independent, an expert entrusted with the duty of issuing certificates under contractual arrangements between two other parties is nevertheless under a duty to act fairly and impartially, as explained in 15.4.

---

[22] *Midland Montagu Leasing (UK) Ltd v. Tyne & Wear Passenger Transport Executive and Ernst & Whinney*, unreported, Chancery Division, February 23, 1990.
[23] *Woods Hardwick Ltd v. Chiltern Air Conditioning*, October 2, 2000, unreported, H.H. Judge Thornton Q.C., TCC.
[24] *Crusader Resources NL v. Santos Ltd* (1991) 58 S.A.S.R. 74.
[25] 10.7.

In cases where there is a conflict of interest, there is generally a greater willingness on the part of the court to find that the decision is invalid.[26-28]

Two cases about leases

Thus the court may hold that as a matter of construction the expert clause did require the appointment of an expert not closely associated with one of the parties. The court intervened on construction grounds in two cases about service charges under leases: in both cases the expert clause appointed the landlord's agent as the expert to determine the amount of the service charge. In the first case[29] the landlord's agents turned out to be wholly owned by the landlord. It was held that the lease contemplated the appointment of someone other than the landlord, and that agents wholly owned by the landlord did not qualify. In the second case[30] the court disallowed service charges certified by the landlord's usual managing agents because the clause referred to decision by the landlord's surveyor "in case of difference". The words "in case of difference" were held to import an "essentially . . . arbitral" function and an "impartial . . . holding of the balance between landlord and tenant", something the landlord's managing agents could not do, and therefore the landlord ought to have appointed another firm of surveyors to resolve the dispute.

15.5.2

Is the interest known to the parties at the time of appointment?

A decision may also be invalid if the expert had a conflict of interest which was unknown to one of the parties at the time of appointment.[31] This was the result in a construction contract certification case, where the contractor was unaware that the architect had given an assurance to the building-owner that the price would under no circumstances exceed a certain amount.[32]

15.5.3

Auditors

An auditor's lack of independence has been relied on as one of the reasons for refusing an application to strike out a winding-up petition on the unfair prejudice ground (section 459 of the Companies Act 1985).[33] The evidence of the lack of independence was the

15.5.4

[26-28] See 18.3.7.
[29] *Finchbourne Ltd v. Rodrigues* [1976] 3 All E.R. 581.
[30] *Concorde Graphics Ltd v. Andromeda Investments SA* [1983] 1 E.G.L.R. 53.
[31] *Kemp v. Rose* (1858) 1 Giff. 258, *Kimberley v. Dick* (1871) L.R. 13 Eq. 1, *Ludlam v. Wilson* [1901] 2 Ont. L.R. 549 (Canada); see *Hudson's Building and Engineering Contracts* 11th edition, Sweet & Maxwell, 1995, Vol. 1, paras 6–099 to 6–105 and 6–140 for summaries of cases on this point.
[32] *Kemp v. Rose, Kimberley v. Dick* (above).
[33] *Re Boswell & Co. (Steels) Ltd* (1989) 5 B.C.C. 145: and see 3.7.

auditor's involvement in certain transactions to which the company had been a party. Having failed to obtain details of these transactions, the petitioner proceeded to petition to be bought out of the company. The concern for independence shown by the court arose in circumstances in which the court has a discretion to exercise statutory powers and may not apply in cases where the court does not have those powers.

15.6 UNFAIRNESS IN THE PROCEDURE

No general standard

15.6.1 Questions are raised about the fairness of procedures adopted by experts. No one would argue with the general proposition that experts' procedures should be fair. Difficulties arise over how to assess whether a particular procedure followed by an expert is fair, and specifically whether the rule of natural justice requiring "due process"[34] applies to expert determinations. Do the procedures have to allow each side to have its say, and to know what the other side is saying, at all stages? The answer is that there are cases which refer to experts being under a duty to act fairly,[35] but there is no general requirement that the rules of natural justice must always be followed,[36] and there is no objective standard of fairness which must be complied with in all expert determinations. In each case the terms of the contract must be considered in order to decide whether, in the circumstances which have occurred, the decision of the expert is a decision made in accordance with the terms of the contract.

Expert communicating with one party only

15.6.2 Communications between the expert and one of the parties, when the other party is unaware that the communications have taken place, commonly give rise to suspicion. Some communications with one party alone may be unavoidable and are frequently innocuous, but where that is not the case the court may hold that the decision cannot stand. Each case must be decided by reference to the seriousness of what took place in the circumstances in which it occurred. Two cases involving accountants, where the experts' decisions were held to be

---

[34] There are two rules of natural justice. Here the issue is not the first rule, the rule against bias, but the second rule which requires that each party must be heard, be informed of the case against it and given an opportunity to answer it, and that there can be no private communications between one party and the tribunal.

[35] *Sutcliffe v. Thackrah* [1974] A.C. 727 at 737, *Macro v. Thompson (No. 3)* [1997] 2 B.C.L.C. 36 at 64 *et seq.*, *John Barker Construction Ltd v. London Portman Hotel Ltd* (1996) 83 B.L.R. 31.

[36] *Hounslow LBC v. Twickenham Garden Developments Ltd* [1971] Ch. 233, at 269–70; see also the adjudication decisions referred to in 7.5.5.

valid, have already been discussed.[37] A case where the decision was held to be invalid is an Australian case[38] in which the experts made their decision on the basis of a much larger claim which had not been disclosed to the other party. The experts were accountants appointed to assess damages. They were held to have acted outside the terms of the agreement by considering the undisclosed claim. Their terms of reference were contained in a letter written on behalf of both parties: there was no explicit reference to fairness in those terms. The accountants' error lay in receiving and acting upon a further claim which had not been in their terms of reference and had not been notified to the other party. That further claim increased the figure from A$ 50,000 to A$ 212,796. The accountants' contract with the parties was to assess damages claimed in the terms of reference. They broke that contract by taking the later (and much larger) claim into account. The court found that the accountants' determination on the larger amount was not within the terms of the agreement, and remitted that part of the decision to a judge in chambers for consideration of liability on grounds other than the determination.

Should each side be given equal opportunity to present its case?

15.6.3

There are dicta to the effect that the certifier under a construction contract should give both parties an equal opportunity to explain its case.[39] In a New Zealand case, the Court of Appeal decided that communication between the certifier and the employer is not of itself a ground for quashing the certificate, and that something further must have transpired in the course of the discussions which would make it necessary, as a matter of "common justice", that the other party to the contract should be given the opportunity of answering the contentions.[40] However it is doubtful whether a failure by an expert to follow this course would always be sufficient to invalidate the decision. The seriousness of the failure in the particular circumstances is likely to be the determining factor.[41]

---

[37] *Macro v. Thompson (No. 3), Midland Montagu Leasing (UK) Ltd v. Tyne & Wear Passenger Transport Executive and Ernst & Whinney*: see 15.6 .

[38] *Capricorn Inks Pty Ltd v. Lawter International (Australasia) Pty Ltd* [1989] 1 Qd R. 8.

[39] Channell J. in *Page v. Llandaff and Dinas Powis RDC* (1901) H.B.C. (4th edition) Vol. 2, paragraph 316 at 320, quoted in *Hudson's Building and Engineering Contracts*, 11th edition, Sweet & Maxwell, (1995), paragraph 6–222 (see also 6–119 and 6–121).

[40] *Nelson Carlton Construction Company v. A.C. Hatrick (NZ) Ltd* [1965] N.Z.L.R. 144, cited in the Australian case of *John Holland Construction and Engineering Ltd v. Majorca Products* (1996) 16 Const. L.J. 114 at 128.

[41] Compare the cases cited in 15.6.2.

Adjudication

15.6.4 Similar problems arise in adjudications under the Housing, Grants, Construction and Regeneration Act 1996, where the law is still evolving. The position in relation to adjudications appears to be that there is no inflexible rule that a decision will not be enforced if there had been a failure to comply with rules of natural justice, specifically, the rule requiring due process, but where there has been a failure to comply the court may decide not to enforce the adjudicator's decision.[42] The court has declined to enforce the adjudicator's decision in two cases where there were undisclosed communications.[43]

Taking account of submissions

15.6.5 There is little scope for a complaint that an expert failed to take sufficient account of representations made to him or her. There is more scope for robustness in dealing with awkward parties than in arbitration,[44] and an expert should also be permitted to curtail parties having their say. Precisely how to deal with an awkward party and when to curtail submissions has to be judged according to the circumstances of each case.

15.7 DUE PROCESS—EXPRESS OR IMPLIED

Commentators have asked[45] what the effect would be if the parties required their expert to observe due process. This could be done, for instance, by the incorporation of codes of conduct. Commentators have argued that there is no reason why parties should not expect fair procedures to be followed and that the public law decision *Ridge v. Baldwin*[46] requires any person making a decision affecting individuals to follow due process. But the dismissal of a chief constable is very different from a company's claim for damages. Denning L.J. stated[47] that a domestic tribunal must observe those principles. However that was in the context of the right of an individual member of a trade union to be given a reasonable opportunity to meet a charge, amounting to an attempt to expel the member from the union.

---

[42] See 7.5.5.
[43] *Discain Project Services Ltd and Opecprime Development Ltd* [2000] B.L.R. 402, H.H. Judge Bowsher Q.C., TCC, and *Woods Hardwick Ltd v. Chiltern Air Conditioning*, October 2, 2000, unreported, H.H. Judge Thornton Q.C., TCC: see 15.4.4.
[44] See 13.6.7.
[45] Burke and Chinkin in [1989] I.C.L.R. 401.
[46] [1964] A.C. 40.
[47] In *Lee v. Showmen's Guild of Great Britain* [1952] 2 Q.B. 329 at 342.

There is more recent authority to the effect that a disciplinary tribunal of the governing body of a sport is obliged to conduct its proceedings fairly.[48] Other cases also refer to a duty to act fairly,[49] but fairness does not necessarily bring with it the whole doctrine of due process. There is no machinery[50] for the setting aside of experts' decisions for failing to observe due process as there is with arbitration awards; and expert determinations, as decisions made under private contracts, are not susceptible to judicial review[51] for failing to comply with due process.[52] The published guides for surveyors and chemical engineers have withdrawn the advice they both previously gave to experts to comply with the rules of natural justice.[53] This is an important feature in distinguishing expert determination from arbitration, statutory adjudication of construction disputes, and judicial review.[54] It is doubtful whether the Human Rights Act 1998 has any application to expert determination, except in cases where parties are obliged by the State to curtail their rights to a "fair" hearing[55] by submitting their disputes to expert determination.[56]

UNFAIRNESS IN THE DECISION ITSELF 15.8

Unfair decision likely to be binding

The cases referred to above have been concerned with unfairness in the decision-making process, as opposed to allegations that the decision itself is a wrong decision and therefore unfair. In most cases the answer would be that the parties must abide by the decision of their chosen decision-maker even if it is wrong.[57] But the 15.8.1

---

[48] *R. v. Disciplinary Committee of the Jockey Club, ex parte Aga Khan* [1993] 1 W.L.R. 909, *obiter*, and therefore not part of the Court of Appeal's decision in that case, by Hoffmann L.J. at 953, *Wilander and Novacek v. Tomin and Jude* [1997] 2 Lloyd's Rep. 293 at 300, Lord Woolf M.R.
[49] See 15.6.
[50] For arbitration awards it is provided by Arbitration Act 1996, s. 68.
[51] Under RSC, Ord. 53.
[52] *Jockey Club* case cited above.
[53] *Guidance Notes for Surveyors acting as Arbitrators or as Independent Experts in Commercial Property Rent Reviews*, RICS Books, used to say that the expert should "observe at least the most fundamental of the rules of natural justice and of evidence", but the 7th edition dropped this assertion. A similar change has been made between the first and the second editions of *Expert Procedures*, published by the Institution of Chemical Engineers.
[54] Arbitration 17.7: statutory adjudication of construction disputes 7.5.5: judicial review 18.8.
[55] Human Rights Act 1998, Schedule 1, Article 6.
[56] See 1.1.5; see also 7.5.5 in relation to construction adjudication under the Housing Grants, Construction and Regeneration Act 1996.
[57] See 15.12.

courts are more willing to hold the decision of an expert to be invalid on the ground of unfairness if the expert is the agent of one of the parties and the contract provides no machinery for review of the decision.

A "fundamentally flawed" decision

15.8.2   A construction contract certification case illustrates how the court may approach a case where the contract provides no machinery for review of an unsatisfactory decision by one party's agent.[58] An architect's determination of an extension of time was held to be invalid on the ground that it was not a fair determination and was not based on a proper application of the provisions of the contract. This was an unusual case, as the parties had deleted from the contract the standard clause which provides for review of the architect's decision by arbitration.[59] The finding that the decision was not based on a proper application of the provisions of the contract may be regarded as a finding that the expert departed from instructions in a material respect.[60] However the judgment was also based on the finding that the decision was an unfair determination, being "fundamentally flawed in a number of respects".[61] This is harder to reconcile with other authorities, which were not referred to in the judgment,[62] but can be explained by reference to the judge's interpretation of the requirements of the contract, given the unusual facts. If the parties had intended that the grounds of challenge were intended to be so limited as to exclude challenge in the case of "an aberrant, uninformed or unfair decision" (provided that there was no fraud or patent excess of powers) he would have expected the contract to say so. As it did not say so, the judge found that it was an implied requirement of a valid decision that the expert should act lawfully and fairly.[63] The judgment is not easy to reconcile with the general principle that an expert's decision cannot be challenged on the ground that the expert has answered the right question in the wrong way.[64] Its applicability is probably limited to cases where the parties have failed to make express provision for review of a decision made by a certifier who is the agent of one of the parties.[65]

---

[58] *John Barker Construction Ltd v. London Portman Hotel Ltd* (1996) 83 B.L.R. 31.
[59] The case predates the decision of the House of Lords in *Beaufort Developments (NI) Ltd v. Gilbert-Ash NI Ltd* [1999] A.C. 266—see 18.3.7.
[60] See 15.12.6 .
[61] At pp. 61–62.
[62] *Jones v. Sherwood Computer Services plc* [1992] 1 W.L.R. 277, *Nikko Hotels (UK) Ltd v. MEPC plc* [1991] 2 E.G.L.R. 103.
[63] At p. 45.
[64] See 15.12.9.
[65] See also *Balfour Beatty Civil Engineering Ltd v. Docklands Light Railway Ltd* (1996) 78 B.L.R. 42, where the decision of an employee of one of the parties

Grounds of challenge other than fraud, partiality, unfairness and mistake 15.9

No agreement or no decision

The determination may be invalid because the formal steps required in order to appoint the expert have not been properly completed.[66] The courts also refuse to enforce a decision which is unclear[67] or inconclusive.[68] 15.9.1

Revocation of expert's authority

One party to the reference cannot challenge the decision by claiming to have revoked the authority of the expert.[69] There are statutory limitations on the revocability of the authority of an arbitrator.[70] 15.9.2

Death of party

The death of one of the parties to an agreement which provided for a valuation to be made was held, on the construction of that agreement, to have brought it to an end, even though the valuation had taken place and there remained only to write the award.[71] Statute enacted the contrary for arbitration[72] and the case would probably not be followed today. 15.9.3

Illegality

The court does not enforce a decision made in relation to an agreement which has an illegal purpose.[73] 15.9.4

Expert appointed who cannot act

The court sets aside a decision if it was taken by someone who was not or could not be appointed as the expert. In *Jones (M) v. Jones (R R)*[74] an agreed court order said that the liquidator of a company 15.9.5

> was unreviewable, and it was conceded that his decisions could be impeached on the ground of legal mis-direction, dishonesty, unfairness or unreasonableness; see 18.3.7.

[66] See 11.4.
[67] *Hopcraft v. Hickman* (1824) 2 Sim. & St. 130.
[68] See 15.13.6.
[69] *Mills v. Bayley* (1863) 2 H. & C. 36 at 41; *Thomson v. Anderson* (1870) L. R. 9 Eq 523 at 532.
[70] Arbitration Act 1996, s. 23.
[71] *Blundell v. Brettargh* (1810) 17 Ves. 232.
[72] Arbitration 1996, s. 8.
[73] *Parken v. Whitby* (1823) Turn. & R. 367 where the effect of the agreement would have been to evade the gaming laws; see also *Rourke v. Short* (1856) 5 E. & B. 904.
[74] [1971] 1 W.L.R. 840.

was to appoint any expert he might select to value the company's machinery. The liquidator appointed himself to value the machinery and the court gave a declaration that this was contrary to the agreement and therefore of no effect.

Determination made by someone other than the expert

15.9.6 The appointed expert must carry out the determination personally, and not delegate it to an employee or third party, unless the parties agree.[75] Where an auditor, appointed to value shares under articles of association, was inexperienced in the complex speciality of share valuation and acted on the advice of specialist share valuers in its entirety, it was held that the decision was still the decision of the auditor and that there had not been unauthorised delegation.[76]

Jurisdiction arguments

15.9.7 Opportunities for challenge based on arguments about jurisdiction can survive a reference and prevent an expert's decision being enforced. A reference may be controversial from the start with allegations that the question referred for decision is outside the terms of the expert clause. A reference which is outside the scope of the expert's jurisdiction stays outside the expert's jurisdiction, and the issue is unaffected by the expert having purported to make a decision about it.[77] However if the scope of the task which the expert intends to perform is clear from the outset, a party which fails to raise the point at that time may be unable to do so later.[78]

Have conditions precedent been complied with?

15.9.8 There may be scope for similar challenges to an expert's decision arising from other aspects of the contract between the parties: for instance, the conditions precedent to the right to refer a dispute to expert determination may not have been met, in which case the entire reference is premature.[79]

Has the contract been varied?

15.9.9 Serious difficulties can arise when a contract is amended or varied without proper consideration of the effect of the variation on the

---

[75] *Ess v. Truscott* (1837) 2 M. & W. 385, *Kollerich & Cie S.A. v. The State Trading Corporation of India* [1980] 2 Lloyd's Rep. 32, CA (see 11.4.3). See also the cases on certificates in *Keating on Building Contracts*, 7th edition, Sweet & Maxwell, 2001, at paras 5–35 to 5–36.
[76] See Chapter 12. *Macro v. Thompson (No. 3)* [1997] 2 B.C.L.C. 36 at 66
[77] See 12.7.3.
[78] See 12.2.4.
[79] See 9.2.9.

expert clause.[80] For instance, a contract may be amended by postponing the time for performance by one of the parties. If the expert clause had been drafted incorporating the original timings and they are not amended there may be a dispute leading to either the threat of, or the reality of, a court application.

Clerical errors

What is to happen when the expert's decision contains a clerical error or slip? In a building adjudication under the Housing, Grants, Regeneration and Construction Act 1996 the court held that there is an implied term that the adjudicator has the power to correct an error arising from an accidental error or omission, or to clarify or remove any ambiguity in the decision, provided that it is done within a reasonable time and without prejudicing the other party.[81] There is a similar statutory power to correct an arbitration award, within 28 days of the award.[82] It is likely that it would be held that a similar implied term applies in the case of an expert determination.[83] Thus where the expert's reasons as a whole make it plain what the expert intended to decide but the decision contains a clerical error which the expert has acknowledged, there should be no difficulty in enforcing the expert's decision in its corrected form. Where however the expert does not acknowledge the error, it may be held that the mistake cannot be treated as being no more than a clerical error.[84]

15.9.10

---

[80] There was a dispute about whether part of the expert clause had been amended in *Neste Production Ltd v. Shell UK Ltd* [1994] 1 Lloyd's Rep. 447.
[81] *Bloor Construction (UK) Ltd v. Bowmer & Kirkland (London) Ltd* [2000] B.L.R. 764, H.H. Judge Toulmin Q.C., TCC, citing arbitration law authority: Arbitration Act 1996, s. 57(3), *Mutual Shipping Corporation v. Bayshore Shipping Co. Ltd, The Montan,* [1985] 1 W.L.R. 625 and *King v. Thomas McKenna Ltd* [1991] 2 Q.B. 480.
[82] *Bloor Construction (UK) Ltd v. Bowmer & Kirkland (London) Ltd,* unreported, April 5, 2000, H.H. Judge Toulmin Q.C., TCC, citing arbitration law authority: Arbitration Act 1996, s. 57(3), *Mutual Shipping Corporation v. Bayshore Shipping Co. Ltd, The Montan,* [1985] 1 W.L.R. 625 and *King v. Thomas McKenna Ltd* [1991] 2 Q.B. 480.
[83] See also *Gosden v. Funnell* (1899) 15 T.L.R. 547, where vendor and purchaser each appointed valuers and both valuers failed to notice a clerical error which halved the amount of one part of the stock to be valued. The court said that it was not a case in which "by any conscious act of the mind the valuers by an erroneous exercise of judgment came to a wrong conclusion", but was a slip which could and should be corrected. The purchaser failed in his action to recover the excess part of the purchase price.
[84] Compare *Bouygues UK Ltd v. Dahl-Jensen UK Ltd,* [2000] B.L.R. 522, also a building adjudication case; see 15.12.10.

15.10 MISTAKE: EARLIER HISTORY

An old problem

15.10.1 The law of mistake in expert determination involves different considerations from the general law of contract applicable to mistakes between contracting parties.[85] Judgments on mistake in expert determination point to the conflict between the parties' agreement that a decision shall be final and the injustice of enforcing a defective decision. This conflict is apparent from the earliest case reports. In *Belchier v. Reynolds*[86] the court said that differences between valuations of an estate could never be a reason to set the valuation aside and ordered specific performance, but as it was a hard case on the defendants, ordered each party to bear its own costs.

Early attempts at a solution

15.10.2 The nineteenth century judges sought to define mistake (sometimes using the word "miscarriage"). Lord Eldon was credited[87] with the principle that:

> ". . . the court . . . must act on the valuation unless there be proof of some mistake or improper motive . . . as if the valuer has valued something not included or had valued it on a wholly erroneous basis . . ."

The practical difficulties of applying this principle are apparent from Lord Eldon's own judgment in *Emery v. Wase*,[88] where the difference between valuations of £4,000 and £6,000 was said to warrant judicial suspicion that the valuation had not been made with attention to accuracy. The case was decided on another ground altogether, the court's duty to protect the property of married women. *Parken v. Whitby*[89] is sometimes cited for the proposition that the court does not specifically enforce an agreement where it believes that the price settled by valuers is considerably below the true value of the property; but the case was decided on the grounds of illegality. Neither case is an authority on how serious a discrepancy or inaccuracy has to be for a challenge on the ground of mistake to succeed. In *Weekes v. Gallard*[90] the fact that property had been undervalued did not stop the court ordering specific performance of the contract of sale at that low valuation.

---

[85] On which see *Chitty on Contracts*, 28th edition (Sweet & Maxwell 1999), Chapter 5.
[86] (1754) 3 Keny. 87 at 88.
[87] In *Collier v. Mason* (1858) 25 Beav. 200.
[88] (1803) 8 Ves. 506.
[89] (1823) Turn. & R. 367.
[90] (1869) 21 L.T. 655.

Mistake: more recent developments 15.11

Dean v. Prince: examples of mistakes

Modern cases have involved the same issues, and up to 1976 followed a similar approach. In *Dean v. Prince*[91] Lord Evershed M.R. said that the most obvious case of mistake would be if the valuer omitted altogether to take account of some substantial asset or made a serious arithmetical miscalculation in regard to a single but material part of the whole process. In the same case[92] Denning L.J. gave more examples in the following passage and summarised the circumstances in which he thought the court would interfere:

15.11.1

"... if the expert added up the figures wrongly; or took something into account which he ought not to have taken into account, or conversely: or interpreted the agreement wrongly: or proceeded on some erroneous principle. In all these cases the court will interfere. Even if the court cannot point to the actual error, nevertheless, if the figure is so extravagantly large or so inadequately small that the only conclusion is that he must have gone wrong somewhere, then the court will interfere in much the same way as the Court of Appeal will interfere with an award of damages if it is a wholly erroneous estimate. These cases about valuers bear some analogy with cases on domestic tribunals, except of course that there need not be a hearing. On matters of opinion, the courts will not interfere; but for mistake of jurisdiction or of principle, and for mistake of law, including interpretation of documents, and for miscarriage of justice, the courts will interfere: see *Lee v. Showmen's Guild of Great Britain* [1952] 2 Q.B. 329."

Later sections of this chapter show how much of this approach has now been discarded: practically every principle contained in it has been reversed.

Wrong basis of valuation

In *Jones (M) v. Jones (R R)*[93] a company's factory premises and shops were valued on a break-up basis when the contract called for valuation on a going-concern basis. This was held to be a mistake sufficient to overturn the decision.

15.11.2

Commodity certificates

Lord Denning, in the Court of Appeal, found that a certificate about the quality of wheat issued by an inspector appointed by the United

15.11.3

---

[91] [1954] 1 Ch. 409 at 419.
[92] *ibid.,* at 427.
[93] [1971] 1 W.L.R. 840.

15 : Challenging the decision

States Secretary for Agriculture was conclusive even though it had subsequently been shown to be incorrect. He said:

> "... a mistake by a certifier, even when afterwards admitted by him to be a mistake, does not invalidate the certificate. It remains binding between seller and buyer and all down the chain."

The decision was approved by the House of Lords, Lord Diplock describing it as "plainly right".[94]

Campbell v. Edwards

15.11.4 In *Campbell v. Edwards*[95] Lord Denning M.R. seemed to exclude mistake altogether, except in the case of speaking decisions.[96] The case was about a challenge to a surveyor's valuation of the surrender price for a lease. The surveyor was duly appointed by the parties under the lease. The surveyor's price had been £10,000 but the tenant later found two more surveyors who said that the price should be much lower, £3,500 and £1,250 respectively. The Court of Appeal dismissed the tenant's appeal and held that the parties were bound by the honest valuation fixed by the agreed valuer. Lord Denning said[97]:

> "It is simply the law of contract. If two persons agree that the price of property should be fixed by a valuer on whom they agree, and he gives that valuation honestly and in good faith, they are bound by it. Even if he has made a mistake they are still bound by it. The reason is because they have agreed to be bound by it. If there were fraud or collusion, of course, it would be very different. Fraud or collusion unravels everything."

This case marked the beginning of a different approach to allegations of mistake, and it is clear from a later passage in his judgment[98] that Lord Denning had very much in mind the recent decision of the House of Lords in *Arenson v. Casson Beckman Rutley & Co.*[99] holding that a negligent valuer owed a duty of care and could be liable for damages.[1]

Although *Campbell v. Edwards* was not cited in *Re Imperial Foods Ltd's Pension Scheme*[2], the court came to a similar conclusion[3].

---

[94] *Alfred C Toepfer v. Continental Grain Co.* [1974] 1 Lloyd's Rep. 11, approved in *Gill & Duffus SA v. Berger & Co. Inc.* [1984] A.C. 382 at 394. See 5.7, in particular 5.7.3.
[95] [1976] 1 W.L.R. 403.
[96] See 15.13.
[97] [1976] 1 W.L.R. 403 at 407.
[98] *ibid.* at 408B; see *per* Dillon L.J. in *Jones v. Sherwood* [1992] 1 W.L.R. 277 at 287.
[99] [1977] A.C. 405.
[1] See 16.5.
[2] [1986] 1 W.L.R. 717.
[3] See 4.3.

Baber v. Kenwood

15.11.5 The primacy of the law of contract in assessing challenges to experts' decisions was reaffirmed by Sir David Cairns in *Baber v. Kenwood Manufacturing Co. Ltd and Whinney Murray & Co.*[4] He said[5]:

> ". . . whether a valuation . . . is binding . . . must depend on the terms of the contract (including any implied terms), on the nature of any circumstances relied on to vitiate the valuation, and the nature of the proceedings on which the issue arises. If the valuation has not been made in accordance with the express terms of the contract then it is clearly not binding. If it is made in accordance with the express terms, the next question is whether there were any implied terms that have not been complied with. Here there may arise a conflict between two principles, one that the court will not imply a term unless it is one which reasonable men would obviously have agreed to if their minds had been directed to the point, the other that a contract should if possible be interpreted in such a way as to achieve fairness between the parties . . . mistake is a much more difficult problem . . . [than fraud or partiality]."

With the other members of the Court of Appeal in that case, he followed *Campbell v. Edwards.*[6]

Robust refusal to intervene

15.11.6 The Judicial Committee of the Privy Council considered a disputed rent review with a valuer acting as an expert in *Hudson (A) Pty Ltd v. Legal & General Life of Australia Ltd.*[7] The question was whether part of the floor area should be included and if so at what price. The tenants preferred to use the contentious area as air space for the benefit of the lower ground floor rather than selling space for the benefit of the ground floor. The Privy Council upheld the valuer's determination in favour of the landlords with the comment that there was no discernible mistake in the valuation either in fact or in law. Lord Templeman was not prepared to consider the kinds of mistake which might justify interference by the court with the valuation of an expert:

> "In general [we] consider that it would be a disservice to the law and to litigants to encourage forensic attacks on valuations by experts where those attacks are based on textual criticisms more appropriate to the measured analysis of fiscal legislation."

Expert's decision binding on matters of opinion

15.11.7 An expert surveyor's valuation of development land was alleged to contain fundamental errors in *Campbell and Palmer v. Crest*

---
[4] [1978] 1 Lloyd's Rep. 175.
[5] At 181.
[6] See 15.11.4.
[7] [1986] 2 E.G.L.R. 130.

Homes (Wessex) Ltd.[8] The allegations were all based on the opinion of another expert surveyor and related to what matters should or should not be taken into consideration. The judge said it was quite impossible to say that any error was shown by these matters on the face of the determination and that the parties were, on a matter of opinion, bound by the opinion of their chosen expert.

15.12 MISTAKE: THE PRESENT POSITION

A further retreat by the courts

15.12.1 The non-interventionist trend was intensified by the Court of Appeal's judgment in *Jones v. Sherwood Computer Services plc,*[9] and *Nikko Hotels (UK) Ltd v. MEPC plc,*[10] though other recent cases reveal a willingness to intervene where the court feels able to do so without departing from the principles established in *Jones v. Sherwood.*[11]

Jones v. Sherwood Computer Services plc

15.12.2 In *Jones v. Sherwood*[12] there was a sale and purchase agreement with part of the consideration deferred. Payment of that deferred consideration depended on the amount by which the acquired company's sales exceeded a certain figure. The vendors' and the purchasers' accountants were then to review the sales figure and try to agree it with each other. If they disagreed, which they did, a third accountant was to determine the figure and to provide a report stating the figure. For some reason, *all*[13] the accountants in the case (not just the third accountant) were said to be acting as experts and not as arbitrators and the determination was to be final and binding for all purposes.

Expert accountants appointed

15.12.3 The claimant vendors sought to set aside the expert's decision and to have the court decide the matter, but the defendant purchasers said that the claimants could not do that because the contract bound them to accept the expert's decision. The claimants' accountants were Deloitte, Haskins & Sells and the defendants'

---

[8] Unreported, Chancery Division, November 13, 1989.
[9] [1992] 1 W.L.R. 277; the judgment was delivered in December 1989.
[10] [1991] 2 E.G.L.R. 103.
[11] See 15.20.
[12] [1992] 1 W.L.R. 277.
[13] The draftsman may have stated that all the accountants were experts to ensure that, if the vendors' and the purchasers' accountants had agreed, their joint decision would then have had the status of an expert determination. The designation is not necessary to achieve that result.

accountants were Peat, Marwick, Mitchell. Deloittes thought that two categories of transaction should be included as sales, but Peats thought they should not be included. The expert firm then appointed was Coopers & Lybrand who set out their terms of reference in some detail, including the difference of opinion between Deloittes and Peats and its financial effect.

Coopers' decision

15.12.4 Coopers' determination was a brief letter referring to the sale agreement and what they had been asked to determine, and stating the answer: "We determine that the sales amount to £2,527,135." The claimants said this letter was a nullity because the sale agreement had called for a report, but the Court of Appeal did not agree that the use of the word "report" required the expert to set out the reasoning or calculations which led to the conclusion.

Mistakes of mixed fact and law

15.12.5 By referring back to the earlier documents it was obvious that Coopers had agreed with the Peats figure and disagreed with Deloittes. It did not follow that Coopers reached the same conclusion as Peats by following the same reasoning. The claimants' case was that Peats and Coopers had made mistakes of mixed fact and law and that they were entitled to ask the court to determine whether or not Coopers had made those mistakes.

Coopers' determination upheld

15.12.6 Giving the judgment of the Court of Appeal, Dillon L.J. stated that the correct approach was as follows[14]:

> "On principle, the first step must be to see what the parties have agreed to remit to the expert, this being, as Lord Denning M.R. said in *Campbell v. Edwards*,[15] a matter of contract. The next step must be to see what the nature of the mistake was, if there is evidence to show that. If the mistake made was that the expert departed from his instructions in a material respect—*e.g.*, if he valued the wrong number of shares, or valued shares in the wrong company, or if, as in *Jones (M) v. Jones (R R)*,[16] the expert had valued machinery himself whereas his instructions were to employ an expert valuer of his choice to do that— either party would be able to say that the certificate was not binding because the expert had not done what he was appointed to do."

The Court of Appeal held that Coopers had not made mistakes of this type. They had determined the sales and that is what they

---

[14] At p. 287.
[15] [1976] 1 W.L.R. 403 at 407G.
[16] [1971] 1 W.L.R. 840.

had been asked to do. The claimants would have had the right to review Coopers' decision only if there could be implied into the original agreement words permitting a challenge to the decision which qualified the final and binding description of the decision in the appropriate manner.

An investigation by the court would involve "yet more accountants"

15.12.7 The Court of Appeal in *Jones v. Sherwood*[17] also addressed the practical problem of how the alleged mistake could be rectified by the court. "Yet more accountants" would have been needed to give expert evidence. The only way for the court to decide on a matter of accountancy opinion is to obtain the expert evidence of accountants acting as expert witnesses.

Material departure from instructions

15.12.8 The grounds on which a decision may be challenged in reliance on *Jones v. Sherwood* are not confined to cases of mistake. The basis of the decision was that the decision of an expert is not binding on the parties if the expert has departed from instructions in a material respect. A fundamental mistake may be one illustration of a material departure from instructions. However other types of material departure from instructions can also provide grounds for challenge,[18] such as an expert using a different computer mapping package from the one specified in the agreement,[19] or an expert valuing machinery when the instructions are to choose and appoint someone else to do the work.[20]

Asking the right questions

15.12.9 In *Nikko v. MEPC*[21] Knox J. said that an expert's decision cannot be challenged unless it could be shown that the expert had not performed the task assigned by the parties. If the expert had answered the right question in the wrong way, the decision would be binding. If the expert had answered the wrong question, the decision would be a nullity. The judge went on to say that this would be the case for any dispute whether of fact or law, and that there was no rule of public policy preventing parties from agreeing to remit a question of

---

[17] [1992] 1 W.L.R. 277.
[18] See Lightman J. in *British Shipbuilders v. VSEL Consortium plc* [1997] 1 Lloyd's Rep. 106 at 109.
[19] *Shell UK Ltd v. Enterprise Oil plc* [1999] 2 Lloyd's Rep. 456.
[20] *Jones (M) v. Jones (R R)* [1971] 1 W.L.R. 840, cited with approval in *Jones v. Sherwood* at p. 287.
[21] [1991] 2 E.G.L.R. 103, approved by Buxton L.J. in *Dahl-Jensen UK Ltd v. Bouygues UK Ltd*, [2000] B.L.R. 522; see also *Pontsarn Investments Ltd v. Kansallis-Osake-Pankki* [1992] 1 E.G.L.R. 148 at 151M.

law to the exclusive and final jurisdiction of an expert. It is therefore hardly surprising that the expression "judge-proof" started to be applied to experts' decisions.[22] Few decisions made by experts are likely to involve a material departure from instructions or asking oneself the wrong question.

Cases on mistake since *Jones v. Sherwood*

In *Macro v. Thompson (No. 3)*[23] the Court of Appeal held, disagreeing with the judge at first instance, that valuing shares in one company by reference to value of the assets of another company involved a departure from the expert's instructions, so that the expert's decision was open to challenge. In another case the Court of Appeal held that valuing a roadway as being subject to limited rights of way when it was already subject to unlimited rights of way was not a valuation of the wrong property.[24]

15.12.10

The principle that the court has no power to intervene where the expert has answered the right question in the wrong way[25] was confirmed by the Court of Appeal in a case concerning a building adjudication.[26] The parties agreed there had been a mistake, although of course they did not agree about the consequences: the adjudicator did not admit there had been a mistake. The Court of Appeal held that the adjudicator's decision was binding on the parties, because the mistake was made within the adjudicator's jurisdiction. The adjudicator's mistake was described by the court as an error that arose in making calculations to answer the question of whether payments thus far made under a contract represented an overpayment or an underpayment. The adjudicator overlooked the fact that the assessment should be made on the contract sum presently due for repayment, *i.e.* the contract sum less the retention, rather than the gross contract sum. The court said that the adjudicator answered exactly the questions put, and the case was quite different from Dillon L.J.'s example of valuing the wrong parcel of shares.[27]

Clerical errors

Where the expert acknowledges having made a clerical error, the decision can probably be corrected.[28]

15.12.11

---

[22] See Jonathan Gaunt Q.C. "What makes an award judge-proof?", [1991] 28 Estates Gazette 70.
[23] [1997] 1 B.C.L.C. 626.
[24] *Morgan Sindall plc v. Sawston Farms (Cambs) Ltd* [1999] 1 E.G.L.R. 93.
[25] *Nikko Hotels (UK) Ltd v. MEPC plc* [1991] 2 E.G.L.R. 103.
[26] *Bouygues UK Ltd v. Dahl-Jensen UK Ltd*, [2000] B.L.R. 522 (see 7.5.5).
[27] *Jones v. Sherwood Computer Services plc* [1992] 1 W.L.R. 277 at 287A.
[28] See 15.9.10.

15.13 SPEAKING AND NON-SPEAKING DECISIONS

Definition

15.13.1 The decision of an expert may be known either as "speaking" or "non-speaking". A speaking decision is one which gives the reasons and calculations behind the decision, whereas a non-speaking decision does not. The expressions are also used with the words "certificates", "decisions", "determinations" and "valuations", and are sometimes found in describing whether reasons accompany an arbitration award; and an expert decision is often referred to as an award. Hence the expressions "speaking award" and "non-speaking award" can be used to describe both expert decisions and arbitration awards.

Speaking decisions previously more vulnerable

15.13.2 Until 1989 (when *Jones v. Sherwood* was decided) the courts had said that a speaking decision could be upset if it contained an obvious error. Thus, if the decision gave its reasons or calculations, and there were obvious errors in them, the decision could be set aside. A speaking decision was overturned in *Johnston v. Chestergate Hat Manufacturing Co Ltd*[29] where the auditors' certificate showed that the amount due was calculated according to the wrong principle.

Burgess v. Purchase

15.13.3 *Johnston v. Chestergate*[30] was the principal authority relied on in *Burgess v. Purchase & Sons (Farms) Ltd*,[31] where auditors explained how their valuation of the shares in question had been arrived at, in a speaking valuation. Nourse J. summarised the effect of the previous authorities as follows: a speaking valuation made on a fundamentally erroneous basis could be impugned; a non-speaking valuation made of the right property by the right individual and in good faith could not be impugned, although it might be possible, if the transaction had not been completed, for equitable relief (such as specific performance) as opposed to damages to be refused. He held that the allegations that the valuation had been made on a fundamentally erroneous basis were sufficient to allow the action to proceed. The merits of the claimant's objections to the means of valuation do not appear from the report, and did not need to, because this was a striking-out application[32] which allows no evidence to be heard about the case that the claimant wished to make.

---

[29] [1915] 2 Ch. 338.
[30] *ibid*.
[31] [1983] Ch. 216.
[32] RSC, Ord. 18, r. 19 (now CPR 3.4).

An unreal distinction?

15.13.4 In his judgment in *Jones v. Sherwood*,[33] Dillon L.J. held that there was no relevant distinction between speaking and non-speaking decisions[34]:

> "Even speaking valuations may say much or little; they may be voluble or taciturn if not wholly dumb. The real question is whether it is possible to say from all the evidence which is properly before the court, and not only from the valuation or certificate itself, what the valuer or certifier has done and why he has done it."

Balcombe L.J. agreed with Dillon L.J. *Burgess v. Purchase*[35] was disapproved.

It therefore does not follow that the right to challenge depends on whether the decision is a speaking decision or a non-speaking decision, or that speaking decisions may be challenged and non-speaking decisions may not. Each decision must be examined to see what it discloses. However, as a practical matter, a non-speaking decision is very hard to challenge. In a case where the expert's decision dealt with each disputed item but did not show detailed workings, the expert was alleged to have failed to take the effect of tax into account. The Court of Appeal refused to invalidate the decision, but did say that, if it could be proved that materials relevant to the tax issue had not been put before the expert, the decision might be questioned.[36] The point was made graphically in a later case[37]:

> "The whole point of instructing a valuer to act as an expert (and not as an arbitrator) is to achieve certainty by a quick and reasonably inexpensive process. Such a valuation is almost invariably a non-speaking valuation, with the expert's reasoning and calculations concealed behind the curtain. The court should give no encouragement to infer, from ambiguous shadows and murmurs, what is happening behind the curtain."

Mistake not apparent from the decision

15.13.5 The question whether a party could allege that the expert had made a mistake which was not apparent from the decision or the reasons was raised in *Dean v. Prince*,[38] where, at first instance, the

---

[33] [1992] 1 W.L.R. 277.
[34] *ibid*. at 284. The same view was taken of architects' certificates in *Lubenham Fidelities and Investment Co. Ltd v. South Pembrokeshire District Council* (1986) 33 B.L.R. 39 at 55 (May L.J.).
[35] [1983] Ch. 216.
[36] *Healds Foods Ltd v. Hyde Dairies*, unreported, CA, December 6, 1996. (http://www.bailii.org/cgi-bailii/disp.pl/ew/cases/EWCA/1996/2049.html).
[37] *Morgan Sindall plc v. Sawston Farms (Cambs) Ltd* [1999] 1 E.G.L.R. 93, CA, *per* Robert Walker L.J. at 92M.
[38] [1953] 1 Ch. 590.

judge held that he could look at documents other than the auditors' certificate and the balance sheet and that cross-examination of the auditors would be allowed.[39] In *Jones v. Sherwood* Dillon L.J. stated that it was permissible to refer to evidence outside the valuation or certificate itself.[40] More recently, it has been held that the expert should not be ordered to attend to give evidence.[41] In the related field of construction adjudication the position is probably that the court cannot look beyond the adjudicator's award to determine what question the adjudicator has answered.[42]

In many cases it may be unnecessary to call other expert evidence.[43] Where there has already been a decision made by a third expert following submissions made by experts representing each party the court is likely to be reluctant to permit evidence to be adduced from yet more experts.[44] However in a complex case it may be necessary to call expert evidence to explain whether an error has been made and whether the alleged error is a material error.[45]

Effect of qualifying words

15.13.6   What is the effect of a speaking decision which contains words which could be said to qualify the decision? This question was considered by Knox J. in *Midland Montagu Leasing (UK) Ltd v. Tyne & Wear Passenger Transport Executive and Ernst & Whinney*.[46] A finance leasing agreement said that the auditors for the owners acting as experts "shall . . . conclusively certify . . . [the rental]". The auditors said in their certificate that they had used one methodology rather than another and that it was not clear from the clause in the lease which methodology they should use. In the certificate the auditor did not just recite the clause, he specifically raised the methodology point. He was later asked to delete the qualification from the certificate and refused. The court found that the certificate was conclusive. (The court also looked at the methodology and decided that the expert had been right about it anyway.) The adverb "conclusively" qualifying the word "certify" may be no more than the more commonly encountered

---

[39] The point was not considered in the appeal at [1954] 1 Ch. 409. Contrast the Australian case of *Mayne Nickless Ltd v. Solomon* [1980] Qd R. 171, where the court held that the mistake must appear from a reading of the decision and not from cross-examination of the valuer.
[40] [1992] 1 W.L.R. 277 at 284, quoted above.
[41] See 15.19.1.
[42] *Bouygues UK Ltd v. Dahl-Jensen UK Ltd*, [2000] B.L.R. 522.
[43] E.g. *Shorrock Ltd v. Meggitt plc* [1991] B.C.C. 471.
[44] Cf. *Jones v. Sherwood Computer Services plc* [1992] 1 W.L.R. 277, per Dillon L.J. at 288G.
[45] *Conoco (UK) Ltd v. Phillips Petroleum* [1998] A.D.R.L.J. 55 (a gasfield re-determination case), *Shell (UK) Ltd v. Enterprise Oil plc* [1999] 2 Lloyd's Rep. 456 (an oilfield re-determination case).
[46] Unreported, Chancery Division, February 23, 1990.

provision that the expert's decision will be final. Subject to the precise words used, it is always likely to be a contractual obligation, binding the expert and the parties, that the decision be final.

If a certificate is found not to be conclusive or final when the contract or terms of reference say it should be, that finding will provide good grounds for challenge. In *Shorrock Ltd v. Meggitt plc*[47] qualifying words rendered a certificate inconclusive and therefore invalid. Auditors certified the amount of the net deficit of a company under the terms of an agreement for the sale and purchase of that company, but stated that they were unable to determine the adequacy or otherwise of a provision made by the directors in respect of potential legal claims against the company. The Court of Appeal said:

> "It was open to the . . . auditors to certify that the . . . deficit was [a particular figure] or, if they felt unable to do that, to refuse to certify. But I do not think it was open to them to state a sum constituting the . . . deficit and then say in effect they were not sure if the sum was correct. That defeats the whole purpose of requiring a certificate, since it destroys the certainty which the parties required by providing for the certificate."

This led the Institute of Chartered Accountants in England and Wales to issue a memorandum[48] warning against the use of the word "certificate" where an accountant could only use professional expertise and judgment to express an opinion. Matters could be certified only where the accountant could be certain of them.

Reasons

Can the expert be compelled to produce reasons for the decision? This would have the effect of either: **15.13.7**

(a) turning a non-speaking decision into a speaking one, where the expert had not been specifically instructed beforehand to produce a speaking decision; or
(b) giving more detail to an existing speaking decision.

In the latter context, the court has regarded this prospect with some alarm. It should not be easier to challenge a reasoned award issued by an expert than a reasoned award issued by an arbitrator.[49] The court has not encouraged applications[50] for orders that

---

[47] [1991] B.C.C. 471.
[48] "The involvement of accountants in commercial agreements", memorandum reference number TR 853, issued by the Institute of Chartered Accountants in England and Wales on November 18, 1991.
[49] *Campbell and Palmer v. Crest Homes (Wessex) Ltd*, unreported, Chancery Division, November 13, 1989.
[50] Previously under Arbitration Act 1979, s. 1(5); this has now been repealed and the new provision is Arbitration Act 1996, s. 70(4).

arbitrators give reasons.[51] The court is therefore very unlikely to insist on an expert giving reasons where the obligation to give reasons was not agreed beforehand. However, where an expert is contractually bound to give the reasons but produces none, presumably the court would view an application more favourably on the ground of the expert's breach of contract. Whether an expert can be ordered to give evidence at the trial to explain the decision is discussed at 15.19.

15.14 QUESTIONS OF INTERPRETATION OF THE WORDS IN THE AGREEMENT

A question of law

15.14.1 Interpretation of words in the agreement is treated as a matter of law because of the common law tradition. This was explained by Lord Diplock in *The Nema*[52] where he said that the English system treated the construction of written agreements as questions of law because of the legacy of trial by juries who might not all be literate. The context of these remarks was his preference for allowing arbitrators to make final decisions on questions of construction. However what is termed a matter of construction may simply be the meaning of an ordinary word of the English language, which Lord Reid said is not a question of law.[53]

Traditional ground for challenge

15.14.2 Interpretation or construction of the contractual terms setting out the manner in which the expert should have resolved the issue has in the past been a fruitful line for challenge to decisions. Until *Jones v. Sherwood* was decided in 1989 the court generally adopted the position that the court always had jurisdiction to decide questions of law.[54]

Are questions of interpretation to be determined by the court or by the expert?

15.14.3 *Jones v. Sherwood Computer Services plc*[55] and *Norwich Union Life Assurance Society v. P&O Property Holdings Ltd*[56] appeared to reduce the scope for challenges on the basis that the reference to

---

[51] *Universal Petroleum Co. Ltd v. Handels und Transport GmbH* [1987] 1 W.L.R. 1178.
[52] *Pioneer Shipping Ltd v. BTP Tioxide Ltd (The Nema)* [1982] A.C. 724 at 736.
[53] *Cozens v. Brutus* [1973] A.C. 854 at 861C-D, referred to by Dillon L.J. in *Norwich Union Life Assurance Society v. P&O Property Holdings Ltd* [1993] 1 E.G.L.R. 164 at 168G when considering the use of the word "completed" to describe the stage of development of a shopping centre.
[54] See 12.5.
[55] [1992] 1 W.L.R. 277; discussed in 15.12.
[56] [1993] 1 E.G.L.R. 164; discussed in 12.6.3.

QUESTIONS OF INTERPRETATION OF THE WORDS IN THE AGREEMENT

the expert involved not only questions of fact but also questions as to the meaning of the words in the agreement. However later cases have shown that the court will still intervene if the terms of the particular agreement and the circumstances in which it was made justify the inference that the parties intended that questions of interpretation and other points of law were to be determined exclusively by the court, and not by the expert. Examples are *Mercury Communications Ltd v. Director General of Telecommunications*[57] and *National Grid plc v. M25 Group Ltd,*[58] discussed at 12.6.[59] In each case, the decision is reached on the basis of the particular agreement before the court.

Cases where questions of interpretation have not been referred to the expert

Where the expert's decision depends on a decision on a question of interpretation which should have been decided by the court, the court may rule that the decision of the expert is a nullity.[60]   15.14.4

OTHER POINTS OF LAW   15.15

The approach applicable to questions of interpretation of the agreement also applies to other points of law, unless the terms of the agreement provide otherwise.

SPECIFIC INSTRUCTIONS FOR THE EXPERT   15.16

Examples

Expert clauses and terms of reference may characterise the decision the expert is to make by the use of certain adjectives or longer, more elaborate qualifications. For instance, a clause providing for auditors to value shares may state that the auditor is to certify their fair value or similar words[61]; a minority holding of shares is to be valued without regard to the fact that it is a minority holding[62]; surveyors have to assume certain facts and disregard others in establishing a rental.[63] Instructions of those kinds are contained in the contract. Specific instructions may also be found in the terms of reference after the dispute has arisen.   15.16.1

---

[57] [1996] 1 W.L.R. 48.
[58] [1999] 1 E.G.L.R. 65.
[59] See also 12.5.4.
[60] See 12.7.3.
[61] See 3.5.
[62] See 3.7.
[63] See 2.3.4.

15 : Challenging the decision

Ability to challenge dependent on reasons

15.16.2 Specific instructions of this type are unlikely to provide opportunities for challenge unless experts set out their reasons.[64] Where reasons are set out, it may be possible to mount a challenge on the basis that there has been a material departure from instructions.[65]

15.17 "In the absence of manifest error"

Expert clauses often provide that the decision is to be final and binding "in the absence of manifest error".[66] Applying *Jones v. Sherwood*, "the fact that [the expert] may be patently wrong does not mean that he has not done what he was appointed to do nor that he has asked himself the wrong question",[67] and unless there are words such as "in the absence of manifest error" a patently wrong decision is usually unchallengeable. The inclusion of these words clearly widens the scope for a challenge based on mistake beyond the circumstances referred to in *Jones v. Sherwood*. However, in a case where the expert does not set out the reasons for the decision it is very difficult to show that an error is manifest or a mistake is obvious, and therefore the provision may be of limited assistance in showing that a mistake has been made. Generally, a party cannot call the expert as a witness to give evidence as to how the decision was reached.[68]

In the words of Lord Lindley:

> "All errors are manifest when discovered; but such clauses ... are intended to be confined to oversights and blunders so obvious as to admit of no difference of opinion."[69]

Reference has also been made to the definition in *Chambers Twentieth Century Dictionary*: an error "that may easily be seen by the eye or perceived by the mind".[70]

---

[64] See 13.8.3.
[65] *Shell UK Ltd v. Enterprise Oil plc* [1999] 2 Lloyd's Rep. 546.
[66] *Healds Foods Ltd v. Hyde Dairies Ltd*, unreported, November 23, 1994, Queens Bench Division, Commercial Court, Potter J; affirmed by Court of Appeal, unreported, December 6, 1996 (http://www.bailii.org/cgi-bailii/disp.pl/ew/cases/EWCA/1996/2049.html); *Conoco (UK) Ltd v. Phillips Petroleum Company* [1998] A.D.R.L.J. 55; *Dixons Group plc v. Jan Andrew Murray-Oboynski* (1997) 86 B.L.R. 16.
[67] *Pontsarn Investments Ltd v. Kansallis-Osake-Pankki* [1992] 1 E.G.L.R. 148, *per* Judge Paul Baker Q.C. at 151M; in *Conoco* at p. 70 Morrison J. referred to manifest error and failure to perform the task allocated as being independent grounds of challenge.
[68] *Dixons v. Murray-Oboynski* (1997) 86 B.L.R. 19 at 30.
[69] Lindley, *Partnership*, 16th edition, p. 162, referring to a stipulation between parties that annual accounts, once approved and signed, should be regarded as conclusive, save in respect of manifest error; cited in *Heald* and *Conoco*.
[70] *Dixons v. Murray-Oboynski* (1997) 86 B.L.R. 19 at 32.

In a case where manifest error has been established, the decision is of no effect, even if it is not established that the error made a material difference to the result.[71]

Consequence of an ineffective decision   15.18

Is a new valuation needed?

In *Jones (M) v. Jones (R R)*[72] the court considered what the fate should be of a valuation made on an erroneous principle. The court said that there was no general rule that a valuation made on an erroneous principle (which presumably means the same as a mistaken decision) had to stand unless it were also shown that a valuation on the right principle would produce a materially different figure from the figure of the erroneous valuation. If there were such a rule, it would place on the objector the extra burden of making a fresh valuation which in its turn might also be rejected. Thus a valuation or any other kind of decision made on an erroneous principle should fall with proof that the principle is erroneous.   15.18.1

A mistake may not vitiate the decision

In *Frank H Wright (Constructions) Ltd v. Frodoor Ltd*,[73] a valuation stated that some assets had not been included when in fact they had been. The result was not affected by this error and it was held that there was no need for the court to correct the valuation. However in *Jones (M) v. Jones (R R)* Ungoed-Thomas J. held that there was no general principle requiring proof that the error has made a material difference[74]:   15.18.2

> "I do not conclude that there is any requirement of general application that where a valuation is made on an erroneous principle, yet the valuation nevertheless stands unless it is also shown that a valuation on the right principle would produce a materially different figure from the figure of the valuation that he made. (This would incidentally place on the objector the onus, not only of proving that the selected expert has acted on a wrong principle, but of incurring what might be the very heavy burden and expense of a completely new valuation, which itself might not be accepted as conclusive between the parties and merely leading to yet another valuation.) The authorities thus to my mind establish that if a valuation is erroneous in principle, it is vitiated and cannot be relied upon even though it is not established that the valuation figure is wrong."

---

[71] *Per* Morrison J. in *Conoco (UK) Ltd v. Phillips Petroleum Company* [1998] A.D.R.L.J. 55 at 71.
[72] [1971] 1 W.L.R. 840.
[73] [1967] 1 W.L.R. 506.
[74] [1971] 1 W.L.R. 840 at 856.

It has also been held that where the expert clause includes the words "save in the case of manifest error", the decision is of no effect even if it is not proved that the error made a material difference to the result, provided that the error is more than just a minor infraction with no consequences of any kind.[75]

Can the court fill the gap?

15.18.3 The usual consequence of a mistake or a material departure from instructions is that the expert must come to a new decision in accordance with the instructions, as clarified by the court, and it is not usually appropriate for the court to fill the gap by ordering an inquiry. The court may however in an appropriate case substitute its own alternative machinery for the machinery specified in the contract.

In *Macro v. Thompson (No. 3)*[76] it was held that a new valuation by the same auditor would not be satisfactory for a number of reasons, including the auditor's lack of specialist expertise in share valuation. In reaching this conclusion the court relied on *Sudbrook Trading Estate Ltd v. Eggleton*[77] where the court made an order for an inquiry following a failure to appoint an expert, but this was an extension of what had been decided in *Sudbrook*. In a case where the court found that the failure in the decision-making process was so serious that the court concluded that the contractual machinery had broken down, the court decided (for a combination of reasons including passage of time and absence of notes) that it was no longer possible for the appointed expert to arrive at a satisfactory determination and proceeded to reach its own decision on the substantive question.[78] The court again relied on *Sudbrook v. Eggleton*. In a Canadian case[79] the court decided that a valuation was a nullity as it had been carried out on the wrong basis, and then ordered that the values were to be determined by a court-appointed referee unless the parties agreed the matter could be referred back to the same valuers who had carried out the original valuation.

15.19 EVIDENCE FROM THE EXPERT

The general position

15.19.1 The evidence of the expert might be thought useful in an attempt to challenge a decision. As has been noted[80] the court may not allow the expert to be joined in the action. Another ploy could be to call

---

[75] *Per* Morrison J. in *Conoco*, at p. 71.
[76] [1997] 2 B.C.L.C. 36 at 68–73 (see 15.4.3).
[77] [1983] A.C. 444.
[78] *John Barker Construction Ltd v. London Portman Hotel Ltd* (1996) 83 B.L.R. 31, Toulson J. at 61–63.
[79] *Irwin v. Campbell* (1915) 23 D.L.R. 279.
[80] See 15.2.2.

the expert as a witness, and, where the request is refused, to obtain a court order requiring the expert to attend the trial to give evidence: where an expert had not had to give reasons,[81] the court order was set aside on the basis that the evidence "properly before the court"[82] did not include oral explanation or elaboration by the determining expert in the face of the objection from the other party.[83] The position is probably the same where the expert did give or had been required to give reasons, but this has not so far been decided. It has been held that a claim to set aside the valuation for mistake could not be left pending while the claimant tried to obtain disclosure of the valuation methodology in proceedings for negligence brought against the valuers.[84]

Contractual exclusions

Some terms of appointment or terms of reference contain words to the effect that the expert is not to be required to give evidence in any subsequent connected proceedings. There is no rule of law which prevents a term of this sort being enforceable.[85]   15.19.2

THE PROSPECTS FOR CHALLENGES IN THE FUTURE   15.20

Despite the general trend towards non-intervention since *Jones v. Sherwood*, cases do still arise in which the courts decide that a decision reached by an expert is not binding, and it can be expected that they will continue to do so in cases where this is possible without departing from the principles established in *Jones v. Sherwood*. The possible grounds for challenge which are most likely to arise in practice are as follows:

---

[81] *Healds Foods Ltd v. Hyde Dairies Ltd*, unreported, November 23, 1994, Queen's Bench Division, Commercial Court, Potter J. (affirmed without referring to this point) unreported, December 6, 1996 (*http://www.bailii.org/cgi–bailii/disp.pl/ew/cases/EWCA/1996/2048.html*), followed in *Dixons Group plc v. Murray-Oboynski* (1997) 86 B.L.R. 19.

[82] Quoting Dillon L.J. in *Jones v. Sherwood Computer Services plc* [1992] 1 W.L.R. 277 at 284H.

[83] The words of Lord Denning in *Campbell v. Edwards* [1976] 1 W.L.R. 403 at 407 quoted at 15.11.4 were also relied on here.

[84] *Re Benfield Greig Group plc, Nugent v. Benfield Greig Group plc* [2000] 2 B.C.L.C. 488 at 515, para. 65, Arden J.

[85] In *Healds Foods* (cited above), *E Rotheray & Sons Ltd v. Carlo Bedarida & Co.* [1961] 1 Lloyd's Rep. 220 was distinguished on the ground that the apparently similar exclusion related to arbitration and was so wide that its effect would have been to exclude from the court's consideration the material necessary to exercise its statutory functions in respect of arbitration. The court has no statutory function to review expert determinations. A contractual restraint of this type is not contrary to public policy except in cases involving crime or, sometimes, insolvency.

(a) The expert has reached a decision on the interpretation of the agreement which the parties did not intend to refer to the expert. Cases decided in the period 1991 to 1993 suggested that the courts would usually decide that these issues should be left to the expert to decide, but more recent cases show a greater willingness to intervene. The main cases on this point are cases where one party applied to the court before the expert's decision: *Mercury Communications Ltd v. Director General of Telecommunications*[86] and *National Grid plc v. M25 Group Ltd,*[87] discussed at 12.6. But the same approach applies after the expert has reached the decision (so long as the aggrieved party has not left it too late to complain).

(b) The expert has made a mistake which involves a departure from instructions in a material respect or has otherwise departed from instructions in a material respect, such as using a different procedure from the procedure stipulated in the agreement or mistakenly valuing the wrong number of shares. The courts do not readily decide that this has occurred,[88] but are prepared to do so in an appropriate case. Recent examples are *Shell UK Ltd v. Enterprise Oil plc,*[89] where the expert used a different computer mapping package from the one specified in the agreement, and *Macro v Thompson (No. 3),*[90] where the expert valued shares in one company by reference to the value of the assets of another company.

(c) The expert has reached a decision which is not a fair determination and is not based on a proper application of the provisions of the contract. This was the decision reached in *John Barker Construction Ltd v. London Portman Hotel Ltd,*[91] where the decision was made by the agent of one party, with no contractual procedure for review, but it is questionable how far that decision will be followed in other cases: see 15.8.

(d) There is a greater willingness by the court to intervene or to decide that questions of law are to be decided by the court where the decision-maker is the agent of one of the parties, in particular where there is no contractual procedure for review.[92]

---

[86] [1996] 1 W.L.R. 48.
[87] [1999] 1 E.G.L.R. 65.
[88] See *e.g. Morgan Sindall plc v. Sawston Farms (Cambs) Ltd* [1999] 1 E.G.L.R. 93 (see 15.12.10 and 15.13.4) and *Bouygues UK Ltd v. Dahl-Jensen UK Ltd* [2000] B.L.R. 522, CA (see 7.5.5).
[89] [1999] 2 Lloyd's Rep. 456.
[90] [1997] 1 B.C.L.C. 626, CA.
[91] (1996) 83 B.L.R. 31.
[92] *John Barker Construction Ltd v. London Portman Hotel Ltd* (above), *West of England Shipowners Mutual Insurance Association (Luxembourg) v. Cristal Ltd ("The Glacier Bay")* [1996] 1 Lloyd's Rep. 370. See 18.3.7.

CHAPTER 16

RIGHTS AND DUTIES OF EXPERTS

SUMMARY 16.1

This chapter considers:

(a) experts' rights to fees and expenses (16.2);
(b) arbitral immunity for experts before 1975 (16.3);
(c) the change in the law on certifiers' liability (16.4);
(d) the current law under which experts are not immune (16.5);
(e) the obsolete concept of the quasi-arbitrator (16.6);
(f) the liability of experts for professional negligence (16.7);
(g) five suggested specific duties of experts (16.8 to 16.12);
(h) the liability of experts in tort (16.13).

FEES AND EXPENSES 16.2

Contract establishes the right to be paid

An expert's right to receive fees or expenses is usually established by agreement with the parties. Where there is no express agreement to pay, the court may be able to infer an agreement to pay from the circumstances. Thus the law of contract governs the entitlement to collect fees and expenses from either or both of the parties, or from some third party; the amount of the fees and expenses; and when the entitlement is to be paid.[1] An expert who does not ensure that the question of fees and expenses is determined in advance might, if the question were subsequently disputed, have to sue both to establish the fact of the debt (either as a matter of contract or *quantum meruit*) and to justify the amount.   16.2.1

Should be decided along with other terms of reference

While the expert clause itself may lay down that the parties are to be responsible for the fees and expenses of the expert in equal shares, which is quite common, or that they are to be met by some   16.2.2

---

[1] It might be useful to provide for progress payments in a lengthy reference.

other party,[2] the clause itself may not be sufficient to establish the expert's entitlement unless its terms are clearly incorporated into the expert's contract to conduct the reference. The amounts of the fees and expenses are still likely to be at large because expert clauses never lay down the amounts. Fees are often calculated as a percentage of the amount at issue and expenses cannot be considered before a reference. The expert should therefore have the question of fees and expenses agreed with the parties in the terms of reference.[3]

Calculating the fees

16.2.3 The amount of the expert's fees depends on negotiation unless it has been established by the expert clause. The amount may be determined either as a percentage, a fixed sum arrived at on some other basis, or an hourly rate. It is unusual to see hourly rates spelled out in terms of reference but it may save arguments later. The expert should bear in mind that the parties may settle the matter before the determination is complete.

No procedure for control

16.2.4 There is no specific procedure for control by the courts of the amount of an expert's fees as there is with arbitrators.[4] If an expert sues for fees, the entitlement and/or the amount could be challenged in court only by reference to the contract made by the parties about the fees. Questions about the reasonableness of the amount charged would arise only if specific rates had not been agreed.

Entitlement to expenses also a matter of contract

16.2.5 The expert's expenses such as the cost of seeking outside legal advice are generally recoverable only if the parties have agreed to the expense.

No entitlement if reference invalid

16.2.6 An expert may have no entitlement to fees and expenses if the expert has not been properly appointed,[5] unless it has been specifically agreed that the expert should be paid in those circumstances.

---

[2] See 9.12.
[3] See 13.5.
[4] Under Arbitration Act 1996, s. 64.
[5] As appears to have been the consequence in *Darlington Borough Council v. Waring & Gillow (Holdings) Ltd* [1988] 2 E.G.L.R. 159 discussed at 11.4.4.

Securing payment

16.2.7 An expert may find it necessary to take steps to secure the payment of fees and expenses by, for instance, making payment of fees a condition of publishing the decision. The existence of a common law lien is uncertain, so an expert might seek to impose a condition of this kind at the time of appointment. The practice is for each party to pay half the fees and expenses on collecting the decision: if one party does not wish to co-operate, the other party may have to pay the whole amount in order to obtain the decision. The amounts paid by the parties may then be adjusted according to any orders made about the incidence of costs in the decision. Some experts go further and ask the parties to deposit the full amount of the fees and expenses before any work is done at all.

Resignation

16.2.8 There is no authority on the circumstances in which an expert may resign, or on the consequences of the resignation on the right to fees. Circumstances can easily arise where the expert may decide to resign, with a greater or lesser degree of justification.[6] The entitlement to fees depends on interpreting the fee arrangement.

Limitation

16.2.9 There is a six-year limitation period for collecting fees and expenses, unless the expert is appointed under seal in which case it is 12 years.[7]

ARBITRAL IMMUNITY FOR EXPERTS UNTIL 1975   16.3

Quasi-arbitral status: *Pappa v. Rose*

16.3.1 A number of attempts to sue experts featured in the law reports in the years before 1975, but it was decided invariably that the experts were quasi-arbitrators and therefore could not be sued. Traditionally, arbitrators have benefited from immunity at common law: this has now been made statutory, subject to the relevant act or omission being shown to have been in bad faith.[8] This concept of quasi-arbitrators was raised in *Pappa v. Rose*,[9] where a broker deciding whether raisins were "fair average quality"[10] in his opinion was held to be in the position of a quasi-arbitrator[11] or in the nature of an

---

[6] For one instance, see 13.6.7. For the parallel position of arbitrators who resign, see Arbitration Act 1996, s. 25.
[7] Limitation Act 1980, ss. 5 and 8.
[8] Arbitration Act 1996, s. 29(1).
[9] (1872) L.R. 7 C.P. 525.
[10] An expression commonly used in these assessments.
[11] See 16.6.

arbitrator. The broker was said to have acted honestly and in good faith and that was all that was required of him. There was no implied contract that he would have any degree of skill.

Jenkins v. Betham

16.3.2 For Mr Rose, the defendant in *Pappa v. Rose*, to escape liability, the courts had to distinguish *Jenkins v. Betham*.[12] Two differences were identified. The first was what stage the dispute, if any, had reached, and the second was the professed ability of the defendants. In *Jenkins v. Betham* two valuers of ecclesiastical property had been appointed, one to advise the representatives of a deceased rector, the other to advise the incoming rector. The incoming rector's valuers were incompetent and ignorant of the subject and caused their client loss. There was an implied term in the contract appointing the valuers that they were qualified to act and understood the subject, and the valuers were in breach. The matter never proceeded to what was then called umpirage, *i.e.* the appointment by the party-appointed valuers of an umpire and consideration of the matter by the umpire. The court at first instance in *Pappa v. Rose*[13] thought it significant that umpirage had not been reached because in its view there could be no real dispute before that stage. The appeal court in *Pappa v. Rose*[14] noted that the valuers in *Jenkins v. Betham* had declared themselves to be persons possessed of proper skill for valuations of ecclesiastical property, whereas Mr Rose was only a selling broker expressing his opinion. The court therefore dismissed the claim against Mr Rose.

Tharsis Sulphur v. Loftus

16.3.3 In *Tharsis Sulphur & Copper Co. Ltd v. Loftus*[15] the court decided that an average adjuster appointed under a contract to determine cargo damage was also in the nature of an arbitrator between the parties, and followed *Pappa v Rose*.[16]

Turner v. Goulden

16.3.4 *Turner v. Goulden*[17] was similar to *Jenkins v. Betham*.[18] The claimant asked the defendant to value a bookselling business that he wished to purchase. The defendant met the vendor's valuer and agreed the valuation of the goodwill on a basis which the claimant

---

[12] (1855) 15 C.B. 168.
[13] (1871) L.R. 7 C.P. 32.
[14] (1872) L.R. 7 C.P. 525.
[15] (1872) L.R. 8 C.P. 1.
[16] (1872) L.R. 7 C.P. 525.
[17] (1873) L.R. 9 C.P.D. 57.
[18] (1855) 15 C.B. 168.

alleged was the wrong basis. The court allowed interrogatories to be administered against the valuer, in a claim against him for negligence, because the procedure was a valuation and not an arbitration.

Architects' certificates

16.3.5 An architect certifying amounts payable to a contractor under a building contract was held to be in the position of an arbitrator in *Stevenson v. Watson*[19] and therefore not liable to the contractor, and, by a considerable extension of the same argument, not liable to the employer either in *Chambers v. Goldthorpe*.[20] The judgment in *Chambers v. Goldthorpe* gave a prominent role to the influential concept of a professional holding the scales between the parties.

Surveyors' valuations

16.3.6 In *Boynton v. Richardson*[21] the court said that surveyors appointed under a contract to value timber had to hold the scales between the two parties and were quasi-arbitrators. They had to be able to exercise their judgment free from the embarrassment of a possible action for negligence.[22]

Finnegan v. Allen

16.3.7 In *Finnegan v. Allen*[23] the Court of Appeal struck out a claim against an accountant who, it was alleged, had not valued shares in accordance with the instructions in the agreement under which he had been appointed. The court did not inquire into the nature of his departure from the instructions, and said that as a quasi-arbitrator all he had to do was to act honestly.

SUTCLIFFE V. THACKRAH — 16.4

Architects lose immunity

16.4.1 In *Sutcliffe v. Thackrah*[24] the House of Lords overruled *Chambers v. Goldthorpe*[25] and held that an architect certifying payments due to a contractor under a building contract was liable for professional negligence to his client the employer. It did not follow that, because the architect was under a duty to act fairly in making a valuation for the certificates, he was acting in a judicial capacity and therefore

---

[19] (1879) 4 C.P. 148.
[20] [1901] 1 Q.B. 624.
[21] [1924] W.N. 262.
[22] A similar line was taken in *O'Brien v. Perry & Daw* (1941) 85 S.J. 142.
[23] [1943] 1 K.B. 425.
[24] [1974] A.C. 727.
[25] [1901] 1 Q.B. 624: see 16.3.5.

16 : Rights and Duties of Experts

immune from liability to his principal for loss caused to him by a negligent valuation. Lord Reid said[26]:

> "There is modern authority to the effect that if the valuer knows his valuation will affect or bind another person besides his client . . . then he can claim an arbitrator's immunity. But why should that be? . . . I do not believe a professional man would . . . be influenced in any significant way because he knew that the interests of some other person beside his employer would be affected by the conclusion which he reached."

Duty of care owed to non-client

16.4.2 In the same case Lord Salmon stated[27] that it was generally well established that professionals owed their clients a duty to exercise reasonable skill and care. The heresy was that:

> "if a person engaged to act for a client ought to act fairly and impartially towards the person with whom his client is dealing, then he is immune from being sued by his client—however negligent he may have been."

Lord Salmon gave as an example two instances of the valuation of a picture, the first for a client who does not tell him the reason for the valuation, and the second where the client tells him the valuation is needed because the client is about to sell the picture to a friend. Lord Salmon said he could find no sensible basis for the astonishing proposition that the valuer should be liable for negligence in the first instance, but not in the second.

16.5 ARENSON V. CASSON BECKMAN

Shares undervalued by a factor of six

16.5.1 In *Arenson v. Casson Beckman Rutley & Co.*[28] an agreement provided that shares in a private company had to be sold back to the claimant's uncle on the claimant's leaving the business. The price of the shares was to be the fair value as determined by the company's auditors, whose valuation acting as experts and not as arbitrators was to be final and binding on all parties. The company secretary orally requested the auditors to give a valuation, which they duly did, and the claimant sold his shares at that price. The company was floated shortly after that with the shares selling at six times the auditors' valuation. The House of Lords held that the valuer could be liable in negligence. To establish immunity it would be necessary for the valuer to show a formulated dispute[29] had been put to him to

---

[26] [1974] A.C. 727 at 736F.
[27] *ibid.*, at 758C.
[28] [1977] A.C. 405.
[29] See 17.5.

resolve in a judicial manner; or, in other words, that the valuer had been an arbitrator. The decision in *Sutcliffe v. Thackrah*[30] was very recent, and the Lords justified their view mainly on public policy grounds that the primary rule is that those who commit breaches of a duty of care should be liable to those affected.

Duty identical in contract and tort?

16.5.2 Neither the claimant nor his uncle had a contract with the auditors. The company secretary had simply passed on an oral instruction. It was not known whether the auditors had charged a fee for their valuation. The Lords did not see that these factors made a difference. They saw the duty of the auditor, whether in contract or tort, as identical, following the decision of the House of Lords in *Hedley Byrne & Co. Ltd v. Heller & Partners Ltd.*[31]

The current position

16.5.3 The decision in *Arenson* was followed in *Palacath Ltd v. Flanagan.*[32] The trend in negligence cases since *Arenson* rules out the possibility of any challenge to *Arenson*. The only defence usually available to a valuer who has been negligent is that the valuer did not act as an expert but as an arbitrator in the full sense. It is no longer possible to say that the valuer acted as a quasi-arbitrator, because the category is obsolete.[33] Chapter 17 discusses the distinction between experts and arbitrators and sets out the factors for an assessment of which category a referee belongs to.

Policy considerations

16.5.4 A referee providing a final and binding resolution of a dispute can therefore do so either with or without the benefit of immunity. If the referee acts as an expert, there is no immunity unless the contract is negotiated to that effect. However, if the referee acts as an arbitrator, full statutory immunity provides protection from claims by the parties to the contract, and from claims by any other party as well. If a referee appointed as an expert has sufficient bargaining power, the parties can be required to give that expert immunity, limitation on claims and possibly also indemnities from suit by any other party.[34] The result is that the commercially weaker experts remain liable, while the powerful ones are immune and indemnified. In the two House of Lords cases discussed above the judges were balancing

---

[30] [1974] A.C. 727.
[31] [1964] A.C. 465: see 16.13.
[32] [1985] 2 All E.R. 161.
[33] See 16.6.
[34] This is the practice of the largest international accounting firms, though the exclusion of liability may not be enforceable—see 16.7.12.

two competing principles of public policy. The first principle was that persons acting in a judicial capacity should be immune from claims. The second was that professionals should be liable in damages for the consequences of their negligence. The judges took the view that a valuer was not acting in a judicial capacity, and that therefore the immunity could not apply.[35] More recent decisions point both ways. Expert witnesses have limited immunity,[36] but barristers and solicitors acting as advocates in court proceedings do not have immunity.[37] The question for the twenty-first century is a wider one: why should not all private referees and dispute resolvers, experts, mediators, conciliators and early neutral evaluators, have the benefit of the statutory immunity afforded to arbitrators?

16.6 QUASI-ARBITRATORS

An obsolete status providing immunity for experts

16.6.1 In many of the cases brought against experts, where full arbitral status did not seem appropriate, an expert's immunity was said to derive from the status of a "quasi-arbitrator"; it was said that an expert was in the position of an arbitrator, or that an expert was in the nature of an arbitrator. As far as immunity is concerned, the concept seems to have been killed off by *Sutcliffe v. Thackrah*.[38]

Avoiding a definition

16.6.2 Goddard L.J. (as he then was) in *Finnegan v. Allen*[39] said that the distinction between an arbitrator and what the courts have called a quasi-arbitrator was not capable of precise definition. He then gave commodity arbitrations as an example.[40]

A quasi-arbitrator can represent one of the parties only

16.6.3 A distinction was drawn between arbitrators and quasi-arbitrators in a case[41] where the person appointed to certify that repairs had been satisfactorily carried out was the surveyor appointed to act on behalf of the ship-owner and was therefore the ship-owner's agent. The House of Lords held that the surveyor was discharging the duties of both expert and quasi-arbitrator.

---

[35] See *e.g. Arenson v. Casson Beckman* [1977] A.C. 405 at 423 (Lord Simon).
[36] *Stanton v. Callaghan* [2000] Q.B. 75.
[37] *Arthur J S Hall & Co. v. Simons* [2000] 3 W.L.R. 543.
[38] [1974] A.C. 727.
[39] [1943] 1 K.B. 425 at 436.
[40] See 17.6.5 to 17.6.7.
[41] *Panamena Europea Navigacion (Compania Limitada) v. Frederick Leyland & Co. Ltd (J Russell & Co.)* [1947] A.C. 428.

Illogical basis for theory

In *Sutcliffe v. Thackrah*[42] Lord Reid said:

> "For some reason not clear to me a theory has developed and is reflected in many decided cases to the effect that where the architect has agreed or is required to act fairly he becomes what has often been called a quasi-arbitrator . . . Persons who undertake to act fairly have often been called 'quasi-arbitrators'. One might suppose that to be based on the completely illogical argument—all persons carrying out judicial functions must act fairly, therefore all persons who must act fairly are carrying out judicial functions. There is nothing judicial about an architect's function in determining whether certain work is defective . . ."

16.6.4

and[43]:

> "If immunity [of an arbitrator or quasi-arbitrator] is claimed then it is for the person claiming it to show that the functions in the performance of which he was negligent were sufficiently judicial in character."

Lord Morris said[44]:

> "There may be circumstances in which what was in effect an arbitration is not one that is within the provisions of the Arbitration Act. The expression 'quasi-arbitrator' should only be used in that connection. A person will only be an arbitrator or quasi-arbitrator if there is a submission to him either of a specific dispute or of present points of difference or of defined differences that may in future arise and if there is agreement that his decision will be binding."

Reductio ad absurdum: but really a matter of public policy

Lord Simon showed what a difficult concept this is when he reviewed various possible definitions of quasi-arbitrator in *Arenson v. Casson Beckman Rutley & Co.*[45] He said that it could mean:

16.6.5

(a) a third party whose duty it is, in deciding a question, to "hold the scales fairly" and who is "likely to be shot at by both sides" (this was formulated three different ways); or

(b) "an arbitrator at common law in contradistinction from one under the Arbitration Act" (an obscure concept: presumably only for oral arbitration agreements or agreements specifically excluding the operation of the Act); or

---

[42] [1974] A.C. 727 at 737.
[43] *ibid*. at 738G.
[44] *ibid*. at 752H.
[45] [1977] A.C. 405 at 422G.

16 : Rights and Duties of Experts

(c) "a person who is not an arbitrator under the Arbitration Act ... but nevertheless acts in a judicial capacity or character or fulfils a judicial function."

Lord Simon said that the argument that the defendant in *Arenson* was a quasi-arbitrator entitled to immunity had to be rejected as it was inconsistent with *Sutcliffe v. Thackrah*.[46] But he also said that the immunity of arbitrators was a secondary issue of public policy. The primary issue of public policy was the duty to act with care with regard to another person. In the same case, Lord Kilbrandon said[47]:

> "I am as mistrustful of the phrase 'mere valuer' as I know some of your Lordships are of the office of 'quasi-arbitrator'".

The condescending expression "mere valuer" appears in several of the cases where valuers are contrasted with arbitrators.

Quasi-arbitrator cannot be defined

16.6.6 Judges in more recent cases have refused to enter the arena. Mars-Jones J. in *Palacath Ltd v. Flanagan*[48] decided that a surveyor was not immune without specifically denying that he had acted as a quasi-arbitrator. Scott J. in *North Eastern Co-operative Society Ltd v. Newcastle upon Tyne City Council*[49]:

> "A declaration that someone was acting as a 'quasi-arbitrator' would be likely itself to be the subject of a future application to the court as to what the declaration meant . . ."

and[50]:

> ". . . I do not understand any accurate meaning that can be ascribed to such an expression as quasi-arbitrator."

Death of the concept

16.6.7 Let us hope therefore that quasi-arbitrators have made their final appearance.[51] The concept was artificially devised in order to give immunity to professionals and was incomprehensible.

---

[46] [1974] A.C. 727.
[47] [1977] A.C. 405 at 429G.
[48] [1985] 2 All E.R. 161.
[49] [1987] 1 E.G.L.R. 142 at 143K.
[50] *ibid*. at 146E.
[51] The expressions "quasi-arbitral position" and "quasi-arbitral powers" appear in the judgment in *John Barker v. London Portman Hotel*, 83 B.L.R. 31 at 45E, to refer to the certifying architect's duty to act fairly and lawfully.

Liability for breach of contract and for negligence

Categories and consequences of claims against experts

16.7.1 Since the decision in *Arenson v. Casson Beckman Rutley & Co.*[52] it has been established that an expert making a decision may owe duties to the parties immediately affected by the decision and has no immunity from claims by those parties. The expert is usually a professional person, and, like other professionals, is required by law to exercise the level of skill and care of a reasonably competent member of that profession.[53] The expert's liability for what is known generally as professional negligence may be based on breach of contractual obligations or, in cases where there is no direct contract between the expert and the party aggrieved by the decision, on breach of a duty of care in tort.[54] If the expert is held to have been in breach of duty the expert may not only lose the right to fees and expenses but may also be liable for damages, to the extent that the breach of duty has caused loss.

Breach of contract claims

16.7.2 The following breach of contract claims might be made:

(a) failure to carry out the reference properly, adequately, or at all;
(b) unauthorised delegation;
(c) failure to deliver a timely decision;
(d) failure to follow the parties' instructions.

Failure to carry out the reference properly, adequately, or at all.

16.7.3 Whether the expert has failed to carry out the reference properly depends on either the specific instructions given to the expert or arguments about the expert's implied duties in conducting the reference.[55] Whether the expert has not carried out the reference at all is a question of fact.

Unauthorised delegation

16.7.4 The work of an expert cannot be delegated to an employee or a third party without the parties' permission.[56] If the decision was not made by the designated expert, it is invalid.[57]

---

[52] [1977] A.C. 405.
[53] Or whatever higher standard is claimed by the expert: see 16.7.8 to 16.7.9.
[54] For professional negligence generally, see Jackson and Powell, *Professional Negligence*, 4th edition (Sweet & Maxwell 1997).
[55] See possible examples at 16.8 to 16.12.
[56] *Ess v. Truscott* (1837) 2 M. & W. 385 (employee—not permitted); *Kollerich v. State Trading* [1980] 2 Lloyd's Rep. 32 (certificates were to be issued by one of two agencies named in the contract—issue by another agency not permitted).
[57] See 15.9.6.

16 : Rights and Duties of Experts

Failure to deliver a timely decision

16.7.5 Failure to deliver a decision within a reasonable time is a breach of the implied statutory duty to perform the contract within a reasonable time,[58] unless there is a specific time provision or the duty has been expressly excluded by agreement with the parties.

Duty of care in tort

16.7.6 Cases occur where the expert does not have a contract with either or both of the parties, but as the relationship is a close one based on reliance, the expert is likely to be held to owe a duty of care similar to the contractual duty.[59] However, in order to avoid disputes the prudent course is to ensure that the expert is appointed under a contract between the expert and the parties to the dispute.

Claims against experts generally

16.7.7 Several attempts to sue experts are discussed below. The fact that in the cases which have been reported the claim usually fails does not mean that they rarely succeed. Where there is a considerable risk of liability being established, the professional indemnity insurers will try to negotiate a settlement, as their policy is to avoid cases against their insured reaching the stage of an adverse judgment.

Failure to keep to professional standard

16.7.8 The elements of this are as follows. The expert's liability is usually considered by reference to expert evidence from other experts in the same professional field; some guidance may be obtained from successful actions against members of the same profession in cases where the expert is acting for a single client, for instance where a valuation is prepared for a buyer and not for both buyer and seller. The standard of competence required from a professional is the standard of skill and care expected from a reasonably competent member of that profession.[60] An expert who claims greater qualifications than he or she in fact possesses is judged by the standard claimed.[61] This principle was applied in *Whiteoak v. Walker*[62] considered below.

---

[58] Supply of Goods and Services Act 1982, s. 14.
[59] See 16.13.
[60] *Bolam v. Friern Hospital Management Committee* [1957] 1 W.L.R. 582, now section 13 of the Supply of Goods and Services Act 1982.
[61] *Wilsher v. Essex Area Health Authority* [1987] Q.B. 730; a point which survived the appeal at [1988] A.C. 1074.
[62] (1988) 4 B.C.C. 122.

Auditors

16.7.9 In *Whiteoak v. Walker*[63] an accountant was sued for negligence in valuing shares under pre-emption provisions in the company's articles. The accountant was the company's regular auditor and the articles said he was to certify the fair value acting as an expert and not as an arbitrator.[64] The claimants' case was that the standard of care required was that of a reasonably competent chartered accountant who professed specialist skills in valuing unquoted shares. The court noted that the claimants had wanted to obtain a fair result quickly and cheaply and they chose the company's auditor. In those circumstances the auditor could not have been expected to act as a specialist valuer and was therefore not liable for failing to reach that higher standard. The court also examined several detailed allegations of negligence against that standard, and found that the accountant had not been negligent. For judicial criticism of an accountant's competence where negligence was not the issue, see 15.4.3.

Rent review

16.7.10 In *Singer & Friedlander v. John D Wood & Co*,[65] the judge said that valuation is not a precise task; the fact that experts reach different conclusions did not show that any of them did so through incompetence or lack of care. However, if the rent determined by the expert is significantly outside the "bracket" which the evidence shows to be acceptable, that may be evidence of negligence on the expert's part. In *Belvedere Motors Ltd v. King*[66] the expert was alleged to have reached a figure so significantly below the right figure that this must have been caused by negligence and there were detailed criticisms of the method adopted. Neither the general allegation nor any of the particular allegations were found to be substantiated. In the course of his judgment the judge said that it was not his task to assess the rent, but to find whether the expert had failed to consider some matter which he ought to have considered, or taken into account some matter which he ought not to have taken into account, or in some way failed to adopt the procedures accepted as standard in his profession and so failed to exercise the care and skill he held himself out as possessing. In *Wallshire Ltd v. Aarons*[67] numerous detailed allegations of negligence were rejected. The judgment also contained a statement about the duty to make one's own investigations.[68]

---

[63] *ibid*.
[64] See Chapter 3.
[65] [1977] 2 E.G.L.R. 84.
[66] [1981] 2 E.G.L.R. 131.
[67] [1989] 1 E.G.L.R. 147.
[68] See 16.8.3.

The principal authority is *Zubaida v. Hargreaves*.[69] The Court of Appeal confirmed that it was not enough to show that another expert would have given a different answer. Even if a valuation was on the high side, that was not enough to show that the expert had not performed his duty with reasonable professional competence. The issue was not whether the expert was right; it was whether he had acted in accordance with practices regarded as acceptable in his profession.[70] A very substantial attack was mounted on a surveyor expert in *Lewisham Investment Partnership v. Morgan*,[71] but this failed because the court found that the surveyor expert's assessment was not so far away from what a reasonably competent surveyor would have determined. The same result was achieved in *Currys Group plc v. Martin*.[72]

Excluding or limiting liability—disclaimers

16.7.11 Experts naturally look for ways to minimise their exposure to claims: the liability of adjudicators is excluded specifically by the wording of the Engineering and Construction Contract documents.[73] Experts could seek to exclude the implied duty of skill and care in individual references.[74] An exclusion is subject to the requirement of reasonableness[75] unless it was contained in a specially negotiated contract, and will not be enforced if it is unreasonable. The implied duty of skill and care is excluded for arbitrators,[76] and they also have statutory immunity unless the relevant act or omission is shown to have been in bad faith.[77] These provisions do not protect experts. Experts therefore need to seek contractual exclusions from the implied obligations of skill and care. Some might also seek to exclude the implied obligation to deliver a decision within a reasonable time.[78] Some experts go even further and seek indemnities from those who appoint them. The large international firms of accountants try to limit their liability, but it may not be possible to seek contractual exclusions in some cases, for instance share valuation where there are numerous shareholders potentially affected: in *Killick v. PricewaterhouseCoopers*[79] it was

---

[69] [1995] 1 E.G.L.R. 127.
[70] Hoffmann L.J. (as he then was) in *Zubaida* at 128B.
[71] [1997] 2 E.G.L.R. 150.
[72] [1999] E.G.C.S. 115.
[73] In both the first (1991) and second (1995) editions of the standard form of these contracts.
[74] Compare *Hedley Byrne & Co. Ltd v. Heller & Partners Ltd* [1964] A.C. 465 at 492–493, and *Pacific Associates Inc. v. Baxter* [1990] Q.B. 993 at 1008, 1021–3, 1032 and 1038, CA, discussed at 16.13.2.
[75] Unfair Contract Terms Act 1977, ss. 2 and 3.
[76] Supply of Goods and Services Regulations 1985 (S.I. 1985 No. 1).
[77] Arbitration Act 1996, s. 29(1).
[78] See 16.7.5.
[79] Unreported, July 5, 2000, Neuberger J.

held that a limitation clause did not prevent a duty of care being owed to a shareholder who was unaware of the limitation clause in the expert's contract with the company.

Reluctance to give reasons

16.7.12 Experts prefer to issue non-speaking decisions; *i.e.* those not disclosing their reasons. This stems from the fact that the less an expert discloses, the less anyone can find fault with it. The provision of reasons increases an expert's vulnerability to claims because details of the workings and calculations may be the very evidence that would otherwise be lacking. An expert cannot be compelled to give reasons for the decision unless it is part of the remit.[80] It is a matter determined by the terms of the expert's contract. Some experts accept appointments only on the basis that they will not be giving reasons. It is common in rent review for reasons to be given only if the parties pay the expert higher fees.

General dispute resolution

16.7.13 The potential liability of an expert who decides all disputes under a contract, both technical and non-technical, has yet to be considered by the courts. Consider the case of the Sydney shopping complex, where all disputes were to be decided by an engineering expert.[81] Does an engineer who decides all matters in dispute, such as issues relating to planning regulations, design liability and quantification of damages have the same liability for the decisions on those matters as for the decisions on engineering matters and if so, on what basis? A construction dispute comprising all those features would, if determined by arbitration or litigation, probably need expert witnesses from four different professional disciplines as well as lawyers. An expert taking on the task of deciding a dispute of this kind would be well-advised to establish terms excluding claims.[82]

Can the expert be sued in the same proceedings as the challenge of the decision?

16.7.14 It was held in a case decided in 1976 that a claimant cannot join the expert in proceedings against the other party to the decision in which the decision is being challenged.[83] The same point might well be decided differently now, as the court's reasoning depended on it being possible to set aside a negligent decision by an expert on the ground that it was wrong, which may no longer be possible.[84]

---

[80] See 15.13.7.
[81] See 8.7.2.
[82] See 8.7.4.
[83] *Campbell v. Edwards* [1976] 1 W.L.R. 303 at 409.
[84] See 15.2.2.

Limitation

16.7.15 The limitation period for claims against experts for breach of contract is six years from the date when the breach of contract occurred (usually the date of the decision), unless the expert is appointed under seal, in which case it is 12 years.[85] The period in tort may be longer, as time does not start to run until loss has been suffered, and may be extended where the claimant was unaware of facts relevant to the existence of the claim.[86]

16.8 A DUTY TO MAKE INDEPENDENT INVESTIGATIONS

Does the duty exist?

16.8.1 One of the reasons for referring a question to an expert is that the expert should be sufficiently qualified, if not actually to know the answer, at least to know where to look for it. On the other hand, the parties are usually only too eager to let the expert know what they think the answer should be. Is the expert supposed to carry out independent investigations beyond the material submitted by the parties?

What has the expert been asked to do?

16.8.2 This has to be approached by looking at the expert clause and other instructions given to the expert. If there is a specific obligation to carry out independent investigations the expert would be at fault in not doing so. It is therefore not surprising that some experts accept appointments on the basis that they do not consider any evidence other than the evidence the parties have themselves submitted to them.

Is there a *need* to make an independent investigation?

16.8.3 Where there is no specific provision, the duty depends on whether the parties have submitted sufficient material on which to make a decision. In *Wallshire Ltd v. Aarons*[87] it was argued that a surveyor conducting a rent review as an expert should have looked at more evidence of comparable lettings. The court decided that in this case there was already sufficient evidence presented by the parties.

The allegation may rebound on the party making it

16.8.4 An expert may need to carry out independent investigations if the parties have not submitted adequate material on which to make a

---

[85] Limitation Act 1980, ss. 5 and 8.
[86] See 16.13.5.
[87] [1989] 1 E.G.L.R. 147.

decision and the expert might be liable for negligence for not doing so. Proving that the negligence caused loss is likely to be difficult because of the uncertainty of the results of that independent investigation, and the party making the allegation might have the damages reduced on account of contributory negligence for not having drawn the matter to the expert's attention during the course of the reference.

Arbitrators

By contrast, an arbitrator who carries out his or her own independent investigation risks removal for serious irregularity unless the results of the investigation are put to the parties with an opportunity for rebuttal before the award.[88]

16.8.5

Parties can prevent independent investigations

The parties could agree to prevent the expert from carrying out independent investigations either in the expert clause[89] or at the start of a reference.[90]

16.8.6

A DUTY TO ACT FAIRLY

16.9

Unfairness, partiality and fraud

Cases in which it has been held that an expert has a duty to act fairly and impartially have been referred to in Chapter 15.[91] However the breach of this duty may involve two different types of situation which need to be examined separately. One type of situation is where it is alleged that the expert has conducted the reference improperly, for example there has been collusion between the expert and one of the parties. The other type of situation is where it is alleged that the expert failed to act fairly and/or impartially, but there is no allegation of collusive behaviour or other deliberate impropriety.

16.9.1

In the first type of situation, the aggrieved party would usually be in a position to have the expert's decision itself declared invalid on the grounds considered in 15.4 to 15.6.[92] It would usually be sufficient for the aggrieved party to follow this course, and for this reason claims against the expert based on improper conduct are rare. The aggrieved party may wish to pursue a claim against the expert, for example if the other party is no longer solvent, or if

---

[88] See 17.6.3.
[89] See 9.15.8.
[90] See 13.7.3.
[91] See 15.4; in particular *Macro v. Thompson (No. 3)* [1997] 2 B.C.L.C. 36 at 64 et seq.
[92] *E.g. Hickman v. Roberts* [1913] A.C. 229, HL.

substantial costs (such as legal costs and wasted management time) have been incurred in the course of an abortive reference in which the decision has been declared invalid on the ground of the expert's improper conduct.

However, in the second type of situation, where there is an allegation of lack of fairness or impartiality, but no allegation of collusive behaviour or other deliberate impropriety, it would not usually be possible for the aggrieved party to upset the decision of the expert, as in most cases the decision is binding on the parties even if it is mistaken.[93] The aggrieved party's remedy can only be against the expert, but the focus of the complaint is on whether the decision can be justified rather than on the manner in which the decision was reached.

A claim that the expert's conduct of the reference has rendered the decision invalid might be pursued on the basis that it was an implied term of the contract between the parties and the expert that the expert would not conduct the reference in a manner which would result in the decision being invalid and unenforceable, but there is no case in which an implied term along those lines has been considered. In cases where there is no direct contract between the aggrieved party and the expert (such as claims by contractors against architects), the claim would be a claim in tort and must therefore be based on breach of a duty of care.[94]

Cases in which the expert has been sued on the ground of failure to act fairly and impartially

16.9.2 In *Michael Salliss & Co. Ltd v. Calil*[95] Judge Fox-Andrews Q.C. held, on a preliminary issue, that the architect could be liable for damages in tort suffered as a result of his alleged unfairness in failing to act impartially. That decision, in the context of tort claims by contractors against architects and engineers, was doubted in *Pacific Associates v. Baxter*.[96] The decision could however still be relevant as showing that in an appropriate case an expert might be liable to one of the parties for damages for breach of contract resulting from failure to act fairly and impartially. The thrust of the

---

[93] See 15.12.6 to 15.12.10.

[94] In *John Holland Construction and Engineering Ltd v. Majorca Products* (discussed in 16.9.2) the judge questioned whether the duty to exercise skill and care and the duty to act with fairness and impartiality could be treated as part of a single duty (see pp. 123 and 143).

[95] (1987) 13 Con. L.R. 68 (the claim was made against the architect following a decision in another case (*Northern Regional Health Authority v. Derek Crouch (Construction) Co. Ltd* [1984] 1 Q.B. 644) which meant that it would be difficult to attack the architect's certificate in proceedings against the building-owner); see also *Shui On Construction Ltd v. Shui Kay Company Ltd* (1985) 4 Const. L.J. 305, a Hong Kong case in which Hunter J. held a similar claim to be arguable.

[96] [1990] Q.B. 993; discussed at 16.13.2.

plaintiff's case was that the architect's decision was wrong, and the case was of the second type referred to in 16.9.1.

In the Australian case of *John Holland Construction and Engineering Ltd v. Majorca Products*[97] the claim was brought by a building contractor against the architect because the building-owner had gone into liquidation. The claim included an allegation that the architect had sought and/or received representations from the building-owner intended to influence it without giving the contractor the opportunity of answering the representations, and by having regard exclusively or predominantly to the interests of the building-owner. The court held, consistently with the English Court of Appeal in *Pacific Associates*, that the architect owed the contractor no duty of care, and went on to reject the allegations of breach of duty on the facts. In the course of his judgment the judge accepted that want of impartiality might be inferred from "an error ... so egregious or persistent that an impartial or fair-minded certifier would not have made it".[98]

Fairness of the procedure

Whilst it is clear that an expert owes in general terms a duty to the parties to conduct the determination fairly, it is harder to define precisely what this requires in particular cases. Fairness is not governed by an objective standard, but is to be determined by reference to the contracts between the parties.[99] The wording of the expert clause, the terms of the contract between the parties and the expert, and any terms of reference all need to be considered. Relevant also might be how determinations are carried out in the particular commercial or industrial context: as can be seen from other chapters in this book, different traditions are found.[1]

16.9.3

A DUTY TO APPLY THE LAW

16.10

An arbitral tribunal has a duty to decide the dispute in accordance with the law, or "such other considerations" as may be agreed by the parties.[2] Parties are likely to expect that an expert should adopt the same approach, where there are legal issues to be decided. In the absence of any wording to the contrary, the court would generally interpret the contract as requiring the expert to reach a decision in accordance with the terms of the contract,

---

[97] (1996) 16 Const. L.J. 114 (Supreme Court of Victoria).
[98] At p. 130.
[99] See 15.4 to 15.16.
[1] Two examples: accountants rarely give reasons, while other professionals generally do give them; and representations to experts are made in a number of different ways.
[2] Arbitration Act 1996, s. 46.

properly construed, and in accordance with applicable legal principles, and would consequently hold the expert to be in breach of duty if he or she negligently reached a decision which was not in accordance with the terms of the contract or applicable legal principles.[3] Failure to obtain legal advice may be alleged to amount to negligence,[4] particularly if one of the parties had specifically asked that the expert should obtain legal advice. Disregarding an undisputed legal opinion obtained by one of the parties might also be relied on as amounting to negligence. Where no reasons are given for the decision, it may be hard to tell what considerations have been applied, and impossible to prove that the expert has not applied the law.[5] Parties agreeing the terms of an expert clause could address these points by stipulating firstly that the expert's terms of reference should include an express requirement to apply the law and secondly that the expert's decision should include reasons.

16.11 A DUTY TO REACH A FINAL AND BINDING DECISION

An expert's instructions are often to reach a final and binding decision, and where it is not an express requirement it should usually not be difficult to imply an obligation on the part of the expert to reach a final and binding decision[6]. An expert who does not do so may be in breach of contract and liable to the parties in damages for the consequences. This duty could include a duty to reach a decision which is not invalid and unenforceable as a result of the expert's failure to act fairly and impartially.[7]

For two contrasting examples of where experts were alleged to have produced an inconclusive decision, see 15.13.7. Where the work done by the expert is not inconclusive but simply not concluded, the court investigates the facts to see whether a final decision has or has not been reached.[8]

16.12 A DUTY OF CONFIDENTIALITY

Parties would generally expect their appointed expert to keep their affairs confidential. It is likely to be an implied term of the appointment that the expert should do so, although there is no

[3] *John Barker Construction Ltd v. London Portman Hotel Ltd* (1996) 83 B.L.R. 31 at 44–5 (discussed at 15.8.2), *Lewisham Investment Partnership Ltd v. Morgan* [1997] 2 E.G.L.R. 150 at 158L.
[4] The allegation was made in *Lewisham Investment Partnership Ltd v. Morgan* (above).
[5] See 18.5.3.
[6] See also 9.8.3.
[7] See 16.9.1.
[8] As in *Gordon v. Whitehouse* (1856) 18 C.B. 747.

decision to this effect. Some expert clauses and/or terms of reference impose a specific duty of confidentiality on the expert. This duty can be overridden by, for instance, the service of a witness summons, the validity of which is not challenged or which, if it is challenged, is upheld by the court.[9]

TORTIOUS LIABILITY
16.13

Where there is no contractual relationship

An expert may have no contractual relationship with the parties either directly or indirectly through an appointing authority. The expert may be appointed by a third party, such as a company secretary instructing auditors to value shares, which is what happened in *Arenson v. Casson Beckman Rutley & Co.*[10] Arguably the company secretary was acting as agent for the shareholders. That kind of arrangement should present no problems, and Lord Salmon certainly thought it did not prevent the expert owing a duty of care in tort[11]:
16.13.1

> "We do not know whether the [auditors] were asked to make the valuation on behalf of the company (which presumably was interested in the value of its own shares) or on behalf of [the buying and selling shareholders], nor do we know whether the [auditors] charged any fee for this valuation, and, if so, to whom, or whether they made their valuation as part of their ordinary duties as the company's auditors. Nor do I think this matters because, since the decision of [the House of Lords] in *Hedley Byrne*[12] ... it is clear that quite apart from any contractual obligation, the respondents must have owed a duty to [both shareholders] to use reasonable skill and care in making their valuation."

Where the valuer denies that the circumstances gave rise to a duty of care owed to the claimant, the court decides whether a duty of care was owed by examining

(a) the foreseeability of the damage;
(b) the proximity of the parties; and
(c) whether it is just and reasonable in all the circumstances that the duty should exist.[13]

---

[9] This is unlikely; see 15.19.
[10] [1977] A.C. 405.
[11] *ibid.* at 434; followed in *Killick v. PricewaterhouseCoopers*, unreported, July 5, 2000, Neuberger J.
[12] [1964] A.C. 465.
[13] Lord Oliver in *Caparo Industries plc v. Dickman* [1990] 2 A.C. 605 at 633B.

Experts do owe tortious duties of care

16.13.2 The circumstances in which a duty of care is owed by one person who gives advice to another person are typically as follows[14]:

(a) The advice must be required for a purpose, whether particularly specified or generally described, which is made known either actually or inferentially to the adviser when the advice is requested.

(b) The adviser knows either actually or inferentially that the advice will be communicated to the advisee, either specifically or as a member of an ascertainable class, in order that it should be used by the advisee for that purpose.

(c) It is known either actually or inferentially that the advice so communicated is likely to be acted upon by the advisee for that purpose without further inquiry.

(d) It is so acted upon by the advisee to his detriment.

The word "advice" is used, although in *Caparo v. Dickman* the advice consisted of the audit of a company, which is more similar to an expert determination than advice given for instance by a lawyer.

From these criteria it usually follows that an expert making a determination under a contract between two parties owes a duty of care to both those parties because both rely on the expert, and no one else, to get the determination right, if for no other reason than that they will be bound by it. However, the general rules applicable to liability for damages for financial loss as a result of negligence have to be borne in mind. The issue of the expert's liability always depends on all the circumstances, including the purpose of the expert's determination, the context in which it is made, the availability of other remedies such as review mechanisms provided in the contract, and the presence of any reservations, qualifications or disclaimers. A construction contract certification case provides an illustration of the point. It has been held by the Court of Appeal that an engineer certifying payments to a contractor under an engineering contract did not owe a duty of care to the contractor so as to be liable to the contractor for damages in the event of negligent under-certification[15]; one of the reasons for deciding that there was no duty of care was that the contractor could claim relief from the consequences of the engineer's

---

[14] *ibid.* at 638.

[15] *Pacific Associates Inc. v. Baxter* [1990] Q.B. 993; see Timothy Trotman "*Pacific Associates v. Baxter*: Time for Re-Consideration?" (1999) 15 Const. L. J. 449 for a criticism of this decision in the light of more recent authorities. In *John Holland Construction and Engineering Ltd v. Majorca Products* (1996) 16 Const. L. J. 114 an Australian court reached the same conclusion as the Court of Appeal in *Pacific Associates*.

negligence by commencing an arbitration against the employer in which the decisions of the engineer could be reviewed.[16] In the same case, the Court of Appeal held that a clause in the contract between the contractor and the employer which purported to protect the engineer from claims excluded the creation of a direct duty owed by the engineer to the contractor.[17] Purchas L.J. doubted two first-instance decisions in which it had been held that a certifier under a construction contract could be liable in tort for breach of a duty of care or a duty to act fairly, or that it was arguable that such duties existed.[18]

An expert can be liable in respect of the same circumstances concurrently in both contract and tort.[19] In some circumstances the expert's duty of care in tort may be wider than the duties imposed by the contract.[20]

Triggers

16.13.3

Sometimes an expert is asked to issue a certificate under one contract which triggers events under another contract.[21] The application of general principles as to liability for negligent mis-statement often means that an expert has no liability in those circumstances to persons who are party only to the second contract: the expert owes no duty of care in tort if there has been no reference to that expert by the parties to the second contract and the expert is unaware that there are third parties who will be affected by the decision. (This applies only to the expert's tortious liability to parties with whom there is no contractual relationship.)

Experts who are agents of one of the parties

16.13.4

In cases concerning certificates under building contracts the certifier is typically the agent of the building-owner. A claim by the building-owner against the certifier is likely to be a claim for breach of contract.[22] A claim by the contractor could only be pursued as a claim in tort. It was held in *Pacific Associates v.*

---

[16] [1990] Q.B. 993, at 1023, 1029, 1031, 1037 and 1039. The arbitration between the contractor and the employer was settled before the action against the engineer was commenced (see at 1003E of the judgment of Purchas L.J.).
[17] [1990] Q.B. 993, at 1008, 1021–3, 1032 and 1038.
[18] *ibid.*, at 1018–20. The cases were *Michael Salliss & Co. Ltd v. Calil* (1987) 13 Con. L.R. 68, in which Judge Fox-Andrews Q.C. held that the architect could be liable for damages in tort suffered as a result of his unfairness in failing to act impartially, and *Shui On Construction Ltd v. Shui Kay Company Ltd* (1985) 4 Const. L.J. 305, Hunter J. at 309 (Hong Kong).
[19] *Henderson v. Merrett Syndicates Ltd* [1995] 2 A.C. 145.
[20] *Holt v. Payne Skillington* (1996) 77 B.L.R. 51 at 73, *Tesco Stores Ltd v. The Norman Hitchcox Partnership Ltd* (1997) 56 Con. L.R. 42 at 164-5.
[21] See 7.4.5.
[22] For example, *Sutcliffe v. Thackrah* [1974] A.C. 727, HL.

Baxter[23] that the contractor had no claim against the engineer, at any rate where the certificate could be reviewed in an arbitration, thereby providing the certifier with a degree of immunity. However, the decision has been criticised.[24]

Limitation period

16.13.5 An expert may therefore be liable concurrently in both contract and tort, which may help a claimant as the limitation period may be longer in tort. Time does not start to run in respect of a tort claim until loss has been suffered, and the limitation period may be extended where the claimant was unaware of facts relevant to the existence of the claim.[25]

---

[23] [1990] Q.B. 993—discussed at 16.13.2.
[24] See "*Pacific Associates v. Baxter*: Time for re-consideration?" by Timothy Trotman (1999) 15 Const. L. J. 449. But see the Australian case of *John Holland* referred to at 16.13.2.
[25] Limitation Act 1980, s. 14A.

CHAPTER 17

ARBITRATION IS DIFFERENT

SUMMARY 17.1

This chapter seeks to distinguish arbitration from expert determination by considering:

(a) confusion between whether references have been to experts or arbitrators (17.2);
(b) how the court interprets express words in the contract about a referee's status (17.3);
(c) the key indicators of the referee's status (17.4 to 17.9);
(d) the procedural differences between arbitrations and references to experts (17.10); and
(e) the different consequences of an expert's decision and an arbitration award (17.11).

IS THE REFERENCE TO AN EXPERT OR AN ARBITRATOR? 17.2

A great controversy

This question has occupied the courts more than any other raised 17.2.1
by the whole subject of expert determination.[1] Some of the problems have arisen from lawyers being simply confused.[2] The question has been so controversial because of earlier uncertainty about the law relating to arbitrators and experts generally, and because of the differences between the consequences of an expert's decision and the consequences of an arbitration award. The differences

---

[1] See Mark McGaw in *Travels In Alsatia*, in *Construction Law: Themes and Practice: Essays in honour of Ian Duncan Wallace*, Sweet & Maxwell, 1998, pp. 131–187. This very authoritative essay analyses the separate growth of arbitration and non-arbitral contractual discretionary powers, notably for the period up to the mid-nineteenth century.
[2] See 17.5.7. If lawyers are confused, it is hardly surprising that journalists are too: see the press accounts of the *Texas Homecare* determination cited in the footnote to 1.1.2.

between those consequences have themselves varied over the years[3]: the current position is set out at 17.11.

Background from earlier chapters

17.2.2 Chapter 14 demonstrates that arbitration awards are easier to enforce than experts' decisions. Chapter 15 shows the very limited potential for challenge to experts' decisions compared to the procedure for arbitration appeals described in this chapter. Chapter 16 shows how experts have become liable for breach of duty while arbitrators are immune.

Reasons for raising the controversy

17.2.3 Arbitration is different. A dissatisfied party may want to establish that the reference was made to an expert to facilitate an action against the dispute resolver, or to establish that the reference was made to an arbitrator to facilitate an appeal against the award. Again there may be differences in rights of enforcement prompting the claim that an arbitration was a reference to an expert, or vice versa. An awkward party may simply want to raise it as a tactical obstacle.

17.3 EXPRESS WORDS

Considered with other evidence about the reference

17.3.1 The court looks at the words of the expert clause which, if unambiguous, may be significant evidence of the intentions of the parties about the procedure that eventuated.[4] However, that evidence has to be considered along with what issue the referee had to consider and what actually happened in the reference.

Express words not conclusive . . .

17.3.2 For instance, in *Taylor v. Yielding*[5] the court said: "The cases are quite clear that you cannot make a valuer an arbitrator by calling him so or *vice versa*." The report is very brief, but it is a telling remark. The cases relied on were mainly about references involving

---

[3] In the second half of the eighteenth century and the first half of the nineteenth century, the distinction between the consequences was sharpened by stamp duty legislation: Mark McGaw, in *Travels In Alsatia*, in *Construction Law: Themes and Practice*: *Essays in honour of Ian Duncan Wallace*, Sweet & Maxwell, 1998, pp. 131–187 at p. 175.

[4] For a simple example, where it was clear that a valuation and not an arbitration was intended by the use of the word "valuers", see *Re Laidlaw and Campbellford Lake Ontario and Western Railway Company* (1914) 19 D.L.R. 481.

[5] (1912) 56 S.J. 253.

umpires being valuations and not arbitrations. For instance, in *Re Hammond and Waterton*[6] arbitrators were designated by the parties' agreement to assess the amount of compensation to be paid by an outgoing tenant of a market garden to his landlord. The judge said he believed the parties intended the reference to be a valuation, because of the appointment as the arbitrators of a seedsman and a market gardener, both being, in his view, eminently suitable persons to assess the compensation by exercising their own skill and knowledge without any evidence or witnesses being called before them. The use of the word "adjudication" in a construction context might suggest that the means of dispute resolution was a type of expert determination, but was held in one case to be a reference to arbitration.[7] Thus the use of particular words is not conclusive proof of the intentions of the parties. In another context, the House of Lords has expressed this principle trenchantly:

> "The manufacture of a five pronged instrument for digging results in a fork even if the manufacturer, unfamiliar with the English language, insists that he has intended to make, and has made, a spade."[8]

... but still very persuasive

17.3.3 However, the clearer the words used, the more difficult a contrary view becomes. In *Palacath Ltd v. Flanagan*[9] the terms of a lease stated that the rent reviewer was to act as an expert and not as an arbitrator. The rent reviewer sought to defend an action for negligence on the basis that he was an arbitrator or quasi-arbitrator. The judge agreed with the dictum in *Taylor v. Yielding*[10] and said that the clause in the lease was not conclusive. But the judge did find the wording to be a very potent factor and, after reviewing the indicators discussed below, he found that the decision had indeed been that of an expert.

Wording not clear

17.3.4 Where the wording of the expert clause does not state expressly what method of determination is intended, the court will first try to reach a conclusion based on the wording of the expert clause,[10a] but may also look at the other words in the document to resolve the ambiguity.[11] There have been some instances where a clause in a

---

[6] (1890) 62 L.T. 808.
[7] *Cape Durasteel Ltd v. Rosser and Russell Building Services Ltd* (1996) 46 Con L.R. 75.
[8] *Street v. Mountford* [1985] A.C. 809: Lord Templeman.
[9] [1985] 2 All E.R. 161.
[10] (1912) 56 S.J. 253.
[10a] *Wilson (David) Homes Ltd v. Surrey Services Ltd (in liquidation) & anr*: [2001] E.W.C.A. Civ. 34—Court of Appeal (Civil Division)—Thorpe L.J., Longmore J., January 18, 2001
[11] See 12.8.2.

lease states that the rent reviewer is to be a surveyor without specifying whether the surveyor is to act as an expert or as an arbitrator. In one case[12] the lease contained an underlease immediately preceding the rent review clause; there were express words in the underlease specifying arbitration and the disputed clause did not use any of those words. The judge decided that the surveyor was to be an expert. In another case,[13] the reasons given for stating that the lease called for the appointment of an expert were that there was a deliberate non-adoption of any express reference to arbitration by clear contrast to the main body of the lease; the relevant part of the lease did not presuppose a dispute[14]; and the nature of the exercise—the determination of rent under a rent review—was particularly suitable for expert procedures. The use of the word "umpire" is neutral.[15]

Confused drafting

17.3.5   Clauses are sometimes encountered which state that an expert is to be appointed but then go on to state that the person will act as an arbitrator or, alternatively, that an arbitrator is to be appointed and then go on to say that that person will act as an expert.[16] The confusion created by this can be very wasteful. Apart from creating the excuse for a dispute about the procedure to be used to resolve a dispute, it also perpetuates the misunderstanding of the differences between expert determination and arbitration.[17]

Where the reference has not yet taken place

17.3.6   If a dispute about the dispute clause comes to a head before the reference has taken place, the words of the contract are the only evidence of the parties' intentions, and the test is whether the parties intended that differences should be settled by a judicial function, in which case the reference is to arbitration.[18]

---

[12] *Langham House Developments Ltd v. Brompton Securities Ltd* [1980] 2 E.G.L.R. 117.
[13] *Fordgate Bingley Ltd v. Argyll Stores Ltd* [1994] 2 E.G.L.R. 84.
[14] See 17.5.
[15] *Safeway Food Stores Ltd v. Banderway Ltd* [1983] 2 E.G.L.R. 116.
[16] For two examples, see *Norwich Union Life Assurance Society v. P&O Property Holdings Ltd* [1993] 1 E.G.L.R. 164, where the expert was called an "arbiter", the Latin and Scots word for an arbitrator, and *Cott UK Ltd v. FE Barber Ltd* [1977] 3 All E.R. 540, where the dispute clause was headed "Arbitration" and said that the person was to be an "independent consultant" and to act "as an expert and not as an arbiter".
[17] See 17.5.7.
[18] *Cape Durasteel Ltd v. Rosser and Russell Building Services Ltd* (1996) 46 Con L.R. 75, quoting *Keating on Building Contracts*, 6th edition (Sweet & Maxwell, 2001) pp. 264–5, now 7th edition, para 16–13.

KEY INDICATORS 17.4

Lord Wheatley's list

Where a reference, or part of one, has taken place, the courts consider a number of factors to establish whether the reference was to an expert or an arbitrator. Those factors were called "indicia" by Lord Wheatley in *Arenson v. Casson Beckman Rutley & Co.*[19] In this book the word "indicators" is used. There are many cases on the distinction: *Arenson* is the starting-point for the modern law on the subject. In that case the defendant auditors claimed immunity from an action for negligence. Following the (then) recent decision in *Sutcliffe v. Thackrah*[20] which had decided that a certifier under a building contract did not have arbitral immunity, the issue in *Arenson* was whether the defendants' valuation of shares was an arbitration. Lord Wheatley said[21] that although each case had to be decided on its own facts, there were four indicators to assist in determining whether the valuer had the benefit of arbitral immunity. If the following were present, this would usually indicate that the decision-maker was an arbitrator rather than an expert: 17.4.1

(a) There is a dispute or a difference between the parties which has been formulated in some way or other (see 17.5).
(b) The dispute or difference has been remitted by the parties to the person to resolve in such a manner that the person is called on to exercise a judicial function (see 17.6).
(c) Where appropriate, the parties must have been provided with an opportunity to present evidence and/or submissions in support of their respective claims in the dispute (see 17.7).
(d) The parties have agreed to accept the decision (see 17.8).

Indicators—and therefore not conclusive

The following sections seek to evaluate these indicators. No indicator is conclusive on its own, and a combination of them may not be either. 17.4.2

A FORMULATED DISPUTE 17.5

The traditional distinction between experts and arbitrators

The notion that a formulated dispute (*i.e.* an issue on which the parties have taken defined positions) is necessary to make the valuer or expert into an arbitrator is deep-rooted. In *Collins v. Collins*,[22] 17.5.1

---

[19] [1977] A.C. 405.
[20] [1974] A.C. 727.
[21] At 428E-F.
[22] (1858) 26 Beav. 306 at 312.

where parties had entered into a contract to buy a brewery and plant at a price to be fixed by arbitrators and an umpire, Sir John Romilly M.R. said:

> "... fixing the price of a property may be 'arbitration' ... but ... an arbitration is a reference to the decision of one or more persons ... of some matter ... in difference between the parties ... It is very true that in one sense it must be implied that although there is no existing difference, still that a difference may arise between the parties: yet I think the distinction between an existing difference and one which may arise is a material one, and one which has properly been relied on in this case ... It may well be that the decision of a particular valuer appointed might fix the price and might be equally satisfactory to both: so it can hardly be said there is a difference between them. Undoubtedly, as a general rule, the seller wants to get the highest price for his property, and the purchaser wishes to give the lowest, and in that sense it may be said that an expected difference between the parties is to be implied in every case, but unless a difference has actually arisen, it does not appear to me to be an 'arbitration'. Undoubtedly, if two persons enter into an arrangement for the sale of any particular property, and try to settle the terms, but cannot agree, and after dispute and discussion respecting the price, they say, 'We will refer this question of price to AB, he shall settle it', and thereupon they agree that the matter shall be referred to his arbitration, that would appear to be an 'arbitration', in the proper sense of the term ...; but if they agree to a price to be fixed by another, that does not appear to me to be an arbitration."

This authority was followed in a subsequent case[23] about the auction of property, where a condition of the sale stated that mistakes in the description of the property would not annul the sale, but compensation should be settled by two referees, one to be appointed by each party to the sale, and an umpire. The court held that the reference was of the amount of the compensation, and not a reference to arbitration of an existing or future difference.

Allied to this is the concept of the distinction between preventing disputes and resolving disputes:

> "... there are cases in which a person is appointed to ascertain some matter for the purpose of preventing differences arising, not of settling the disputes that have arisen, and where the case is not one of arbitration but of mere valuation".[24]

This concept of preventing disputes was relied on in a Hong Kong case.[25] The court did not adopt the argument but nevertheless

---

[23] *Bos v. Helsham* (1866) L.R. 2 Exch 72.
[24] *Re Carus-Wilson and Greene* (1886) 18 Q.B.D. 7 at 9, Lord Esher M.R., applied in *David Wilson Homes Ltd v. Surrey Services Ltd (in liquidation)*, January 18, 2001, CA, unreported.
[25] *Mayers v. Dlugash* [1994] 1 H.K.C. 755, Kaplan J.

decided that the accountant who was to determine the manner of distribution of the business, assets and liabilities of a company owned jointly by the parties was to act as an expert, partly because a dispute about the terms on which the parties should bring their commercial relationship to an end was not a sufficiently formulated dispute.

Can a case with no dispute be an arbitration?

In *Tharsis Sulphur & Copper Co. Ltd v. Loftus*[26] the court found that the amount of an average adjustment was in question between the parties under the terms of their agreement to refer, and therefore appears to have concluded that the reference to the average adjuster to apportion cargo damage was the reference of a dispute to arbitration. However, as Lord Salmon said in *Sutcliffe v. Thackrah*[27]:

17.5.2

> ". . . there does not seem to have been any dispute between the parties [in *Tharsis Sulphur*]. They both knew that a loss had been suffered which had to be apportioned between them, but there is nothing to show that they had any idea, let alone conflicting ideas, of what the correct apportionment should be. Each of them might have engaged a separate average adjuster to advise him: had these not agreed, a dispute could have arisen between the parties which they might have submitted to arbitration—a somewhat unusual course in business of this kind. Instead, they sensibly decided to avoid disputes and differences by jointly employing one average adjuster to advise them on how the loss should be apportioned and agreed to accept and act on his advice."

It has been held that an arbitration cannot be started without there first being a difference or dispute between the parties. This requires the making of a claim by one party and its rejection by the other party.[28]

But a dispute resolver need not be an arbitrator

While arbitration requires a dispute, the existence of a dispute does not necessarily enable one to infer that the system used to resolve the dispute is arbitration:

17.5.3

> "There may be cases of the intermediate kind, where, though a person is appointed to settle disputes that have arisen, still it is not intended that he shall be bound to hear evidence and arguments. In

---

[26] (1872) L.R. 8 C.P. 1, Bovill C.J. during argument.
[27] [1974] A.C. 727 at 762C and D.
[28] *Cruden Construction Ltd v. Commission for the New Towns* (1994) 75 B.L.R. 134: *Monmouthshire County Council v. Costelloe and Kemple Ltd* (1965) 5 B.L.R. 83, Lord Denning M.R.

such cases it may often be difficult to say whether he is intended to be an arbitrator or to exercise some function other than that of an arbitrator".[29]

An architect's certificate is not the decision of a dispute

17.5.4 In *Chambers v. Goldthorpe*[30] the Court of Appeal had to assert, at some length, that a formulated dispute was *not* necessary to give arbitral immunity to an architect certifying payments due to a contractor under a building contract. This issue was therefore of major importance for the House of Lords when they overruled *Chambers v. Goldthorpe* in *Sutcliffe v. Thackrah*.[31] They held that the architect's interim certificate was not the decision of a dispute between the claimant and his builders, and that there would need to be a dispute for the architect to qualify as an arbitrator.[32] They did not decide, because they did not need to for the purposes of the particular case, whether the dispute had to be formulated or what that expression might mean.

Auditors as arbitrators?

17.5.5 In *Leigh v. English Property Corporation Ltd*[33] a company's articles of association were silent as to whether its auditors should value its shares as experts or as arbitrators. Brightman J. at first instance said that because the articles showed that the auditors were not to be called in until the parties showed they were in disagreement, it was arguable that the auditors were to act as arbitrators; the Court of Appeal affirmed his decision. This raises the question of whether a partnership, such as a firm of accountants or a corporation, can act as arbitrators. An arbitral tribunal is often composed of three or sometimes of five individuals, but all those individuals take a full part in the proceedings. Some modern firms of accountants number hundreds of partners, and their appointment as arbitrators would be inconsistent with the concept of all the members of a tribunal playing a full role by, for instance, attending the hearing. The question of whether a firm could be appointed as arbitrator was not considered in *Leigh v. English Property Corporation Ltd*. Since that case was decided, it has been enacted that an arbitrator's function is personal and ceases on death.[34] From this it follows that a partnership cannot act as arbitrators.

---

[29] *Re Carus-Wilson & Greene* (1886) 18 Q.B.D. 7 at 9, Lord Esher M.R.
[30] [1901] 1 Q.B. 624.
[31] [1974] A.C. 727.
[32] *ibid.*, Lord Reid at 737H. For a discussion of certifiers in construction contracts, see 7.4.
[33] [1976] 2 Lloyd's Rep. 298.
[34] Arbitration Act 1996, s. 26(1).

A dispute can be referred to an expert

Scott J. considered the question in *North Eastern Cooperative Society Ltd v. Newcastle upon Tyne City Council*,[35] a case about ambiguous provisions in a lease dealing with the status of the rent reviewer:

17.5.6

> ". . . there was, of course, a dispute between the parties at the time in question in the sense that they could not agree on the amount of the yearly rent; but it was not a dispute in which each had formulated a view which was then placed for decision before the independent surveyor. The independent surveyor asked for their submissions in order to assist him in his task. He did not proceed on the footing that he was obliged to have their submissions."

This passage contains the important recognition that the existence of a dispute does not preclude a reference to an expert. Scott J. said that the distinction lay in whether the parties would have been prepared to allow the matter to be decided on the basis of views which had not been formulated.

Ipswich v. Fisons

The indicator of whether a dispute has been formulated between the parties was restated in *Ipswich Borough Council v. Fisons plc*.[36] The headnote in the Law Reports is wrong: it states that the lease provided that disputes were to be referred to arbitration, whereas in fact the lease between Ipswich and Fisons said that if Fisons did not accept Ipswich's terms the matter should be referred to an independent expert. The serious consequences of confusion between experts and arbitrators are underlined by the fact that the subject matter of this case that the Court of Appeal had to deal with was nothing more than the rent of a car park. Purporting to act under the terms of the lease, the parties appointed an arbitrator, and Ipswich appealed against the award. The case is important for establishing the circumstances in which the courts allow an appeal from an arbitration award. It is also important for expert determination because of the words of Lord Donaldson M.R.[37]:

17.5.7

> "[The expert] was not determining the rights and obligations of the parties. They were not in dispute. He was fixing the terms in the exercise of his professional skill and judgment . . . Undoubtedly the parties did not see it like this. They seem to have concluded that the *independent expert would be acting as an arbitrator* . . ." (emphasis added).

---

[35] [1987] 1 E.G.L.R. 142; the quotation comes from 146A.
[36] [1990] Ch. 709.
[37] *ibid.* at 725G.

This goes to the heart of how some judges would like to define the essential difference between experts and arbitrators. The curious facts of *Ipswich v. Fisons* enable the court to draw a distinction between cases considered suitable for expert determination, where there was no dispute as to the parties' respective rights and obligations, and cases considered suitable for arbitration, where there was a dispute about the parties' respective rights and obligations. Lord Donaldson was suggesting that the parties made an informed decision that the matter had to be referred to arbitration on the basis that they had a formulated dispute where their rights and obligations were to be determined. Probably the true position in this case (as in many others) was that the parties and their lawyers were not familiar with the distinction and were just confused, and may not even have realised that there is a distinction.

Transition to the next indicator

17.5.8 Commenting on this indicator in *Capricorn Inks Pty Ltd v. Lawter International (Australasia) Pty Ltd*,[38] the judge said:

> ". . . the existence of a 'dispute', although a factor, is not necessarily a decisive factor in determining whether arbitration or appraisement is involved. It is quite possible for parties to become involved in a dispute about something, such as the value of premises or goods, which they agree to submit for appraisal without intending that an arbitration should follow. The distinction depends on a range of factors of varying importance and weight depending on the circumstances; but generally what must be in contemplation is that there will be 'an inquiry in the nature of a judicial inquiry'".

This leads to the next indicator.

17.6 A JUDICIAL FUNCTION

A judge is not an expert

17.6.1 To be an arbitrator, the referee has to be shown, in deciding the matter between the parties, to have exercised the functions of a judge. It is not the function of a judge to use his or her own expertise in a given area outside the law and the administration of justice. For instance,[39] the Court of Appeal has criticised a judge for having:

> "turned himself into a handwriting expert and compared examples of the defendant's signature . . . A judge should not be seen as a witness who held himself capable of comparing handwriting and reached conclusions of the comparisons".

---

[38] [1989] 1 Qd R. 8 at 15. The last phrase is a quotation from the judgment of Lord Esher M.R. in *Re Carus-Wilson and Greene* (1886) 18 Q.B.D. 7 at 9.
[39] *R. v. Simbodyal, The Times*, October 10, 1991.

This was a criminal case but the principle is the same in civil cases.

This indicator often overlaps with the next one, which relates to the manner in which judicial inquiries are conducted, with particular reference to evidence and submissions.

Re Hopper

17.6.2 The line of authority starts with *Re Hopper*.[40] The court took the view that the case raised issues that were sufficiently difficult (illustrated by the fact that the arbitrators differed considerably in their views and the fact that the parties were represented at the hearing by counsel) to justify the decision that the procedure had been an arbitration. In *Sutcliffe v. Thackrah*[41] Lord Salmon explained the point as follows:

> "In *Re Hopper* Cockburn CJ ... was ... saying that the question whether anyone was to be treated as an arbitrator depended on whether the role which he performed was invested with the characteristic attributes of the judicial role. If an expert were employed to certify, make a valuation or appraisal or settle compensation as between opposing interests, this did not, of itself, put him in the position of an arbitrator. He might ... do no more than examine goods or work or accounts and make a decision accordingly. On the other hand, he might, as in *Re Hopper*, hear the evidence and submissions of the parties, in which case he would clearly be regarded as an arbitrator ..."

Arbitrators using their own expertise

17.6.3 Where arbitrators behave more like experts and rely on their own expertise, their awards may be set aside. One example is *Annie Fox v. P G Wellfair Ltd (in liquidation)*[42] the respondents did not take part in the proceedings but the applicants produced expert evidence at the hearing. The court said that the conclusion the arbitrator had come to could only have been reached by, in effect, giving evidence to himself in flat contradiction to the evidence given by the applicants' expert witness. The arbitrator was guilty of misconduct[43] in failing to observe the rules of natural justice, and the award was set aside and the arbitrator removed. In *Top Shop Estates v. Danino*[44] a surveyor conducted a rent review of a shop as an arbitrator. Without telling the parties, he collected a series of pedestrian counts which he considered relevant. His award was also set aside, Leggatt J. remarking that the arbitrator's function

---

[40] (1867) L.R. 2 Q.B. 367.
[41] [1974] A.C. 727 at 763D.
[42] [1981] 2 Lloyd's Rep. 514.
[43] Now renamed and redefined as serious irregularity in the Arbitration Act 1996, s. 68.
[44] [1985] 1 E.G.L.R. 9.

was not to play the part of Perry Mason[45] where he felt that the submissions or evidence of the parties might usefully be supplemented. However, a rent review arbitrator was allowed rather more latitude in disagreeing with the expert witnesses of both parties about the assessment of valuation criteria in *Lex Services plc v. Oriel House BV.*[46] Expensive court cases have been mounted concerning the distinction to be drawn between the general expertise arbitrators may have from their knowledge of an area of business on the one hand and the specifics of the dispute in question on the other hand. The distinction is not always easy to apply.[47] These problems do not arise if the referee is an expert who is expected to rely on his or her own expertise.[48]

The ultimate test

17.6.4 The ultimate test of whether or not the decision-maker is to act as an arbitrator was said by Mars-Jones J. in *Palacath Ltd v. Flanagan*[49] to be:

> "... how is he [the referee] to arrive at his decision? Was he obliged to act wholly or in part on the evidence and submissions made by the parties? Or was he entitled to act solely on his own expert opinion? If the answer to the question is the latter, then the [referee] could not be exercising a judicial function or a quasi-judicial function, if there is any such distinction".

In an action by a tenant against the surveyor who had represented him in a rent review,[50] the surveyor was found liable for the consequences of failing to put in representations by the date stipulated by the expert; the court said that the expert could have ignored representations put in unilaterally after that date, because the rent reviewer was acting as an expert and not as an arbitrator *dependent on evidence.*[51] In a recent Hong Kong judgment[52] the referee was an accountant who could, if he thought fit, investigate the whole of the accounts, dealings and transactions of the company concerned. The referee was described by the judge as having inquisitorial powers not normally given to an arbitrator and was held to be acting as an expert. However, unless the parties disagree, an arbitrator can take the initiative in ascertaining the facts and the

---

[45] An attorney in an American television series in the 1970s.
[46] [1991] 39 E.G. 139.
[47] *Russell on Arbitration*, 21st edition, David Sutton, John Kendall and Judith Gill, Sweet & Maxwell, 1997, at 4–159.
[48] See 16.8.
[49] [1985] 2 All E.R. 161 at 166.
[50] *Rajdev v. Beckets (a firm)* [1989] 2 E.G.L.R. 144.
[51] Emphasis added.
[52] *Mayers v. Dlugash* [1994] 1 H.K.C. 755, Kaplan J.

law, but having done so is still obliged to allow each party to deal with the results of the investigation.[53]

Commodity arbitrations

Some commodity arbitrations relating to quality and price seem to be in a separate category in this respect. Commodity arbitrations of this type are conducted and administered under the rules of commodity trade associations in the City of London. Some of these arbitrations are about the quality and/or condition of commodities like rice or coffee. The arbitrators' task is to look at and sniff the sample of the commodity and to apply their trade experience to determine its quality or condition. Derek Kirby Johnson writes[54] on how cocoa beans would be assessed:

17.6.5

> "[The arbitrators] open the sample and cut the beans with a pen knife and examine the interior for slatiness, mould or other defects, such as a smoky or hammy smell or taste . . . On the results of their cutting, [the arbitrators] agree whether an allowance [reducing the price] should be given, and if so, how much. This is entirely a matter of their personal skill and judgment".

A recognised categorisation

These arbitrators are experts in the non-legal sense of the word and they do not perform a judicial function. Here is an analysis:

17.6.6

> "Although called arbitrations, these determinations [in look-sniff arbitrations] lie outside modern concepts of arbitration and modern arbitration statutes. They are essentially summary determinations or appraisals owing their binding force to the pre-contract of the parties and not attended by procedural requirements of ordinary arbitrations. They share with litigation and arbitration the characteristic of the dispute being resolved by the imposition of a third party's decision. They share with arbitration and mediation the characteristic that they derive from pre-contract between the disputants. But they are themselves a separate and distinct ADR procedure described in modern usage as expert appraisal or expert determination".[55]

However, the categorisation of this procedure as arbitration is traditional and deeply rooted. In any case, the courts recognise the practice. For instance, in *Finnegan v. Allen*,[56] Goddard L.J. said:

> "The person appointed will be an expert in the trade who will look at the sample . . . This is constantly done in Mincing Lane [a street in the

---

[53] Arbitration Act 1996, s. 34(2)(g) and s. 33.
[54] In *Handbook of Arbitration Practice*, edited by Ronald Bernstein, John Tackaberry, Arthur L. Marriott and Derek Wood 3rd edition (Sweet & Maxwell in conjunction with The Chartered Institute of Arbitrators,1998), at para. 3–140
[55] Sir Laurence Street, "The Language of Alternative Dispute Resolution", [1992] A.D.R.L.J. 144–8.
[56] [1943] 1 K.B. 425 at 436.

City of London], and the person who acts in this way is, perhaps, a quasi-arbitrator or even an arbitrator, but he is an arbitrator of a particular sort, and it is not intended that there should be the same judicial proceeding on his part as there would be in the case of an arbitrator appointed under a formal submission".

This judge saw valuers/experts as quasi-arbitrators because he believed they should not be sued. He addressed the question again in *Mediterranean and Eastern Export Co. Ltd v. Fortress Fabrics (Manchester) Ltd.*[57] The issue here was whether a chamber of commerce textile arbitration should have heard expert evidence. In this judgment there is no mention of quasi-arbitrators: it is fully accepted that the question of the quality of the textile was determined by arbitrators acting on their own knowledge and experience.

Courts support arbitration rules

17.6.7 Look/sniff arbitrations, as these arbitrations have become known, have to be seen as an exception to this indicator. The courts have not tried to change commercial practice in this respect. Rather, the courts have upheld commercial contracts incorporating the rules of commodity associations. Those rules specifically say that the arbitration is going to be conducted in this way.

The most significant indicator

17.6.8 With the important exception of look/sniff arbitrations, this indicator of a judicial function is probably the most important. As well as expertise, it covers the rules of natural justice, as now interpreted in the statutory standard of fairness in arbitrations.[58] In an 1894 case[59] where arbitrators had met the tenant without the landlord being present, the court said: "Arbitrators are not merely valuers; they have judicial functions to perform. . . . They must observe the fundamental rules which govern judicial proceedings." (This must now be read subject to the arbitrator's power to take the initiative in ascertaining the facts and the law.[60])

This issue is dealt with in more detail in the next section.

17.7 EVIDENCE AND SUBMISSIONS

Presentation an essential feature of an arbitration

17.7.1 The presentation, where appropriate, to the referee of evidence and submissions in support of the parties' respective claims in the dispute was Lord Wheatley's third indicator. He said that if evidence

---

[57] [1948] 2 All E.R. 186.
[58] Arbitration Act 1996, s. 33.
[59] *Re an arbitration between Gregson and Armstrong* (1894) 70 L.T. 106.
[60] See 17.6.4.

and submissions are not present the procedure cannot be an arbitration. This indicator has not attracted as much comment as the previous two, and has sometimes been seen as part of the second one.

An exception to this principle

17.7.2
In *Re Hopper*[61] the court said that a judicial inquiry was conducted on the principle of hearing the parties and the evidence of their witnesses. However, in *Bottomley v. Ambler*[62] an arbitration award was allowed to stand although the principle had not been followed. An umpire was appointed to determine the rent of a mill. The umpire gave no notice to the parties or their solicitors, examined no witnesses, but merely heard the statement of the two arbitrators and inspected the premises. In his award he said that he had heard, examined, and considered the allegations, witnesses and evidence of all the parties. The Court of Appeal held that there was no ground for disturbing the award as the arbitrators and the umpire were all experts and it was evidently the intention of the parties that they should settle the value and not act as formal arbitrators. The court said that the arbitrators had incurred enormous expense in calling witnesses, which was entirely thrown away, for as soon as the arbitrators saw the property they knew at once what ought to be done.

How do arbitrators and experts stand in relation to this indicator?

17.7.3
The presentation of submissions and evidence at a formal hearing (with witnesses available to be cross-examined) is a universal characteristic of litigation in England. The questions remain whether an arbitrator is obliged to follow the litigation practice and whether an expert is prohibited from doing so. The answers are as follows:

(a) An arbitrator is obliged to adopt procedures suitable to the circumstances of the particular case, avoiding unnecessary delay or expense, so as to provide a fair means for the resolution of the matters falling to be determined.[63] An arbitrator decides all procedural and evidential matters, subject to the right of the parties to agree any matter[64]; this includes whether and to what extent there should be oral or written evidence or submissions. In practice, the tendency is for arbitrators to follow the litigation practice in order to avoid an allegation of serious irregularity,[65] unless the arbitration

---

[61] (1867) L.R. 2 Q.B. 367.
[62] (1878) 38 L.T. 545.
[63] Arbitration Act 1996, s. 33(1)(b).
[64] Arbitration Act 1996, s. 34.
[65] Arbitration Act 1996, s. 68.

rules concerned specifically preclude those procedures or the parties both agree they need not be followed. An arbitrator who sought to proceed to final award without a hearing at which the parties could call their own evidence and have the opportunity of cross-examining witnesses on the other side was removed: the judge found that the process the arbitrator had adopted was really that of a valuation, rather than an arbitration.[66]

(b) The position of an expert depends first on whether the parties have any specific requirements. Subject to that, an expert is not prohibited from following these litigation-style procedures, but would be unwise to do so because the reference may subsequently be held to have been an arbitration and in any event take longer and be more costly.

Two modern exceptions

17.7.4 The qualifying words "where appropriate" in Lord Wheatley's phrase[67] may point to certain types of arbitrations where evidence and submissions are not heard. These are the look/sniff arbitrations[68] and documents-only arbitrations.[69] It may be helpful to consider an example of each.

Commodity arbitrations

17.7.5 From the description of the cocoa arbitration at 17.6.5, it is immediately apparent that there are no submissions or evidence. It is difficult to see what use submissions or evidence would be. Presumably each side would want to state its position about the quality or condition of the sample, and the evidence would be about other samples said to be of various qualities or conditions. But the arbitrator is sufficiently expert and can decide just by inspection of the goods in dispute.

Documents-only arbitrations

17.7.6 Documents-only arbitrations are procedures where the issues are decided on the basis of written submissions only and there is no oral presentation of submissions or evidence. Documents-only arbitrations have been set up to provide a simple means of resolving complaints by consumers in a number of industries, such as travel and telephones. Arbitration is written into the standard form contracts as the form of dispute resolution to be used. The

---

[66] See *Town & City Properties (Development) Ltd v. Wiltshier Southern Ltd and Gilbert Powell* (1988) 44 B.L.R. 109.
[67] See 17.4.1(3).
[68] See 17.6.5.
[69] See 17.7.6.

contracts say that a consumer who is dissatisfied with certain types of consumer service covered by one of these schemes has to refer the matter to a documents-only arbitration. But the consumer has the choice between arbitration and the County Court, as statute[70] overrules the compulsory arbitration clause.

Procedure in documents-only arbitrations

In documents-only arbitrations[71] there is no formal hearing and no oral evidence: the documents consist of an application form, a claim form and a defence, each accompanied by copies of relevant documents such as the contract and correspondence, and the claimant's comments on the defence. It is on the basis of those documents that the arbitrator then makes the award. The documents-only procedure is also used in property valuation disputes and rent reviews.[72] The procedure in documents-only arbitrations is difficult to distinguish from the procedure in some references to an expert. 17.7.7

These exceptions resemble expert determination

Look/sniff arbitrations bear a strong resemblance to expert determinations, and documents-only arbitrations to determinations of general disputes by an expert.[73] But they are arbitrations which contractually-incorporated rules and commercial practice make exempt from the requirement of submissions and oral evidence. 17.7.8

Rules of evidence

The rules of evidence may be applied in arbitrations but do not apply to expert determinations.[74] 17.7.9

AGREEMENT TO ACCEPT THE DECISION 17.8

An expert's decision is usually final and binding

Lord Wheatley's fourth and last indicator was that the parties had agreed to accept the referee's decision. This is often expressly 17.8.1

---

[70] Arbitration Act 1996, s. 91(1).
[71] See Margaret Rutherford, "Documents-only arbitrations in consumer disputes", in *Handbook of Arbitration Practice*, edited by Ronald Bernstein, John Tackaberry, Arthur L. Marriott and Derek Wood 3rd edition, Sweet & Maxwell in conjunction with The Chartered Institute of Arbitrators,1998, at part 8.
[72] See Ian V. Oddy, "Rent review and property valuation arbitration", in Ronald Bernstein, John Tackaberry, Arthur L. Marriott and Derek Wood, *Handbook of Arbitration Practice*, 3rd edition, Sweet & Maxwell in conjunction with The Chartered Institute of Arbitrators,1998, at para. 6–23.
[73] See 8.7.
[74] See 17.10.3.

stated in expert clauses,[75] by providing that the decision of the expert will be final and binding.[76] In appropriate cases, the court infers that the decision is to be final and binding, even if this is not expressly stated.[77]

Arbitration appeals used to be commonplace

17.8.2 The essential difference here is that an arbitration award is subject to appeal to or review by the High Court. In the past this right was frequently exercised under what was known as the case stated procedure. This led to comments like the following:

> "Why do the parties provide that the auditors 'shall be considered to be acting as experts and not as arbitrators'? For the simple reason that, if they were to be considered as arbitrators, there would be at least a danger that one party or the other might be able to require a case to be stated before a court of law, by which means it could be suggested that the award was not binding because of some error in it."[78]

Substantial restrictions on right to appeal

17.8.3 In 1979 the case stated procedure for appeals to the court against arbitration awards was abolished.[79] The position now is that the right to appeal on a point of law can be excluded in all cases, by agreement at any stage.[80] Where there is no exclusion agreement, review and appeal are available only if the determination of the question will substantially affect the rights of one or more of the parties, the question is one the tribunal was asked to determine, and either the award is obviously wrong or the matter is one of general public importance and the award is at least open to serious doubt, and it is just and proper in all the circumstances for the court to determine the question.[81] Appeals are not provided for in cases of disputed facts. Appeals are still possible on the ground of lack of jurisdiction[82] and serious irregularity.[83] In expert determination there is no right of appeal, and enforcement of the decision can be resisted only on limited grounds related to the contractual requirements for the

---

[75] See 9.8.
[76] But see Chapter 7 on interim determinations.
[77] See 9.3.3.
[78] *Baber v. Kenwood Manufacturing Co. Ltd and Whinney Murray* [1978] 1 Lloyd's Rep. 175 at 179, Megaw L.J.
[79] Arbitration Act 1979, s. 1(1). The 1950, 1975 and 1979 Arbitration Acts have now been repealed in their entirety by the Arbitration Act 1996, which has further restricted appeals.
[80] Section 87 of the Arbitration Act 1996 has not been brought into force and will not be: see *Russell on Arbitration*, 21st edition, David Sutton, John Kendall and Judith Gill, Sweet & Maxwell, 1997, 2-022.
[81] Arbitration Act 1996, s. 69.
[82] *ibid.*, s. 67.
[83] *ibid.*, s. 68.

decision.[84] There is no machinery for remission for serious irregularity in procedure in expert determination, as there is in arbitration.[85]

Consequences of restriction of rights of appeal in arbitrations

Since it is now possible for parties to agree to exclude appeals from arbitration awards on points of law, a provision that a determination is to be final and binding is less likely than it used to be to imply that the clause provides for arbitration as opposed to expert determination.

17.8.4

REVIEW OF THE INDICATORS 17.9

The indicators are not conclusive

Based on the above, the following points can be made: 17.9.1

(a) An arbitration cannot be commenced unless there is a formulated dispute,[86] but the fact that there is a formulated dispute is not conclusive of whether the reference is to arbitration or expert determination.

(b) A judicial function and the judicial procedures of submissions and evidence are generally present in arbitrations. However arbitrators have power, subject to the parties' agreement, to decide that there should be no oral hearing, and contractually-incorporated rules may provide that there should be no oral hearing. Another exception is where, in accordance with commercial practice, no formal hearing takes place.[87]

(c) The agreement to accept the decision is not conclusive, because the right of appeal in arbitration has become so much more restricted.[88]

Diminishing importance of the controversy

The changes in arbitration law may make this question less important in the future; a finding that a reference was an arbitration does not usually improve the chances of a successful challenge, because the opportunities for appeals from arbitration awards are now so scarce.[89] The issue will, however, continue to be important

17.9.2

---

[84] See 17.11.3.
[85] Arbitration Act 1996, s. 68(3)(a) for serious irregularity; s 69(7)(c) on a point of law.
[86] See 17.5.2.
[87] See 17.6 and 17.7.
[88] See 17.8.
[89] See 17.8.3.

for negligence claims where the defendant wishes to seek immunity on the grounds of having acted as an arbitrator, as in *Palacath Ltd v. Flanagan*.[90]

A third category?

17.9.3 The debate about categorising private contractual dispute procedures tends to start from the basis that any reference must be either to an expert or to an arbitrator. This rather difficult question is discussed further in Chapter 18.

17.10 PROCEDURAL DIFFERENCES

Expert determination procedure depends on contract

17.10.1 Chapter 11 discussed the procedure for expert determination. There is no official model and the procedure for any given reference depends on the expert clause in the original contract between the parties and subsequent directions by the expert. The parties' rights in the resulting procedure are established by the law of contract.

Current trends in the reform of arbitration procedure

17.10.2 Arbitration is used in a wide range of disputes, and procedures can be tailored to suit the occasion although arbitrators and the parties' lawyers are understandably cautious, given the grave consequences of an allegation of serious irregularity.[91] Some English lawyers wish to detach arbitration from close adherence to litigation procedures, and there is now by law much more flexibility in the choice of procedure. One important litigation-type procedure available in arbitrations is the right to obtain a court order requiring witnesses to attend arbitrations.[92] In rent review arbitrations, this authorises the extraction, under threat of imprisonment for contempt of court, of evidence from third parties with no direct involvement in the dispute.[93]

Evidence

17.10.3 Rules of evidence may be applied to arbitrations,[94] but they do not apply to expert determinations. The difference this can make has become apparent in rent reviews where the court has held[95] that

---

[90] [1985] 2 All E.R. 161: see 16.5.3.
[91] Arbitration Act 1996, s. 68.
[92] Arbitration Act 1996, s. 43; and see UNCITRAL Model Law, art. 27.
[93] See John Kendall and Steven Dark "Countering Confidentiality Agreements", (1991) Law Society's Gazette, Vol. 31, p. 14.
[94] Arbitration Act 1996, s. 34(2)(f).
[95] *Land Securities plc v. Westminster City Council* [1993] 1 W.L.R. 286.

the award of an arbitrator in one rent review arbitration (and, by analogy, the decision of an expert) is inadmissible in other rent review arbitrations. There is nothing to stop evidence of this sort being considered by an expert in an expert determination.

Expert witnesses

17.10.4 Expert witnesses appear before independent experts and perform a very similar function to that which they perform in arbitration and litigation. The court has imposed specific requirements on the conduct of expert witnesses.[96] This guidance does not apply to expert determinations unless the parties and the expert decide to adopt it and/or the guidance has been applied to the expert witnesses by their professional body. Because of concern that the standards for expert witnesses in rent review expert determinations were lower than those obtaining for rent review arbitrations, the RICS made it clear that exactly the same rules—issued by the RICS—apply to expert witnesses giving evidence under either system. The rules relate to honesty as to opinion, completeness as to coverage of relevant matters, independence, objectivity and impartiality.[97]

Is there to be a hearing?

17.10.5 Parties to an arbitration can agree whether there is to be a hearing; if not, the tribunal decides whether there should be one.[98] In expert determinations, it is a matter for agreement between the expert and the parties, subject to what the expert clause says about the expert's right to make directions.

Serious irregularity

17.10.6 Statute[99] gives the right to apply to the court to set aside an award on the ground of serious irregularity affecting the tribunal, the proceedings or the award. This statutory right has no common law analogue in expert determination.

Two types of arbitration more like expert determination

17.10.7 The procedure in look/sniff and documents-only arbitrations is very close to that of expert determination.[1]

---

[96] CPR 35.3, 35.10 and Practice Direction Part 35, para. 1; see also *The Ikarian Reefer* [1993] 2 Lloyd's Rep. 68 at 81–2, Cresswell J.
[97] *Practice Statement and Guidance Note for Surveyors acting as Expert Witnesses,* RICS books.
[98] Arbitration Act 1996, s. 34(2)(h).
[99] *ibid.* s. 68.
[1] See 17.7.8.

Tactics

17.10.8 The differences in procedure between expert determination and arbitration may be only potential in some cases. But any one of those differences can be very important tactically where one party is prepared to exploit the opportunity. Allegations of serious irregularity by the arbitrator are an obvious example of a tactic available in arbitration and not in expert determination.[2] The parties' legal costs are recoverable in arbitrations but not in expert determinations unless specific provision is made.[3]

17.11 THE DIFFERENT CONSEQUENCES OF AN EXPERT'S DECISION AND AN ARBITRATION AWARD

General

17.11.1 Parties faced with an expert's decision or an arbitration award need to know how the decision or award may be enforced, whether they can appeal against the decision or award, and whether they can sue the expert or arbitrator.

Enforcement

17.11.2 An expert's decision cannot be enforced by the courts without issuing proceedings and obtaining judgment, and it is not enforceable internationally without court proceedings in at least one country. An arbitration award can be enforced by a simple procedure, and is enforceable internationally.[4]

Appeals from experts' decisions

17.11.3 Strictly speaking, there can be no appeal from a decision of an expert, but the court may be asked to review the validity of a decision if, for instance, enforcement is resisted. Generally, the court's powers are limited to ordering that the decision is either valid or invalid. The grounds of challenge are very limited and are based on application of the principles of the law of contract. A decision is declared invalid only:

(a) if the expert lacked jurisdiction to decide the issue or has decided the wrong issue;
(b) if the expert has asked himself or herself the wrong question;
(c) if the expert has materially departed from instructions or failed to follow the procedure expressly or impliedly required by the terms of the contract;

---

[2] See 17.10.6.
[3] See 9.13.
[4] See 14.7.

(d) if there are other reasons why the decision cannot be regarded as a decision made in accordance with the requirements of the contract, such as partiality, fraud, collusion or bad faith.[5]

Procedural unfairness, of a kind which would amount to serious irregularity in an arbitration, rarely provides a basis for challenging the decision of an expert. The only ground is where the unfairness is of such a kind that the court can infer that the decision has not been made in accordance with the requirements of the contract.[6]

Appeals from arbitration awards

17.11.4 There is no appeal from an arbitrator's decision on a question of fact. A party who wishes to appeal from an arbitration award on a question of law is be able to do so only:

(a) if the right to appeal has not been excluded; and
(b) if the determination of the question will substantially affect the rights of one or more of the parties, the question is one the tribunal was asked to determine, and either the award is obviously wrong or the matter is one of general public importance and the award is at least open to serious doubt, and it is just and proper in all the circumstances for the court to determine the question.[7]

A dissatisfied party to an arbitration also has the right to appeal on the ground of serious irregularity affecting the tribunal, the proceedings or the award.[8]

The court may make a variety of orders, including varying or setting aside the whole or part of the award and remitting the award to the tribunal.[9]

Suing experts and arbitrators

17.11.5 A party who wishes to sue an expert has to prove negligence or some other breach of contract. An arbitrator is immune from suit except for acts or omissions in bad faith.[10]

---

[5] See Chapters 12 and 15.
[6] See 15.8.
[7] Arbitration Act 1996, s. 69; see 17.8.3.
[8] See 17.10.6.
[9] Arbitration Act 1996, s. 67 and s. 68.
[10] *ibid.* s. 29.

Chapter 18

A THIRD CATEGORY?

18.1 Summary

Should every contractual system for private decision-making be classified as either expert determination or arbitration? This is not an entirely academic question. If some decisions under commercial contracts are neither expert determination nor arbitration, but something else, it is important to know what they are to be able to advise on how those decisions would be treated by the court.

This chapter:

(a) notes that there is a much wider range of possibilities (18.2);
(b) considers the various possibilities in turn (18.3 to 18.8);
(c) notes the special circumstances which mark these possibilities out from commercial dispute resolution (18.9.1); and
(d) concludes that the law applicable to expert determinations by independent third parties is largely the same as the law applicable to other private decisions made under a contract which are not arbitration awards and where none of the special, non-commercial factors apply (18.9.2 to 18.9.5).

18.2 The range of systems

There are several other systems for dispute resolution under contract as well as arbitration and the system of expert determination by an independent third party which is the main subject of this book:

(a) decisions by one party or the agent of one party only;
(b) decisions by reference to a document or formula;
(c) competitions and wagers;
(d) decisions concerning membership of associations;
(e) statutory adjudication; and
(f) public administration.

At first sight therefore there would appear to be several contenders for other categories.

DECISIONS BY ONE PARTY (OR ITS AGENT) ONLY 18.3

Not a third party

An expert is most naturally a third party: one of the parties, or its agent, is not an independent third party who can convincingly be referred to as "expert". The identification of the decision-maker is however a matter for the parties as they express their intentions in the contract,[1] and the same general principles of the law of contract apply in each case; examples of this are set out at 18.3.4 to 18.3.7. As these principles require the contract to be construed in its actual context, a contract requiring a decision to be made by one of the parties may however be construed differently from a similar contract requiring a decision to be made by an independent third party.[2]

18.3.1

Not independent, but may be required to reach an independent decision

A decision taken by one of the parties or its agent risks being seen as lacking independence. The courts declare invalid an expert determination which has been obtained by fraud or where there is proven bias. They do not intervene just because an expert is not independent. However in two reported instances where an expert clause provided for decision by an agent of one of the parties the court has intervened, on the ground that on their true construction, the expert clauses showed an intention that the party appointed as referee should be independent. The use of the word "expert" was relied on for this in one of the cases, but not the other.[3]

18.3.2

Where the decision-maker is an independent third party, the decision-maker is required to reach an impartial and independent decision. But where the decision-maker is one party or its agent, whether the decision-maker is required to reach an independent decision depends on interpretation of the contract in all the circumstances; where the decision-maker is not required to be independent there may be no implied term that the parties will not seek to influence the decision-maker.[4]

No magic in the word "expert"

The presence of the word "expert" may assist construction arguments, but there is no fundamental objection to the role of one of the parties or its agent acting as expert.

18.3.3

---

[1] See 10.5.2.
[2] See 18.3.7.
[3] Discussed at 15.5.2.
[4] *Minster Trust Ltd v. Traps Tractors Ltd* [1954] 1 W.L.R. 963 at 973–5.

Conclusive evidence clauses

18.3.4 Some bank guarantees contain a clause which states that a notice of default by one of the parties shall be conclusive evidence of the amount of the other party's liability. The Court of Appeal has held a conclusive evidence clause to be effective, dismissing arguments that the clause was contrary to public policy as it ousted the court's jurisdiction and made one of the parties judge in its own cause.[5]

Building and engineering contracts

18.3.5 Decisions by the agent of one party only are found in many building and engineering contracts. Often they are interim, and reviewable in arbitration. The same general legal principles apply to a conclusive decision by an architect or an engineer acting for the building-owner as to a conclusive decision by an independent third party.[6] In particular, certifiers under building and engineering contracts are required to reach an impartial and independent decision.[7]

Two-tier expert systems

18.3.6 There are some instances of expert determinations by one party only where this is part of a two-tier expert system. At the first level, a decision is made by one of the parties. This decision is final as well as binding unless there is an appeal to a disinterested third party with appropriate experience.[8]

Jurisdiction of decision-maker and issues of law

18.3.7 Generally speaking, the same legal principles apply to a decision by one of the parties or by his or her agent as to a decision by a neutral third party. The most important principle is that the court aims to ascertain and enforce the intentions of the parties as expressed in their contract. However in considering a clause conferring decision-making powers on one of the parties or on his/her agent, the court is more likely to adopt a narrow view of the scope of the decision-maker's authority to reach decisions.

In particular, it would be rare for the court to find that a contract had conferred on one of the parties the power to decide a disputed

---

[5] *Bache & Co, (London) Ltd v. Banque Vernes et Commerciale de Paris SA* [1973] 2 Lloyd's Rep. 437. For a telling criticism of the judgment, see Lawrence Collins and Dorothy Livingston, "Aspects of Conclusive Evidence Clauses" [1974] Journal of Business Law, p. 212. See also 5.10. Other cases are cited at *Halsbury's Laws of England* 4th edition, Vol. 20, para. 182.

[6] See 7.4.1.

[7] See 7.4.2.

[8] See 5.5.2, 5.7.3 and 8.6.1.

issue as to the meaning of the contract. In *The Glacier Bay*,[9] the Court of Appeal considered a dispute as to the status of decisions under a reinsurance contract by one of the parties, Cristal Ltd, which administered the Cristal contract and the Cristal fund. The contract provided that Cristal Ltd was to be sole judge of the validity of claims made. Neill L.J., with whom the other members of the Court of Appeal agreed, referred to the fact that the agreement, which was an unusual one, was an international agreement to which oil companies throughout the world were parties, and to the fact that each of the parties to the agreement was required to become a member of Cristal Ltd. Reversing the first instance decision,[10] the Court of Appeal decided that the words "sole judge" were "sufficient to show that the determination was to be final and binding for all purposes on matters of fact, subject of course to any question of unfairness, bad faith or perversity".[11] It was however conceded by counsel that decisions of law could be reviewed by the court.[12] Neill L.J.[13] referred to the principle that an agreement wholly to oust the jurisdiction of the courts is against public policy and void, and referred to cases where the parties have agreed to refer some matter to an independent expert as being an exception to this principle. This would provide the basis for an argument that the decision-making power of one of the parties to the contract (as opposed to an independent third party) cannot extend to issues of law. The position is probably not so inflexible: there could be limited issues of law or construction which might properly be left to one of the parties to decide.

A further illustration of a narrow interpretation of the decision-making authority of a party to the contract is *Balfour Beatty Ltd v. Docklands Light Railway Ltd*,[14] where in an engineering contract decisions were to be made by an employee of the defendant. The Court of Appeal held that the effect of the contract was that there was no power to review a proper exercise of judgment by the employee. However counsel conceded[15] that a decision by the employee could be impeached in the courts on the ground of legal misdirection, dishonesty, unfairness or unreasonableness. In a later

---

[9] *West of England Shipowners Mutual Insurance Association (Luxembourg) v. Cristal Ltd ('The Glacier Bay')* [1996] 1 Lloyd's Rep. 370. But see also the cases cited in the footnotes to 18.3.8.
[10] [1995] 1 Lloyd's Rep. 560, Waller J.
[11] [1996] 1 Lloyd's Rep. 370 at 379. This would be different from expert determination law: 15.14.
[12] *ibid*. at 379.
[13] *ibid*. at 378. Neill L.J. also stated: "It may be that in the future new methods of resolving disputes by a tribunal chosen and agreed by the parties to a dispute may lead to some further relaxation of the rule, but for the purposes of the present case it is not necessary to explore this point further."
[14] (1996) 78 B.L.R. 42; see 7.4.3.
[15] See *ibid*. at 56 and 58.

case the House of Lords held that the Court of Appeal's decision was wrong, and that the court should be slow to find that a certificate by an architect (the building-owner's agent) is unreviewable.[16]

Conclusion

18.3.8 In cases where the decision is to be made by a party or its agent, the court is more likely to find, on the wording of the contract in question, reasons for intervention by the court. But if the clause is held to be binding, the court generally applies the same general principles derived from the law of contract as it would apply if the decision was to be made by an independent third party.

18.4 DECISIONS BY REFERENCE TO A DOCUMENT OR FORMULA

Where a contract provides that an issue is to be determined by reference to a document, such as the accounts of a company,[17] or by the application of a formula such as those used in quality/price adjustments in commodity contracts[18] and oil and gasfield re-determinations,[19] the courts approach disputes about those determinations in the same way as they do when an expert has made the determination. For instance, compensation for termination of a contract was to be an amount three times the annual average profit of a company before tax, the profit figure to be ascertained by reference to the company's accounts. The Court of Appeal was prepared to decide issues relating to the construction of this clause, but refused to go behind the company's accounts to deal with other disputed issues[20]:

> "This . . . is not a case in which the parties have agreed that the company's net profits should be determined by an expert or third party. They had defined the term by reference to a document: to wit, the published audited accounts for the relevant period. Nevertheless, in my judgment similar principles apply. The parties can go behind the relevant document if, but only if, they establish (i) that it has been produced as the

---

[16] *Beaufort Developments (NI) Ltd v. Gilbert-Ash NI Ltd* [1999] AC 266 at 276, 281-2 and 292. The House of Lords overruled *Northern Regional Health Authority v. Derek Crouch Construction Co Ltd* [1984] 1 Q.B. 644, where the Court of Appeal had held that the review powers of an arbitrator could not be exercised by the court. See also *John Barker Construction Ltd v. London Portman Hotel Ltd* (1996) 83 B.L.R. 31, discussed at 15.8.2, where the arbitration clause in a building contract had been deleted, and the court held that the architect's decision was fundamentally flawed and was reviewable as the contractual machinery had broken down.
[17] *Highway Contract Hire Ltd v. NWS Bank plc*, unreported April 17, 1996, CA.
[18] See 5.7.
[19] See 6.4.2.
[20] *Highway Contract Hire Ltd v. NWS Bank plc*, unreported, April 17, 1996 CA: Millett L.J.

result of what is described, perhaps inaptly in this context, as fraud or collusion, or (ii) that it has been prepared on a different basis from that contemplated by the contract. In either case it is simply not the document which conforms to the contractual definition."

Thus the provision setting out how the determination is to be made is analogous to an expert clause, and the court construes a provision of that sort on the same basis as an expert clause. But the court does not investigate the document by reference to which the determination is to be made, unless fraud, collusion or preparation on a different basis from that contemplated by the contract is shown: the same exceptional circumstances where an expert determination may be challenged. In this case the documents by reference to which the determination was to be made were published audited accounts for periods later than the date of the agreement. Similar use is made of published economic statistics such as the retail price index. A determination is to be made on the basis of a document to be prepared in the future by some identified or identifiable party, and on the basis that that document should not, generally, be questioned. A formula, while being known at the time of the contract, is also likely to contain variables whose values will only become known in the future. Indeed, the whole purpose of agreements like this is to make arrangements for the future on the basis of information that itself will only be available in the future.

The judge thought the reference to fraud or collusion inapt, presumably because the accounts were not prepared specifically for the purposes of establishing the sum to be paid as compensation for the termination of the agreement, although in a private company auditors are often thought to be too close to one of the shareholder/directors, Where a document is prepared for other purposes there are likely to be fewer opportunities for fraud or collusion than in the case of a one-off expert determination. There is no difficulty in adapting the concept of difference from the contractual basis to reference to a document or a formula. The contract refers to the accounts of company A, but the accounts of company B are used. The contract calls for formula C, but formula D is used. Where the contractual document or the formula no longer exists, the clause may fail.

COMPETITIONS AND WAGERS   18.5

Competitions and sports

Sports and competitions provide interesting comparisons. The   18.5.1
court cannot substitute its own opinion, in place of the opinion of the stewards or organisers, as to who won a race or a competition. However, the court may be able to review the result if it believes

18 : A THIRD CATEGORY?

there has been unfairness, for example where a winner is disqualified for disciplinary reasons. The owner of the winner of a horse race challenged the decision of the Jockey Club to disqualify on the ground that the horse's urine was found to contain a prohibited substance. The rules of the Jockey Club govern racing in England. The court stated that this was a matter of private contract, and that judicial review was not available to an aggrieved horse-owner who was a party to that contract. The court held that it could generally intervene only on the basis of that private contractual obligation. Hoffmann L.J. held that it was an implied term of the contract that the Jockey Club would conduct its disciplinary proceedings fairly, and the aggrieved owner would have a remedy based on that duty if the Jockey Club did not act fairly.[21]

Wagers

18.5.2 Would the court enforce a contract under which the parties agreed that in the event of a dispute, the dispute would be determined by the toss of a coin? Many issues are settled that way every day but probably not in circumstances where the parties intend their agreement to be legally enforceable. In any case, enforcement might be refused on the grounds that the contract was a contract of wager. The court has refused to enforce the decision of a valuer where the result of the valuation triggered consequences which seemed out of proportion on the ground that the contract was one of wager.[22]

Relevance to expert determination

18.5.3 Comparisons with competition results and with wagers are not inapt because the decision of an expert is often non-speaking, *i.e.* just the answer (or result) without any reasons or calculations. It is very difficult to find how an expert has reached a decision: it may actually have been by the toss of a coin.[23]

18.6 DECISIONS CONCERNING MEMBERSHIP OF ASSOCIATIONS

The attempt to expel a member from a trade guild has been said to be subject to the rules of natural justice.[24] There is a close analogy with decisions by the governing body of a sport, and there is likely to

---

[21] *R v. Disciplinary Committee of the Jockey Club, ex parte Aga Khan* [1993] 1 W.L.R. 909, Hoffmann L.J. at 933, also Farquharson L.J. at 930. In *Wilander and Novacek v. Tomin and Jude* [1997] 2 Lloyd's Rep. 293 at 300, Lord Woolf M.R. in the Court of Appeal stated that the Appeals Committee of the International Tennis Federation also had an obligation derived from private contract to conduct its proceedings fairly.

[22] See the strange story in *Rourke v. Short* (1856) 5 El. & Bl. 904.

[23] Rabelais' Judge Bridlegoose decided cases by throwing dice: *Gargantua and Pantagruel*, Book Three, Chap. 39.

[24] *Lee v. Showmen's Guild of Great Britain* [1952] 2 Q.B. 329, Denning L.J. at 342.

be an obligation to conduct the proceedings fairly.[25] A duty to act fairly need not include a duty to comply with the rules of natural justice.[26]

STATUTORY SYSTEMS 18.7

Private rights

Some statutes provide for the regulation of private rights by a statutory system of adjudication. Where a statute regulates public rights the procedure is subject to judicial review.[27]   18.7.1

Party wall awards

Party wall awards are decisions made by a surveyor operating under a procedure laid down by statute[28] for the settlement of disputes between the owners of adjoining buildings. Both owners appoint surveyors and a third surveyor is appointed to resolve differences. The status of the procedure was considered by the court,[29] which concluded that a party wall award was not an arbitration award: it was in a category of its own and more in the nature of an expert determination. The court was looking at the right of appeal to the court which is provided by statute, and held that this right of appeal was not restricted to the original evidence before the surveyor and could look at all aspects, including the competence of the third surveyor. The court noted that there were very few cases on party wall awards, which suggested the scheme was successful.   18.7.2

Statutory arbitration

Disputes under certain types of contract are referred to specific arbitration tribunals by statute.[30] This type of arbitration is therefore a statutory system and a hybrid closer to statutory adjudication than private dispute resolution.   18.7.3

Adjudication in construction contracts

There is now a statutory system for interim determination of construction disputes.[31] It is clear that it is not arbitration, and is to be treated as analogous to expert determination.[32]   18.7.4

---

[25] See 18.5.1.
[26] See 15.6 to 15.7.
[27] See 18.8.
[28] London Building Acts (Amendment) Act 1939, applying to the London area only; the scheme has been extended to other parts of the country: Party Wall etc. Act 1996.
[29] *Chartered Society of Physiotherapy v. Simmonds Church Smiles* [1995] E.G.C.S. 25.
[30] For instance, Agricultural Holdings Act 1986, s. 12.
[31] See 7.5.4.
[32] *Bouygues UK Ltd v. Dahl-Jensen UK Ltd* [2000] B.L.R. 522, CA (see 7.5.5).

18.8 Public administration

Experts' decisions not subject to judicial review

18.8.1 Decisions by experts are not subject to the public law remedies of judicial review. A judge offers the following reasons[33]:

> "Tribunals have been imposed from outside by Parliament to adjudicate on disputes between executive authorities and citizens, or sometimes between citizens and citizens. Some control over those tribunals is necessary for the preservation of order in the legal system as it affects public administration. By contrast an expert's jurisdiction is a matter purely of contract between the parties: it is not imposed from outside. Either party can apply to the court on questions of law, and an expert can be sued for negligence."

Public valuations

18.8.2 In the same way that the courts have kept judicial review out of private contractual disputes the courts have also kept public law disputes out of the private law arena. Decisions by valuers operating under statute, such as district valuers, have sometimes been asserted to be matters of private law.[34] The arguments have been rejected and valuations of this type are now subject to judicial review like other public administrative decisions.[35]

So where is the boundary?

18.8.3 The boundary between public and private law has been considered in three recent court decisions. Decisions of the governing body of horse-racing were held not be susceptible to judicial review where a private law remedy was available.[36] The court refused an application for judicial review of a decision by the Football Association.[37] In the third case,[38] the Director General of Telecommunications was also held to be operating under private contract law. The Director's decision was taken under powers arising under statute in respect

---

[33] *Pontsarn Investments Ltd v Kansallis-Osake-Pankki* [1992] 1 E.G.L.R. 148.
[34] *Woodley v. Robert Newman & Son* [1950] W.N. 141; *In re Malpass Dec'd, Lloyds Bank plc v. Malpass* [1983] 1 Ch. 42; *R. v. Kidderminster District Valuer, West Midlands Police Authority and Secretary of State for the Home Department, ex parte Powell and West Midlands Branch of the Police Federation of England and Wales, The Times,* July 23, 1991, [1992] C. O. D. 381.
[35] Under RSC Ord. 53.
[36] *R. v. Disciplinary Committee of the Jockey Club, ex parte Aga Khan* [1993] 1 W.L.R. 909. See also *Wilander and Novacek v. Tobin and Jude* [1997] 2 Lloyd's Rep 293 (International Tennis Federation).
[37] *R. v. Football Association Ltd, ex parte Football League Ltd* [1993] 2 All E.R. 833.
[38] *Mercury Communications Ltd v. Director General of Telecommunications* [1996] 1 W.L.R. 48.

of a licence but the interpretation of the terms of the conditions in the licence was a dispute between two companies about the terms of a contract. The House of Lords said that it was "of particular importance . . . to retain some flexibility as the precise limits of . . . public law and . . . private law".[39]

Conclusion 18.9

Special, non-commercial features override contract law

The preceding sections have provided a brief review of the systems for decision under contracts other than expert determination by an independent third party and arbitration. They are all applied in circumstances somewhat different from commercial dispute resolution between parties of equal bargaining power. This may make a crucial difference. The type of decision where contract law is thought not to be applicable arises where the court has to step in to protect the public interest. In the case of wagers the law has evolved special rules within the law of contract but again deriving from public policy. In some cases statute has laid down an adjudication system. The essential issues raised when considering whether contract law takes precedence are not simply what law to apply: they are whether the decision can be made by the private tribunal, the extent of review of that decision by a court, and whether the court can take over the decision-making process. This arises from the nature of the contract, the parties agreeing to a private decision-making process rather than the jurisdiction of the courts. English law allows contract law to prevail between parties of equal bargaining status.[40]

18.9.1

Same law applied where the decision is made by one party or its agent

Somewhat surprisingly, the same general legal principles apply where the decision is made by one of the parties to the contract or its agent rather than by an independent third party.[41]

18.9.2

Decision by reference to a document or a formula

The validity of the settlement of questions by reference to a document or a formula is established by rules equivalent to those applicable to expert determination.

18.9.3

---

[39] Lord Slynn in *Mercury* at 57D.
[40] See 12.4.
[41] See 18.3.

Special cases

18.9.4 Competitions, wagers and membership of associations are all different from commercial dispute resolution and need their own rules. Statutory systems operate according to rules laid down by statute, which may or may not involve some borrowing from contract law.

Judicial review

18.9.5 Judicial review is applied to regulate tribunals imposed by Parliament to determine public law disputes. The presence of a private commercial contract in a public law dispute can take resolution of the dispute back to contract law.

In commercial arm's length contracts, decision-making is either arbitration or expert determination

18.9.6 Where none of the special factors applies, and the reference of a commercial dispute to a third party is not arbitration, it is likely to be governed by the law of expert determination, which depends on the law of contract. Contract law applies to every aspect: the expert clause, the qualifications and appointment of experts, jurisdiction, procedure, enforcement, challenge, rights and duties, and the implication of terms. Regard must be paid to the exact words of every contract for any special terms. For instance, an expert can make independent investigations but there is nothing to stop the parties restricting those investigations.[42] An expert is not immune from liability but the parties can agree to exclude their right to sue.[43] Decisions are generally to be final and binding, but that usually arises from express words to that effect, and it is a simple matter to provide that they are to be interim; if they are never to be binding, decisions really cease to be decisions at all.[44] English law is pragmatic and does not invent categories where there is no need. Expert determination is a convenient label for all non-arbitral references of commercial contract disputes.

---

[42] See 16.8.6.
[43] See 16.7.
[44] See 1.1.7.

APPENDIX A

PRECEDENTS FOR AN ACCOUNTANCY EXPERT

I   Expert Clause
II   Appointment Letter
III Terms of Reference
IV Procedural Directions
V   Decision

IMPORTANT NOTE

These precedents are by way of example and need careful adaptation for particular applications. They can also be used, suitably adapted, for references to experts other than accountants. See Bernstein and Reynolds for rent review precedents.

I EXPERT CLAUSE

1 If the Vendors and the Purchasers are unable to agree on [the sales figure] by [date] the matter in dispute shall be referred, at the request of either the Vendors or the Purchasers, for decision to an independent Chartered Accountant (the "Independent Accountant") who shall be appointed by agreement between the Vendors and the Purchasers, or, if they have not agreed within 14 days of the [first date above – or – date of request to refer by one of the parties], by the President for the time being of the Institute of Chartered Accountants in England and Wales ["the President"] on the application of either party. If an Independent Accountant has been appointed but is unable to complete the reference another Independent Accountant shall be appointed by the parties, or if they have not agreed on the appointment within 14 days of the request to do so by one of the parties, by the President.

2 The Independent Accountant shall act as an expert and not as an arbitrator. The parties shall each have the right to make representations to the Independent Accountant. The decision of the Independent Accountant shall, in the absence of manifest error, be final and binding on the parties. All costs incurred by the Independent Accountant shall be borne by the Vendors and the Purchasers in equal shares unless the Independent Accountant determines

otherwise. The amount (if any) which becomes payable by the Purchasers to the Vendors, or, as the case may be, repayable by the Vendors to the Purchasers, as a result of the Independent Accountant's decision shall become due and payable within seven days of publication of the decision. The Independent Accountant shall have the power to direct that interest on that amount, at the rate equal to [1%–a compensatory rate] above the base rate of [clearing] bank, shall be paid by the Purchasers to the Vendors or repaid by the Vendors to the Purchasers as compensation for delay in receipt in respect of the period following the date on which the matter was referred to expert determination.

3 If the amount payable as a result of the Independent Accountant's decision is not paid by either the Vendors or the Purchasers within the period of seven days after publication of the Independent Accountant's decision, interest will accrue on that amount at the rate of [4%–a penal rate] above the base rate of [clearing] bank.

II Appointment Letter

This form can be used where parties agree on the appointment of an expert without needing to apply to an appointing authority: in the other precedents it is assumed that the appointment is made by the President of the Institute of Chartered Accountants. Some appointing authorities have their own standard forms for application and appointment, and a fee is payable.

1 We refer to Clause [number] of the agreement between the Vendors and the Purchasers dated [date] by which the Purchasers acquired the whole of the issued share capital of XYZ plc from the Vendors ("the Agreement"): a copy of the agreement is enclosed.

2 Clause [number] of the Agreement provided that if the parties could not agree on [the sales figure], they should appoint an independent accountant to determine the figure. They have not been able to agree.

3 Accordingly the parties jointly* request you [ABC] to determine [the sales figure].

4 Draft terms of reference are enclosed, which the parties have agreed: if you are prepared to accept the appointment, please indicate whether you also approve these draft terms.

---

* Or, if it is the case, one party only: see 9.7.3. In these cases the letter should set out the part of the expert clause allowing one party only to appoint and the circumstances in which the other party has not joined in the application.

III Terms of Reference

1 We refer to the agreement [date] ("the Agreement") between [parties] by which the Vendors sold to the Purchasers the whole of the issued share capital of XYZ plc; the Purchasers' liability to make additional payments to the Vendors or, as the case may be, the Vendors' liability to make repayments to the Purchasers depends on whether, and, if so, by how much, XYZ plc's sales exceeded or fell short of the sum of [*e.g*, £2 million] in the year ended [—].

2 Clause [number of expert clause] of the Agreement provided that if the parties had not agreed on [the sales figure] in clause [number] by [date] the matter was to be referred to an Independent Accountant acting as an expert and not as an arbitrator whose decision was to be final and binding and whose fees would be shared equally between the parties unless the Independent Accountant determined otherwise.

3 The parties disagree about the [sales figure]. As the parties were also unable to agree on who the Independent Accountant should be, they applied to the President of the Institute of Chartered Accountants requesting that he appoint an Independent Accountant.

4 The President of the Institute of Chartered Accountants appointed ABC to be the Independent Accountant, by a letter dated [date].

5 The issue referred to ABC is whether the [sales figure should include the sales of widgets by a subsidiary which are unconnected with the main business of XYZ plc].

6 The parties agree to pay ABC's fees in equal shares and that the fees shall be charged at the rate of £xxx per hour plus reasonable expenses [or to pay ABC's fees and expenses as ABC directs].

[7 ABC shall decide whether either the Vendors or the Purchasers are to pay or contribute to the costs incurred by the other party.]

[8 Provision to replace ABC if s/he becomes incapacitated during the reference, if this is not contained in the expert clause.]

[9 Provision for the decision to include interest if not in the expert clause.]

Signed and dated by the expert and the parties.

IV Procedural Directions

1 ABC will receive from the Vendors acting as agents for both the Vendors and the Purchasers [here list the basic documents—the contract and other specified documents].

APPENDIX A

2 The Vendors* will send ABC a letter setting out their case by [date–say 28 days from date of directions]. All documents relied on and/or referred to by the Vendors must be attached to that letter, unless they have already been supplied to ABC under direction 1 above. The Vendors will send the Purchasers a copy of their letter and attachments at the same time as they are sent to ABC.

3 The Purchasers* will send ABC a letter setting out their case by [date–say 28 days from date of Vendors' letter]. All documents relied on and/or referred to by the Purchasers must be attached to the letter, unless they have already been supplied to ABC under direction 1 or 2 above. The Purchasers will send the Vendors a copy of their letter and attachments at the same time as they are sent to ABC.

[4 Optional provision for further submissions.]

5 Neither party has the right to call for a hearing at which witnesses would be examined. However, ABC may meet the parties' accountants [and the parties themselves] either separately or together at his/her discretion.

6 ABC may request either party or both parties to make further submissions, to be provided to ABC and copied to the other party within [21] days of the request.

7 If ABC decides it is necessary to take legal advice on the issue to be determined, ABC shall instruct the [DEF] law firm after notifying the parties and obtaining their agreement to pay [DEF]'s fees.

[8 Arrangements to inspect a site or object–not usually necessary for accountancy experts.]

9 Either party has the right to apply to ABC on two working days' notice given to ABC and the other party.

10 ABC shall issue a [non-]speaking decision within [10] weeks of the date of the latest submission[+].

11 All communications are to be sent to [list postal and e-mail addresses for communications, with telephone and fax numbers]. All communications are to be sent by [fax—or e-mail] with a confirming copy sent by post.

Signed and dated by the expert and the parties.

---

* Note that in some cases orders are made for simultaneous submissions.
[+] But see 9.18.6.

V Decision

1 I [ABC] was appointed to decide [define the issue: *e.g.* whether the sales figure included the sales of widgets by the subsidiary etc] between the Vendors and the Purchasers under an agreement between the parties [dated].

2 [Here all the points in the terms of reference may be either recited or the terms of reference themselves may be referred to by the following: the circumstances of the reference, the issue to be decided, my appointment and my fees were all provided for in Terms of Reference between the parties and myself [dated].]

3 Procedural directions for the reference were agreed on [date], and the parties made their submissions to me in accordance with those directions.

4 My decision is that the [sales of widgets by the subsidiary should be included in the sales figure]. [It will depend on the wording of the Agreement whether ABC needs to go further and say what the sales figure is as a consequence, and how much interest the Purchasers should pay the Vendors following the lapse of time since the issue arose.]

[5 Reasons for the decision.]

[6 The Purchasers shall pay the Vendors' costs assessed at £xxx.]

7 My fees are £xxx and my expenses are £xx, payable [in equal shares by the Vendors and the Purchasers] or [payable by the Purchasers].

Signed[   ] [ABC].

Dated..

Appendix B

APPOINTMENT OF ARBITRATORS BY THE PRESIDENT OF THE LAW SOCIETY: GUIDANCE NOTES

Reproduced by kind permission of the Law Society

Introduction

The President of the Law Society is always pleased to appoint (or nominate an independent expert) to deal with a dispute when duly empowered to do so. A number of appointments are made each year, in a wide range of cases, which include partnership disputes, commercial agreements, insurance disputes and rent reviews.

The Advantages of Arbitration

Arbitration as a method of resolving disputes has a number of advantages over conventional litigation in the courts. It is quick, private and usually cheaper. Although it is best if the parties to a dispute can agree their own arbitrator, this is not always possible, and in such cases it is sensible if an independent authority, such as the President of the Law Society, can be named in the agreement as the person to make the appointment if the parties cannot agree.

Even where the dispute does not involve a document with an arbitration clause, the parties can jointly agree to submit it to arbitration with the President choosing the arbitrator, and the Law Society can supply a simple draft agreement for this purpose.

The Procedure For Applying

Attached to these notes is an application form, which should be completed and returned, marked **Private & Confidential**, to:-

>Joanne Cooper
>Administration Manager
>The Law Society
>113 Chancery Lane
>London WC2A 1PL
>DX: 56 London/Chancery Lane

The form should be accompanied by a copy of the agreement which contains the arbitration clause giving the President the power to appoint, together with a cheque (made payable to "**The Law Society**") for the appointment fee. The fee is calculated by reference to the scale below which relates to the sum in dispute:-

Amount in Dispute	Total Fee Payable (Including VAT)
Below £25,000	£293.75
£25,001 - £50,000	£352.50
£50.001 – £100,000	£528.75
£100,001 - £250,000	£646.25
Above £250,000	£1175.00

In cases where the sum in dispute is not quantified the basic fee of £293.75 applies.

How The Law Society Handles The Arbitration

Once the application and accompanying documentation (including the fee) have been received, they will be acknowledged and steps will quickly be taken to identify a suitable candidate for appointment by the President. Once the President has signed the appointment, it will be sent to the arbitrator together with the copy of the agreement, and copies of the appointment will be sent to the parties or their advisers. Thereafter, the parties or their advisers should contact the arbitrator to make the necessary arrangements for the arbitration to proceed. We aim to turn all appointments round within one calendar month from receipt of the appointment fee and the completed application form. We can expedite the procedure if necessary.

Who will be Appointed?

The normal arbitration clause nominating the President as the appointing authority will give him a complete discretion over whom is appointed, although on occasion a member of a particular profession of a particular seniority may be specified. Subject to this, the President will other things being equal wish to appoint an appropriately qualified and experience solicitor to conduct the arbitration. The Society has a database of information about solicitors who have indicated that they are willing to accept Presidential appointments and (where a solicitor is appointed) the appointee will normally but not invariably be drawn from this database. The views (if any) of the parties on the qualifications of the arbitrator will be taken into account by the President but he will exercise a complete discretion in the matter. The Society also maintains a database of arbitrators from other professions who may be appointed if a solicitor is not the right choice, and liaises with other professional bodies if the right person is not in the database. Candidates for appointment will always be asked if there is any conflict of interest which would disqualify them from taking the appointment. It is not possible to supply extracts from the Society's database of potential arbitrators, as this is compiled exclusively to assist the President and not as a general panel of arbitrators.

General Conditions Governing the Appointments Procedure

Once the arbitrator has taken over responsibility for the case, the Law Society will take no further action in the matter, any challenge to the arbitrator's authority or to the way he or she conducts the arbitration should be raised in the first instance with him or if necessary application made to the court under the Arbitration Acts. Similarly, if one of the parties contests the need for arbitration at all, or disputes that the President is entitled to make the appointment, then this again should be raised with either the arbitrator or the court, and neither the President nor the Law Society can deal with such claims.

No responsibility is accepted by either the President or the Law Society for the payment of the arbitrator's fees, which will form part of the overall cost of the arbitration (as will the fee to the Law Society for the appointment of the arbitrator) and will be paid as ordered by the arbitrator at the conclusion of the arbitration.

Further Information

Further information about the appointments procedure can be obtained by telephoning 020 7320 5698.

THE LAW SOCIETY

APPLICATION FOR THE APPOINTMENT OF AN ARBITRATOR BY THE PRESIDENT

I/We .... hereby request the President of the Law Society to appoint an arbitrator in the dispute details of which are set out below:-

Name and Address of Applicant ....

....

....

Name and Address of Applicant's Solicitors (and their File Reference)

....

....

....

Name(s) and Address(es) of Other Parties to the Proposed Arbitration..........................

....

....

....

....

....

Name(s) and Address(es) of Other Parties' Solicitors (and their file references)................

....

....

....

....

....

Details of persons considered to be disqualified for appointment ....

....

....

....

....

See Over

Nature and Date of Agreement Containing Arbitration Clause ....

....

....

(A FULL COPY OF THE AGREEMENT MUST BE ENCLOSED)

Please state briefly the nature of the dispute ....

....

....

Amount in Dispute £ ....
(If unliquidated this should be stated)

Please state any views relative to the qualifications of the arbitrator ....

....

....

....

....

I/We confirm that efforts have been made to agree an arbitrator between the parties as required by the arbitration clause (copies of relevant correspondence must be enclosed)

I/We enclose a cheque (payable to "The Law Society") in the sum of £ ....

I/We acknowledge that no liability will attach to the President or the Law Society in respect of any fees or expenses connected with the arbitration (including the arbitrator's fees)

Signed ....

Date ....20...........

Notes

1. This form should also be used for the nomination of an independent expert or valuer and amended accordingly.

2. Where the President is out of the country or unable to make the appointment for any other reason, the Vice-President of the Law Society will make the appointment on his behalf, and similarly the Deputy Vice-President of the Law Society will make the appointment on the President's behalf where both the President and Vice-President are unable to act.

3. If additional information needs to be given, this can be given in a separate letter attached to the form.

Appendix C

PRECEDENT FOR SHARE VALUATION

1 The expression "Fair Price" means the price which the auditors of the Company state in writing to be in their opinion the fair value of the shares on a sale between a willing seller and a willing purchaser (taking no account of whether the shares do or do not carry control of the Company) and, if the Company is then carrying on business as a going concern, on the assumption that it will continue to do so. The Fair Price shall be assessed at the date of service of the Transfer Notice and by reference to the information available to the company at that date.

2 In stating the Fair Price the auditors (whose charges shall be borne by the Company) shall be considered to be acting as experts and not as arbitrators and their decision shall be final and binding on the parties.

APPENDIX D

RICS APPLICATION FORM (OPPOSITE)

Reproduced by kind permission of the RICS

RICS APPLICATION FORM

Form AS1 (August 2000)

Dispute Resolution Service

THE ROYAL INSTITUTION OF CHARTERED SURVEYORS

APPLICATION FOR APPOINTMENT / NOMINATION OF AN ARBITRATOR / INDEPENDENT EXPERT BY THE PRESIDENT OF THE ROYAL INSTITUTION OF CHARTERED SURVEYORS
(COMMERCIAL PROPERTY RENT REVIEW)

You are encouraged to type or print all details

I / We _____ hereby request the President of the Royal Institution of Chartered Surveyors to [appoint / nominate] an [Arbitrator / Independent Expert] *(delete as appropriate)* to act in the case below

OR

The application for the appointment / nomination of an Arbitrator / Independent Expert to which the following details refer was made in a letter from:

dated: _____ ref: _____

Address of Premises for which Rent is to be Reviewed (It is essential for the computerised processing of applications that the correct full post code is quoted)	Post Code
Type of Premises, and short description of premises (eg High Street Shop, Storage Warehouse, Retail Warehouse, Office Suite)	Agreed or alleged date of review
Present Rent	Date of Lease
Name and Address of Present Landlord	
Name and Address of Present Tenant	
Name of Original Landlord	
Name of Original Tenant	
Parent, Subsidiary or any Associated Company of Landlord	
Parent, Subsidiary or any Associated Company of Tenant	

Please also confirm any other individuals, organisations or interests the arbitrator / independent expert should take into account when undertaking conflict checks within his / her firm. (This particularly relates to any associated companies of the parties, if appropriate). Continue on a separate sheet if necessary.

RICS Business Services Ltd Registered in England: No 1526902 Registered Office: Surveyor Court Westwood Way Coventry CV4 8JE

Continued overleaf

APPENDIX D

Name, Address, Telephone Number and Reference of Present Landlord's Representative (eg solicitor, surveyor, company official) ie person or firm to whom communication should be sent	
Name, Address, Telephone Number and Reference of Present Tenant's Representative	

Conflicts of Interest
Please state below the names of any Chartered Surveyors who, in your view, should not be considered for appointment / nomination (continue on a separate sheet if necessary). It is emphasised that, while the President will give careful consideration to any representations, he will reach his own decision as to who shall be appointed / nominated. **Please note that objections will not be entertained unless full reasons are given.**

Agreement to Refer
Which clause in the lease gives the President power to make this appointment / nomination? ....
Please detail below any special requirements contained in the lease, and name the clause in which they appear. Eg "...the surveyor shall be a specialist in letting similar properties in the locality and shall give his decision within two months of his/her appointment".

A copy of the duly executed (not draft) lease should accompany this application. **Whilst the President may have regard to the lease, this application form is the contract between the applicant and the President and he will rely entirely upon the information contained herein.**

We accept that in some circumstances the appointment will be made by the President through one of his Vice-Presidents or duly appointed agents and this is the basis upon which the application is submitted to you and upon which the application will be entertained. We accept that in special circumstances (to be decided by the President) it may be inappropriate for the President to effect the appointment and in these circumstances the appointment may be effected by a Vice President in his own name.

Fees
A fee of £275.00 (inclusive of VAT) which is solely for administrative costs must accompany all applications for appointment / nomination by the President. The fee is non-returnable whether or not the President makes the appointment (eg if the matter is settled by agreement). **I / We enclose** a cheque for £275.00 (made payable to RICS Business Services Ltd).

I / We undertake to ensure that the reasonable professional fees and costs of the Surveyor appointed / nominated are paid, including any fees and costs arising where a negotiated settlement is reached before the award or determination is taken up.

Signed ....

Dated.. ....

To be returned to : The Dispute Resolution Service, RICS, Surveyor Court, Westwood Way, Coventry, CV4 8JE
Tel: 020 7222 7000 (or Local Calls: 024 7669 4757) Fax: 020 7334 3802

Appendix E

PRECEDENT FOR EXPERT DETERMINATION OF ALL DISPUTES UNDER A CONSTRUCTION CONTRACT

Note. This precedent is suitable for a main contract. Subsidiary contracts should contain a clause making the decision of the expert appointed under the main contract binding on the parties to the subsidiary contracts and providing that the same expert may determine all disputes under the subsidiary contracts with the same absence of formality.

1. All disputes between the Developer and the Contractor shall be determined by an expert as follows. Either the Developer or the Contractor may initiate the reference by proposing to the other party the appointment of an expert ("the Expert"). The Expert shall be an Architect/Engineer/Surveyor/Lawyer and shall be appointed by agreement between the Developer and the Contractor, or, if they have not agreed within 14 days of the date of the request to refer by one of the parties, by the President for the time being of [appropriate appointing authority] ("the President") on the application of either party. If the Expert has been appointed but is unable to complete the reference another Expert shall be appointed by the parties; or if they have not agreed on the appointment within 14 days of a request to do so by one of the parties, by the President.

2. The Expert shall act as an expert and not as an arbitrator. The parties shall have the right to make representations to the Expert. There will be no formal hearing. The decision of the Expert shall be final and binding on the parties and can include orders that one or both of the parties are to pay the Expert's costs. The amount (if any) which becomes payable by one party to the other as a result of the Expert's decision shall become due and payable within seven days of publication of the decision. The Expert shall have the power to direct that interest on that amount, at a rate equal to 1% above the base rate of [clearing bank] shall be paid by one party to the other as compensation for delay in respect of the period following the date on which the matter was referred to expert determination.

3. If the amount payable as a result of the Expert's decision is not paid within seven days of the publication of the decision, interest will accrue on that amount at the rate of 4% above the base rate of [clearing bank].

Appendix F

PRECEDENT FOR *AD HOC* REFERENCE OF CONSTRUCTION DISPUTE WITH FORMAL HEARING

Note. This precedent is for use where the contract contains an arbitration clause instead of arbitration after an arbitration notice has been served.

1. The parties agree that the dispute relating to [ ] as referred to in the notice of arbitration dated [ ] should be referred to [named expert ("the Expert"] for final and binding determination, and that in reaching the determination, the Expert shall act as an expert and not as an arbitrator.

2. The parties agree the terms of reference for resolving the dispute are as follows:

   (a) Party A to serve points of claim by [ ].
   (b) Party B to serve points of defence by [ ].
   (c) Parties to exchange factual and expert evidence and any further pleadings by [ ].
   (d) Parties to agree on the files to be sent to the Expert by [ ].
   (e) The hearing will commence on [ ] and last for [ ] days without interruption.
   (f) The hearing may include oral submissions and cross-examination of witnesses as directed by the Expert.

3. The parties agree that each party can request disclosure of specific documents or classes of documents from the other, and inform the Expert of any failure to provide documents.

4. The Expert shall have the following powers:

   (a) To award interest. The amount (if any) which becomes payable by one party to the other as a result of the Expert's decision shall become due and payable within seven days of publication of the decision. The Expert shall have the power to direct that interest on that amount, at a rate equal to one per cent above the base rate of [clearing bank] shall be paid by one party to the other as compensation for delay in respect of the period following the date on which the matter was referred to expert determination.

[N.B. The contract should also include provision for interest on late payment of the amount due under the decision.]

(b) To award the costs of the reference to one or the other party, or to make the award of costs the Expert considers appropriate. If the Expert does not assess the costs personally s/he shall be entitled to refer the question of their assessment to an independent costs draftsman to be agreed between the parties or to be nominated by the Chairman for the time being of the Association of Law Costs Draftsmen.

APPENDIX G

PRECEDENT FOR REFERENCE TO PANEL OF EXPERTS: CHANNEL TUNNEL

Here is the edited text of Clause 67 of the contract for the construction of the Channel Tunnel, providing for the interim resolution of disputes by a panel of experts[1]:

Settlement of disputes

(1) If any dispute or difference shall arise between the employer and the contractor during the progress of the works (but not after the issue of the maintenance certificate for the whole of the works or the last of such certificates . . . or after abandonment of the works . . . or alleged termination of the contract), then . . . such dispute or difference shall at the instance of either the employer or the contractor in the first place be referred in writing and settled by a panel of three persons (acting as independent experts but not as arbitrators) who shall unless otherwise agreed by both the employer and the contractor within a period of 90 days after being requested in writing by either party to do so, and after such investigation as the panel think fit, state their decision in writing and give notice of the same to the employer and the contractor.

(2) The contractor shall in every case continue to proceed with the works with all due diligence and the contractor and the employer shall both give effect forthwith to every such decision of the panel (provided that such decision shall have been made unanimously) unless and until the same shall be revised by arbitration as hereinafter provided. Such unanimous decision shall be final and binding upon the contractor and the employer unless the dispute or difference has been referred to arbitration as hereinafter provided.

(3) . . . if (i) either the employer or the contractor be dissatisfied with any unanimous decision of the panel given under clause 67(1), or (ii) the panel shall fail to give a unanimous decision for a period of 90 days, or such other period as may be agreed by both the employer and the contractor, after being requested by either party to do so, or (iii) any unanimous decision of the panel is not given

---

[1] Reprinted from *Channel Tunnel Group Ltd and another v. Balfour Beatty Construction Ltd and others* [1993] A.C. 334 at 345–6.

effect in accordance with clause 67(2) then either the employer or the contractor may within 90 days after receiving notice of such decision or such other period as may be agreed by the employer and the contractor (as the case may be) notify the other party in writing that the dispute or difference is to be referred to arbitration. If no such notice has been given by either party to the other within such periods, the panel's decision shall remain final and binding upon the parties. . . .

(4) [Expanded ICC arbitration clause, with seat in Brussels, and certain other provisions.] . . .

Appendix H

PRECEDENT FOR CLAIMS TRIBUNAL FOR COMPANY VOLUNTARY ARRANGEMENT

The following is an extract from the Company Voluntary Arrangement for the *Olympia and York Canary Wharf Limited* administration. It is discussed at chapter 5.12.1.

Definitions

claims panel means the persons appointed in accordance with [provisions below] by the President for the time being of the Law Society of England and Wales in consultation with the Presidents for the time being of the Institute of Chartered Accountants in England and Wales and of the Royal Institution of Chartered Surveyors to determine disputed claims by way of expert determination and not by way of arbitration;

claims tribunal means the persons selected from the claims panel in accordance with the [provisions below] to act as experts (and not as arbitrators) for the purpose of the determination of claims;

creditor means any person who has a claim [as further defined];

supervisor means [any of the three administrators].

Tribunal provisions

1. There shall be a claims panel of six persons. The six persons shall be two practising solicitors or barristers of ten years' standing, two fellows of the Institute of Chartered Accountants in England and Wales and two fellows of the Royal Institution of Chartered Surveyors.

2. The claims panel shall be constituted by the President for the time being of the Law Society of England and Wales on the application of the supervisors.

3. Members of the claims panel shall be appointed by the President for the time being of the Law Society of England and Wales in consultation (where necessary) with the Presidents for the time being of the Institute of Chartered Accountants in England and Wales and the Royal Institution of Chartered Surveyors.

4. The President for the time being of the Law Society of England and Wales may appoint substitutes, replacements and/or additional members to the claims panel where he is satisfied that this is reasonably required for the proper functioning of the claims tribunal. Such appointments shall be made as set out in paragraph 3 above.

5. The claims tribunal shall consist of one or of three persons chosen from the claims panel.

6. The decision of the number of members of any claims tribunal shall be by agreement between the supervisors and the creditor. Where the parties do not agree on the number of members, the party who requires the larger number of persons shall prevail.

7. The claims tribunal shall be comprised as follows:

   7.1 on all claims tribunals with one member that member shall be either a solicitor or a barrister; and
   7.2 all claims tribunals of three members shall be chaired by either a solicitor or a barrister whose decision shall prevail only where otherwise no decision emerges.

8. Where the supervisors and the creditor cannot agree on any matter concerning the composition of the claims tribunal from the members of the claims panel (other than the number of members; see paragraph 7 above) the appointments to the claims tribunal shall be made from the claims panel by the President for the time being of the Law Society of England and Wales in consultation as set out in paragraph 3 above and in accordance with the requirements of paragraphs 5, 6, and 7.

9. In the event that for any reason it is not possible to constitute a claims tribunal from the members of the panel, the appointment of the claims tribunal shall be made by the President for the time being of the Law Society of England and Wales, in consultation as set out in paragraph 3 above and in accordance with the provisions of paragraph 5, 6, and 7, save only that he may select as members of the claims tribunal persons other than members of the claims panel.

10. The claims tribunal shall meet in London and their proceedings shall be conducted in English.

11. There shall be no formal hearing.

12. The claims tribunal shall determine its own procedure save that the creditor and the supervisors shall have the right to make written presentations to the claims tribunal.

13. If the creditor fails to comply with directions of the claims tribunal or if the claims tribunal determines that the creditor is failing to pursue the proceedings with reasonable despatch, the claims tribunal may, in its discretion, reject the creditor's claim.

14. The claims tribunal shall have no power to award costs.

15. The claims tribunal shall have no power to award interest.

16. The determination of the claims tribunal on each and every issue before them shall be final and binding on the creditor, the company and the supervisors.

17. The claims tribunal shall be entitled to rely for the purposes of its determination on the advice of counsel (of not less than ten years' standing) instructed by it on any aspect of its work and on any legal issues, including issues of *quantum*, arising in the course of making its determinations.

Appendix I

CEDR'S BROCHURE ON EXPERT DETERMINATION (OVERLEAF)

Reproduced by kind permission of CEDR

APPENDIX I

INTRODUCTION

Expert Determination

- is quick, inexpensive and confidential
- is informal
- produces a binding result

Expert Determination is used for a wide variety of commercial applications. The most commonly encountered are

- rent review
- valuation of shares in private companies
- price adjustment in take-overs
- transfers of pension rights
- long-term commodity supply contracts
- valuations of partners' interests in oil and gas field projects
- construction contracts
- IT contracts.

Expert Determination can be chosen as the method of dispute resolution either of

- specific issues; or
- all disputes arising under a contract;

and it can be chosen

- at the time of signing the contract; or
- later when a dispute arises.

Expert Determination differs from arbitration in its greater informality. Unless the parties agree that it should be, it is not subject to "due process" and can therefore be more flexible. In particular there is no need for a trial-type hearing. Unless the Parties agree otherwise, the Expert may conduct investigations independently of the Parties, and make the Decision based on those investigations without reference to the Parties. Parties should obtain legal advice when embarking on an Expert Determination, but do not strictly need to be legally represented during the procedure.

The expression "Expert" is much more commonly used to refer to expert witnesses. In Expert Determination, the appointed Expert makes the Decision, and is not in any sense a witness.

MODEL EXPERT DETERMINATION AGREEMENT

Text in italics indicates where information has to be added.
Text in square brackets indicates where a choice has to be made.

Please refer to the guidance notes for commentary on and help with the completion of this Agreement.

DATE

PARTIES

1 .... ("Party A")

2 .... ("Party B")

3 .... ("Party C") etc
                                  Add full names and addresses

(jointly "the Parties")

4 .... ("the Expert")

5 .... ("the Pupil")

6. Centre for Dispute Resolution Limited trading as Centre for Dispute Resolution (CEDR) of Princes House, 95 Gresham Street, London EC2V 7NA.

DISPUTE
("the Dispute")

Here set out details of the contract(s) or other legal relationship(s) and brief details of the dispute(s) to be resolved by Expert Determination.

....
....
....
....
....
....
....
....
....
....
....

CEDR'S BROCHURE ON EXPERT DETERMINATION

1. **Appointment of Expert**
   CEDR has appointed the Expert to resolve the Dispute. The Parties agree that the Expert will resolve the Dispute by Expert Determination. The Expert will act as an expert and not as an arbitrator.

2. **Purpose of Expert Determination**
   Unless the Parties subsequently agree otherwise, this Expert Determination leads to a decision ("the Decision") being issued by the Expert. The Decision will be final and binding on the Parties.

3. **Confidentiality**
   The Expert Determination process is private and confidential. The Parties, the Expert, the Pupil and CEDR will keep it confidential except to the extent that it is necessary in order to implement the Decision or is required by law.

4. **Independence**
   The Expert, the Pupil and CEDR are independent of the Parties, neutral and impartial, and do not act as advisers to the Parties.

5. **Conduct of Expert Determination**
   The Expert will conduct the Expert Determination in accordance with procedural directions which the Expert will seek to agree with the Parties. If they cannot be agreed, the Expert's directions will prevail.

6. **Challenge to the Procedure**
   The Parties agree that they [are/are not] permitted to challenge the Expert's rulings on issues arising during the procedure including those on the Expert's own jurisdiction.

7. **Mediation Option**
   At any time before the issue of the Expert's decision the Parties may agree to refer the Dispute to mediation, in accordance with CEDR's Model Mediation Procedure. In that case each of the Parties notifies the Expert and CEDR, and the Expert Determination is suspended. The parties would be free to appoint the Expert and/or the Pupil as mediator(s). If the dispute is settled by mediation, the Expert Determination comes to an end and the Parties settle the fees and expenses of the Expert and of CEDR. If the dispute is not settled by mediation, the Expert Determination resumes, and if they have been acting as mediators the Expert and the Pupil may take up their previous roles.

8. **Reasons in the Decision**
   The Decision of the Expert [shall/shall not] include reasons.

9. **Interest**
   The Expert is empowered to award interest as part of the Decision.

10. **Fees and Expenses**
    Unless the Parties agree otherwise, the fees and expenses of the Expert Determination will be borne by the Parties in equal shares. The fees and expenses will be estimated by CEDR and paid to CEDR as a condition precedent for the Expert Determination to start. The Expert will be paid fees and expenses, and the Pupil will be paid expenses. Interim bills may be raised by CEDR to cover the Expert's fees at the Expert's option. A final account of the fees and expenses will be sent to the Parties by CEDR when the Decision is ready for issue to the Parties and the Decision will be released on payment by the Parties of any further amounts due. CEDR will reimburse the Expert. If the Parties agree not to proceed with Expert Determination, CEDR will refund a proportionate amount of the fees and expenses advanced, depending on the amount of work done by the Expert and CEDR.

11. **Implementation of the Decision**
    The Parties agree to implement the Decision within . [e.g. - seven] days of its being published to them.

12. **Challenge to the Decision**
    The Parties agree they [are/are not] permitted to challenge the Decision in any legal proceedings or otherwise.

13. **No Liability**
    The Parties expressly acknowledge that neither the Expert, nor the Pupil, nor CEDR shall be liable to the Parties for any act or omission whatsoever in connection with this Expert Determination.

14. **Role of Pupil**
    The Pupil [observes/takes a full part in] the Expert Determination, but the Decision is the responsibility of the Expert.

15. **Role of CEDR**
    CEDR appoints the Expert and makes arrangements for the Pupil. The Expert is responsible for the procedure from then on. CEDR may be consulted by any of the Parties to this Agreement in case of difficulty. Should the Expert be unable to complete the task, CEDR will appoint a substitute Expert within a reasonable time.

16. **After the Decision**
    None of the Parties will call the Expert, Pupil or CEDR (or any employee, consultant, officer or representative of CEDR) as a witness, consultant, arbitrator or expert in any litigation or arbitration in relation to the Dispute and the Expert and CEDR will not voluntarily act in any such capacity without the written agreement of all the Parties.

17. **Law and Jurisdiction**
    This Agreement shall be governed by English law and under the jurisdiction of the English courts. All the Parties to this Agreement agree to refer any dispute arising in connection with it to mediation first.

....
Signed on behalf of Party A

....
Signed on behalf of Party B

....
Signed on behalf of Party C

....
Signed by the Expert

....
Signed by the Pupil

....
Signed on behalf of CEDR

SCHEDULE

CEDR appointment fee	£	
Expert's fees	£	per hour
Payment to be made on account by each Party	£	by [date]

© CEDR 1999

1st edition/Aug 99

APPENDIX 1

GUIDANCE NOTES

Essential Information
The CEDR Model Expert Determination Agreement includes any Pupil and CEDR as well as the Parties to the Dispute and, of course, the Expert. The roles of the Pupil and of CEDR are defined in clauses 10 and 11 of the Agreement.

The section "Dispute", when completed, sets out how the dispute arose with a brief description of the issue(s).

Clauses 1 and 2 establish the appointment of the Expert, that the process is Expert Determination, and that the result is a Decision which will be final and binding on the Parties. Clauses 3 and 4 establish the confidentiality of the process and the independence of the Expert, the Pupil and CEDR.

The Procedure
Once appointed, the Expert will wish to establish the procedure. Clause 5 states that the Expert will seek to agree the procedure with the Parties, and that if agreement cannot be reached, the Expert's directions will prevail.

Procedural directions may deal with any or all of the following:

- a timetable for the submission of case summaries and supporting documents to the Expert with copies to each other
- whether submissions are to be simultaneous or sequential
- whether there should be one or two rounds of submissions
- whether the Expert has the power to call for documents
- whether the Expert has the power to award costs.

Challenge to the Procedure
Clause 6 gives the Parties the choice whether they have the right to challenge the Expert Determination procedure before the Decision is issued. CEDR strongly encourages Parties to give up this right. This enhances the use of Expert Determination, is in the spirit of ADR and allows the Expert to do the work for the Parties as agreed without the time and expense of court applications.

Mediation Option
Clause 7 provides that the Parties may agree to refer the dispute to mediation at any time before the Decision is made, provided the fees and expenses to date are paid, and that CEDR will organise the mediation. There is no reason in principle why the Expert and the Pupil should not act as mediators, but the Parties may agree to appoint other mediators. There are obvious savings in time and cost in appointing the same people in the two different capacities. However the Parties may have difficulty in being entirely frank with a mediator who may later act as Expert, and the Expert may have difficulty in dealing with confidential material disclosed during the mediation.

Reasons in the Decision
Clause 8 gives the Parties a choice as to whether to include reasons in the Decision. The inclusion of reasons increases the cost, but may make the resolution of the Dispute by this means more attractive and therefore worth the extra cost.

Interest
The Expert does not have the power to award interest unless the Parties agree, so clause 9 gives the Expert that power.

Fees and Expenses
Clause 10 deals with fees and expenses, some of which are payable in advance.

Consequences of the Decision
Clauses 11 and 12 deal with the consequences of the Decision: the Parties agree to implement it within an agreed period (CEDR recommends seven days), and have a choice whether to challenge the Decision. A Decision can be challenged only on very limited grounds arising from its fundamental validity, and not from differences on issues of fact, law or professional opinion. The effect of excluding the right to challenge a Decision is uncertain.

No Liability
Clause 13 gives immunity from liability to the Expert, the Pupil and CEDR.

Role of Pupil
The Pupil is a trainee who is gaining experience of the process and receiving guidance from the Expert. Clause 14 gives a choice as to the extent of the role that the Pupil plays, but makes the essential point that the appointed Expert is solely responsible for the Decision.

Role of CEDR
Clause 15 explains CEDR's role, in making the appointment and other arrangements, and collecting the fees and expenses.

After the Decision
Clause 16 ensures that those involved in the Expert Determination do not get involved in future proceedings without the consent of all the Parties.

Law and Jurisdiction
Clause 17 establishes English law as the governing law of the Agreement, with disputes referred first to mediation and then to the English court. It may be necessary in international cases to provide that the language of the Expert Determination is to be English.

LIST OF APPOINTING AUTHORITIES

The Academy of Experts
2 South Square
Gray's Inn London
WC1R 5HT
Tel: 020 7637 0333
Fax: 020 7637 1893
E-mail: admin@academy-experts.org
Website: www.academy-experts.org

The British Computer Society
BCS Headquarters
1 Sanford Street
Swindon SN1 1HJ
Tel: 01793 417424
Fax: 01793 417473
E-mail: marketing@hq.bcs.org.uk
Website: www.bcs.org.uk

The Centre for Dispute Resolution – CEDR
Princes House
95 Gresham Street
London EC2V 7NA
Tel: 020 7600 0500
Fax: 020 7600 0501
E-mail: mediate@cedr.co.uk
Website: www.cedr.co.uk

The Chartered Institute of Arbitrators
International Arbitration Centre
12 Bloomsbury Square
London WC1A 2LP
Tel: 020 7421 7444
Fax: 020 7404 4023
E-mail: info@arbitrators.org
Website: www.arbitrators.org

The Chartered Institute of Management Accountants
63 Portland Place
London W1B 1AB
Tel: 020 7637 2311
Fax: 020 7631 5309
E-mail: [surname.firstname]@cimaglobal.com

LIST OF APPOINTING AUTHORITIES

Website: www.cimaglobal.com
The City Disputes Panel
International Dispute Resolution Centre
8 Breams Buildings
Chancery Lane
London EC4A 1HP
Tel: 020 7440 7373
Fax: 020 7440 7374
E-mail: info@disputespanel.com
Website: www.disputespanel.com

The Electricity Arbitration Association
5 Meadow Road
Great Gransden
Sandy
Bedfordshire
Tel: 01767 677043
Fax: 01767 677043
E-mail: N/A
Website: N/A

The General Council of the Bar of England and Wales
3 Bedford Row
London WC1R 4DB
Tel: 020 7242 0082
Fax: 020 7831 9217
E-mail:[name]@barcouncil.org.uk
Website: www.barcouncil.org.uk

The International Centre for Expertise
The International Chamber of Commerce
38, Cours Albert 1er
75008 Paris
France
Tel: 00 331 49 53 28
Fax: 00 331 49 53 28 59
E-mail: icc@iccwbo.org
Website: www.iccwbo.org

The Institute of Actuaries
Staple Inn Hall
High Holborn
London WC1V 7QJ
Tel: 020 7632 2100
Fax: 020 7632 2111
E-mail:[name]@actuaries.org.uk
Website: www.actuaries.org.uk

LIST OF APPOINTING AUTHORITIES

The Institute of Chartered Accountants in England and Wales
Chartered Accountants' Hall
P.O. Box 433
London EC2P 2BJ
Tel: 020 7920 8100
Fax: 020 7920 0547
E-mail: LSCA@lsca.co.uk
Website: www.icaew.co.uk

The Institution of Chemical Engineers
Davis Building
165–189 Railway Terrace
Rugby CV21 3HQ
Tel: 01788 578214
Fax: 01788 560833
E-mail: [initial surname (no space or dot)]@icheme.org.uk
Website; www.icheme.org.uk

The Institute of Petroleum
61 New Cavendish Street
London
W1M 8AR
Tel: 020 7467 7100
Fax: 020 7255 1472
E-mail: [name]@petroleum.co.uk
Website: www.petroleum.co.uk

The Law Society of England and Wales
113 Chancery Lane
London
WC2A 1PL
Tel: 020 7242 1222
Fax: 020 7831 0344
E-mail: info.services@lawsociety.org.uk
Website: www.lawsociety.org.uk

Royal Institute of British Architects
66 Portland Place
London W1B 1AD
Tel: 020 7580 5533
Fax: 020 7255 1541
E-mail:admin@inst.riba.org
Website: www.architecture.com

LIST OF APPOINTING AUTHORITIES

The Royal Institution of Chartered Surveyors
12 Great George Street
London SW1P 3AE
Tel: 020 7222 7000
Fax: 07334 3802
E-mail: [name]@rics.org
Website: www.rics.org

GLOSSARY

Every subject grows its own jargon and borrows jargon from its neighbours. Here is a list, with a brief explanation, of some of the technical expressions used in this book or appearing in other textbooks or in the law reports.

Ad hoc reference: A reference arranged after a dispute has arisen: see 9.2.4. It can have this meaning in arbitration law, but can also mean an arbitration which is not supervised by an institution: see 11.2.3. There are no instances of a supervised reference to an expert.

Adjudication: A system for interim determination of construction disputes: see 7.5.

Adjudicator: The referee in an adjudication.

Appointing authority: A body specified by the parties to appoint an expert (or an arbitrator) if they cannot agree on one: see 11.2.3 and 11.5.

Appointment: An act by which the parties or an appointing authority establish the identity of the expert to conduct the reference. Sometimes used as a synonym for nomination.

Appraisal or appraisement: The act of valuation.

Appraiser: Valuer.

Arbitration: A form of private dispute resolution between the two parties to a contract, subject to the law of arbitration: an unavoidably circular definition. For a full account of the differences between arbitration and expert determination, see Chapter 17.

Arbitrator: An individual charged with resolving a dispute submitted to arbitration.

Award: The judgment issued by an arbitrator. This expression is sometimes used for an expert's decision as well.

Certificate: The form of decision issued by certain experts, such as accountants: not to be confused with certificates issued under a construction contract (see 7.4) or a share certificate.

Conflicted out: Prevented from accepting an appointment as expert by a conflict of interest: see 11.8.3.

Construction: Means either (i) interpretation; or (ii) building/engineering.

Decision: Issued by an expert at the conclusion of the reference; otherwise known as an award, certificate or determination.

Determination: See Decision; also a descriptive label for the subject, derived from the decision-making process.

Dispute Review Board: A system of generally non-binding review of construction disputes: see 7.6.

Disputes clause: The clause in a contract which says how disputes are to be handled: *e.g.*, by reference to an expert, arbitration or litigation.

Expert: A natural or legal person (or persons) appointed by parties to a contract to decide an issue in accordance with the terms of that contract and in a manner not subject to the law of arbitration; for the differences from being an arbitrator, see Chapter 17.

Expert clause: The expression used in this book for the clause containing the machinery for referring questions to an expert for decision: see Chapter 9.

Expert determination: The process by which an expert decides questions, or a descriptive label for the subject as a whole.

Formulated dispute: An issue on which the parties have taken defined positions and traditionally thought only referable to an arbitrator, and not to an expert, for that reason: see 17.5.

Impeach, impugn: These words mean the challenge of experts' decisions by parties and the court declaring decisions invalid.

Indicia: The plural of indicium.

Indicium: A Latin word meaning a sign, and translated "indicator" in this book: see 17.4.

Nomination: The act by which a party proposes an expert (or an arbitrator) for appointment.

Glossary

Non-speaking valuation or decision: A decision unaccompanied by reasons or calculations: see 15.7.

Official Referee: The former title of a judge dealing mainly with building/engineering cases, now known as a judge of the Technology and Construction Court.

Panel of experts: A board of adjudicators or a tribunal of experts: see 7.5.6.

Quasi-arbitrator: Status of expert or other referee giving conferring immunity from suit, now obsolete: or, simply describing a referee's position as being similar to that of an arbitrator: see 16.6.

Referee: The person to whom an issue is referred, in whatever capacity. Not to be confused with Official Referee.

Reference: The procedure under which an expert (or an arbitrator) decides a dispute.

Speaking valuation or decision: A decision which provides reasons and/or calculations: see 15.7.

Terms of reference: Terms agreed between the parties and usually the expert as well about the matters to be decided by the expert, the appointment of the expert and the procedure to be followed in the reference: see 13.5. The expression is also used in a similar way in arbitration.

Umpirage: The process by which an umpire decides between the views of two party-appointed experts. An obsolete expression: for an example, see 16.3.2.

Umpire: A third expert, usually appointed by two party-appointed experts: see 10.8. In arbitrations it is not uncommon for the umpire to be known as the "third arbitrator" or the "president", and for that person to be appointed by the appointing authority supervising the arbitration.

FURTHER READING

BOOKS

Bernstein, Ronald; Tackaberry, John; Marriott, Arthur L.; and Wood, Derek, *Handbook of Arbitration Practice*, (3rd ed. Sweet & Maxwell in conjunction with the Chartered Institute of Arbitrators 1997).

Bernstein, Ronald and Reynolds, Kirk, *Handbook of Rent Review*, (Sweet & Maxwell, continuously updated).

Brown, Henry and Marriott, Arthur, *ADR Principles and Practice*, (2nd ed., Sweet & Maxwell, 1999).

Chitty and Guest, *Chitty on Contracts*, (28th ed., Sweet & Maxwell, 1999).

Keating on Building Contracts, (7th ed., Sweet & Maxwell, 2001).

Mackie, Karl; Miles, David; Marsh, William; Allen, Tony, *The ADR Practice Guide: Commercial Dispute Resolution*, (Butterworths, 2000).

Mustill, Sir Michael, and Boyd, Stewart, *Commercial Arbitration*, (2nd edn Butterworths, 1989).

Russell on Arbitration, edited by Sutton, David; Kendall, John and Gill, Judith, (21st ed., Sweet & Maxwell, 1997).

Construction law: themes and practice: essays in honour of Ian Duncan Wallace Q.C., (Sweet & Maxwell, 1998).

Hudson's Building and Engineering Contracts, (11th Ed., Sweet & Maxwell, 1995).

ARTICLES

Buhler, Michael, "Technical expertise: an additional means for preventing or settling commercial disputes". Journal of International Arbitration, March 1989, pp. 135–57.

Burke, Terence and Chinkin, Christine, "Expert determination as a viable alternative to arbitration and litigation" [1989] International Construction Law Review, p. 40.

Burke, Terence and Chinkin, Christine, "Drafting alternative dispute resolution clauses" [1990] International Construction Law Review, p. 444.

Capper, Phillip, "The Adjudicator under NEC 2nd edition: a new approach to disputes", in Engineering, Construction and Architectural Management, Vol. 2, No. 4, December 1995, Blackwell Science.

Collins, Lawrence and Livingston, Dorothy, "Aspects of conclusive evidence clauses" [1974] Journal of Business Law, p. 212.

de Fina, A. A., "Australian courts look at expert determination" 1999 A.D.L.R.J. 3 (Sep) 148–152.

Gaunt, Jonathan Q.C., "What makes an award judge-proof?" [1991] Estates Gazette, 28, p. 70.

Greeno, E.P., "Expert Determination—the use of experts in energy contracts", IBA SBL Conference Paper PP252, Paris September 1995.

Jaffe, Paul A. "Judicial supervision of commercial arbitration in England" (1989) Arbitration, Vol. 55, p. 184.

Jones, Doug, "Is expert determination a 'final and binding' alternative?" Arbitration (1997) Vol. 63, No. 3, p. 213 at 217.

Kendall John, and Dark, Steven "Countering confidentiality agreements" (1991) Law Society's Gazette, Vol. 31, p. 14.

Kendall, John, "Ousting the Jurisdiction", Law Quarterly Review, July 1993, 384–5.

Kendall, John, "Let the experts decide", The Arbitration and Dispute Resolution Law Journal, Part 4, December 1993, 210–A.

Kendall, John, "Expert Determination: a European and American Survey", International Business Lawyer, November 1994, 458–60.

Kendall, John, "Expert Determination in Major Projects", International Business Lawyer, April 1997, Vol. 25, No. 4, pp. 171–179

Kendall, John, "Expert Determination: its use in resolving art and antiquity disputes", in Art Antiquity and Law, Vol. 2, Issue 4, December 1997, pp. 325–330.

Kendall, John, "Role of the Expert/Adjudicator in Support of Arbitration in International Long-Term Contracts", International Business Lawyer, May 1999, Vol. 27, No. 5, pp. 201–207.

Kendall, John, "The effect of the *National Grid* case on the law of expert determination", Landlord & Tenant Review, Vol. 3, Issue 3, pp. 66–68.

Kendall, John, "Choosing a System for Resolving Commercial Disputes", International Company and Commercial Law Review, March 2000, Vol. 11, No. 3, pp. 82–86.

Kendall, John, "How fundamental does an expert's mistake have to be?" Landlord & Tenant Review, Vol. 4, Issue 3, pp. 51–53.

King, Ronnie, "The accountability of experts in unitisation determinations" [1994] Oil and Gas Law and Tax Review, Vol. 6, p. 185.

McGaw, Mark C., "Adjudicators, experts, and keeping out of court", Current Developments in Construction Law, fifth annual construction conference organised by the Centre of Construction Law and Management, King's College, London, 1991.

Morgan, Paul, "Suing an independent valuer in negligence", Rent Review and Lease Renewal (1988–9) Vol. 9, No. 2, p. 118.

Newmark, Christopher and Hill, Richard, "Can a Mediated Settlement Become an Enforceable Arbitration Award?" (2000) Arbitration International Vol. 16, No. 1 at pp. 81–7.

Patocchi, Paolo Michele, and Schiavello, Giuseppe, "Arbitrato irrituale: how it should be handled in a non-Italian jurisdiction? A discussion from a Swiss perspective" A.D.L.R.J. 1998 2 (Jun) 132–151.

Vigrass, Christopher, "The limited role of the courts in expert determination", in International Commercial Litigation, special supplement of April 1996.

Wilson, David, "Disputes on the E & P sector of the oil industry: the viewpoint of the expert", IBA SBL Conference Paper PP253, Paris September 1995.

Webber Lesley ,"Independent experts – Where has the law got to?", Blundell Memorial Lectures 1999.

INDEX

(All references are to paragraph numbers except for those prefixed "App." which refer to the appendices.)

"Absence of manifest error"
  challenging decisions, and, 15.17
Accountants
  certification of items in company accounts, and, 4.2.3
  conflicts of interest, and, 11.8.3
  precedent for appointment
    appointment letter, App. A
    decision, App. A, II
    expert clause, App. A, I
    procedural directions, App. A, IV
    terms of reference, App. A, III
  rent review, and, 2.3.5
Acquiescence
  challenging decisions, and, 15.2.4
"Act as an expert and not as an arbitrator"
  generally, 9.6.1—9.6.2
  meaning, 6.2.3
Actuaries, role of
  pension schemes, and, 4.3.2
Ad hoc expert clauses
  construction disputes, for, App. F
  generally, 8.10.2, 9.2.4
Adjudication
  construction contracts
    Channel Tunnel project, 7.5.6
    decision, 7.5.5
    FIDIC boards, 7.5.7
    jurisdiction, 7.5.3
    meaning, 7.5.1
    nature, 7.5.2
    procedure, 7.5.5
    statute, under, 7.5.4
  generally, 8.6.5
Adjudicator, 1.1.5
Agent of party
  certification by

Agent of party—*cont.*
  condition precedent, 7.4.4
  introduction, 7.4.1
  liability of certifier, 7.4.2
  meaning of certificate, 7.4.6
  practical completion triggers, 7.4.5
  review, 7.4.3
  decisions by
    building contracts, 18.3.5
    conclusive evidence clauses, 18.3.4
    engineering contracts, 18.3.5
    generally, 18.3.1—18.3.8
    independence, 18.3.2
    jurisdiction of decision-maker, 18.3.7
    two-tier systems, 18.3.6
  independence, and, 15.5.1
  tortious liability, and, 16.13.4
  unsatisfactory decision by, 15.8.2
Agreement for lease
  land valuation, and, 2.6.1
Agreement to accept decision
  generally, 17.8.1—17.8.4
Aid to mediation
  generally, 8.10.4
Alternative dispute resolution (ADR)
  dispute clauses, in, 8.6.4
  expert determination as related to, 1.1.7
Alternatives to expert determination or arbitration
  competitions, 18.5.1—18.5.3
  conclusion, 18.9.1—18.9.6
  decisions by one party
    building contracts, 18.3.5
    conclusive evidence clauses, 18.3.4
    engineering contracts, 18.3.5

Alternatives—*cont.*
   generally, 18.3.1—18.3.8
   independence, 18.3.2
   jurisdiction of decision-maker, 18.3.7
   two-tier systems, 18.3.6
  decisions by reference to document, 18.4
  membership of associations, 18.6
  public administration, 18.8.1—18.8.3
  range of
   competitions, 18.5.1—18.5.3
   decisions by one party, 18.3.1—18.3.8
   decisions by reference to document, 18.4
   generally, 18.2
   membership of associations, 18.6
   public administration, 18.8.1—18.8.3
   sports, 18.5.1—18.5.3
   statutory adjudication, 18.7.1—18.7.4
   wagers, 18.5.2
  sports, 18.5.1—18.5.3
  statutory systems
   party wall awards, 18.7.2
   private rights, 18.7.1
   statutory arbitrations, 18.7.3
  wagers, 18.5.2
Appeals from arbitration awards
  generally, 17.11.4
Appeals from experts' decisions
  generally, 17.11.3
Applications of expert determination
  and see under individual headings
  commercial
   auctions, 5.14
   banking, 5.10
   broadcasting, 5.13
   capital markets, 5.5
   commodities, 5.7
   convertible preference shares, 5.6
   employee remuneration, 5.2
   finance leasing, 5.4
   insolvency, 5.12

Applications—*cont.*
   insurance, 5.9
   intellectual property, 5.16
   investment, 5.11
   partnership agreements, 5.3
   share options, 5.2
   shipping, 5.8
   sports tribunals, 5.15
  computer contracts, 6.6
  construction contracts
   adjudication, 7.5
   certification, 7.4
   decision not final and binding, 7.2—7.3
   general dispute resolution, 7.9
   joint ventures, 7.7
   panels of experts, 7.6
   specific issue resolution, 7.8
  energy and mining contracts, 6.4
  engineering contracts, 6.7
  land
   boundary disputes, 2.9
   certificates triggering obligations, 2.6
   development agreements, 2.8
   fittings, products and machinery, 2.5
   freeholds, 2.2
   leaseholds, 2.4
   mortgage portfolios, 2.7
   rent review, 2.3
   specific dispute resolution, 2.10
  mining contracts, 6.4
  sale and purchase of businesses
   certification of figures in accounts, 4.2
   pension rights, 4.3
   summary, 4.1
   tax liabilities, 4.4
  shares in private companies, 3.2
   articles of association, 3.3
   auditors, 3.4
   fair value, 3.5
   liability to third parties, 3.9
   limitation of liability, 3.10
   minority shareholder petitions, 3.7—3.8

Applications—*cont.*
  specific valuation instructions, 3.6
  shipbuilding contracts, 6.5
  telecommunications contracts, 6.8
Applications to court
  expert clause, and
    after decision, 9.16.2
    during reference, 9.16.1
  jurisdiction of expert, and
    after decision, 12.7.3
    before reference, 12.7.1
    challenges to jurisdiction, 12.3.2
    during reference, 12.7.1
    generally, 12.3.2
    procedure, 12.7.3
    specific prohibition, 12.7.2
Apply law, duty to
  generally, 16.10
Appointing authorities
  advantages, 11.5.1
  appointment of expert by
    application, 11.6.1
    fees, 11.6.2
    forms, 11.6.2
  list of, 11.5.3
  role of President, 11.5.4
  willingness to act, 11.5.2
Appointment of auditors
  shares in private companies, and introduction, 3.4.1
  reasons, 3.4.3
  status, 3.4.2
Appointment of expert
  absence of effective machinery,
    in by one party, 11.3.4
    generally, 11.3.1—11.3.5
  acceptance, 11.9
  appointing authorities, by
    advantages, 11.5.1
    application procedure, 11.6.1—11.6.3
    fees, 11.6.2
    list of, 11.5.3
    role of President, 11.5.4
    willingness to act, 11.5.2
  challenges to
    generally, 11.6.1
    injunctions, 11.6.2

Appointment of expert—*cont.*
  conflicts of interest
    accountancy firms, 11.8.3
    agents, 11.8.4
    other commercial relationships, 11.8.1
    RICS policy statement, 11.8.2
  expert clause, in
    agreement, by, 9.7.1
    jointly, 9.7.3
    one party, by, 9.7.4
    professional body, by, 9.7.2
  immunity, and, 11.9
  injunctions, and, 11.6.2
  one party, by, 11.3.4
  parties, by
    advance identification, 11.2.1
    appointing authorities, 11.2.3
    other situations, 11.2.2
  President of appointing authority, by
    generally, 11.5.4
    procedure, 11.6.1—11.6.3
  validity
    acts of appointing authority, 11.4.5
    correspondence between parties, 11.4.4
    generally, 11.4.1—11.4.2
    wording of expert clause, 11.4.3
Appointment of replacement expert
  generally, 9.7.5
Arbitral immunity, *see* Immunity
Arbitration
  commodity contracts, and, 5.7.1
  distinguished from expert determination
    consequences of result, 17.11.1—17.11.5
    interpretation of express words about referee's status, 17.3.1—17.3.6
    key indicators of referee's status, 17.4—17.9
    nature of reference, 17.2.1—17.2.3
    procedural differences, 17.10.1—17.10.8

Arbitration—*cont.*
  documents-only
    generally, 17.7.6
    procedure, 17.7.7
  rent review, and, 2.3.7
  statute, under
    adjudicators, 1.1.5
    construction contracts, and, 7.5.4
    generally, 18.7.3
    party wall awards, and, 18.7.2
    private rights, and, 18.7.1
Architects' certificates
  formulated dispute, and, 17.5.4
  liability of expert
    pre-*Sutcliffe* case law, 16.3.5
    Sutcliffe v. Thackrah, 16.4.1—16.4.2
Articles of association
  valuation of shares, and, 3.3.1
"As an expert and not as an arbitrator"
  first appearance, 6.2.3
  generally, 9.6.1—9.6.2
Associations
  generally, 18.6
Assumptions
  capital markets, and, 5.5.3
  rent review, and, 2.3.4
Auctions
  conditions of sale, 5.14
Auditors
  formulated dispute, and, 17.5.5
  lack of independence, and, 15.5.4
  valuation of shares in private companies, and
    introduction, 3.4.1
    reasons, 3.4.3
    status, 3.4.2
Auditors, role of
  certification of items in company accounts, 4.2.3
  partnership agreements, and, 5.3.1

Banking
  conclusive evidence clauses, 5.10
Bias
  challenging decisions, and, 15.4.1—15.4.5
  duty to act fairly and, 16.9.1

Binding results, 1.6.9
Bond
  construction contracts, and, 7.9.2
  performance bond, 5.9.4
Boundary disputes
  land valuation, and, 2.9
Breach of contract, liability for
  examples
    failure to carry out reference properly, adequately or at all, 16.7.3
    failure to deliver timely decision, 16.7.5
    unauthorised delegation, 16.7.4
  exclusion of liability, 16.7.11
  introduction, 16.7.2
  limitation of liability, 16.7.11
  reasons for decision, and, 16.7.12
  time limits, 16.7.15
Breach of duty of care, liability for
  examples
    auditors, 16.7.9
    failure to keep to professional standard, 16.7.8
    rent reviews, 16.7.10
    share valuation, 16.7.9
  exclusion of liability, 16.7.11
  introduction, 16.7.6—16.7.7
  limitation of liability, 16.7.11
  reasons for decision, and, 16.7.12
  time limits, 16.7.15
Breach of warranty
  sale and purchase of businesses, and, 4.2.2
Broadcasting contracts
  generally, 5.13
By-passing expert clauses, 1.5.3

Calculation agents
  swaps and derivatives, and, 5.5.2
Capital markets
  assumptions, 5.5.3
  swaps and derivatives, 5.5.2
  trustee remuneration, 5.5.1
Case review
  construction contracts, and, 7.2

INDEX

CEDR
  brochure on expert
    determination, App. I
Certificates triggering obligations
  agreement for lease, 2.6.1
  funding agreements, 2.6.2
Certification
  items in company accounts, of
    amount of consideration, 4.2.1
    breach of warranty, 4.2.2
    common calculations, 4.2.4
    procedure, 4.2.5
    relevant issues, 4.2.3
    unreasoned determinations, 4.2.6
  practical completion, of
    condition precedent, 7.4.4
    introduction, 7.4.1
    liability of certifier, 7.4.2
    meaning of certificate, 7.4.6
    practical completion triggers, 7.4.5
    review, 7.4.3
Challenging decisions
  "absence of manifest error", 15.17
  acquiescence, and, 15.2.4
  clerical errors
    generally, 15.9.10
    mistake, and, 15.12.1
  collusion, 15.4.1—15.4.5
  conditions precedent, and, 15.9.8
  consequence of ineffective
    decision, 15.18.1—15.18.3
  death of party, 15.9.3
  delay, and, 15.2.4
  delegated decision, 15.9.6
  evidence of expert, and
    contractual exclusions, 15.19.2
    general rule, 15.19.1
  fraud, 15.4.1—15.4.5
  future prospects, 15.20
  grounds
    clerical errors, 15.9.10
    collusion, 15.4.1—15.4.5
    death of party, 15.9.3
    delegated decision, 15.9.6
    fraud, 15.4.1—15.4.5
    illegality, 15.9.4
    incapacity of expert, 15.9.5

Challenging decisions—*cont.*
    inconclusive decision, 15.9.1
    introduction, 15.3
    invalidity of appointment, 15.9.5
    lack of independence, 15.5.1—15.5.4
    mistake, 15.10—15.12.11
    partiality, 15.4.1—15.4.5
    prematurity, 15.9.8
    revocation of expert's authority, 15.9.2
    unfairness, 15.6—15.8
    variation of contract, 15.9.9
  illegality, 15.9.4
  incapacity of expert, 15.9.5
  inconclusive decision, 15.9.1
  interpretation of words in
    agreement, 15.14.1—15.14.4
  invalidity of appointment of
    expert, 15.9.1, 15.9.5
  jurisdiction, relating to, 15.9.7
  lack of independence, 15.5.1—15.5.4
  mistake
    background, 15.10.1—15.10.2
    present position, 15.12.1—15.12.11
    recent case law, 15.11.1—15.11.7
  negligence of expert, and, 15.2.2
  non-speaking decisions
    definition, 15.13.1
    effect of qualifying words, 15.13.6
    generally, 15.13.2—15.13.4
    mistake not apparent from decision, 15.13.5
    reasons for decisions, 15.13.7
  partiality, 15.4.1—15.4.5
  points of law, on
    generally, 15.15
    interpretation of words in
      agreement, 15.14.1—15.14.4
  prematurity, 15.9.8
  relevant proceedings
    decision-related issues, 15.2.1
    negligence of expert, 15.2.2

295

Challenging decisions—*cont.*
  revocation of expert's authority, 15.9.2
  speaking decisions
    definition, 15.13.1
    effect of qualifying words, 15.13.6
    generally, 15.13.2—15.13.4
    mistake not apparent from decision, 15.13.5
    reasons for decisions, 15.13.7
  specific instructions to expert, 15.16.1—15.16.2
  time limits, 15.2.3—15.2.4
  unfairness
    decision, in, 15.8.1—15.8.2
    due process, 15.7
    introduction, 15.6.1—15.6.5
  variation of contract, 15.9.9
Channel Tunnel
  construction contracts, and, 7.5.6
  precedent for reference to panel of experts, App. G
Choice of means of determination
  cost, 8.9.2
  enforcement, 8.9.9
  finality, 8.9.5
  legal questions, 8.9.4
  privacy, 8.9.7
  procedure, 8.9.3
  recourse against expert, 8.9.6
  relationship of parties, 8.9.8
  speed, 8.9.1
Classification societies
  shipbuilding contracts, and, 6.5.2
Clerical errors
  generally, 15.9.10
  mistake, and, 15.12.11
Collusion
  challenging decisions, and, 15.4.1—15.4.5
Commercial transactions
  auctions
    conditions of sale, 5.14
  banking
    conclusive evidence clauses, 5.10
  broadcasting contracts, 5.13
  capital markets
    assumptions, 5.5.3

Commercial transactions—*cont.*
  capital markets—*cont.*
    swaps and derivatives, 5.5.2
    trustee remuneration, 5.5.1
  commodity contracts
    adjustment of price, 5.7.5
    fixing price, 5.7.6
    generally, 5.7.1
    inspection certificates, 5.7.2
    price and volume, 5.7.4
    public policy, 5.7.3
  convertible preference shares, 5.6
  employee remuneration
    generally, 5.2.1
    share options, 5.2.2
  finance leases, 5.4.1—5.4.2
  insolvency
    claims against insolvent companies, 5.12.1
    claims between insolvent companies, 5.12.2
    insurance company, of, 5.9.5
  insurance
    insolvency of insurance company, 5.9.5
    introduction, 5.9.1
    legal questions, 5.9.2
    performance bonds, 5.9.4
    technical questions, 5.9.3
  intellectual property agreements, 5.16
  investment agreements, 5.11
  know-how licences, 5.16
  loan agreements
    conclusive evidence clauses, 5.10
  partnership agreements
    auditors' certificates, 5.3.1
    extent of valuation exercise, 5.3.2
  performance bonds, 5.9.4
  share options, 5.2.2
  shipping contracts, 5.8
  sports tribunals, 5.15
  summary, 5.1
  swaps and derivatives, 5.5.2
  trustee remuneration, 5.5.1
Commodity arbitrations
  evidence and submissions, and, 17.7.1—17.7.9
  judicial function, and, 17.6.5

Commodity contracts
  adjustment of price, 5.7.5
  fixing price, 5.7.6
  generally, 5.7.1
  inspection certificates, 5.7.2
  price and volume, 5.7.4
  public policy, 5.7.3
Companies
  certification of items in accounts
    amount of consideration, 4.2.1
    breach of warranty, 4.2.2
    common calculations, 4.2.4
    procedure, 4.2.5
    relevant issues, 4.2.3
    unreasoned determinations, 4.2.6
  experts, as
    generally, 10.2.1—10.2.4
    holding particular position, 10.4
    named company, 10.3.2
  sale and purchase of
    breach of warranty, 4.2.1
    certification of items in accounts, 4.2.1— 4.2.6
    pension schemes, 4.3.1—4.3.3
    summary, 4.1
    tax liabilities, 4.4
Company voluntary arrangement
  precedent for claims tribunal, App. H
Comparables
  rent review, and, 2.3.3
Competitions
  generally, 18.5.1—18.5.3
Completion triggers
  construction contracts, and, 7.4.5
Computer contracts
  generally, 6.6
Conclusive evidence clauses
  banking, and, 5.10
Conditional fee agreement, disputes relating to
  role of lawyers, and, 8.8.5
Conditions of sale
  auctions, and, 5.14
Conditions precedent
  challenging decisions, and, 15.9.8

Conditions precedent—*cont.*
  construction contracts, and, 7.4.4
  expert clause, and, 9.2.9
  Q.C. clause, and, 8.8.3
  Scott v. Avery clauses, and, 12.5.2
Conduct of hearings
  generally, 13.7.5
Conduct of investigation
  conduct of hearings, 13.7.5
  defamatory statements, 13.7.6
  disclosure of documents, 13.7.4
  impartiality, 13.7.2
  independent investigation, 13.7.3
  informality, 13.7.1
  negotiations, 13.7.7
Confidentiality
  expert clause, and, 9.15.10
  sources of law, and, 1.2.6
Confidentiality, duty of
  generally, 16.12
Conflicts of interest
  accountancy firms, 11.8.3
  agents, 11.8.4
  independence, and
    challenging decisions, and, 15.5.1—15.5.4
    meaning, 10.7.1—10.7.2
    specific exclusions, 10.7.3
  other commercial relationships, 11.8.1
  RICS policy statement, 11.8.2
Construction contracts
  adjudication
    Channel Tunnel project, 7.5.6
    decision, 7.5.5
    FIDIC boards, 7.5.7
    jurisdiction, 7.5.3
    meaning, 7.5.1
    nature, 7.5.2
    procedure, 7.5.5
    statute, under, 7.5.4
  case review, and, 7.2
  certification
    condition precedent, 7.4.4
    introduction, 7.4.1
    liability of certifier, 7.4.2
    meaning of certificate, 7.4.6

Construction contracts—*cont.*
certification—*cont.*
practical completion triggers, 7.4.5
review, 7.4.3
Channel Tunnel project, 7.5.6
completion triggers, 7.4.5
condition precedent, 7.4.4
dispute review, and, 7.2
Dispute Review Boards, 7.6
early neutral evaluation, and, 7.2
FIDIC boards, 7.5.7
final determination
all issues, 7.9.1—7.9.2
specific issues, 7.8
general dispute resolution, 7.9.1—7.9.2
interim determinations
generally, 7.2
use in construction contracts, 7.3.1
use in other situations, 7.3.2
joint ventures, 7.7
panels of experts, 7.6
precedents
ad hoc reference, App. F
expert determination clause, App. E
reference procedure, and, 13.9.2
Construction, rules of
contract basis, 12.8.1
implied terms, 12.8.3
resolution of ambiguity, 12.8.2
Contract law
primacy of
generally, 1.5.6
jurisdiction of expert, 12.4.1—12.4.2
sources of law, and, 1.2.2
Contractual disputes
role of lawyers, and, 8.8.6
Convertible preference shares
generally, 5.6
Co-operation
implied duty, 9.3.9, 9.15.9, 11.3.5, 13.3.2, 13.4.2, 13.6.3, 13.6.7, 13.10.1
Costs, award of
assessment, 9.13.3
generally, 9.13.1—9.13.2

Court applications
expert clause, and
after decision, 9.16.2
during reference, 9.16.1
jurisdiction of expert, and
after decision, 12.7.3
before reference, 12.7.1
challenges to jurisdiction, 12.3.2
during reference, 12.7.1
introduction, 12.3.2
procedure, 12.7.3
specific prohibition, 12.7.2
Court-appointed expert, 1.1.6

Date for payment of amount determined
expert clause, and, 9.9
Death of party
challenging decisions, and, 15.9.3
Decisions
circulation of draft, 13.8.5
financial provisions, 13.8.4
form, 13.8.2
procedure, 13.8.1
reasons, 13.8.3
Decisions by one party
building contracts, 18.3.5
conclusive evidence clauses, 18.3.4
engineering contracts, 18.3.5
generally, 18.3.1—18.3.8
independence, 18.3.2
jurisdiction of decision-maker, 18.3.7
two-tier systems, 18.3.6
Decisions by reference to document
generally, 18.4
Defamatory statements
generally, 13.7.6
Default of directions
expert clause, and, 9.15.11, 13.6.7
Delay
challenging decisions, and, 15.2.4
Delegated decision
challenging decisions, and, 15.9.6
Development agreements
land valuation, and, 2.8

INDEX

Development potential, land with
  generally, 2.2.1
Directions
  default, 9.15.11, 13.6.7
  inspections, 13.6.3
  inquisitorial procedure, 13.6.6
  lawyer's role, 13.6.5
  legal advice, 13.6.4
  parties with unequal bargaining power, 13.6.8
  representations, 13.6.1
  time limits, 13.6.2
Disclaimer
  and see Immunity and Limitation of liability
  professional negligence, and, 16.7.11
  shares in private companies, and, 3.10
Disclosure of documents
  generally, 13.7.4
Dispute resolution
  ad hoc expert clauses, 8.10.2
  adjudication, 8.6.5
  ADR, 8.6.4
  aid to mediation, 8.10.4
  choice of means of determination
    cost, 8.9.2
    enforcement, 8.9.9
    finality, 8.9.5
    legal questions, 8.9.4
    privacy, 8.9.7
    procedure, 8.9.3
    recourse against expert, 8.9.6
    relationship of parties, 8.9.8
    speed, 8.9.1
  context, 1.6.1—1.6.13
  ICC Rules for Technical Expertise, 8.6.6
  land valuation, and
    general disputes, 2.10.2
    specific disputes, 2.10.1
  lawyers, role of
    conditional fee agreement disputes, 8.8.5
    contractual disputes, 8.8.6
    drafting of leases, 8.8.2
    expert tribunals, 8.8.7
    generally, 8.8.1
    interpretation of contracts, 8.8.4

Dispute resolution—*cont.*
  lawyers, role of—*cont.*
    Q.C. clauses, 8.8.3
  multi-party disputes, 8.5
  multi-tier clauses
    choice of forum, 8.6.1
    dispute of choice of forum, 8.6.2
    solution to problem, 8.6.3
  overview, 1.4.2
  proposal of expert determination
    ad hoc expert clauses, 8.10.2
    aid to mediation, 8.10.4
    contractual choice of forum, 8.10.1
    courts' role, 8.10.3
  Q.C. clauses, 8.8.3
  referral of all disputes to expert
    courts' role, 8.7.2
    introduction, 8.7.1
    objections to general clause, 8.7.3
    practical problems, 8.7.4
  stay of litigation
    reasons for grant, 8.4.1
    reasons for refusal, 8.4.2
Dispute review boards (DRBs)
  construction contracts, and, 7.6
Disregards
  rent review, and, 2.3.4
District valuer, 1.1.5
Divorce
  land valuation, and, 2.2.4
Documents-only arbitrations
  generally, 17.7.6
  procedure, 17.7.7
Drafting of leases
  role of lawyers, and, 8.8.2
Due process, 1.6.10, 7.5.5, 15.6.1, 15.6.4, 15.7
Duties of experts
  apply law, to, 16.10
  confidentiality, of, 16.12
  fairly, to act
    case law examples, 16.9.2
    procedural fairness, 16.9.3
    unfairness, partiality and fraud, 16.9.1
  final and binding decision, to reach, 16.11

Index

Duties of experts—*cont.*
  independent investigation, to make
    distinguished from position of arbitrators, 16.8.5
    generally, 16.8.1—16.8.4
    prevention of, 16.8.6
Duty of care, liability for breach of
  examples
    auditors, 16.7.9
    failure to keep to professional standard, 16.7.8
    rent reviews, 16.7.10
    share valuation, 16.7.9
  exclusion of liability, 16.7.11
  introduction, 16.7.6—16.7.7
  limitation of liability, 16.7.11
  reasons for decision, and, 16.7.12
  time limits, 16.7.15

Early neutral evaluation (ENE)
  construction contracts, and, 7.2
Economic grounds, termination on
  gas and oil supply agreements, 6.4.4
Effectiveness of expert determination, 1.5.1
Electricity supply agreements
  generally, 6.4.7
Employee remuneration
  generally, 5.2.1
  share options, 5.2.2
Energy contracts
  electricity supply agreements, 6.4.7
  gas and oil supply agreements
    establishing quantity, 6.4.3
    fixing price, 6.4.2
    introduction, 6.4.1
    re-determination disputes, 6.4.6
    termination on economic grounds, 6.4.4
    unitised projects, 6.4.5
  mining contracts, 6.4.8
  nuclear industry agreements, 6.4.9
Enforcement of decision
  arbitration clause, effect of, 14.4
  distinguished from arbitrations, 17.11.3

Enforcement of decision—*cont.*
  foreign countries, in, 14.7.1—14.7.3
  injunction, 14.3.2
  insolvency
    demand for payment, 14.5.1
    effectiveness, 14.5.2
    generally, 14.2.4
  procedures
    injunction, 14.3.2
    insolvency, 14.2.4
    introduction, 14.2.1—14.2.3
    leases, 14.2.5
    summary judgment, 14.3.1
  set-off, 14.6.1—14.6.2
  summary, 14.1
  summary judgment, 14.3.1
  time limits, 14.8.1—14.8.2
Engineering contracts
  generally, 6.7
Evidence and submissions, 17.7.1—17.7.9
Establishing quantities
  gas and oil supply agreements, 6.4.3
Expenses of expert
  basis of entitlement, 16.2.1—16.2.2
  invalid appointment, and, 16.2.6
  prior approval, 16.2.5
  resignation, on, 16.2.8
  security for payment, 16.7
  time limits, 16.2.9
"Expert"
  meaning, 6.2.1—6.2.2
Expert clause
  act as expert not as arbitrator, 9.6.1—9.6.2
  analysis of elements, 9.4—9.18
  applications to court
    after decision, 9.16.2
    during reference, 9.16.1
  appointment of expert
    agreement, by, 9.7.1
    jointly, 9.7.3
    one party, by, 9.7.4
    professional body, by, 9.7.2
  appointment of replacement expert, 9.7.5
  conditions precedent, and, 9.2.9
  confidentiality, 9.15.10

Expert clause—cont.
  contractual rights, and, 9.2.8
  costs, award of
    assessment, 9.13.3
    generally, 9.13.1—9.13.2
  date for payment of amount
    determined, 9.9
  default of directions, 9.15.11
  elements
    implied terms, 9.3.2
    introduction, 9.3.1
  final and binding decision
    conclusiveness, 9.8.6
    construction contracts, 9.8.4
    form of decision, 9.7
    generally, 9.8.1—9.8.2
    implied term, 9.8.3
    qualifying words, 9.8.5
  form, 9.2.2
  immunity of expert, 9.17
  implied terms
    act as expert, 9.6
    appointment of expert, 9.7
    costs, 9.13
    date for payment of amount
      determined, 9.9
    final and binding decision, 9.8
    generally, 9.3.2
    interest, 9.10
    issue to be determined, 9.4
    late payment of amount
      determined, 9.11
    non-payment of fees, 9.14
    qualifications of expert, 9.5
    reference procedure, 9.15
    remuneration of expert, 9.12
    types, 9.3.3
  incorporation
    after dispute arises, 9.2.4
    generally, 9.2.3
    oral agreement, by, 9.2.5
    prior agreement, by, 9.2.1
    separate agreement, by, 9.2.6
  interest, award of
    case where power is needed, 9.10.2
    delay by liable party, 9.10.4
    generally, 9.10.1
    late payment, for, 9.11
    rent reviews, 9.10.3

Expert clause—cont.
  interpretation
    generally, 12.8.1—12.8.3
    introduction, 9.3.4
  issue to be determined
    jurisdiction, 9.4.1
    referral of dispute, 9.4.2
  late payment of amount
    determined, 9.11
  legal advice, 9.15.12
  meaning of expression, 1.1.4
  pre-operation steps, 9.2.7
  provision of information, 9.15.9
  qualifications of expert, 9.5
  reference procedure
    confidentiality, 9.15.10
    default of directions, 9.15.11
    legal advice, 9.15.12
    provision of information, 9.15.9
    representations, 9.15.1—9.15.8
  remuneration of expert
    generally, 9.12
    non-payment, 9.14
  rent reviews
    interest, 9.10.3
    reference procedure, 9.15.4
    time limits, 9.18.5
  representations
    company applications, for, 9.15.2
    dispute resolution, for, 9.15.5
    generally, 9.15.1
    procedure, 9.15.8
    rent reviews, 9.15.4
    right to make, 9.15.6
    sale of businesses, 9.15.3
    time limits, 9.15.7
  separability, 1.5.3, 9.2.6
  summary, 9.1
  time limits
    decision of expert, for, 9.18.6
    effect, 9.18.2
    enforcement, 9.18.3
    extension, 9.18.4
    generally, 9.18.1
    rent reviews, 9.18.5
    representations, for, 9.15.7
    statutory period, 9.18.7
Expert tribunals
  role of lawyers, and, 8.8.7

Expert witness
  distinguished from experts, 1.6.3, 17.10.4
Experts
  agent of party as decision maker, *see* Party
  apply law, duty to, 16.10
  confidentiality, duty of, 16.12
  duties
    application of law, 16.10
    confidentiality, 16.12
    fairness, 16.9
    final and binding decision, 16.11
    independent investigations, 16.8
    summary, 16.1
  expenses
    basis of entitlement, 16.2.1—16.2.2
    invalid appointment, and, 16.2.6
    prior approval, 16.2.5
    resignation, on, 16.2.8
    security for payment, 16.7
    time limits, 16.2.9
  fairly, duty to act
    case law examples, 16.9.2
    procedural fairness, 16.9.3
    unfairness, partiality and fraud, 16.9.1
  fees
    basis of entitlement, 16.2.1—16.2.2
    calculation, 16.2.3—16.2.4
    invalid appointment, and, 16.2.6
    resignation, on, 16.2.8
    security for payment, 16.7
    time limits, 16.2.9
  final and binding decision, duty to reach, 16.11
  immunity
    and see Immunity
    post-*Sutcliffe* case law, 16.5.1—16.5.4
    pre-*Sutcliffe* case law, 16.3.1—16.3.7
    quasi-arbitrators, 16.6.1—16.6.7
    Sutcliffe v. Thackrah, 16.4.1—16.4.2

Experts—*cont.*
  independent investigations
    distinguished from position of arbitrators, 16.8.5
    generally, 16.8.1—16.8.4
    prevention of, 16.8.6
  liability
    immunity for, 16.3—16.6
    negligence, for, 16.7
    tort, in, 16.13
  party as decision maker, *see* Party
  professional negligence
    breach of contract claims, 16.7.2—16.7.5
    duty of care in tort claims, 16.7.6—16.7.10
    exclusion of liability, 16.7.11
    general disputes, for, 16.7.13
    generally, 16.7.1
    limitation of liability, 16.7.11
    procedure, 16.7.14
    reasons for decision, and, 16.7.12
    time limits, 16.7.15
  tortious liability
    agents of party, 16.13.4
    generally, 16.13.1
    nature of duty of care, 16.13.2
    time limits, 16.13.5
    trigger events, 16.13.3
  use of
    resolve dispute, to, 8.2
    witness, as, 8.3

Fair value basis, valuation on
  certainty, 3.5.2
  generally, 3.5.1
  mistaken basis of decision, 3.5.3
Fairly, duty to act
  and see Unfairness
  case law examples, 16.9.2
  decision, in, 15.6
  procedural fairness, 16.9.3
  procedure, in, 15.8
  unfairness, partiality and fraud, 16.9.1
Fees and expenses of experts
  basis of entitlement, 16.2.1—16.2.2

Fees and expenses—*cont.*
  calculation, 16.2.3—16.2.4
  invalid appointment, and, 16.2.6
  prior approval, 16.2.5
  resignation, on, 16.2.8
  security for payment, 16.7
  time limits, 16.2.9
FIDIC boards
  construction contracts, and, 7.5.7
Final and binding decision
  conclusiveness, 9.8.6
  constructions contracts
    adjudication, 7.5
    certification, 7.4
    decision not final and binding, 7.2—7.3, 9.8.4
  expert's duty, 16.11
  form of decision, 9.7
  generally, 9.8.1—9.8.2
  implied term, 9.8.3
  qualifying words, 9.8.5
Final determination of construction contracts
  all issues, 7.9.1—7.9.2
  specific issues, 7.8
Finance leases
  generally, 5.4.1—5.4.2
Firms as experts
  generally, 10.2.1—10.2.4
  holding particular position, 10.4
  named company, 10.3.2
Fittings, products, machinery and furniture
  land valuation, and, 2.5
Fixing price
  commodity contracts, and, 5.7.6
  gas and oil supply agreements, and, 6.4.2
Formulated dispute
  generally, 17.5.1—17.5.8
Fraud
  challenging decisions, and, 15.4.1—15.4.5
Freehold land, valuation of
  agreement for purchase, 2.6.1
  development potential, with, 2.2.1
  divorce, on, 2.2.4

Freehold land, valuation of—*cont.*
  sale contract, in, 2.2.2
  successive adjacent plots, of, 2.2.3
"Fundamentally flawed" decision
  unfairness, and, 15.8.2
Funding agreements
  land valuation, and, 2.6.2

Gas supply agreements
  establishing quantity, 6.4.3
  fixing price, 6.4.2
  introduction, 6.4.1
  re-determination disputes, 6.4.6
  termination on economic grounds, 6.4.4
  unitised projects, 6.4.5
Going concern basis, valuation on
  challenging decision, 3.6.2
  generally, 3.6.1

Housing Grants, Construction and Regeneration Act 1996
  adjudication, 7.5.4

ICC Rules for Technical Expertise, 8.6.6
Identification of expert
  company
    holding particular position, 10.4
    named company, 10.3.2
  deadlock, and, 10.3.3
  firm
    holding particular position, 10.4
    named company, 10.3.2
    generally, 10.2.1—10.2.4
  individual
    holding particular position, 10.4
    named company, 10.3.1
Illegality
  challenging decisions, and, 15.9.4
Immunity
  acceptance of appointment, and, 11.9
  architects' certificates, and
    pre-*Sutcliffe* case law, 16.3.5
    Sutcliffe v. Thackrah, 16.4.1—16.4.2

Immunity—*cont.*
  case law
    post-*Sutcliffe*, 16.5.1—16.5.4
    pre-*Sutcliffe*, 16.3.1—16.3.7
    Sutcliffe v. Thackrah, 16.4.1—16.4.2
  commodity contracts, and, 5.7.1
  expert clause, and, 9.17
  quasi-arbitrators
    current status of law, 16.6.1—16.6.7
    introduction, 16.3.1—16.3.7
  share valuations, and
    post-*Sutcliffe* case law, 16.5.1—16.5.2
    pre-*Sutcliffe* case law, 16.3.7
  surveyors' valuations, and, 16.3.6

Impartiality
  challenging decisions, and, 15.4.1—15.4.5
  conduct during the reference, 13.7.2

Implied submission
  jurisdiction of expert, and, 12.2.4

Implied terms
  act as expert not as arbitrator, 9.6.1—9.6.2
  appointment of expert
    agreement, by, 9.7.1
    jointly, 9.7.3
    one party, by, 9.7.4
    professional body, by, 9.7.2
  appointment of replacement expert, 9.7.5
  confidentiality, 9.15.10
  costs, award of
    assessment, 9.13.3
    generally, 9.13.1—9.13.2
  date for payment of amount determined, 9.9
  default of directions, 9.15.11
  final and binding decision
    conclusiveness, 9.8.6
    constructions contracts, 9.8.4
    form of decision, 9.7
    generally, 9.8.1—9.8.2
    implied term, 9.8.3
    qualifying words, 9.8.5
  generally, 9.3.2

Implied terms—*cont.*
  interest, award of
    case where power is needed, 9.10.2
    delay by liable party, 9.10.4
    generally, 9.10.1
    late payment, for, 9.11
    rent reviews, 9.10.3
  issue to be determined
    jurisdiction, 9.4.1
    referral of dispute, 9.4.2
  late payment of amount determined, 9.11
  legal advice, 9.15.12
  provision of information, 9.15.9
  qualifications of expert, 9.5
  remuneration of expert
    generally, 9.12
    non-payment, 9.14
  representations
    company applications, for, 9.15.2
    dispute resolution, for, 9.15.5
    generally, 9.15.1
    procedure, 9.15.8
    rent reviews, 9.15.4
    right to make, 9.15.6
    rules of construction, 12.8
    sale of businesses, 9.15.3
    time limits, 9.15.7
  types, 9.3.3

Incapacity of expert
  challenging decisions, and, 15.9.5

Inconclusive decision
  challenging decisions, and, 15.9.1

Incorporation of expert clause
  after dispute arises, 9.2.4
  generally, 9.2.3
  oral agreement, by, 9.2.5
  prior agreement, by, 9.2.1
  separate agreement, by, 9.2.6

Independence of expert
  challenging decisions, and, 15.5.1—15.5.4
  conflicts of interest, and
    accountancy firms, 11.8.3
    agents, 11.8.4
    other commercial relationships, 11.8.1

Independence of expert—*cont.*
　conflicts of interest—*cont.*
　　RICS policy statement, 11.8.2
　　meaning, 10.7.1—10.7.2
　　specific exclusions, 10.7.3
Independent investigation
　distinguished from position of
　　arbitrators, 16.8.5
　generally, 16.8.1—16.8.4, 13.7.3
　prevention of, 16.8.6
Informality of hearing
　generally, 13.7.1
Information, provision of
　expert clause, and, 9.15.9
Injunctions
　appointment of expert, and, 11.6.2
　enforcement of decision, and,
　　14.3.2
Insolvency
　claims against insolvent
　　companies, 5.12.1
　claims between insolvent
　　companies, 5.12.2
　enforcement of decision, and
　　demand for payment, 14.5.1
　　effectiveness, 14.5.2
　　introduction, 14.2.4
　insurance company, of, 5.9.5
Inspection certificates
　commodity contracts, and, 5.7.2
Institution of Chemical Engineers
　Conditions of Contract for
　　Process Plant, 13.9.3
Insurance
　insolvency of insurance
　　company, 5.9.5
　introduction, 5.9.1
　legal questions, 5.9.2
　performance bonds, 5.9.4
　technical questions, 5.9.3
Insurance Ombudsman
　introduction, 1.1.5
Intellectual property agreements
　generally, 5.16
Interest, award of
　case where power is needed,
　　9.10.2
　compound, 9.10.1
　delay by liable party, 9.10.4
　generally, 9.10.1
　late payment, for, 9.11

Interest, award of—*cont.*
　rent reviews, 9.10.3
　simple, 9.10.1
Interim determinations
　generally, 7.2
　use in construction contracts,
　　7.3.1
　use in other situations, 7.3.2
International Association of
　Classification Societies
　shipbuilding contracts, and, 6.5.2
Interpretation of contracts
　role of lawyers, and, 8.8.4
Interpretation of expert clause
　challenging decisions, and,
　　15.14.1—15.14.4
　generally, 12.8.1—12.8.3
　introduction, 9.3.4
Invalidity of appointment of expert
　acts of appointing authority,
　　11.4.5
　challenging decisions, and,
　　15.9.1, 15.9.5
　correspondence between
　　parties, 11.4.4
　fees and expenses, and, 16.2.6
　generally, 11.4.1—11.4.2
　wording of expert clause, 11.4.3
Investment agreements
　generally, 5.11

Joint ventures
　construction contracts, and, 7.7
Judicial function
　generally, 17.6.1—17.6.8
Judicial review
　generally, 18.8.1—18.8.3
Jurisdiction of expert
　applications to court
　　after decision, 12.7.3
　　before reference, 12.7.1
　　challenges to jurisdiction,
　　　12.3.2
　　during reference, 12.7.1
　　introduction, 12.3.2
　　procedure, 12.7.3
　　specific prohibition, 12.7.2
　challenges to
　　consideration by expert, 12.3.1
　　grounds, 15.9.7
　　introduction, 1.5.4

Jurisdiction of expert—*cont.*
  challenges to—*cont.*
    procedure, 12.3.2
    construction, rules of
      contract basis, 12.8.1
      implied terms, 12.8.3
      resolution of ambiguity, 12.8.2
    extent
      construction of terms of contract, 12.6.1
      interpretation of terms of contract, 12.6.2
      Jones v. Sherwood, 12.6.3
      lack of general principle, 12.6.6
      Mercury v. DG of Telecommunications, 12.6.4
      National Grid v. M25 Group, 12.6.5
      Norwich Union v. P&O, 12.6.3
      other cases, 12.6.8
      rent review clauses, 12.6.7
    generally, 9.4.1
    implied submission, 12.2.4
    limitations, 12.2.3
    ouster of court's jurisdiction
      general principle, 12.5.1
      Re Davstone, 12.5.3—12.5.5
      Scott v. Avery clauses, 12.5.2
    primacy of contract law, 12.4.1—12.4.2
    rules of construction
      contract basis, 12.8.1
      implied terms, 12.8.3
      resolution of ambiguity, 12.8.2
    scope and nature
      generally, 12.2.1
      implied submission, 12.2.4
      limitations, 12.2.3
      wording of expert clause, 12.2.2
    Scott v. Avery clauses, 12.5.2
Just and equitable winding-up
  alternative remedy, 3.8
  generally, 3.7.1

Key indicators of referee's status
  agreement to accept decision, 17.8.1—17.8.4
  effect of, 17.9.1—17.9.3
  evidence, 17.7.1—17.7.9
  formulated dispute, 17.5.1—17.5.8

Key indicators of referee's—*cont.*
  introduction, 17.4.1—17.4.2
  judicial function, 17.6.1—17.6.8
  submissions, 17.7.1—17.7.9
Know-how licences
  generally, 5.16

Lack of independence
  challenging decisions, and, 15.5.1—15.5.4
Land, valuation of
  boundary disputes, 2.9
  certificates triggering obligations
    agreement for lease, 2.6.1
    funding agreements, 2.6.2
  development agreements, 2.8
  dispute resolution
    general disputes, 2.10.2
    specific disputes, 2.10.1
  divorce, on, 2.2.4
  fittings, products, machinery and furniture, 2.5
  freeholds
    agreement for purchase, 2.6.1
    development potential, with, 2.2.1
    divorce, on, 2.2.4
    sale contract, in, 2.2.2
    successive adjacent plots, of, 2.2.3
  leaseholds, 2.4
  mineral extraction, compensation for, 2.4
  mortgage portfolios, 2.7
  options
    development potential, land with, 2.2.1
    freehold reversion, to purchase, 2.4
    sale contract, in, 2.2.2
    successive adjacent plots, of, 2.2.3
  rent review
    accountants' role, 2.3.5
    assumptions, 2.3.4
    comparables, 2.3.3
    disregards, 2.3.4
    interest, 2.3.6
    PACT scheme, 2.3.8
    purpose of clause, 2.3.1
    standard form, 2.3.2

Land, valuation of—*cont.*
  service charges, 2.4
  specific dispute resolution, 2.10
  successive adjacent plots, 2.2.3
  surrender of leases, 2.4
Late payment of amount
    determined
  expert clause, and, 9.11
Law reports
  sources of law, and, 1.2.3
Law Society
  appointment of arbitrators,
    App. B
  Model Forms of Rent Review
    Clause, 2.3.2
  PACT scheme, 2.3.8
Lawyers, role of
  conditional fee agreement
    disputes, 8.8.5
  contractual disputes, 8.8.6
  drafting of leases, 8.8.2
  expert tribunals, 8.8.7
  interpretation of contracts,
    8.8.4
  introduction, 8.8.1
  Q.C. clauses, 8.8.3
Leases, valuation of
  mineral extraction,
    compensation for, 2.4
  options to purchase freehold
    reversion, , 2.4
  service charges, 2.4
  surrender of leases, 2.4
Legal advice
  expert clause, and, 9.15.12
Liability of experts
  breach of contract, for
    failure to carry out reference
      properly, adequately or at
      all, 16.7.3
    failure to deliver timely
      decision, 16.7.5
    introduction, 16.7.2
    time limits, 16.7.15
    unauthorised delegation,
      16.7.4
  duty of care in tort, for
    auditors, 16.7.9
    failure to keep to professional
      standard, 16.7.8
    introduction, 16.7.6—16.7.7

Liability of experts—*cont.*
    rent reviews, 16.7.10
    share valuation, 16.7.9
    time limits, 16.7.15
  immunity , and
    and see Immunity
    post-*Sutcliffe* case law,
      16.5.1—16.5.4
    pre-*Sutcliffe* case law,
      16.3.1—16.3.7
    quasi-arbitrators, 16.6.1—
      16.6.7
    Sutcliffe v. Thackrah, 16.4.1—
      16.4.2
  professional negligence, for
    breach of contract claims,
      16.7.2—16.7.5
    duty of care in tort claims,
      16.7.6—16.7.10
    exclusion of liability, 16.7.11
    general disputes, for,
      16.7.13
    introduction, 16.7.1
    limitation of liability, 16.7.11
    procedure, 16.7.14
    reasons for decision, and,
      16.7.12
    time limits, 16.7.15
  tortious
    agents of party, 16.13.4
    introduction, 16.13.1
    nature of duty of care,
      16.13.2
    time limits, 16.13.5
    trigger events, 16.13.3
Liability to third parties
  shares in private companies,
    and, 3.9
Limitation of liability
  professional negligence, and,
    16.7.11
  shares in private companies,
    and, 3.10
Limitation period
  and see Time limits
  reference procedure, and, 13.2
Loan agreements
  conclusive evidence clauses,
    5.10
"Look-sniff" arbitrations
  generally, 17.6.6, 17.67.8

Index

Lord Wheatley's list of key indicators
  agreement to accept decision, 17.8.1—17.8.4
  effect of, 17.9.1—17.9.3
  evidence, 17.7.1—17.7.9
  formulated dispute, 17.5.1—17.5.8
  introduction, 17.4.1—17.4.2
  judicial function, 17.6.1— 17.6.8
  submissions, 17.7.1—17.7.9

Manifest error
  challenging decisions, and, 6.4.6, 9.8.5, 15.17
  vitiating decision, and, 15.18.2
Membership associations
  generally, 18.6
Mineral extraction, compensation for
  land valuation, and, 2.4
Mining contracts
  generally, 6.4.8
Minority holding basis, valuation on
  challenging decision, 3.6.2
  generally, 3.6.1
Mistake
  challenging decisions, and
    background, 15.10.1—15.10.2
    present position, 15.12.1—15.12.11
    recent case law, 15.11.1—15.11.7
  fair value basis, and, 3.5.3
Model Forms of Rent Review Clause
  generally, 2.3.2
Mortgage portfolios
  land valuation, and, 2.7
Multi-party disputes
  generally, 8.5
Multi-tier clauses
  choice of forum, 8.6.1
  dispute of choice of forum, 8.6.2
  solution to problem, 8.6.3

Negligence of expert
  breach of contract, for
    failure to carry out reference properly, adequately or at all, 16.7.3

Negligence of expert—*cont.*
  breach of contract, for—*cont.*
    failure to deliver timely decision, 16.7.5
    introduction, 16.7.2
    time limits, 16.7.15
    unauthorised delegation, 16.7.4
  challenging decisions, and, 15.2.2
  duty of care in tort, for
    auditors, 16.7.9
    failure to keep to professional standard, 16.7.8
    introduction, 16.7.6—16.7.7
    rent reviews, 16.7.10
    share valuation, 16.7.9
    time limits, 16.7.15
  exclusion of liability, 16.7.11
  general disputes, for, 16.7.13
  introduction, 16.7.1
  limitation of liability, 16.7.11
  procedure, 16.7.14
  reasons for decision, and, 16.7.12
  time limits, 16.7.15
Negotiations
  generally, 13.7.7
"Net after tax rate of return"
  finance leasing, and, 5.4.2
Non-speaking decisions, challenging
  definition, 15.13.1
  effect of qualifying words, 15.13.6
  generally, 15.13.2—15.13.4
  mistake not apparent from decision, 15.13.5
  reasons for decisions, 15.13.7
Nuclear industry agreements
  generally, 6.4.9

Oil supply contracts
  establishing quantity, 6.4.3
  fixing price, 6.4.2
  introduction, 6.4.1
  re-determination disputes, 6.4.6
  termination on economic grounds, 6.4.4
  unitised projects, 6.4.5
One party, decisions by *see* Party, decisions by one

Open market basis, valuation on
  shares in private companies,
  and, 3.5.1
Options, valuation of
  development potential, land with,
    2.2.1
  freehold reversion, to purchase,
    2.4
  sale contract, in, 2.2.2
  successive adjacent plots, of,
    2.2.3

PACT scheme
  rent review, and, 2.3.8
Panels of experts
  construction contracts, and, 7.6
  precedent for reference, App. G
Partiality
  challenging decisions, and,
    15.4.1—15.4.5
  duty to act fairly and, 16.9.1
Partnership agreements
  auditors' certificates, 5.3.1
  extent of valuation exercise, 5.3.2
Party, decisions by one
  agent of one party as decision
    maker, 7.4, 15.5.1, 15.8.2,
    18.3
  building contracts, 18.3.5
  conclusive evidence clauses,
    18.3.4
  enforceability, 12.5.4
  engineering contracts, 18.3.5
  generally, 12.5.4, 18.3.1—18.3.8
  independence, 18.3.2
  jurisdiction of decision-maker,
    18.3.7
  two-tier systems, 18.3.6
Party wall awards
  generally, 18.7.2
Performance bonds
  generally, 5.9.4
Pension schemes
  actuaries' role, 4.3.2
  challenging decision, 4.3.3
  transfer of pension rights, 4.3.1
Points of law, challenging on
  generally, 15.15
  interpretation of words in
    agreement, 15.14.1—
    15.14.4

Practice and procedure
  and see under individual
    headings
  appointment of expert
    appointing authorities, 11.5
    conflicts of interest, 11.7
    court's role, 11.6
    immunity, 11.8
    invalidity, 11.4
    method, 11.2—11.3
  challenging decision
    future prospects, 15.20
    grounds, 15.3—15.19
    relevant proceedings, 15.2
  enforcement of decision
    arbitration clause, 14.4
    foreign countries, in, 14.7
    insolvency, 14.5
    methods, 14.2—14.3
    set-off, 14.6
    time limits, 14.8
  expert clause
    analysis of elements, 9.4—
      9.18
    effect, 9.2
    elements, 9.3
  jurisdiction of expert
    applications to court, 12.6
    challenges, 12.3
    construction rules, 12.7
    definition, 12.2
    extent, 12.5
    ousting, 12.4
    summary, 12.1
  qualifications of expert
    effect of specific requirements,
      10.6—10.7
    identification of expert, 10.2
    referral practice, 10.3—10.5
    umpires, 10.8
  reference, for
    conduct of investigation,
      13.7
    consequences of failure,
      13.10
    directions, 13.6
    form of decision, 13.8
    generally, 13.3—13.4
    limitation, 13.2
    specific applications, 13.9
    terms of reference, 13.5

Prematurity
　challenging decisions, and, 15.9.8
President of appointing authority
　generally, 11.5.4
Primacy of contract law
　introduction, 1.5.6
　jurisdiction of expert, and, 12.4.1—12.4.2
Privacy of expert determination
　introduction, 1.2.6
Private rights
　statutory systems
　　party wall awards, 18.7.2
　　private rights, 18.7.1
　　statutory arbitrations, 18.7.3
　wagers, 18.5.2
Procedural fairness
　generally, 16.9.3
Professional Arbitration on Court Terms (PACT)
　rent review, and, 2.3.8
Professional negligence
　breach of contract, for
　　failure to carry out reference properly, adequately or at all, 16.7.3
　　failure to deliver timely decision, 16.7.5
　　introduction, 16.7.2
　　time limits, 16.7.15
　　unauthorised delegation, 16.7.4
　challenging decisions, and, 15.2.2
　duty of care in tort, for
　　auditors, 16.7.9
　　failure to keep to professional standard, 16.7.8
　　introduction, 16.7.6—16.7.7
　　rent reviews, 16.7.10
　　share valuation, 16.7.9
　　time limits, 16.7.15
　exclusion of liability, 16.7.11
　general disputes, for, 16.7.13
　introduction, 16.7.1
　limitation of liability, 16.7.11
　procedure, 16.7.14
　reasons for decision, and, 16.7.12
　time limits, 16.7.15
Provision of information
　expert clause, and, 9.15.9

Public administration
　generally, 18.8.1—18.8.3
Public policy
　commodity contracts, and, 5.7.3
　introduction, 1.6.13

Q.C. clauses
　generally, 8.8.3
Qualifications of expert
　company
　　holding particular position, 10.4
　　named company, 10.3.2
　firm
　　holding particular position, 10.4
　　named company, 10.3.2
　holding particular position, by, 10.4
　identification of expert, and
　　deadlock, and, 10.3.3
　　company, firm or individual holding particular position, 10.4
　　introduction, 10.2.1—10.2.4
　　named company or firm, 10.3.2
　　named individual, 10.3.1
　in expert clause, 9.5
　independence
　　meaning, 10.7.1—10.7.2
　　specific exclusions, 10.7.3
　individual
　　holding particular position, 10.4
　　named company, 10.3.1
　profession, by
　　with qualifications, 10.5.1
　　without qualifications, 10.5.2
　responsibility of appointing authority
　　generally, 10.6.2
　　implied term, 10.6.3
　　tortious, 10.6.4
　suitability criteria
　　generally, 10.6.1
　　responsibility of appointing authority, 10.6.2—10.6.4
　umpires, 10.8
Quasi-arbitrators
　current status of law, 16.6.1—16.6.7
　introduction, 16.3.1—16.3.7

Re-determination disputes
  gas and oil supply agreements, 6.4.6
Referral of all disputes to expert
  courts' role, 8.7.2
  introduction, 8.7.1
  objections to general clause, 8.7.3
  practical problems, 8.7.4
Reference procedure
  conduct of hearings, 13.7.5
  conduct of investigation
    conduct of hearings, 13.7.5
    defamatory statements, 13.7.6
    disclosure of documents, 13.7.4
    impartiality, 13.7.2
    independent investigation, 13.7.3
    informality, 13.7.1
    negotiations, 13.7.7
  consequences of failure, 13.10.1—13.10.5
  decision
    circulation of draft, 13.8.5
    financial provisions, 13.8.4
    form, 13.8.2
    procedure, 13.8.1
    reasons, 13.8.3
  defamatory statements, 13.7.6
  directions
    default, 13.6.7
    inspections, 13.6.3
    inquisitorial procedure, 13.6.6
    lawyer's role, 13.6.5
    legal advice, 13.6.4
    parties with unequal bargaining power, 13.6.8
    representations, 13.6.1
    time limits, 13.6.2
  disclosure of documents, 13.7.4
  expert clause, in
    confidentiality, 9.15.10
    default of directions, 9.15.11
    legal advice, 9.15.12
    provision of information, 9.15.9
    representations, 9.15.1—9.15.8
  impartiality, 13.7.2

Reference procedure—*cont.*
  independent investigation, 13.7.3
  informality, 13.7.1
  limitation period, and, 13.2
  location of, 13.3.1—13.3.4
  negotiations, 13.7.7
  no contract, if, 13.4.1—13.4.2
  RICS Guidance Notes, 13.9.1
  specific applications
    construction disputes, 13.9.2
    other disputes, 13.9.4
    process plant, 13.9.3
    rent reviews, 13.9.1
  terms of reference, 13.5.1—13.5.2
  without prejudice communications, 13.7.7
Remuneration of expert
  generally, 9.12
  non-payment, 9.14
Rent review
  accountants' role, 2.3.5
  assumptions, 2.3.4
  comparables, 2.3.3
  disregards, 2.3.4
  expert clause, and
    interest, 9.10.3
    reference procedure, 9.15.4
    time limits, 9.18.5
  interest, 2.3.6
  PACT scheme, 2.3.8
  purpose of clause, 2.3.1
  reference procedure, and, 13.9.1
  standard form, 2.3.2
Replacement expert
  appointment, 9.7.5
Representations
  company applications, for, 9.15.2
  dispute resolution, for, 9.15.5
  generally, 9.15.1
  procedure, 9.15.8
  rent reviews, 9.15.4
  right to make, 9.15.6
  sale of businesses, 9.15.3
  time limits, 9.15.7
Resignation of expert
  fees and expenses, and, 16.2.8
Revocation of expert's authority
  challenging decisions, and, 15.9.2

INDEX

RICS
  application for appointment,
    App. D
  conflict of interest policy
    statement, 11.8.2
  Guidance Notes on procedure,
    13.9.1
  Model Forms of Rent Review
    Clause, 2.3.2
  PACT scheme, 2.3.8
Rules of construction
  contract basis, 12.8.1
  implied terms, 12.8.3
  resolution of ambiguity, 12.8.2

Sale and purchase of businesses
  certification of items in
    accounts
      amount of consideration,
        4.2.1
      breach of warranty, 4.2.2
      common calculations, 4.2.4
      procedure, 4.2.5
      relevant issues, 4.2.3
      unreasoned determinations,
        4.2.6
  pension schemes
    actuaries' role, 4.3.2
    challenging decision, 4.3.3
    transfer of pension rights,
      4.3.1
  tax liabilities, 4.4
Scott v. Avery clauses
  jurisdiction of expert, and,
    12.5.2
Service charges
  land valuation, and, 2.4
Set-off
  enforcement of decision, and,
    14.6.1—14.6.2
Share options
  generally, 5.2.2
Shareholder agreements
  valuation of shares in private
    companies, and, 3.3.1
Shares in private companies,
  valuation of
  appointment of auditors
    introduction, 3.4.1
    reasons, 3.4.3
    status, 3.4.2

Shares in private—*cont.*
  fair value basis
    certainty, 3.5.2
    introduction, 3.5.1
    mistaken basis of decision,
      3.5.3
  going concern basis
    challenging decision, 3.6.2
    generally, 3.6.1
  immunity of valuer, and
    post-*Sutcliffe* case law,
      16.5.1—16.5.2
    pre-*Sutcliffe* case law, 16.3.7
  introduction, 1.6.5
  just and equitable winding-up, and
    alternative remedy, 3.8
    generally, 3.7.1
  liability to third parties, 3.9
  limitation of liability, 3.10
  minority holding basis
    challenging decision, 3.6.2
    generally, 3.6.1
  open market value basis, 3.5.1
  precedent, App. C
  procedure
    articles of association, 3.3.1
    representations, 3.3.3
    shareholder agreements, 3.3.1
    usual wording, 3.3.2
  relevant circumstances
    compulsory transfer of shares,
      3.2.2
    shares not traded publicly,
      3.2.1
  summary, 3.1
  unfair prejudice
    minority holdings, 3.7.1
    transfer provisions, 3.7.2
Shipbuilding contracts
  classification societies, 6.5.2
  technical questions, 6.5.1
Shipping contracts
  generally, 5.8
Single joint expert
  introduction, 1.1.6
"Slip rule"
  generally, 15.9.10
  mistake, and, 15.12.11
Sources of law and information
  confidentiality, 1.2.6
  construction contracts, and, 1.2.7

INDEX

Sources of law—*cont.*
  contract law, 1.2.2
  introduction, 1.2.1
  law reports, 1.2.3
  practice, 1.2.4
  statutes, 1.2.5
Speaking decision, challenging of
  definition, 15.13.1
  effect of qualifying words, 15.13.6
  generally, 15.13.2—15.13.4
  mistake not apparent from decision, 15.13.5
  reasons for decisions, 15.13.7
Specific instructions to expert
  challenging decisions, and, 15.16.1—15.16.2
Sports tribunals
  generally, 5.15, 18.5.1—18.5.3
Statutes
  sources of law, and, 1.2.5
Statutory adjudication
  construction contracts, and, 7.5.4
  generally, 18.7.3
  party wall awards, and, 18.7.2
  private rights, and, 18.7.1
Statutory adjudicators and valuers, 1.1.5
Stay of litigation
  reasons for grant, 8.4.1
  reasons for refusal, 8.4.2
Successive adjacent plots
  land valuation, and, 2.2.3
Summary judgment
  enforcement of decision, and, 14.3.1
Surrender of leases
  land valuation, and, 2.4
Surveyors, role of
  boundary disputes, 2.9
  development land, valuation of, 2.2.2
  divorce, on, 2.2.4
  immunity, and
    post-*Sutcliffe* case law, 16.5.1—16.5.2
    pre-*Sutcliffe* case law, 16.3.6
  options to purchase, valuation of, 2.2.3
Swaps and derivatives
  generally, 5.5.2

Telecommunications contracts
  generally, 6.8
Television contracts
  generally, 5.13
Termination on economic grounds
  gas and oil supply agreements, 6.4.4
Terms of reference
  generally, 13.5.1—13.5.2
Time limits
  challenging decisions, for, 15.2.3—15.2.4
  decision of expert, for, 9.18.6
  effect, 9.18.2
  enforcement of, 9.18.3
  enforcement of decision, for, 14.8.1—14.8.2
  extension, 9.18.4
  fees and expenses, for recovery of, 16.2.9
  generally, 9.18.1
  professional negligence, for action for, 16.7.15
  rent reviews, 9.18.5
  representations, for, 9.15.7
  statutory period, 9.18.7
  tortious liability, for, 16.13.5
Tortious liability
  agents of party, 16.13.4
  introduction, 16.13.1
  nature of duty of care, 16.13.2
  time limits, 16.13.5
  trigger events, 16.13.3
Trustee remuneration
  generally, 5.5.1

Umpires
  background, 10.8.1
  modern practice, 10.8.2
  status, 10.8.3
Unfair prejudice
  minority holdings, 3.7.1
  transfer provisions, 3.7.2
Unfairness
  decision, in, 15.8.1—15.8.2
  due process, 15.7
  duty to act fairly, and
    case law examples, 16.9.2
    procedural fairness, 16.9.3
  unfairness, partiality and fraud, 16.9.1

Unfairness—*cont.*
   introduction, 15.6.1—15.6.5
Unitised projects
   gas and oil supply agreements, 6.4.5

Validity of appointment of expert
   acts of appointing authority, 11.4.5
   challenging decisions, and, 15.9.1, 15.9.5
   correspondence between parties, 11.4.4
   generally, 11.4.1—11.4.2
   wording of expert clause, 11.4.3

Valuer
   introduction, 1.1.4
Variation of contract
   challenging decisions, and, 15.9.9

Wagers
   generally, 18.5.2
Warranty, breach of
   sale and purchase of businesses, and, 4.2.2
Without prejudice communications
   generally, 13.7.7